}

This
self

Schoenberg's Musical Imagination

No composer was more responsible for changes in the landscape of twentieth-century music than Arnold Schoenberg (1874–1951), and no other composer's music inspired a commensurate quantity and quality of technical description in the second half of the twentieth century. Yet there is still little understanding of the correlations between Schoenberg's musical thought and larger questions of cultural significance in and since his time: the formalistic descriptions of music theory do not generally engage larger questions in the history of ideas, and scholars without an understanding of the formidable musical technique are ill-equipped to understand the music with any profundity of thought. *Schoenberg's Musical Imagination* is intended to connect Schoenberg's music and critical writings to a larger world of ideas. While most technical studies of Schoenberg's music are limited to a single compositional period, this book traces changes in his attitudes as a composer, and their impact on his ever-changing compositional style over the course of his remarkable career.

MICHAEL CHERLIN is Professor of Music Theory and Founding Director of the Interdisciplinary Program in Collaborative Arts at the University of Minnesota. He is co-editor of *Musical Transformations and Musical Intuitions: A Festschrift in Honor of David Lewin* (1994) and *The Great Tradition and Its Legacy: The Evolution of Dramatic and Musical Theater in Austria and Central Europe* (2003). His work on Arnold Schoenberg has been published in journals devoted to music theory and history, including *Music Theory Spectrum*, the *Journal of the American Musicological Society*, and *Perspectives of New Music*.

Music in the 20th Century

GENERAL EDITOR Arnold Whittall

This series offers a wide perspective on music and musical life in the twentieth century. Books included range from historical and biographical studies concentrating particularly on the context and circumstances in which composers were writing, to analytical and critical studies concerned with the nature of musical language and questions of compositional process. The importance given to context will also be reflected in studies dealing with, for example, the patronage, publishing, and promotion of new music, and in accounts of the musical life of particular countries.

Recent titles

James Pritchett
The music of John Cage

Joseph Straus
The music of Ruth Crawford Seeger

Kyle Gann
The music of Conlon Nancarrow

Jonathan Cross
The Stravinsky legacy

Michael Nyman
Experimental music: Cage and beyond

Jennifer Doctor
The BBC and ultra-modern music, 1922–1936

Robert Adlington
The music of Harrison Birtwistle

Keith Potter
Four musical minimalists: La Monte Young, Terry Riley, Steve Reich, Philip Glass

Carlo Caballero
Fauré and French musical aesthetics

Peter Burt
The music of Toru Takemitsu

David Clarke
The music and thought of Michael Tippett: modern times and metaphysics

M. J. Grant
Serial music, serial aesthetics: compositional theory in post-war Europe

Philip Rupprecht
Britten's musical language

Mark Carroll
Music and ideology in Cold War Europe

Schoenberg's Musical Imagination

Michael Cherlin

CAMBRIDGE UNIVERSITY PRESS
Cambridge, New York, Melbourne, Madrid, Cape Town, Singapore, São Paulo

Cambridge University Press
The Edinburgh Building, Cambridge CB2 8RU, UK

Published in the United States of America by Cambridge University Press, New York

www.cambridge.org
Information on this title: www.cambridge.org/9780521851664

First published 2007

Printed in the United Kingdom at the University Press, Cambridge

A catalogue record for this publication is available from the British Library

ISBN 978-0-521-85166-4 hardback   0521851661

Contents

Music examples and figures

Musical examples

Chapter 1

Chapter 3

Chapter 5

Chapter 6

Chapter 4

Acknowledgements

This is a book that has been some thirty years in the making. Like all such projects, it is the product of countless exchanges with teachers, friends, and family. And needless to say, I risk omitting many in naming a few. David Lewin was my principal teacher and inspiration and he will always have a special place in my memory. Although I never studied formally with Milton Babbitt, it would be impossible to overemphasize his importance as a teacher and friend. Along the way, my Schoenberg studies benefited from other teachers as well, principally Martin Picker and Richard Chrisman at Rutgers University and Allen Forte at Yale University. Over the years, I have shared and refined ideas through conversations and correspondence with colleagues including Paul Wilson, Joseph Straus, Susan McClary, Harald Krebs, Andrew Mead, Steven Cahn, Brian Campbell, Richard Kurth, Henry Klumpenhauer, and Joseph Auner: heartfelt thanks to them all.

I owe a special debt of gratitude to Noah Rogoff, who was an insightful and indefatigable research assistant during the final stages of the project. Noah's contributions ranged from pointing out infelicities of style, to helping with some of the graphics, to formulating the book's index entries and bibliography; for all of this I am very grateful. Special thanks also go to Arnold Whittall who has been more than an insightful and supportive editor. Arnold's interest in my work led to the initial book proposal. His grace, encouragement, patience, and insights throughout the project have been extraordinary. The staff at Cambridge University Press have been a pleasure to work with, and I would like to particularly thank Vicki Cooper and Rebecca Jones for their help in making the book a reality. Thanks also to Zeke McKinney for crucial technical support; Zeke kept the computer going, no mean task.

Financial support allows a scholar to work. The University of Minnesota has been my academic home since the fall of 1988, and I owe the College of Liberal Arts, and the Graduate School a continuing debt of gratitude. A sabbatical during the academic year of 2002–2003 allowed crucial progress in the writing of *Schoenberg's Musical Imagination*. Summer fellowships from the McKnight Foundation (1992, 1998) allowed scholarship that is part of the cumulative process that led to the book. Thanks also for a summer stipend from the National Endowment for the Humanities (2005), supplemented by a grant from the Graduate School of the University of Minnesota. Noel

Zahler, the Director of the School of Music and the University of Minnesota, has been supportive through the final stages of the project, and I want to thank Noel in particular for a release from teaching during the fall of 2005.

My mother Pauline and father Jacob did not live to see me graduate college, but they provided the means and loving family surroundings that nurtured my beginning studies in music. I am blessed with a wonderful wife, Rose, and two sons who make their dad proud, Joseph and Paul. They have shared in my passion for music and for Schoenberg's music in particular over the years. How can one even begin to appreciate the peace of mind and enthusiastic sharing of ideas that a family can bring? This book is lovingly dedicated to my wife Rose Cherlin.

Michael Cherlin, June 2006

Introduction

while we hunger
for a clear and beaming truth to settle our
perspectives down (a foundation upon which to
base a way of life, religion, or musical theory)
we need even more the muddled doubts of our
seeking: for to know is to be at an end . . .
A. R. Ammons, *Glare*, number 103

No composer was more responsible for changes in the landscape of twentieth-century music than Arnold Schoenberg (1874–1951), and no other composer's music inspired a commensurate quantity and quality of technical description in the second half of the twentieth century. Yet the correlations between Schoenberg's musical thought and larger questions of cultural significance in and since his time have not been well addressed by musical scholarship: formalistic descriptions of music theory do not generally engage larger questions in the history of ideas, while scholars without an understanding of the formidable musical technique are ill-equipped to understand the music with any profundity of thought. To cite a case in point, the authors of *Wittgenstein's Vienna* claim "Schönberg, unlike Hanslick, considered the question, how a composition sounds, as having no importance."[1] The reader's ability to hear Schoenberg's music with any comprehension correlates directly to the perceived absurdity of that claim. I cannot imagine anything parallel being said about a major philosopher – X discovered that ideas have no importance.

Music is part of how we make sense of the world and how we place ourselves within it. *Schoenberg's Musical Imagination* intends to place Schoenberg's music and critical writings into larger contexts of human creativity, with the aim to better connect compositional techniques and their expressive ends (i.e. the way the music *sounds*) to more encompassing human concerns.

A second aspect of the book is its range over most of Schoenberg's long career. Technical studies of Schoenberg's music have tended to an extraordinary degree to be circumscribed by his various periods: the chromatic tonality of his earliest works up until 1908, the so-called "atonal" works from 1908 until after World War I, and then the twelve-tone works, from the mid 1920s until his death. Theorists with expertise in one area, say twelve-tone music, rarely have insights into the other periods.[2] Correlating with this division of scholarly labor is a division along lines of reception: more than any other composer that I can bring to mind, those interested in Schoenberg's music tend to be interested in one period above the others. My own position is that Schoenberg composed great works in each period, and moreover that we understand his music most comprehensively when we do not place his compositional periods in isolation.

To frame one of the central issues of the book, we need to take a very long view of the development of Western concepts of harmony. The classical Greek concept of *harmonia* included but was not limited to musical relationships. It applied to the order of the cosmos, and to the "soul" as well.[3] The two most foundational (and conflicting) concepts of harmony can be traced respectively to the Pythagorean school and to Heraclitus of Ephesus.[4] The Pythagoreans emphasized the alternation of concord and discord and held that concord was the more fundamental of the two: discord resolves into concord. In contrast, Heraclitus understood harmony as necessarily entailing opposition or conflict, where conflict is an eternal force (more properly, an eternal aspect of *Logos*), fundamental to the nature of the world, and never to be overcome or transcended. The Pythagorean model has dominated throughout most of the history of Western music. From the "perfections" of medieval music theory to the "perfect cadences" of common-practice tonality, resolution in concord was the expected, and only possible end for all musical compositions.[5] For nearly two thousand years, musical discord was necessarily subordinate to and concluded by musical concord, and it wasn't only "music" that worked that way. Hannah Arendt cites a striking example using the imagery of historian Jacob Burckhardt.[6]

> The beginning, in Jacob Burckhardt's words, is like a "fundamental chord" which sounds in its endless modulations through the whole history of Western thought. Only beginning and end are, so to speak, pure or unmodulated; and the fundamental chord therefore never strikes its listeners more forcefully and more beautifully than when it first sends its harmonizing sound into the world and never more irritatingly and jarringly than when it still continues to be heard in a world whose sounds – and thought – it can no longer bring into harmony.

In the early twentieth century, Arnold Schoenberg begins to imagine music where internal conflict is not resolved, and where closure in "perfection" instead of being the only possibility becomes an impossibility. The implications of this departure have proved to be immense. Schoenberg had arguably abandoned one of the most fundamental "master narratives" of Western civilization: conclusion in perfection is assumed by the entire

Judeo-Christian (and Islamic) tradition. Schoenberg himself could only be vaguely aware of the implications for music. He couldn't even begin to imagine the correlations between his musical thought and developments that had occurred and would yet develop in literature, philosophy and science.

As with questions about "perfection," questions about the nature of time, as ancient as human imagination itself, reach a particularly high pitch in the literature and science of the early twentieth century. Given that music is the temporal art *par excellence* it should come as no surprise that music's ability to shape our experience of time would be central to the musical thought of Schoenberg's generation. And yet relatively little has been written about temporality in Schoenberg's music.[7] One extraordinarily important aspect of time in music is in how music can express our three basic temporal orientations: retrospection, anticipation, as well as a sense of "now." The chapters on the First String Quartet and on *Pelleas und Melisande* in particular focus on how Schoenberg integrates these temporal orientations into a more encompassing concept of musical unfoldings ("form" is too static to capture what is at stake). In Schoenberg's most successful works, these elements combine to form what Elliott Carter, punning on Schoenberg's harmonic concept of "emancipated dissonance," has named "emancipated discourse."[8]

Another aspect of Schoenberg's treatment of temporal flow is studied in Chapter Five. There we develop a theory of uncanny time and its correlate: the *time shard*. Schoenberg's expressions of uncanny time develop out of common practice tonality where the flow of time is regulated by an underlying pulse-stream that remains more or less regular as the work unfolds. Tonal works can create a sense of uncanny time by a number of means that we discuss in the chapter. These include interrupting the pulse-stream itself, or disrupting the sequence of narrative events to create uncanny flashbacks or uncanny foreshadowings. Another development is traced to Schubert's practice where he brings attention to the pulse stream, so that it becomes the signifier of meaning rather than the underlying conveyor of meaning. Schoenberg's develops all of these techniques, but they undergo extraordinary change and take on unforeseeable significance in his post-tonal compositions. In Schoenberg's practice, the regular yet *unheimlich* pulse-streams are shards of time, reminiscent of but alien to the way that time used to go.

Most technical studies of Schoenberg's music have emphasized its radical discontinuities with the past. Developments in set theory and twelve-tone theory over the past forty years and more make the disjunction vivid.[9] Set theory and twelve-tone theory have developed ways of modeling combinations of notes and their intervallic contents that wipe the slate clean, severing all or almost all connections to tonal practice. For many composers and scholars the new ways of modeling music have been liberating. Set theory and twelve-tone theory have directly and indirectly inspired an extraordinary body of compositions and scholarship. In contrast to the ways that set theory and twelve-tone theory have tended to sever the music from its past, Schoenberg's critical writings emphasize connections to his tonal precursors. His compositional pedagogy as well is fully grounded in tonal practice, albeit an idiosyncratic representation of that practice. It is the conflict between holding on to the past while forging a new musical language adequate to the needs of a fleeting present that is essential to Schoenberg's creativity as a composer. There is an ever-present tension between Schoenberg the conservative and Schoenberg the radical, and this dialectic is essential to Schoenberg's genius as a composer. Points of contact with the past are simultaneously points of departure, and I try to capture this interpretive spirit throughout the book.

Set theory and twelve-tone theory, as they have evolved over the past half century, have developed a formidable mathematical apparatus and the ability to generate inexhaustible numerical data about pitch and rhythmic relationships within a musical composition, or within collections of notes that might form the resources for musical composition. Most of this has remained, and will remain in the domain of music theorists and the relatively small number of composers who have the imaginative capacity to transform such data into music. The intellectual and imaginative content of the best of this work speaks for itself, and I intend no critique of that work, explicit or implicit, in abandoning most of the apparatus of set theory in *Schoenberg's Musical Imagination*. On the other hand, set theory has produced a self-engendering body of arcana that too often gets in the way, blocking vivid perception rather than facilitating it. Moreover, its concerns generally do not intersect with those of performance, where the shaping of phrases, balancing of contrapuntal voices, subtle shadings of color, and the like are most essential. For some scholars the solution to this problem is to disparage theory and abandon deep analysis altogether. This too would be antithetical to my own approach.

The foundation of my Schoenberg studies was my 1983 dissertation on Schoenberg's twelve-tone opera *Moses und Aron*, work done under the tutelage of David Lewin.[10] In preparing the dissertation I began to have an understanding of how Schoenberg uses the conflict among mutually exclusive row partitions (e.g. 6 + 6 vs. 4 + 4 + 4) to portray the dramatic conflicts that are at the crux of the opera. I had no idea at the time how important the role of conflict would become in my understanding of Schoenberg's music. In returning to a serious study of the opera after more than two decades of subsequent work on Schoenberg's music, I found my hearing radically transformed. My study of uncanny time altered the ways I understood once familiar passages, and a deeper understanding of cultural context and musical lineage had profoundly changed my orientation to the music. The chapter on *Moses und Aron* draws upon my earlier work, but brings those formal characteristics of the music into larger contexts of meaning by relating Schoenberg's twelve-tone techniques to the concerns that span his entire career, and to a wider world of ideas that they engage.

My 1993 article "Schoenberg and *das Unheimliche*," draws on Freud's celebrated article on the uncanny to interpret repressed tonal structures in Schoenberg's post-tonal music.[11] I have continued to be interested in cross-reading Schoenberg and Freud; we will return to this topic in the final section of this Introduction. The "*Unheimliche*" article also marks the beginnings of my attempts toward interpreting Schoenberg's music in light of other thought within his cultural context. My current approach reaches its first maturity with my 1998 article, "Memory and Rhetorical Trope in Schoenberg's String Trio," which has been adapted to become the final chapter in this book.[12] The study of the Trio engages ideas derived from Nietzsche and Freud to describe the avoidance of closure in that work, Schoenberg's musical depiction of a near-death experience. The chapter also explores the ways that the String Trio engages and remembers a musical past that reaches back to the Classicism of Haydn and Mozart, and continues through the nineteenth and early twentieth centuries. The simultaneous encoding of memory and memorial has profound implications for understanding the creation of musical space within the work. My understanding of these aspects of Schoenbergian composition was subsequently augmented by ideas derived from the writings of Henri Bergson, Gilles Deleuze and Félix Guattari. I was able to begin to employ these ideas in my essay "Motive and Memory in Schoenberg's First String Quartet," which has been adapted to form Chapter Four.[13] Particularly open to further development are ideas concerning musical space that I developed out of Deleuze and Guattari's concepts of *agrarian space* versus *nomadic space*.[14] My article "Dialectical Opposition in Schoenberg's Music and Thought" is adapted to form Chapter Two.[15] It studies the crucial role of conflict in Schoenberg's critical and theoretical writings, placing those writings into larger historical and cultural contexts.

Rhetorical tropes: conflict, flux, and imperfection

While performing musicians interpret musical compositions through sounds prompted by musical notation, scholars and critics use words that provide context and meaning, or describe the structures and processes embodied by the sounds produced in performance or the sounds implied by the score. The performer, using the score as the principal text, reads it against the background of a tradition of musical works in the context of a tradition of performances. In studying a musical composition, the scholar too uses the score as a principal text; like the performer, the scholar reads the composition against a tradition of musical works, but the scholar substitutes a body of scholarly and creative writing for the performer's tradition of musical performances. Substitution runs deep in musical scholarship where one symbol-making system substitutes for another: words for music, creative and scholarly literature for performance practice.

Composers can think directly in sounds, and it would be a gross falsification of the compositional process to reduce it to a conversion from words to sounds. And yet, composers do transform verbal thought, physical gesture and other spatial and temporal orientations (mathematical, painterly, dancerly) into musical sound. Substitution is at the very heart of all of our symbol making. While our different modes of symbolic thought and action fulfill different human potentials as they respond to different human needs, words about music matter because the interactions of our symbolic modes (languages, practices) have the potential to augment one another.

The study of substitution in rhetoric and poetics is the study of tropes, figurative language that constitutes our most basic strategies for knowing or shaping our worlds. In Kenneth Burke's words, to study tropes is to study "their rôle in the discovery and description of 'the truth.'"[16] "The truth," placed in scare quotes, points to a paradox: while "truth" may be imagined to be at the bottom of things, substitution through tropes, like asymptotic freedom, is boundless and without limit. Its play of energies, like the Heraclitean universe, is open ended.

Burke names "four master tropes" that comprise the most fundamental ways that language uses substitution to create meaning: metaphor (perspective), metonymy (reduction), synecdoche (representation), and irony (dialectic). As conceptualized by Burke, metaphoric understanding knows one thing through the perspective of another. Metonymy's basic strategy is to understand something incorporeal or intangible in terms corporeal or tangible. Synecdochic thought represents some whole through a part, or vice versa. And the dialectic of irony results from juxtaposing different perspectives that are not reducible to one another. All of these linguistic strategies have analogues in musical thought. When we recall the first theme of a sonata form through the perspective of the second theme, our process mimics metaphoric thought. Notation itself might be considered a metonymic strategy, reducing the evanescence of sound to a tangible symbol. When we hear a motivic fragment and recall its larger context, our thought is synecdochic. And when we expect one thing and then hear another the juxtaposition of expectation and realization mimics verbal irony. These parallels apply not necessarily because music mimics linguistic thought; the strategies of understanding through substitution are arguably antecedent to language itself.

Building upon Burke's scholarship, Harold Bloom adds two fundamental terms, hyperbole (restitution/repression) and metalepsis or transumption (the trope of a trope).[17] The latter is particularly interesting in our study. To trope a trope is to put a new spin on an old idea, but to do that successfully is to challenge the priority or at least the hegemony of the earlier idea. Schoenberg's reception of tradition is metaleptic through and through.

In addition to its foundational terms, the study of tropes also includes more specific kinds of substitution, images or ideas that take on a life of their own, for example, the complementary tropes of darkness and light as substitutes for ignorance and knowing, bad and good, melancholy and levity, death and life. The three tropes that most fundamentally inform this study are conflict, flux-as-change, and what we will call "imperfection." Conflict or opposition is at the heart of the creative moment – something new opposes something that came before. It is also at the heart of drama, comedic and tragic, and so is therefore at the heart of music conceived along dramatic lines. Flux, in the sense of constant change, like conflict as a constant, is a Heraclitean term, a genealogy that we will consider in Chapter Two. Flux asserts the impermanence of things, and so perpetual gain pitted against perpetual loss. All music is composed of evanescent, fleeting sounds: Schoenberg's music, or so our study will claim, makes evanescence thematic. Imperfection, as we will use it, is the impossibility of reaching a final state of being, which is to say that imperfection asserts the impossibility of perfection.

We can think of conflict and flux-as-change as co-determinants with imperfection as their resultant. Or, we can think of imperfection as the fundamental ontological category, with conflict and flux as its resultants. Or we can think of any of the three terms as a substitute for the others in that any of the three terms suggests the other two.

The familiar terminology of tonal music brings a technical meaning to perfect intervals and perfect cadences, but underlying the technical jargon is an assumption, or so I will claim, about a world that ends in perfection. In this world-view, conflict and flux are subordinated to ultimate perfection. The assumption of perfectibility has deep religious and cultural roots, and I find nothing in Schoenberg's theoretical and critical writings that recognizes the "master narrative" that is challenged by his musical intuitions. On the contrary, in many ways Schoenberg's critical writings cling to a teleological world-view. Yet, Schoenberg's abandonment or repression of tonality was concomitant with the development of a musical syntax that did not, and could not, end in perfection. Despite Schoenberg's formidable contributions to theory and criticism, his intuitions and vision as a composer outstripped his capacity as a theorist and critic. We will argue that perfection is not redefined by Schoenberg's music, it is abandoned.

Canonical Schoenberg and the process of *Bildung*

In contrast to music, a literary canon, reaching as far back as the Hebrew Torah and the Greek Homer, has been in place since antiquity. Literary works have long spoken to and through one another across vast spans of time, and across sea changes in natural language. A competent seventeenth-century English reader of John Milton's *Paradise Lost* would hear echoes and arguments reaching back through Dante to Virgil, to Homer, and from Protestant thought through Catholic scripture back to the Torah. In a similar way, a competent nineteenth-century German reader of Goethe's *Faust* might include all the above in an extended lineage, argument and counter-argument. The depth and complexity of the literary canon has profound implications for the ways we read.

The idea of a musical canon is a surprisingly late invention of the nineteenth century – for the first time in the history of music, musicologists and performers began the process of reviving works, indeed entire musical periods that had fallen out of performance practice. Prior to that, the living presence of musical works might last a generation or two (as students remember the works of their teachers), but generally no longer. It is no small irony that Brahms at the end of the nineteenth century was able to study works that were antecedent to any available to J. S. Bach at the beginning of the eighteenth century. The invention of a musical canon had profound implications for the ways we listen.

The canonical works of literature, both sacred and secular (if one makes the distinction), were not just literary objects of study. They were shaping forces in the ways human beings understood themselves and their place in the world. Canonical works are world-shaping arguments, while the canon itself shapes worlds into galaxies, the forces and counterforces that comprise our imaginative universes.

To conceive music as canonical is to grant it a different aspect of this same shaping force and function. Musical works are not just musical objects of study. They too are world-making arguments; like literature, they help shape the ways we understand ourselves and our place in the world. Music conceived of as canonical enters into the play of symbolic world-making that is so distinctive of being human.

For German-speaking persons of the nineteenth and early twentieth century, the significance of a living, evolving canon is inseparable from the concept of *Bildung*. Hans-Georg Gadamer credits the German philosopher and social critic Johann Gottfried von Herder (1744–1803) with conceptualizing *Bildung*.

> More than anyone, Herder transcended the perfectionism of the Enlightenment with his new ideal of "cultivating the human" (Bildung zum Menschen) thus prepared the ground for the growth of the historical sciences in the nineteenth century. The *concept of self-formation, education, or cultivation* (Bildung), which became supremely important at the time, was perhaps the greatest idea of the eighteenth century, and it is this concept which is the atmosphere breathed by the human sciences of the nineteenth century, even if they are unable to offer any epistemological justification for it.[18]

The concept of *Bildung* is developed and refined in Kant and Hegel, and becomes programmatic in the writings and progressive politics of Wilhelm von Humboldt (1767–1835). The term has its origins in medieval mysticism, and Humboldt develops this aspect of the concept in distinguishing *Bildung* from *Kultur*.

> Bildung here no longer means "culture" – i.e. developing one's capacities or talents. Rather, the rise of the word Bildung evokes the ancient mystical tradition according to which man carries in his soul the image of God, after whom he is fashioned, and which man must cultivate in himself.[19]

Humboldt envisioned *Bildung* as the road to social progress, and his initiatives as Prussian Minister of Education were instrumental in the nineteenth-century "emancipation" of German-speaking Jews.[20] For many German-speaking Jews, *Bildung* became a kind of secular religion, the process of self-formation that would allow them to fully participate in European culture and education.[21]

The process of *Bildung* was internalized and open-ended. Whereas "canonical" might be thought of as comprising a closed set, the canon seen in light of *Bildung* was ongoing. Paul Mendes-Flohr emphasizes this idea in *German Jews: A Dual Identity*. He writes of "the innate contradiction of the very ideas of a [closed] canon to the character of Bildung as a plastic, dynamic conception of culture and learning. Clearly, Bildung *eo ipso* is antagonistic to a closed, authoritative conception of canon."[22]

Schoenberg's understanding of the role of music is not separable from its place as a constituent of *Bildung*.[23] By the time of his generation, the idea had become so fundamental that in a sense it was no longer noticed as being there. Serious music was simply not an "entertainment"; it was an extraordinarily important constituent in the ongoing process of self-formation.

In the world of German literature in the nineteenth century on into the early twentieth century, no one instantiated or depicted the ideal of *Bildung* more quintessentially than Johann Wolfgang von Goethe. Amos Elon, writing specifically about the Jews of Germany emphasizes this connection, one that evidently resonated deeply for Schoenberg.[24]

> Their true home, we now know, was not "Germany" but German culture and language. Their true religion was the bourgeois, Goethean ideal of *Bildung* . . .

Paul Mendes-Flohr also emphasizes the significance of Goethe:[25]

> . . . the poet was honored in virtually every Jewish household. It is said only somewhat hyperbolically that a set of his writings graced every Jewish home and was the standard bar mitzvah and confirmation present. Many a rabbi wove citations from Goethe into his sermons.

In a sketch dated 1 June 1923, for a passage in the Wind Quintet, Schoenberg notes an important breakthrough in his evolving twelve-tone technique by appending a diagram which represents the row partition. Schoenberg writes a note beside the diagram: *Ich glaube Goethe müsste ganz zufrieden mit mir sein* (I believe Goethe would be quite satisfied with me).[26]

Schoenberg, Freud, and Kafka

We do not need to posit a *Zeitgeist* to recognize that the terms, conflict, flux, and imperfection, resonate deeply with the creative thought of others in Schoenberg's generation. Two contemporaries fascinate me most in this regard: Sigmund Freud and Franz Kafka. We will use the remainder of this introduction to explore relationships among the three, so that they might function as a subtext to all that follows.

Freud shared Schoenberg's Vienna, yet I find no evidence that indicates that either had but a passing knowledge of the other's work. Freud evidently had a tin ear, and Schoenberg's understanding of Freud was likely limited to coffee-house conversations.[27] The inclusion of Kafka is even more extreme in this regard. It is a safe bet that neither Freud nor Schoenberg knew of his existence. Kafka was evidently familiar with some of Freud's writings,

but it would be far-fetched to assume any deep influence.[28] It is possible
that Kafka heard some of Schoenberg's music in Prague, but I find no mention of Schoenberg in Kafka's diaries. And so, it is not because of causal
links that I associate this triad. To be sure, the three shared much common
ground: all were German-speaking Jews who grappled deeply with the culture of Western civilization; each radically re-imagined creative thought in
his respective domain; each suffered as perennial outsider; and each within
his domain of thought profoundly develops the nexus of tropes that concerns
us here, conflict-flux-imperfection. And yet to my mind the most compelling
reason for understanding Schoenberg in light of Freud and Kafka, or understanding Freud and Kafka in light of Schoenberg, is the scope and power
of each man's imagination. If I were interested in measuring influences on
Schoenberg, Karl Kraus, Adolph Loos, Stefan George, and many others
would be obvious choices; if I was interested in measuring Schoenberg's
influence on others, I might choose his students, or composers, performers and scholars closer to our own times; but my interest is in developing
the nexus of tropes that are at the core of my interpretive perspective. The
writings of Freud and Kafka and the extraordinary body of scholarly commentary on those writings enter into dialogue with Schoenberg's music
and the body of scholarly commentary on that music in ways that lesser
imaginations cannot.

Although Freud's ideas about mapping the mind change over time, nothing remains more basic to his models of the human psyche than conflict.
Freud's early modeling divided psychic space into three parts – conscious,
preconscious, and unconscious – where the preconsciousness can emerge
into consciousness, but the unconscious proper remains hidden from the
conscious mind. Harold Bloom describes the dynamics of Freud's early
model.[29]

> Freud distinguished his concept of the unconscious from that of his closest
> psychological precursor, Pierre Janet, by emphasizing his own vision of a civil
> war within the psyche, a dynamic conflict of opposing mental forces,
> conscious against unconscious. Not only the conflict was seen thus as being
> dynamic, but the unconscious peculiarly was characterized as dynamic in
> itself, requiring always a contending force to keep it from breaking through
> into consciousness.[30]

Freud's mature map of the mind posited three basic physic functions, *es,*
ich, and *überich* (id, ego, and super-ego). The id is fully unconscious, while
the ego and super-ego are partly conscious, and substantially unconscious.
The dynamics of conflict between the unconscious and conscious mind
continue, but the moral conscience of the super-ego adds another theater
of conflict to the psychic warfare.

Philip Rieff, in his important study *Freud: The Mind of the Moralist*, begins Chapter Two, "Conflict and Character," by emphasizing a different aspect of this Freudian conflict, that between instinct and culture.[31]

> No small part of Freud's impact upon the contemporary moral imagination derives from his idea of the self in conflict. He conceives of the self not as an abstract entity, uniting experience and cognition, but as the subject of a struggle between two objective forces – unregenerate instincts and overbearing culture. Between these two forces there may be compromise but no resolution. Since the individual can neither extirpate his instincts nor wholly reject the demands of society, his character expresses the way in which he organizes and appeases the conflict between the two.

Bloom asserts that Freud's last and greatest period of creativity begins with his paper *Beyond the Pleasure Principle* (1920). It is here that Freud identifies what becomes the most fundamental conflict of all, that between Eros and the death drive (*Todestreib*, and sometimes *Thanatos*, from the Greek word for death).[32]

> It would be a contradiction to the conservative nature of the instincts if the goal of life were a state of things which had never yet been attained. On the contrary, it must be an *old* state of things, an initial state from which the living entity has at one time or other departed and to which it is striving to return by the circuitous paths along which its development leads. If we are to take as a truth that knows no exception that everything living dies for *internal* reasons – becomes inorganic once again – then we shall be compelled to say the '*the aim of life is death*' and, looking backwards, that '*inanimate things existed before living ones*'.

Reflecting on the struggle between these two fundamental instincts, Rieff describes Freud's final thoughts on death.[33]

> In 1938, a year before he died of cancer, he suspected that we die not merely of disease but of the death-wish, locked forever in conflict with Eros. Finally the balance of power shifts. Eros ages; ageless Thanatos asserts itself "until at length succeeds in doing the individual to death."

Bloom provides another striking insight into *Beyond the Pleasure Principle* that will prove important for our own concerns as well. Referring to Freud's paper on the uncanny (*das Unheimliche*), Bloom writes that "what Freud declined to see, at that moment, was the mode of conversion that alienated the 'canny' into the 'uncanny'. *Beyond the Pleasure Principle* clearly exposes that mode as being catastrophe."[34]

> *Beyond the Pleasure Principle*, like the essay on narcissism, is a discourse
> haunted by images (some of them repressed) of catastrophe. Indeed, what
> Freud verges on showing is that to be human is a catastrophic condition . . .
> It is as though for Freud the Creation and the Fall had become one and the
> same event.[35]

In Freud's model, conflict wells up from within the human psyche; the strivings of the conscious mind and the unconscious, and then the id, ego, and super-ego, and finally Eros and Thanatos, are all the mysterious workings of our internal lives. Our very being is in conflict with its "goal," non-being. While it can be argued that Kafka's most delineated characters project these insolvable conflicts onto an external world, the uncanny Kafka can be read just as well to the opposite effect: that the world is full of unfathomable and hostile forces, and that catastrophe always looms close at hand.

In his commentary on *The Metamorphosis*, Kafka scholar Ritchie Robertson takes note of Freud's concept of a divided self, comparing Kafka to his contemporary Arthur Schnitzler.[36]

> Kafka is more radical than Schnitzler in his presentation of the divided self.
> For Schnitzler, the recesses of the self can be explored by sufficiently resolute
> introspection; but for Kafka, as for Dostoyevsky, self-scrutiny is by definition
> impossible. In *Die Verwandlung* Kafka shows the self-estrangement of the
> protagonist in the most drastic terms: Gregor 'fand sich', we are told,
> transformed into an insect; he actually sees his new body with its many
> helpless little legs; but the sight is too unfamiliar to impinge on his
> consciousness, and he decides to go back to sleep and forget his 'Narrheiten'.

Of course, sleep is not the cure for the madness; an inexplicable calamity has overtaken him. The settled world of Gregor Samsa has profoundly changed, and he will never get back to the way that it was.

In his two most extended works, both incomplete, Kafka gives the protagonists the name K., asserting and effacing himself, the one imagining and one imagined. In *The Trial*, K. awakes to find himself accused of some unknowable but evidently critical breaking of the law. Like Samsa in *The Metamorphosis*, K.'s once familiar surroundings take on a new strangeness, in K.'s case as he finds himself the accused who struggles to exonerate himself against charges that remain unknown. *The Castle* takes the opposite approach toward placing K. Instead of the familiar suddenly having become strange, at the beginning of *The Castle* K. finds himself in an unknown location "gazing upward into the seeming emptiness."[37] Who he really is, and where he comes from we are never told, nor is it clear that there is a way home. Informed that he is in the domain of the Castle of Count Westwest, K.'s unobtainable obsession becomes to reach the Castle, so that he can explain himself (and perhaps so that he might find out who he is). K. finds himself displaced in a strange world whose mysterious forces seem to have him in their control.

> K. knew there was no threat of actual compulsion, he had no fear of that, especially not here, but the force of these discouraging surroundings and of the increasing familiarity with even more predictable disappointments, the force of scarcely perceptible influences at every moment, these he certainly did fear, but even in the face of this danger he had to risk taking up the struggle.[38]

Kafka's interrupted syntax captures the sense of being lost, while the pile-up of phrases moves in an ever more ominous direction, from "no threat of actual compulsion," to "the force of scarcely perceptible influences at every moment." While it would be foolish to reduce *die Gewalt der unmerklichen Einflüsse jedes Augenblicks* (the force of scarcely perceptible influences at every moment) to Freud's id, as it would be foolish to reduce the id to some literal meaning, the parallels are striking nonetheless.

I would like to cite one more example of Kafka's fractured, conflicted, and besieged sense of self, this from his diaries, the famous description of a breakdown dated January 16, 1922.

> This past week I suffered a breakdown; the only match to it was that night two years ago; apart from then I have never experienced the like. Everything seemed over with, even today there is no great improvement to be noticed . . . Breakdown, impossible to sleep, impossible to stay awake, impossible to live, or, more exactly to endure the course of life. The clocks are not in unison; the inner one runs crazily on at a devilish or demoniac or in any case unhuman pace, the outer one limps along at its usual speed. What else can happen but that the two worlds split apart, and they do split apart, or at least clash in a fearful manner.[39]

Shakespeare's metaphor of "time out of joint" becomes almost literalized in Kafka's harrowing experience. Bloom likens Kafka's description of fractured time to an image in Lurianic Kabbalah, the breaking of the vessels.[40] I will use the same image in my Chapter Five conception of time shards, and with more pointed reference in my interpretation of the opening of *Moses und Aron*, in Chapter Six.

Schoenberg explores a fractured psyche at war with itself, or at war with its own projections most explicitly in *Erwartung* and *Die glückliche Hand*, but as we will see in Chapter Two, irresolvable conflict takes on many aspects within his musical thought. Conflict is at the heart of Schoenberg's *Grundgestalt*, the seed idea that engenders musical compositions. It is basic to his concepts of harmony and history. Chapter Six is an extended meditation on the role of conflict built into the twelve-tone row that is the conceptual basis of *Moses und Aron.*

Flux or change is our second trope, or the second aspect of our tropical nexus. Freud's celebrated study of dream-work, *Die Traumdeutung*, grapples with the elusive, shifting sense of time and place that are inherent in dream consciousness. The unstable meanings of dream images parallel the instability of dream consciousness itself. Where meaning is always emergent, change is always present, and in this sense flux is as essential to Freud's mapping of the psyche as is conflict.

Freud also recognizes the essential transience of the world that we inhabit in the daytime. His short essay *Vergänglichkeit* ("On Transience") is essentially a meditation on the work of mourning, the painful process of letting go: "libido clings to its objects and will not renounce those that are lost even when a substitute lies ready at hand. Such then is mourning." Mourning is a part of the ways we cope with loss and life's inevitable changes.[41]

For Kafka, flux is inherent in the instability of his protagonist's worlds. Kafka sometimes places world-changing calamity antecedent to the story, so that our first experience of the protagonist finds him already plunged into an altered reality. The openings of the three stories we have already considered, *The Metamorphosis, The Trial,* and *The Castle* all work this way. Kafka uses a different approach in *The Judgment (Das Urteil)*. At the outset, the protagonist Georg Bandemann seems to be living a settled and fairly comfortable life. He writes to a friend, who in Bandemann's eyes has had less good fortune than he, to tell him of his engagement and planned wedding. Having finished writing, Bandemann goes across the hallway into his infirm father's room, which we are told he has not entered for months. He tells his father about the letter, and after some conversation, all seemingly cordial, or at least benign, he carries his infirm parent to bed. Suddenly, and without any forewarning, the father turns on his son, telling him that he is the stronger of the two, that Georg's friend "knows everything a hundred times better than you do yourself, he crumples your letters in his left hand without reading them while he holds up my letters in his right hand to read them!"[42] After a few more angry comments, the father pronounces the dark judgment to which the story's title alludes: "I hereby condemn you now to death by drowning!"[43] The story quickly unravels as Bandemann rushes headlong out of the room, across a roadway toward the river that evidently runs nearby.

> He was already clutching the railing the way a hungry man clutches food. He swung himself over, like the outstanding gymnast he had been in his youth, the pride of his parents. He was still clutching tight with weakening hands

when he spied a bus between the railing bars: it would easily drown out the sound of his fall. He softly cried, "Dear parents, I have always loved you," and let himself drop.

At that moment, a simply endless passage of traffic was passing across the bridge.[44]

Bandemann's doom is unforeseeable, sudden, and catastrophic. Precipitous and catastrophic change is thematic in many of Kafka's stories, but it often runs in tension with its own opposite, the inability to change. In *The Hunter Gracchus* the protagonist has died, or should have died, in a hunting accident. If only death were achievable, Gracchus would be accepting, after all, at the moment that should have led to his death he was doing what he loved best. But he finds himself trapped in an in-between world, no longer alive, yet not able to die. In Gracchus, the precipitous change that should have led to death leads instead to a deathless wandering, without hope and without the possibility of closure. While flux is a concomitant of imperfection, in *The Hunter Gracchus* it is the breakdown of the natural flow of change that ironically leads to imperfection.

Change is no less central for Schoenberg than for Kafka or Freud. Change through constant transformation of musical materials is immanent in most of his music; although flux arguably reaches an apex in *Erwartung*, it continues to be central and essential to Schoenberg's musical thought until the end of his life. In the twelve-tone works, the omnipresence of the row insures a kind of stability, but the row itself is manifest in endless possibilities. Schoenbergian perception is a perception based on the fleeting evanescence of things.

The kind of precipitous change that Kafka explores finds remarkable analogues in Schoenberg. As I will argue in Chapter Three, the massive intrusions of Fate in *Pelleas und Melisande* are more like Kafka than Wagner. The opening of *Das Buch der hängenden Gärten*, and even more powerfully the opening of *Moses und Aron* signal the kind of precipitous change that is so typical in Kafka. Catastrophe that converts the canny into the uncanny is likewise central to both works; in *Das Buch der hängenden Gärten*, love and kingdom have been lost, and the disruption of the normal flow of things results in an uncanny sense of time and place; in *Moses und Aron*, Moses standing before the Burning Bush is plunged into a world-changing new consciousness. For him, time and space will never be the same.

I find a passage in Gilles Deleuze's book, *Proust and Signs*, that is remarkably apposite to the kind of sudden change we have been discussing. The passage is worthy of violating my self-imposed limitation of examples concerning Freud, Kafka, and Schoenberg.[45]

> But the Socratic demon, irony, consists in anticipating the encounters. In
> Socrates the intelligence still comes before the encounters; it provokes them,
> it integrates and organizes them. Proust's sense of humor is of another nature:
> Jewish humor as opposed to Greek irony. One must be endowed for the signs,
> ready to encounter them, one must open oneself to their violence. The
> intelligence always comes after; it is good when it comes after; it is good only
> when it comes after.

Schoenberg opens *Moses und Aron* with Moses listening to the Divine polyphony as he stands before the Burning Bush. Moses comes upon the Burning Bush not because he has been searching for it. It takes him unaware, and nothing afterwards is the same. The wisdom of Freud, Kafka, and Schoenberg always comes after.

Our final trope is imperfection, the impossibility of getting to the bottom of things, or the impossibility of reaching a final state of being. As we have already noted, imperfection takes on many guises in Freud's thought. The unconscious, and then the id are wholly unfathomable, even the ego and super-ego are in great part submerged in inaccessible mystery. The play of substitutions in self-knowing is unending. And every memory that is suppressed is itself suppressed by another, *ad infinitum*. The play of figurative meanings, so basic to Freudian dream analysis, is exactly the same as the emergence of meaning in tropical substitution. Ken Frieden nicely captures this aspect of Freud, one that correlates with Deleuze's remark that intelligence comes after.[46]

> One pragmatic thesis of this book is that no interpretation is intrinsically
> true, because a present truth depends upon the future reality that confirms,
> alters, or gives meaning to the interpretive act. Meaning does not stand
> waiting to be uncovered behind a dream or text, but evolves in front of it,
> actualized by its readers and interpreters who produce new possibilities . . .
> Meaning is made, not discovered.

Emergent meaning is meaning in flux through change that cannot reach perfection.

Kafka's representations of imperfection are among the most extraordinary aspects of his parables and stories. The celebrated image of a doorkeeper in "Before the Law," a parable that is integrated into *The Trial*, provides a striking example. A man comes begging for admittance to the Law. A fearsome doorkeeper blocks his way, and tells of another even more fearsome than he, and another beyond him, an so on without count. The man waits his whole life, never getting past the first doorkeeper. As he is about to expire, the doorkeeper reveals that this door was created only for him, and that now it will be sealed for ever. Another equally striking parable is that of "An Imperial Message" ("*eine Kaiserliche Botschaft*"). Kafka describes a dying Emperor, "who has sent a message [exclusively] to you." The messenger leaves immediately and proceeds with all possible alacrity, but despite his indefatigable determination, he will never reach you, not even were he to travel for thousands of years, for the empire is too large to traverse.[47] Kafka's great masterpiece *The Castle* provides yet another striking example. K. approaches the Castle time and time again, but the way remains mysteriously elusive; K. will never reach his goal. Kafka's tales of imperfection are put into sober relief in that Kafka himself was never able to complete any of his larger works of fiction.

Long before Schoenberg imagined ways to exclude perfection from musical syntax, composers had created musical spaces that suggested the impossibility of emotional closure. Schubert in particular imagines such spaces: *Winterreise* as a whole, and its closing song, "der Leiermann," provide stunning examples. A similar lack of psychological closure is common in Mahler as well. Schoenberg's large-scale tonal works strike me as developing a different orientation to the impossibility of psychological closure. While the broad tonic pedals, so typical of Schoenberg's tonal endings, can be interpreted as arrivals (in the sense of Beethovenian rhetoric), they always strike me otherwise. Schoenberg's codas seem to reflect on a time and place regained from something lost and antecedent to the piece itself. Coda space is afterthought, and the forward moving rhetoric of Schoenberg's tonal masterworks cannot achieve closure. Chapters Two and Five explore such imaginative spaces in *Pelleas und Melisande* and the First String Quartet.

Schoenberg conceptualizes harmonic dissonance as resulting from conflict built into the harmony. The "emancipation of dissonance" does not erase dissonance, so much as it removes its obligation to resolve. It is this basic aspect of Schoenberg's reconception of harmony that opens new musical space, and fully initiates the impossibility of perfection. Imperfection, the impossibility of closure, becomes especially thematic in a number of works including *Erwartung*, *Die glückliche Hand*, and the String Trio. This aspect of *Erwartung* is discussed in the context of Chapter Five. Imperfection is central to my interpretation of the Trio in Chapter Seven, which uses the Freudian terms of Eros and Death Drive locked in conflict. The same drives are posited in my interpretation of *Pelleas und Melisande*. The early work ends as Golaud's bitter memories drive toward the final cadence, a triumph of the death drive. The Trio falls off at the end, into silence, but I posit that here death is not triumphant, for Schoenberg lives on to tell the tale.

Imperfection takes another guise in *Moses und Aron*, despite Schoenberg's attempts otherwise. As others have argued before me, I claim that *Moses und Aron* has reached an impasse at the end of its second act. I do not find

Schoenberg's attempts at a libretto for Act III to be convincing. For me, there is nowhere left to go once Moses utters his last words of Act II, *O Wort, du Wort, das mir fehlt.*

The tropical nexus of conflict, flux, and imperfection may be understood as comprising the central theory of this book: to the degree that any overriding theory is posited at all it is that music analysis should be guided by the quest for an adequate figurative language. But every theory has a conflict of interests. On the one hand it wants to understand the thing, being, or process which it interprets. On the other hand, it wants to prove itself. Interpretation and commentary are always infused with the shadowy life of theory, whether we want it or not.

Gershom Scholem characterized the canonical as that which calls forth endless commentary.[48] Like the examples of Kafka and Freud, there is something in Schoenberg that demands explanation and so calls forth commentary. Yet I am chastened by an observation made by Maurice Blanchot about interpreting Kafka.[49]

> What is strange about books like *The Trial* and *The Castle* is that they send us back endlessly to a truth outside of literature, while we begin to betray that truth as soon as it draws us away from literature, with which, however, it cannot be confused.
>
> This tendency is inevitable.

The truth of the music is in the music, and commentary should always send us back to the music itself.

1 A passing of worlds: *Gurrelieder* as Schoenberg's reluctant farewell to the nineteenth century

> Wir wurden aus dem Paradies vertrieben, aber zerstört wurde es nicht. Die Vertreibung aus dem Paradies war in einem Sinne ein Glück, denn wären wir nicht vertrieben worden, hätte das Paradies zerstört werden müssen.
>
> [We were expelled from Paradise, but Paradise was not destroyed. In a sense our expulsion from Paradise was a stroke of luck, for had we not been expelled, Paradise would have had to be destroyed.]
>
> Franz Kafka, "das Paradies"
[translated by Willa and Edwin Muir]

This chapter will function as an extension to the Introduction; rather than a study of *Gurrelieder* in its own right, the chapter functions as prelude to what follows. Schoenberg famously said that *Gurrelieder* was the key to his entire evolution.[1] It is in that spirit that we approach the work.

Even a passing acquaintance will reveal that Schoenberg's *Gurrelieder* is a work of enormous energy and imagination, a composition of majestic power and scope. Its realization was an incredible act of will by a composer only twenty-six and twenty-seven years old during its original conception and composition, an accomplishment made even more extraordinary in that the work was laid aside for a decade, a time during which its composer had undergone perhaps the most radical sea change in the history of music. In the course of Schoenberg's life's work, there were other major compositions that were put aside in the hope of being completed later. Schoenberg planned an even more massive symphonic work, *Die Jakobsleiter*, that remains only as a fragment. As we have already noted in the Introduction, *Moses und Aron* remains without music for its planned third act. *Gurrelieder* is the only large-scale work that Schoenberg was able to put aside and complete years later.[2]

Its composition began in 1900 and continued on into the next year. Schoenberg could work incredibly fast, but as the project grew in scope from its original conception of a song cycle – nine songs for tenor, soprano and piano – to its final conception in the form we now have – nearly two hours of music requiring one of the largest ensembles of musicians in the entire repertory – even the prodigious Schoenberg could not initially complete the work.[3] With no prospects for performance, and with other pressing matters claiming his energies, the demands of his quickly evolving musical imagination, as well as the mundane practicalities of paying rent and buying food, he put the huge project aside from 1901 until 1910. By the time that Schoenberg returned to *Gurrelieder*, his own musical universe had moved from the expansive forms of late German romanticism to the relatively compact forms of his second maturity, and more important, he had abandoned tonality and the *telos* and closure that are associated with tonal music. In so doing, Schoenberg had abandoned the kinds of narrative and musical structures that *Gurrelieder* embodied. And so, as Schoenberg completed the orchestration for the second half of the work in 1910 and 1911, it already embodied a world that had passed, the comfortable world of tonality and all that it had entailed.

But Schoenberg's reluctant farewell to the nineteenth century is not just a result of his returning to a work composed in an earlier style. The idea of reluctant farewell is profoundly embodied in the music and text itself. At the heart of *Gurrelieder* is a tension, indeed *conflict*, between looking backwards over the ever accumulating weight of the past, and looking forward to an unfolding that lies beyond the present, whose implications remain unknown and unknowable. Within the drama of the work, longing for the past is symbolized by Waldemar's love for Tove; looking toward the future is symbolized by the summer wind and the final sunrise.

As we have noted, Schoenberg claimed that *Gurrelieder* was the key to his entire evolution. Since he did not elaborate, the comment can be taken several ways. Knowing the work might alert listeners to aspects of his compositional style *in nuce*, and so listeners might perceive something of the logic of his later developments by understanding the nature of their precursors. Schoenberg himself described *Gurrelieder* as "propaganda" for his later music. And critics have cited the work to "prove" that Schoenberg knew what he was doing.[4] Schoenberg might also have been referring to the musical *Bildung* immanent within the work. Schoenberg's indebtedness to Wagner is extraordinarily present, especially in the first part, but the imprint of other composers in the Austrian-German tradition is also evident. Most significant are the voices of Brahms, in the work's phrase designs, counterpoint and in some of the approaches toward choral writing; Beethoven, the ultimate source for its motivic unity, and just as important, the probable model for the work's larger trajectory of musical affirmation; Bach, in its cantata-like structure, and in the dramatic functions of the choral parts; and Mahler, whose impact is especially evident in the lucidity of orchestration realized in 1910 and 1911. All of these composers comprise the ground from which Schoenberg springs.

But *Gurrelieder* is the key to Schoenberg's development in another way as well. The conflict between holding on to the past, and imagining the world anew, thematic to both the text and music, lies at the heart of Schoenberg's entire career as a composer. Descriptions of Schoenberg as a reluctant revolutionary, or as a Janus-faced figure are common in the literature, and they strike me as being fundamentally correct.[5] The conflict between holding on to the accomplishments of the past and imagining the world anew is worked out again and again as Schoenberg progresses through his life's work. In this sense, Schoenberg's reluctant farewell to the nineteenth century lasts a lifetime.

The literary background for *Gurrelieder* has been nicely studied by Brian Campbell, and I will summarize Campbell's research here.[6] The text is adopted from a German translation of poems by the Danish poet, novelist, and translator Jens Peter Jacobsen. Jacobsen, in addition to his novels and poems, is remembered as the Danish translator of Charles Darwin, and there is a Darwinian message embedded in the narrative of his *Gurresänge*: that nature will renew us through her own selective processes, irrespective of our more limited vision of self, origin and goal. The poems integrate two myths whose many variants would have been well-known to their Danish and German audiences, the doomed love of King Waldemar (Valdemar in the original) and Tove, and the legend of the "Wild Hunt," where the howling wind is personified as ghost riders in the sky who are damned to a never-ending nocturnal hunt. To these myths, Jacobsen adds a new twist at the end of his story: the world is born anew through the summer's wind and the final sunrise. For Jacobsen, the forces of nature herself cleanse the world of its mythic, accumulated past.

The encoding of memories, their gradual accumulation as the music becomes more and more retrospective, and then their dissipation as the music depicts the new sunrise becomes thematic to the entire work. Figure 1.1 provides an outline of the whole work, emphasizing the musical recollections as they accrue through the first part, and continue to haunt the second part, until they are finally dispersed through the summer's wind.

The work begins with an expansive prelude depicting the twilight of sunset. Example 1.1 shows its first four measures.

There will be nothing quite like this slow, majestic unfolding in all the works to come. Although the expansive prelude has antecedents in the works of Haydn, Mozart, and Beethoven, its chief precursor is Wagner's prelude to *Das Rheingold*, with Schoenberg inverting Wagner's morning (if not dawning) into his depiction of sunset. But whereas Wagner's prelude expansively prolongs a barely adorned tonic triad (E♭ major), Schoenberg begins almost immediately with an added sixth – C natural – and withholds an arrival of an unadorned tonic triad until well into the first song (also E♭, at m. 145 with words "Ruh aus" (Come to rest)). The longing for rest and resolution

Text by Jens Peter Jacobsen, German Translation by Robert Franz Arnold

Part I

Orchestral Prelude:

Depicts sunset, is musically without final resolution, and leads directly into the first song. Initiates the use of tone painting and use of Leitmotivs that will be pervasive in the work.

(Waldemar) "Nun dämpf die Dämm'rung jeden Ton" (Now dusk mutes every sound) – (Tove) "O, wenn des Mondes Strahlen leise gleiten" (Oh, when moonbeams softly glide):

The arrival of evening, images of nature at rest. In addition to new musical motives, the music continues to develop motives derived from the prelude.

(Waldemar) "Ross! mein Ross!" (Horse, my horse) – (Tove) "Sterne jubeln" (The stars rejoice):

The orchestral introduction to Waldemar's song develops what will become a principal motive in Tove's song that follows. "Ross! mein Ross!" introduces anxiety into the work, and in this sense anticipates his later "Es ist Mitternachtszeit." Tove's song transforms Waldemar's anxious music into a music that is joyous and celebratory, but the orchestral music before the next song returns to the unsettled music of "Ross! mein Ross!"

(Waldemar) "So tanzen die Engel vor Gottes Thron nicht" (Never have angels danced before the throne of God) – (Tove) "Nun sag' ich dir zum ersten Mal" (Now for the first time I say to you):

This song pair expresses joy, gratification, and fulfillment. Both are ravishing love songs. Waldemar's song foreshadows later comparisons (in Parts II and III) of the earthly king with God.

(Waldemar) "Es ist Mitternachtszeit" (It is midnight) – (Tove) "Du sendest mir einen Liebesblick" (You send me a loving glance):

This pair expresses a foreboding of death (Waldemar) and an acceptance of death (Tove). Tove's song recollects and transforms musical ideas from her "O, wenn des Mondes Strahlen." The climax of Tove's song embraces death: "So lass uns die goldene Schale leeren ihm, dem mächtig verschönenden Tod" (So let us drain the golden goblet to him, mighty, adorning Death).

(Waldemar) "Du wunderliche Tove!" (You wonderful Tove):

Peace, contentment, and deep love. Transforms material from Waldemar's "Ross! Mein Ross!" and Tove's "Sterne jubeln."

Orchestral Interlude

> Recollects all of Tove's songs, as well as "So tanzen die Engel vor Gottes Thron nicht," and "Du wunderliche Tove!" The orchestral climax is a reprise of the music from "So lass uns die goldene Schale leeren ihm, dem mächtig verschönenden Tod," from Tove's "Du sendest mir einen Liebesblick."

(Waldtaube) "Tauben von Gurre!" (Doves of Gurre):

> Announces the death of Tove. Recollections of "Es ist Mitternachtszeit," "Nun sag ich dir zum ersten Mal," "So tanzen die Engel vor Gottes Thron nicht," and "Du sendest mir einen Liebesblick" occur in counterpoint to the wood dove's litany.

Part II
Orchestral introduction and Waldemar's "Herrgott, weisst du was du tatest," (Lord God, do you know what you have done?):

> Waldemar quarrels with God over his loss of Tove. The orchestral introduction and song are permeated with musical recollections of "Tauben von Gurre!" Tove's "Du sendest mir einen Liebesblick" and Waldemar's "So tanzen die Engel vor Gottes Thron nicht" are also recollected.

Part III
(Waldemar) "Erwacht, König Waldemars Mannen wert!" (Arise King Waldemar's noble men!):

> The orchestra recollects "Es ist Mitternachtszeit" and then Waldemar summons his men to rise from the grave for the wild hunt.

(Bauer) "Deckel des Sarges klappert" (Coffin lids clatter):

> A peasant reports the horrific sight of Waldemar's men rising from their graves for the wild hunt.

(Waldemar's Men) "Gegrüsst, o König" (Greetings, oh King):

> The wild hunt. The men's choir sing the first choral setting of the work, a description of the hunt.

(Waldemar) "Mit Toves Stimme flüstert der Wald" (The wood whispers with Tove's voice):

> Waldemar's pantheistic substitution of Tove for God. Tove's spirit suffuses the world. The music recollects Tove's "Nun sag ich dir zum ersten Mal" and Waldemar's "Es ist Mitternachtszeit."

(Klaus-Narr) "Ein seltsamer Vogel ist so'n Aal" (A strange bird is the eel):

> The king's fool's nonsense song mocks Waldemar. The music ironically recollects Tove's "Nun sag ich dir zum ersten Mal."

(Waldemar) "Du strenger Richter droben" (You harsh judge above):

> Waldemar promises to storm heaven's fortress with his men. The music continues to recollect "Nun sag ich dir zum ersten Mal."

(Waldemar's Men) "Der Hahn erhebt den Kopf zur Kraht" (The cock raises his head to crow):

> Waldemar's men sing of the sunrise, soon to come, and of their longing to return to the peace of their graves. The music begins with recollections of "Ross! Mein Ross" and ends with figures reminiscent of "Nun dämpf die Dämm'rung."

Des Sommerwindes wilde Jagd

(Speaker) "Herr Gänsefuss, Herr Gänsekraut" (Sir Goosefoot, Lady Amaranth):

> The text, ever verging on nonsense, speaks of the stirrings of nature toward a new beginning. The music has glimmerings of the orchestral opening, and wisps of motives from "Nun sag ich dir zum ersten Mal" and from "Es ist Mitternachtszeit," but is dominated by the influx of new material with natural imagery throughout.

(Choir) "Seht, die Sonne" (Behold the sun):

> A grand choral finale depicting the rising sun. The music integrates motives from the opening sunset, but those motives are transfigured in their new context.

Figure 1.1. Overview of Arnold Schoenberg's *Gurrelieder.*

becomes thematic to the work whose ending brings tonal closure, but only with the promise of a new day, quite the opposite of Wagner's universal dissolution that ends the Ring.

Schoenberg's rapidly developing tendency toward musical ideas that undergo constant transformation would soon preclude the kind of slow, reiterative unfolding that characterizes the opening of *Gurrelieder*. In contrast, the imagery of flickering light – first painted in the piccolos, flutes, harps, strings, and horns – exemplifies a significant and recurrent trope for Schoenberg. By the time he composed *Gurrelieder*, Schoenberg had already painted flickering light in some of the most memorable passages in *Verklärte Nacht*. Of course, the light in *Verklärte Nacht* is moonlight, while *Gurrelieder* begins with sunset and ends with sunrise. As in *Verklärte Nacht*, light is depicted in *Gurrelieder* through a complex, rhythmic steady state composed of layered interaction among steady pulse-streams within a framework of

Example 1.1. *Gurrelieder*, first four measures.

harmonic stasis. A fascination with musical depictions of light would stay with Schoenberg through his second maturity, despite profound changes in his musical language; we will consider a number of striking examples in Chapter Five.[7] More important however, is the precedent of a complex rhythmic/harmonic steady state. This technique generalizes beyond depictions of light, to form the basis of Schoenberg's later depictions of uncanny time, our principal topic of Chapter Five.

The expansive prelude flows seamlessly into Waldemar's first song. As in Jacobsen's cycle, Schoenberg's setting of the text begins with a series of nine poems that alternate the voices of Waldemar and Tove. As shown in Figure 1.1, the opening eight poems and their musical settings work in pairs, each pair comprising a statement by Waldemar and a response by Tove. The fourth pair of songs begins with Waldemar's "Es ist Mitternachtszeit," the darkest song up until this point. Tove's response, "Du sendest mir einen Liebesblick," is a love song, but one that also contemplates death. Waldemar's final song of the first part, "Du wunderliche Tove!" is without the ominous forebodings of his previous song, as though Waldemar has forgotten or repressed his earlier anxiety: its music and text express peace and contentment. The song retrospectively takes on a bitter irony: this time there is no response from Tove. Instead, the response to Waldemar's "Du wunderliche Tove!" is the song of the Wood Dove, announcing Tove's death and bringing the first part of the work to its conclusion. In the musical setting, Schoenberg interposes a large-scale orchestral interlude, 135 measures in length, before we get to the Wood Dove's text. And so it is the interlude which first interrupts the series of statements and responses that characterize the music up until this point. The interlude is a retrospective, contrapuntal entangling of motives from six of the previous nine songs, all four of Tove's songs, and the two songs of Waldemar that are most explicitly love songs, "So tanzen die Engel," and "Du wunderliche Tove!" Thus, the music that prepares the news that Tove has died is saturated with musical memory. Its retrospection signifies loss before the Wood Dove makes that loss explicit.

The song of the Wood Dove, sealing the death of Tove, reminds us that we have not heard a duet between Waldemar and Tove, and that now such a duet is an impossibility. Of course, we can think of the alternating but separate poems for Waldemar and Tove as mere poetic convention, a convention followed by Schoenberg in his settings. There is no love duet, the most effective *musical* way to portray the union of Waldemar and Tove, simply because Schoenberg doesn't have a poetic duet available. Nonetheless, in the musical setting, the lack of a duet is at the very least, particularly striking. The missing duet is a palpable void that gives rise to an alternate interpretation of all that has passed, that *all* of the expressions of longing, gratification, and contentment are cast backwards in memory and that the lovers are

Example 1.2. Measures 93–6.

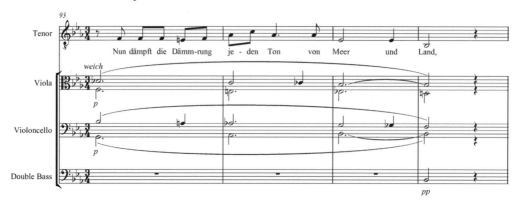

Example 1.3. Measures 139–45.

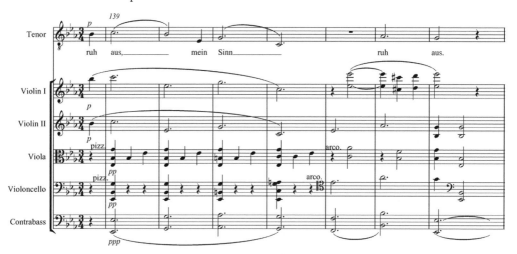

never united within the "now-time" of the work. By this interpretation the retrospection of the orchestral interlude continues and intensifies an implicit sense of loss that pervades the whole, and that is finally made explicit by the Wood Dove.

Examples 1.2 through 1.12 are designed to show how Schoenberg gradually builds up the memories that will eventually saturate the orchestral interlude, memories that will form the retrospective elements that continue into the second and third parts of *Gurrelieder*. Example 1.2 shows the first four measures of Waldemar's first song as it emerges out of the prelude.

The opening harmony and the chromatic descent in the viola continue the dissolution of the prelude as Waldemar adds his descriptive text. The vocal phrase, actually a fragment of a much larger phrase, terminates with a B♭ triad, the dominant of our tonic key, E♭. Example 1.3 shows the measures directly leading to the arrival of the tonic at m. 145.

Example 1.4. Measures 189–96 (texture simplified).

The line in the violins, with its salient added sixth, C-natural, is derived from a motive first heard in m. 3 of the prelude, and extensively developed as the prelude continues. The motive is only slightly embellished by Waldemar's melody "ruh aus, mein Sinn." The second iteration of "ruh aus" brings tonic closure for the first time in the work, and the sense of settling into the tonic triad after 145 expansive measures is extraordinary. Schoenberg then extends this cadence by prolonging the tonic for another fifteen measures up until m. 170. All of this glances backward at the space created by the prelude to create a sense of retrospection that dominates the work from its very beginnings.

Example 1.4 shows the opening music to Tove's first song, "O, wenn des Mondes Strahlen milde gleiten" (Oh, when moonbeams softly glide). Tove's reiterative Gb tonics, embellished by the exquisite voice-leading chords of mm. 194–5, continue the sense of expanse, while they add an increased sense of harmonic relaxation (albeit in the area of Gb). As we shall see in Example 1.10, Tove's melody will return somewhat transformed within her fourth

Example 1.5. Measures 343–9 (texture simplified).

song, "Du sendest mir einen Liebesblick." It is this later transformation of "Mondes Strahlen" that will be recollected in the orchestral interlude.

Example 1.5 shows the introduction to Tove's second song, "Sterne jubeln" (The stars rejoice). The song is Tove's response to "Ross! mein Ross!," Waldemar's first expressions of anxiety as he longs to arrive at Castle *Gurre* to be united with his beloved Tove. Tove's response is joyous and celebratory, in striking contrast to the unsettled music from "Ross! mein Ross!" which precedes it and then returns afterwards. The music of the introduction which functions as an extended dominant upbeat to the song's B major tonic has a giddy quality that is almost carnivalesque.

Example 1.6 shows the music that begins Waldemar's third song, "So tanzen die Engel vor Gottes Thron nicht," his claim that earthly joy with Tove's love is not surpassed even by the celebration of God in heaven. Schoenberg's approximation of chorale style in the string writing is clearly not by accident. The song will take on bitter irony as it is recollected in the orchestral interlude, then in the song of the Wood Dove, and then in Waldemar's "Herrgott, weisst du was du tatest" (Lord God, do you know what you have done), the song comprising Part II of the *Gurrelieder*.

Example 1.6. Measures 444–51 (texture simplified).

Example 1.7. Measures 502–15 (voice part only).

Example 1.7 shows voice part for the first fifteen measures of Tove's "Nun sag ich dir zum ersten Mal." The words, placed in the present tense, are clearly a retrospective and imagined conversation.

Nun sag ich dir zum ersten Mal:	Now for the first time I say:
"König Volmer, ich liebe dich!"	"King Volmer, I love you!"
Nun, küss ich dich zum erstenmal,	Now, I kiss you for the first time,
Und schlinge den Arm um dich.	And encircle you in my arms.
Und sprichst du, ich hätt' es schon früher gesagt	And if you say I have already told you,
Und je meinen Kuss dir geschenkt . . .	Or have ever given you my kiss . . .

The wide, lyrical leaps in Tove's slowly unfolding melody are beautifully expressive and very memorable. The text's message of love "for the first time" will become more and more poignant as "first time" is recollected in the orchestral interlude, and by the Wood Dove. The motive becomes a virtual *idée fixe* within Part III of *Gurrelieder* as it becomes a recurrent thread in Waldemar's "Mit Tove's Stimme flüstert der Wald," Klaus-Narr's mocking "Ein seltsamer Vogel ist so'n Aal," and then Waldemar's "Du strenger Richter droben." "For the first time" will then take on new meaning in its final appearances in "Des Sommerwindes wilde Jagd," where it is expressive of the new dawn to come, while never losing its retrospection of "first times" that have passed.

Example 1.8 shows the opening measures of Waldemar's "Es ist Mitternachtszeit." The harps and string basses toll twelve strokes of time on their octave D-naturals while the celli spin out their mournful and foreboding melody. Waldemar's words – "It is midnight, and unholy beings rise from forgotten, sunken graves" – anticipate the images of Part III, the rising of the dead that form Waldemar's army of the damned. Later in the song (mm. 577–80 and again at 636 and following) time tolls again to the words, "Unsre Zeit ist um" (Our time is over), Waldemar anticipating Tove's death as well and ultimately his own. Like the very different music of the prelude only in this respect, the steady pulse-stream measures out time. We have noted that the flicker light of the prelude anticipates later developments expressive of uncanny time. Here the connection is more explicit; "Es ist Mitternachtszeit" is already uncanny in its anticipation of death. The chiming of uncanny time will return with the song of the Wood Dove.[8]

Example 1.9 shows the opening measures of Tove's final song, "Du sendest mir einen Liebesblick." It is Tove's climactic statement, inspiring some of the most extraordinary orchestration in Part I of *Gurrelieder* (although nothing surpasses the orchestration of Part III). The song begins with twelve solo strings composed of four violins, four violas, and four celli. The orchestration expresses intimacy, tenderness, and a sense of overflowing as it builds toward its more and more impassioned lyricism. The D♯-E motive, an ascending semitone, conveys a sense of longing. Ascending semitones are further developed by the opening vocal line, "Du sendest mir einen Liebesblick" (You send me a loving glance) and then by "liebeweckenden Kuss" (love awakening kiss) whose melody brings the semitone motive back to its original pitches. The melody for "liebeweckenden Kuss" is loosely based on Tove's first song, "O, wenn des Mondes Strahlen milde gleiten" (see Example 1.4, mm. 191–6) with its downward leap of a perfect fifth and scalar ascent. It becomes greatly developed during the orchestral interlude. The expansive climax of the song is heard at mm. 691–8 as Tove sings "So lass uns die goldene Schale leeren ihm, dem mächtig verschönenden Tod" (So let us drain the golden goblet to him, mighty, adorning Death). The opening of this passage is shown in Example 1.10. This music later becomes

Example 1.8. Measures 553–62.

Example 1.9. Measures 653–67 (texture simplified).

the source for the climax of the orchestral interlude beginning at measure 919 and continuing into the dissolution of the interlude and the music that announces the song of the Wood Dove and news of Tove's death.

Waldemar responds to Tove's "Du sendest mir einen Liebesblick" with his own expansive love song, "Du wunderliche Tove!" Example 1.11 shows the open measures of Waldermar's song whose expressive leaps are reminiscent of Tove's earlier "Nun sag ich dir zum ersten Mal" (Example 1.7). Waldemar's second vocal phrase, "So reich durch dich nun bin ich," is enriched by doublings in the violins. It will later generate the opening sequence of the orchestral interlude, as shown in Example 1.12.

Example 1.12 shows the opening measures of the orchestral interlude where memories of the preceding songs begin to saturate the musical texture. The technique is clearly indebted to Wagner, but the contrapuntal virtuosity of composition is very Schoenbergian. The opening six measures develop the melody derived from "So reich durch dich nun bin ich," and then, with the change to 4/4, the viola *espressivo* remembers Tove's "Nun sag' ich dir zum ersten Mal." A *stretto* of recollective fragments quickly piles up as the English horn recalls "Sterne jubeln" and fragments of "ersten Mal" and

Example 1.9. (*cont.*)

Example 1.10. Measures 691–2.

Example 1.11. Measures 722–33.

"Sterne jubeln" continue to weave through the oboe, bassoons, and celli. With the upbeat to m. 827, the clarinet marked *espressivo* plays a fragment of Waldemar's "So tanzen die Engel." As this continues in counterpoint to "ersten Mal" in the violas, the first flute and violins bring the initial constellation of memories to its most expansive statement remembering

Example 1.12. Measures 818–29.

"und je meinen Kuss dir geschenkt" from Tove's "Nun sag ich dir zum ersten Mal" (see Example 1.7, mm. 514–16). The flood of memories continues as the orchestral interlude expands from measure 818 until 953 forming a huge coda to the initial nine songs and separating all that came before from the song of the Wood Dove. All of this then becomes the "before" that separates Part I of *Gurrelieder* from all that remains.

Gurrelieder is a Dionysian vision of birth out of death. This is true both of the larger drama ending with rebirth as the old is swept away, and also within the context of the first part alone. The death of Tove, whose spirit then suffuses Waldemar's world, has its roots in Greek myth, the legends of Dionysus and Orpheus. Schoenberg would return to other variants of Dionysian *sparagmos* in *Pierrot lunaire*, *Moses und Aron*, and arguably in his String Trio as well.[9] From a Freudian perspective, the work exemplifies the most primal of conflicts, the death drive, *Thanatos*, pitted against the life force, *Eros*. This is the primal conflict that Schoenberg would approach differently in *Pelleas und Melisande*, and near the end of his life, in the String Trio. In its depiction of a literal and metaphoric journey through the night, *Gurrelieder* participates in the tradition of heroic questing, one of literature's most basic archetypes, a lineage that includes Homer, Virgil, Dante, and Goethe. The examples of music as quest that Schoenberg would have recognized would certainly include Beethoven and Wagner, and both composers loom large in *Gurrelieder*. As Campbell points out, the number of parallels with and departures from Wagner's dramas are uncanny, especially in that the poet Jacobsen evidently had little interest in Wagner. Needless to say, the parallels would not have escaped Schoenberg.[10] The love-death idea, central to *Tristan und Isolde*, is paralleled by Waldemar and Tove, except that rather than union through love-death as depicted by Wagner, Tove's death results in their eternal separation, Waldemar's "wild hunt," and his feckless promise of storming heaven. There are also relations between *Gurrelieder* and the legend of the Flying Dutchman. The Dutchman is doomed to an eternal journey which parallels the "wild hunt" of Waldemar's men. But whereas the Dutchman is ultimately saved, Waldemar and his ghostly hunt are forgotten, swept away by the summer's wind. Perhaps most striking, the overall trajectory of the work inverts the sunrise to sunset organization of Wagner's Ring. We might recall Debussy's famous comment that Wagner was a sunset mistaken for a sunrise. Schoenberg was a sunrise who could never get over the sunset that had preceded. (It would certainly seem that the reception history of art music since Schoenberg has largely continued to play out this nostalgia for a lost past.)

It seems to me that the final apotheosis of *Gurrelieder*, the depiction of the new sunrise, in its musical manifestation owes at least as much to Beethoven as it does to Wagner. It is surely among the work's most central ironies that Schoenberg depicts the closing sunrise with a massive chorus set firmly in C major, all the more striking because of the extended chromaticism of so much of the music that precedes it. The overwhelming power of that chorus can only be experienced in live performances; it succeeds through its sheer immensity of force. On the page, and even in recordings, the triumph of C major seems a cop-out, a vestige of Beethovenian rhetoric, where diatonicism triumphs over chromaticism, the tried and "true" method of works such as Beethoven's Fifth and Ninth symphonies. As stated earlier, by the time that Schoenberg completed *Gurrelieder* in 1911, he had abandoned this kind of narrative structure. As we will see in our interpretation of the String Trio in Chapter Seven, the ghost of Beethoven will continue to imprint the music of Schoenberg, but the triumph of final tonic was a myth that had been spent.

The creation of a *Volk* myth itself is another aspect of *Gurrelieder*, one that represents another deep connection to and departure from Wagner. Schoenberg as a Jew would eventually realize that no amount of *Bildung* would allow him to participate in the kind of *Volkgeist* that once seemed imaginable. The connection with that *Volkgeist* is not yet severed in *Gurrelieder*. Nature revivified through the summer wind implies a regenerated *Volk* rooted in nature.

The idealization of peoples being rooted in the land was among the most seminal ideas of the entire Romantic movement. Geoffrey Hartman, in *The Fateful Question of Culture*, traces the degradation of the idea of rootedness from William Wordsworth's benign, even salutary understanding of humanity's connection to nature to Heidegger's *bodenloses Denken*, and the anti-intellectualism and anti-Semitism that fed into the Nazi agenda.[11] Hartman contrasts Wordsworth's "faith in a trustworthy rural imagination" with later developments on the continent (italics in the original).[12]

> *It is my view that the failure to carry this imagination into a modern form, the failure to translate into a modern idiom a sensibility nurtured by country life, creates – less in England, because of Wordsworth, than in continental Europe – an unprogressive, over idealized, image of what is lost, and thus a deeply anti-urban sentiment.*

In Hartman's striking phrase, "A man without property becomes too easily a man without properties (qualities, *Eigenschaften*): deracinated, lacking local attachments, abstract in his thinking . . ."[13] Leon Botstein's article, "Schoenberg and the Audience: Modernism, Music, and Politics in the Twentieth Century," brings these same concerns into direct relevance in the reception of Schoenberg's music.[14] To exemplify the kinds of critique that Schoenberg faced in the 1920s, Botstein cites Oscar Bie's comparison of Schoenberg and Bartók.[15]

> Bie unwittingly confirms the idea that Bartók had no need to invent artificially; he could reach back into the cultural roots of his homeland and find natural sources of originality. Bie's unfavorable comparison hides an implicit agreement with the view of the Jew as inferior, foreign, and without genuine roots in Europe.

By the 1920s, Schoenberg had long abandoned music that was grounded in what had come to seem natural. Indeed, the metaphors of groundedness and rootedness were and still are fundamental to our understanding tonal music. Moreover, as a Jew who had never known a Jewish folk tradition (through *Bildung*, Bach, Mozart, Beethoven, Schubert, Brahms, Wagner and others had become his *Volk*), Schoenberg couldn't draw upon folk roots, roots that came so naturally to Bartók, Stravinsky, and others. Even the largely Jewish audiences could only react in discomfort as Schoenberg "challenged the premises of the audience's fragile sense of place."[16] The fragile sense of place is still intact in the final affirmation of the *Gurrelieder*. By the time of its 1913 premiere, which was a great success with the audience and critics alike, Schoenberg could no longer affirm that sense of place. Can it be any wonder that he could not accept the adulation of the audience?

A grounding in nature within *Gurrelieder* is reflected in its pervasive use of naturalistic tone painting. Whereas "voice" had been part of the Jewish imagination from the time of the poet whose work forms the core of Genesis and Exodus, visual images of nature come down to us primarily through the Greek imagination. In his essay "Odysseus' Scar," the literary critic Erich Auerbach compares the narrative technique in Homer to that in the Torah, the Hebrew bible. Whereas Homer's descriptions are full of light and visual detail, in the Torah voices emerge from the darkness; the Torah generally does not describe faces or places.[17]

> It would be difficult, then, to imagine styles more contrasted than those of these two equally ancient and equally epic texts. On the one hand, [in Homer] externalized, uniformly illuminated phenomena, at a definite time and in a definite place, connected together without lacunae in a perpetual foreground; thoughts and feeling completely expressed; events taking place in leisurely fashion and with very little suspense. On the other hand, [in the Torah] the externalization of only so much of the phenomena as is necessary for the purpose of the narrative, all else left in obscurity; the decisive points of the narrative alone are emphasized, what lies between is nonexistent; time and

place are undefined and call for interpretation; thoughts and feeling remain unexpressed, are only suggested by the silence and the fragmentary speeches; the whole, permeated with the most unrelieved suspense and directed toward a single goal . . . , remains mysterious and 'fraught with background.'

Harold Bloom makes a similar observation:

The preferred biblical way of representing an object is to explain *how it was made.* We are not told how the Ark of the Covenant, the Desert Sanctuary, the Temple, and Solomon's Palace looked, because the stories of how they were built is what constitutes depiction. And though we are told that Joseph, David, and Absalom were outstandingly handsome, again we are given only an impression, with no sense of their actual appearance.[18]

Bloom's observations are placed in the larger context of his discussion of the Second Commandment and the "curious sense of interiority [that] marks Jewish thought."[19] The tendency of Schoenberg's music to depict interior, psychological space is pervasive, and will remain central to his musical expressivity until the end of his life. But his musical interiority is not necessarily connected to his being a Jew. Music defining interior space had been well established in the late works of Beethoven and had been central to the Romantic tradition throughout the nineteenth century. Depictions of interior and exterior space commingle throughout the Romantic period and both kinds of space are significant in Schoenberg's music.

Although the physical characteristics of Waldemar, Tove, and the others are not described in Jacobsen's text, its images of nature are vivid, and commonplace throughout. Schoenberg responds to the naturalistic images in the poetry by composing some of the most striking tone painting in his entire career. In fact, naturalistic tone painting, famously explored by Beethoven in his Sixth Symphony, and central to the orchestral techniques of Wagner, is pervasive in *Gurrelieder.* The centrality of natural images in Jacobsen's text, given his Darwinian world-view, comes as no surprise, but it is interesting to think about the preponderance of musical tone painting in light of Schoenberg's evolution as a composer. Although *Gurrelieder* provides the most abundant examples of natural imagery in Schoenberg's music, it is certainly not alone among his compositions in using this technique. Mimesis of nature is conspicuous in a number of central works, both before and after the composition of *Gurrelieder.* To name some examples, we have the moonbeams of *Verklärte Nacht,* the famous depiction of a summer morning by a lake in his Five Pieces for Orchestra, op. 16 (which includes a motif that Schoenberg himself described as a leaping trout), as well as many examples of tone painting in the *Book of the Hanging Gardens, Erwartung,* and *Pierrot lunaire.* Nonetheless, in the context of Schoenberg's entire output, musical evocations of nature play a relatively small role, a role that seems to diminish to a vanishing point in Schoenberg's twelve-tone period, from the mid 1920s until his death in 1951. Naturalistic tone painting is minimally used in Schoenberg's opera *Moses und Aron*, and the technique fades to insignificance in Schoenberg's late works. It is interesting, therefore, to note that Schoenberg's abandonment of tone painting roughly coincides with his return to Judaism. Given the centrality of nature as sublime in the Romantic world-view, the prominence of tone painting in *Gurrelieder* is also part of Schoenberg's reluctant farewell to the nineteenth century.

2 Dialectical opposition in Schoenberg's music and thought

Opposition is true Friendship *The Marriage of Heaven and Hell*

William Blake

Es ist langweilig, wenn die Polizisten interessanter sind als die Räuber. [It is boring if the police are more interesting than the robbers.]

Harmonielehre Arnold Schoenberg

In the Introduction, we began to explore the significance of conflict in Schoenberg's thought and that of his contemporaries, noting there its centrality to Freud's model of the psyche and to the mysterious worlds of Kafka's beleaguered personae.[1] In this chapter we explore the role of conflict within Schoenberg's critical and pedagogical writings, characterizing it as *dialectical opposition*. After an introduction that provides a general context for our inquiry, an historical sketch traces significant precursors to Schoenbergian dialectics by outlining key developments in the history of dialectical thought and adaptations of that thought within musical discourse. The chapter continues by formulating and discussing various categories of *opposition* as they are used in music theory in general and in Schoenberg studies in particular. The next three sections of the chapter separate Schoenbergian dialectics into three principal areas: dialectics of history, dialectical aspects of musical technique, and "systems" as failed dialectics. Each of these sections centers on close readings of passages from Schoenberg's critical and pedagogical writings. The chapter concludes with a brief discussion of the implications of dialectical thought for future analysis.

Introduction

While the creative thought of Arnold Schoenberg cannot be reduced to *any* single, consistent and well defined methodology or world-view, it is possible nonetheless to trace a network of assumptions and values whose components, though loosely affiliated and sometimes mutually contradictory, inform and guide the overall shape as well as the minutiae of details that constitute his creative life's work. Among those assumptions and values, a tendency to think in terms of what we will call *dialectical oppositions* is a basic constituent of Schoenberg's creativity.[2] Dialectical oppositions, at least to some degree, shape his view of history as well as his view of his own place within the history of music. Dialectical oppositions are basic to Schoenberg's understanding of musical technique; these assumptions profoundly affect the development of his musical language. Moreover, in at least one passage in the *Harmonielehre*, Schoenberg ascribes far-ranging moral and musical compromises to weakened or failed dialectical situations.

The importance of specific precursors notwithstanding, it seems safe to assert that Schoenberg's tendency to think in terms of dialectical opposition is culturally based, and not the result of specific readings or self-conscious affiliation with any philosophical, psychological or pedagogical school. In other words, Schoenberg thinks dialectically not because he is a student of Hegel, or Hauptmann, or any specific school of thought, but because he is a product of *fin-de-siècle* Vienna where dialectical thought, at least among the intelligentsia, is pervasive. Of course, the specifics of that thought vary greatly among creative persons. Those specifics take on surprising and momentous proportions at the heart of Schoenberg's creative imagination. Since the word "dialectical" has had a long, complex and changing range of meanings, I will begin by offering a working definition of "dialectical opposition," and proceed from there.

> Definition: *Dialectical Opposition* – the process wherein progress, change or some desired resultant is obtained through antagonisms or other types of opposition applied to matter, ideas, values, emotions, etc. The *opposition* is normally dyadic, where two forces, ideas, values, etc. are pitted against one another or opposed in some way to result in a third force, idea, value, etc. The *opposition* can be conceived of as *necessary* in that the resultant (i.e. the 'third' force, idea, value, etc.) cannot be obtained without it. Although normally dyadic, the concept of *dialectical opposition* can be enlarged to include the resultants from complex force fields of oppositions.

Within the definition I have side-stepped at least three issues that have been significant in the history of dialectical thought. First, there is no mention of an *ideal* versus a *material* basis of things. Second, and more important in our present context, I have avoided the thorny question of *telos*. By the definition, dialectical opposition does not require (or exclude) a goal-oriented view of history. Third, the definition does not address the significant distinction between dialectical systems that assert that opposition is neutralized as it gives rise to a higher unity, as in a Hegelian *Aufhebung*, versus dialectics where opposition is sustained within a higher unity, as in the thought of Heraclitus. My reasons for these avoidances are as follows: 1) while the history of dialectical oppositions includes idealism and materialism as variables, outside of a professed *ontology*, the distinction is moot; in Schoenberg's writings and thought there is no fully developed *ontology*, and moreover, the distinction is generally irrelevant in most practical music making, analysis and criticism; 2) the choice between *telos* and a universe that simply unfolds in a continuous flux is not always clear, or perhaps even consistent in Schoenberg's writings; 3) while a Heraclitean rather than Hegelian view of opposition seems generally more consistent with Schoenberg's writings and practice, Schoenberg is certainly not explicit nor consistent in this, and so I have opted for greater generality in the definition.[3]

Historical sketch

Like most aspects of Western thought, understanding the world in terms of dialectical oppositions can be traced back to ancient Greece. In this case, the Greek source is particularly apposite because the understanding of *music* plays a central role in its origin. The argument between the pre-Socratic philosopher Heraclitus and the Pythagoreans concerning the nature of harmony is a defining historical moment. Historian W. K. C. Guthrie provides a succinct and commanding discussion of the matter.

> The word *harmonia*, a key-word of Pythagoreanism, meant primarily the joining or fitting of things together, even the material peg with which they were joined (Homer, *Od.*, V, 248) then especially the stringing of an instrument with strings of different tautness . . . , and so the musical scale.[4]

This in vivid contrast to Heraclitus for whom the opposition of *contraries* was a fundamental aspect of the universe:

> Harmony is always the product of opposites, therefore the basic fact in the world is strife.[5]

The Pythagoreans certainly had a fully developed concept of opposition or strife, but in their system discord and concord are primarily understood as alternating states (although, cf. Philolaus cited below). Guthrie's comparison of Empedocles and Heraclitus is to the point:

> Empedocles, who followed the Italian tradition dominated by Pythagoras, spoke of alternate states of harmony and discord, unity and plurality . . . Heraclitus with his 'stricter muse' asserted that any harmony between contrasting elements necessarily and always involved a tension or strife between the opposites of which it was composed. The tension is never resolved. Peace and war do not succeed each other in turn: always in the world there is both peace and war. Cessation of struggle would mean disintegration of the universe.[6]

Also of interest are fragments attributed to Philolaus, whose definition of harmony evidently became the source for later writers, including Boethius, who transmitted a version of that definition into the mainline of the Western tradition.

> Nature in the universe was harmonized from unlimiteds and limiters, both the whole universe and things in it.[7]
>
> *Harmonia* comes to be in all respects out of opposites: for *harmonia* is a unification of things multiply mixed, and an agreement of things that disagree.[8]

As we move through the history of Western civilization, from antiquity up until the late eighteenth century, there seems to be little evidence of a Heraclitean opposition of contraries having any significant impact on our thought about music. In great contrast, ideas that may be ultimately derived from the Pythagoreans are highly significant. Pythagorean assumptions of "things fitting together" and of the alternation of "discord and concord" are at the very basis of our musical thought, as common to Boethius as they are to Schenker.[9] Moreover, in the vast preponderance of our current discourse, "things fitting together" takes precedence over the contrariety of discord and concord. Unity, as it is normally described, is a higher level of concord, not, as Heraclitus would have it, a state of continual flux that necessarily involves and sustains tension or strife between opposites.

To my knowledge, the story of the re-emergence of dialectical thought in the late eighteenth and early nineteenth centuries is yet to be fully studied. It is a difficult and complex story to trace, in part because its constituents are diffused throughout European and American culture. Although prominent in the history of philosophy, dialectical thought is not restricted to philosophy. At the very least, theater, music and poetry as well as philosophy and political theory feed into the general growth of thinking about the world in terms of opposition and conflict. And though dialectical opposition emerges as a pervasive constituent of thought at the dawn of the Romantic period, its immediate precursors reach back at least as far as the seventeenth century. A striking example is found in what Arthur Lovejoy calls the principle of *counterpoise*.

> Although philosophers of the 17th and eighteenth centuries, when discoursing on the divine government of the world, often declared it to be axiomatic that the Creator always accomplished his ends by the simplest and most direct means, they also tended to assume that he is frequently under the necessity of employing what may be called the method of counterpoise – accomplishing desirable results by balancing harmful things against one another. This was illustrated in the admirable contrivance on which popular expositions of the Newtonian celestial mechanics liked to dwell, whereby the

planets had within them a centrifugal force which alone would have made them fly off into space in straight lines, and a centripetal force, which alone would have caused them to fall into the sun; happily counterbalancing one another, these two otherwise mischievous forces caused these bodies to behave as they should, that is, to roll round in their proper orbits. And human nature was increasingly conceived after the analogy of such a mechanical system . . . The place of the method of counterpoise in the dynamics of human nature had been tersely pointed out by Pascal before 1660: 'We do not sustain ourselves in a state of virtue by our own force, but by the counterpoise of two opposite faults, just as we stand upright between two contrary winds; remove one of these faults and we fall into the other.'[10]

While *counterpoise* as a model of human nature may have posited the neutralization of negative forces through their interaction, the burgeoning role of theater in the seventeenth century showed a more variegated view of human conflict. *Dramatic* opposition becomes a basic constituent of musical composition during the eighteenth century, a tendency clear, for example, in virtually any work of Mozart. This in turn sets the stage for further developments that take place in the nineteenth century when dialectical opposition becomes one of the principal ways that we understand the universe.

It is generally accepted that developments in English poetry anticipate many of the changes that are the hallmarks of German Romanticism. In this light, some of the central tenets of William Blake – a poet not usually associated with German Romanticism – take on surprising significance. Blake first formulates his principle of opposition of *contraries* in his poem *The Marriage of Heaven and Hell* (1790–3): "Without Contraries is no progression. Attraction and Repulsion, Reason and Energy, Love and Hate, are necessary to Human existence."[11]

Unlike Hegelian dialectics, which develop during the early nineteenth century and which assume that oppositions lead to higher syntheses (the concept of Hegelian *Aufhebung*), Blake's oppositions are based on eternal forces that are always opposed. In this respect, the Blakean concept of *contraries* is in striking agreement with Heraclitus. Indeed, Blake's epigram "Opposition is true Friendship" is most likely a paraphrase of Heraclitus taken from Aristotle.[12]

While Blake may have asserted that "without Contraries is no progression," it is German philosophy of the nineteenth century that brings dialectical opposition to the foreground of intellectual debate. Dialectical opposition becomes the mechanism for universal progress most famously in the works of Hegel, but Hegel's concepts are part of a rich and complex intellectual context.

Not long after Blake's "Marriage," Friedrich Schlegel, in *Athenäum Fragmente* (1797–8), defines "idea" in terms of a self engendering opposition. Although Schlegel and Blake are vastly different thinkers, placing their views on the opposition of contraries side by side reveals a striking congruence.

> An idea is a concept perfected to the point of irony, an absolute synthesis of absolute antitheses, the constantly self-engendering interchange of two conflicting thoughts.[13]

Ian Bent has shown that Schlegel's contemporary and colleague Friedrich Schleiermacher based hermeneutics and the principle of the *hermeneutic circle* on two central modes of opposition: *whole* versus *part* and *objectivity* which he thought was exemplified in "language" versus *subjectivity*, exemplified by "the one who speaks." In Schleiermacher's hermeneutics, the dialectic of the whole versus the part is not restricted to oppositions within a given work. The dialectic operates between works as well; it is the force that generates traditions.[14]

Another key development in the terminology of dialectical opposition is attributed to the philosopher Johann Gottlieb Fichte. Fichte, a student of Kant, formulated three stages – thesis, antithesis, and synthesis – and applied them to his study of history (*Grundzüge des gegenwärtigen Zeitalters*, 1806).[15] As the nineteenth century continued, dialectical oppositions are adapted and profoundly developed by Hegel, and later by Karl Marx. By the late nineteenth century, thought in terms of dialectical oppositions becomes diffused throughout the general culture, and it remains a basic constituent of German and Austrian thought well into the twentieth century. The sociologist Georg Simmel, Schoenberg's contemporary, provides a striking example applied to human interaction.

> The individual does not attain the unity of his personality exclusively by an exhaustive harmonization, according to logical, objective, religious, or ethical norms, of the contents of his personality. On the contrary, contradiction and conflict not only precede this unity but are operative in it at every moment of its existence. Just so, there probably exists no social unit in which convergent and divergent currents among its members are not inseparably interwoven. An absolutely centripetal and harmonious group, a pure "unification" ("*Vereinigung*"), not only is empirically unreal, it could show no real life progress.[16]

It is not surprising therefore that nineteenth- and early twentieth-century music theory would incorporate dialectical models. In the 1830s François-Joseph Fétis formulates the very beginnings of musicological historiography along Hegelian lines.[17] In the 1840s Adolph Bernhard Marx applies dialectical principles toward understanding the motion and rest within the major scale, his paradigm for "the whole science of music."

> We recognize the Tonic therefore as the beginning and end of the scale.
> The latter originates from the Tonic and returns to it. In juxta-position
> to the Tonic – the moment of repose – the scale – the moment of motion –
> is formed. Here we have discovered at last an antithesis which runs through
> the whole science of music – REPOSE and MOTION, TONIC and
> SCALE.[18]

Marx subsequently adapts dialectical thought in his description of musical phrasing – antecedent as thesis and consequent as antithesis – and he applies the same principles to his description of sonata form – where the first part and second part are each divided into thesis/antithesis, and where the whole is characterized as a larger unity embodying repose, motion, repose.[19] As was true for Fétis, A. B. Marx was influenced directly by Hegel, indeed, he lectured at the University of Berlin during the last years of Hegel's life, a period during which Hegel's influence was at its apex.

A thoroughgoing exploration of dialectical opposition in music theory is found in the work of Moritz Hauptmann (*Die Natur der Harmonik und der Metrik zur Theorie der Musik*, 1853). The book is self-consciously based on Hegelian principles and virtually all aspects of harmony and meter are understood as exemplifying the principle of dialectical opposition.[20] Closer to Schoenberg's generation, the various writings of Hugo Riemann (1849–1919) are suffused with dialectical assumptions about music history and musical technique. Between January and December of 1872, Riemann, under the pseudonym of Hugibert Ries, published a series of articles entitled *Musikalische Logik* in the *Neue Zeitschrift für Musik*. This work is explicit in its indebtedness to Hauptmann, and it is thoroughgoing in its application of Fichte's terminology – thesis, antithesis, and synthesis – to aspects of harmonic progression, musical phrasing, and rhythm.[21] While the explicit links with dialectical thought are softened in Riemann's later work, the underlying assumptions still remain intact. In very different ways, dialectical oppositions also inform the work of Heinrich Schenker (1868–1935).[22] And though Adorno singles out Schoenberg as "der dialektische Komponist" for reasons specific to Adorno's own polemics, a more embracing dialectics could have been applied to any number of German-speaking musicians of his generation.[23]

In addition to considering ideas that are explicitly dialectical, in establishing the preconditions for Schoenbergian dialectics we must be cognizant at the very least of two more aspects of musical thought that are conspicuous in the generations leading to his own. First, as already noted, there is the well documented shift that takes hold during the Classical period from a rhetorical model of musical composition to one based on drama.[24] To be sure, the art of rhetoric is inextricably linked with argumentation; the ultimate bases of advocacy in our legal system are derived from the study of rhetoric. Nonetheless, coherence and persuasiveness are at the core of rhetorical argument while *conflict* is the basic constituent of drama. Drama in music gives rise to a wide range of oppositions involving key areas, qualitative affects, textures of timbre and rhythm, and the like. Within Germany and Austria, traditions of theater and musical theater, stimulated in part by August Schlegel's translations of Shakespeare, had a profound impact on emerging German Romanticism and its tendencies to think in terms of opposed forces.[25] Second, discussions of *Mehrdeutigkeit*, ranging as far back as Abbé Vogler, but most important in the work of Gottfried Weber and successive theorists, form a rich tradition of thinking about the elements of music in terms of multiple, opposed meanings.[26] Of course, musical thought in terms of *Mehrdeutigkeit* is not necessarily dialectical, but it does set up significant preconditions for those composers who will think dialectically.

Categories of opposition

Once again, turning back to the ancient Greeks will prove useful in formulating categories of *opposition* in music and in thought about music. The *locus classicus* for the analysis of *opposition* is Aristotle's *Categories*.[27] Aristotle, well over a century after Heraclitus, categorized four basic types of opposition (the examples are those provided by Aristotle): *relatives* (e.g. the double and the half); *contraries* (e.g. the good and the bad); *privation/possession* (e.g. blindness and sight); and *affirmation/negation* (e.g. he is sitting, he is not sitting).[28] Although a deconstruction of Aristotle's categories is easily done – e.g. relatives (two halves) are always contraries (to be left is contrary to being right), involve privation/possession (each half does not include the other), as well as affirmation/negation (this half, not that) – the distinctions are useful and interesting nonetheless.[29] All of the "dialectical oppositions" that we have traced historically, as well as those that will interest us in Schoenberg's music and thought, fit most convincingly into the Aristotelian category of *contraries*. However, before turning to musical modes of *conflict*, it will be helpful to give an overview of the ways music theory employs the other three categories: relatives, privation/possession, affirmation/negation.

Aristotle's category of *relatives* fits comfortably with our current colloquial use of the term.

> Things opposed as *relatives* are called just what they are, *of* their opposites or in some other way *in relation to* them. For example, the double is called just what it is (double) *of* the half.[30]

Within the discourse of music theory, the most common category of opposition is surely that of *relation*. Beyond the obvious examples, from the mundane "relative keys" to the exotic "Z-relations," the category of *relative* is at the basis of our ideas about motivic transformations of most kinds; if we hear x_2 as a transformation of x_1 then we hear the two as related or associated. Complementarity of all kinds is also based primarily on a perception of relation; this is as true for complementary hexachords as it is for the antecedent and consequent of a musical period. When we speak of harmony, it is primarily in terms of relations; all of our terms such as Tonic, Dominant, Subdominant, etc. are relational. Indeed, one of our most prestigious harmony texts defines harmony as "that aspect of music concerned with *relationships* among the chords."[31] The same category is at the basis of set theory; pc set equivalence classes entail formal *relations*. Without doing a statistical count, it seems safe to say that the category of *relation* is also the most prevalent category of opposition in Schoenberg's writings. For example, the 1922 edition of the *Harmonielehre* outlines ways that tonality can be extended. Not only does Schoenberg's outline emphasize what we might call *similarity relations*, there is no mention of anything that might fit into the other categories of opposition.

> IV. Tonality is extended as follows:
> (a) through *imitating* and *copying from* each other the keys become more similar to one another;
> (b) similar things are considered *related* [*verwandt*] and are under certain conditions treated as identical (for example, chords over the same root).[32]

Relations among motives, phrases, and themes dominate Schoenberg's analytic writings throughout, as virtually any of the analytic papers collected in *Style and Idea* will demonstrate. Schoenberg's foundational idea of "developing variation form" emphasizes *relations* first and foremost.

The category of *privation/possession*, though not as pervasive as relationships, is also conspicuous in our field. Privation/possession is at the core of our understanding of consonance as having stability, and dissonance as lacking stability. And though we speak of subset/superset *relations*, the properties that obtain are concerned with privation or possession: e.g. a superset contains (it *possesses*) its subsets; a diatonic collection does not contain "chromaticisms." Although hexachordal combinatoriality is a *relation* (i.e. the two halves of a whole share the same interval content), the opposition of pitch-class content (where complementary hexachords share no notes in common) involves *privation/possession*. The pervasive importance of hexachordal combinatoriality in the twelve-tone works best demonstrates the significance of this category in Schoenberg's thought.

Whenever we speak of musical expectation, we apply the category of *affirmation/negation*. For example, a full cadence affirms the tonic, and a deceptive cadence is a kind of negation (to delay, is to deny "for now"). More generally, any fulfilled expectation is an affirmation and any denied expectation is a negation: i.e. the expectation of x is tantamount to asserting a "truth value" to the statement "x will happen"; if x indeed is realized then the truth value of the statement is affirmed; if x is not realized then the truth value of the statement is negated. To the degree that we assert the expectation of completion in aggregate formation or in patterning of any kind, we exemplify the category of *affirmation/negation*.[33] This category is particularly emphasized in phenomenological hearings.[34] While it can be argued that expectation plays a significant role in Schoenberg's compositions (and hence either affirmation or negation of what is expected), this category is not emphasized in Schoenberg's writings.

The category of *contraries* with some remarkable exceptions, is typically understated within the discourse of contemporary music theory. To be sure, concepts such as bitonality or polymeter imply one key or one meter pitted against another. Yet these terms, or terms like them are the exception rather than the rule. As we have already noted, the privileging of unity understood as the reconciliation of oppositions has been at the core of Western musical ideology since its very beginnings. This is true even during the remarkable florescence of dialectical thought during the nineteenth century, surely more Pythagorean than Heraclitean in its concepts of dialectical opposition. And so, while we recognize consonance and dissonance, and the closely related ideas of passage (with its sense of ongoing) and cadence (with its sense of closure) as basic musical contraries, the role of opposition is usually softened by a characterization wherein dissonance is subordinate to and dependent on consonance. For example, teachers of harmony typically tell their students that they can understand difficult harmonies in an ongoing passage by glancing ahead to the cadence, and interpreting the harmonies in light of their goal. Again, instability is subordinated to stability, and this is tantamount to subordinating dissonance to consonance.

The practice of subordinating conflict, with suitable modifications and obvious exceptions, continues in theories of twentieth-century music. A case in point is set theory, surely the most fully developed and pervasively applied system of theoretical modeling that has been developed for the study of post-tonal musics. While *equivalence* relations are at the very core of set theory, oppositional conflict is generally addressed, if it is addressed at all, on an *ad hoc* basis. To the degree that we theorists and analysts place emphasis on the means through which unity reconciles oppositions, we tend to downplay or marginalize the ways through which opposition is created or intensified in musical thought.

Schoenberg, as critic and teacher, and most importantly as composer, was well aware of the significance of conflict. In the next three sections of this chapter, I have selected passages from Schoenberg's prose all of which begin to flesh out the role of opposed contraries in Schoenberg's music and thought.

Schoenbergian dialectics of history

Schoenberg, in his essay "New Music: My Music" (c. 1930), uses a comical anecdote to convey a sense of historical necessity:

> In the army, a superior officer once said to me: 'So you are this notorious Schoenberg, then.' 'Beg to report, sir, yes,' I replied. 'Nobody wanted to be, someone had to be, so I let it be me.'[35]

As Stephen Cahn points out, the attitude toward history that informs Schoenberg's quip is Hegelian, or at the very least a parody of what in Hegelian terms one would call a "world-historical individual."[36] This is not to say that Schoenberg was self-consciously associating himself with the philosopher. The Hegelian attitude toward history at least in some ways had become normative in German speaking cultures of the time. Yet if Schoenberg is not self-consciously Hegelian, he is certainly being Hegelian without being aware of it.

Be this as it may, Schoenberg's historiography is nonetheless equivocal in its stand toward dialectical opposition in general and *telos* in particular. For example, while dialectical opposition can be inferred in reading his essay "My Evolution" (1949), Schoenberg's language does not particularly support (or refute) such a reading.

> I had been a 'Brahmsian' when I met Zemlinsky. His love embraced both Brahms and Wagner and soon thereafter I became an equally confirmed addict. No wonder that the music I composed at that time mirrored the influence of both these masters, to which a flavour of Liszt, Bruckner, and perhaps also Hugo Wolf was added. This is why in my *Verklärte Nacht* the thematic construction is based on Wagnerian 'model and sequence' above a roving harmony on the one hand, and on Brahms' technique of developing

variation – as I call it – on the other. Also to Brahms must be ascribed the imparity of measures, as, for instance, in measures 50–54, comprising five measures, or measures 320–327, comprising two and one-half measures [sic]. But the treatment of the instruments, the manner of composition, and much of the sonority were strictly Wagnerian. I think there were also some Schoenbergian elements to be found in the length of some of the melodies, in the sonority, in contrapuntal and motival combinations, and in the semi-contrapuntal movement of the harmony and its basses against the melody. Finally, there were already some passages of unfixed tonality which may be considered premonitions of the future.[37]

A dialectical reading of the passage would emphasize that young Schoenberg understood Brahms and Wagner as representing opposing camps – he had been a "Brahmsian" – and that more was at stake than the simple absorption and integration of techniques from the earlier masters. Read in light of Hegelian dialectics, Schoenberg's place in history was to make something new out of the former opposition and it was as though his absorption of both Brahms and Wagner – with Liszt, Bruckner, and Wolf as ancillary forces, essentially in the Wagner camp – allowed his own personal style, those "Schoenbergian elements," to emerge as a third thing. On the other hand, the passage can be read without any dialectical baggage: he learned thus and such from Brahms, thus and such from Wagner, and added a little of himself. One need not interpret a dialectic among oppositions, although given the intellectual context, a dialectical reading is reasonable and revealing.

More important than the ways Schoenberg verbally expressed his relation to precursors, are the ways in which that relation is manifest in his music. If a musical dialectic is to succeed, its force must be perceived *in the music itself*. In Adorno's terms, the dialectic must be *immanent*. Max Paddison's study, *Adorno's Aesthetics of Music*, emphasizes the significance of *immanent* dialectics in numerous guises. Chief among these are two variants of the same theme; one emphasizes the dialectic between "preformed" musical materials and the creative vision of the composer, and the other emphasizes an immanent critique of societal values within the composition. In the first formulation, the composer inherits musical material from the works of those who have preceded him or her within the tradition. Such musical material has taken on what seems to be "a life of its own." It has specific tendencies and implications for its own continuation. When music uses "preformed" materials, musical meaning exists *a priori*; the composer must resist this meaning if new meaning is to emerge. The musical composition becomes the place where the composer both obeys and dialectically opposes those demands.[38] Aspects of the same dialectic take on social significance as we realize that the composer is a socially mediated subject, and that the musical material too is historically and culturally mediated. The material, a social/historical construct, has become a "second nature." The composer's dialectic with that material forms an immanent critique of society.[39]

Schoenberg's paper "A Self-Analysis" (1948) addresses the problem of immanent dialectic by framing it in terms of an opposition between *innovation* and *continuity*. In contrast to the equivocal nature of Schoenberg's "My Evolution," here a dialectical reading is not only consistent with the prose, it is the most reasonable way to understand Schoenberg's argument. The opposition of innovation and continuity results in a new mode of continuing, hence the evolution of tradition through its transformation.

> It is seldom realized that a hand that dares to renounce so much of the achievements of our forefathers has to be exercised thoroughly in the techniques that are to be replaced by new methods. It is seldom realized that there is a link between the technique of forerunners and that of an innovator and that no new technique in the arts is created that has not had its roots in the past. And it is seldom realized that these works in which an innovator prepares – consciously or subconsciously – for the action that will distinguish him from his surroundings furnish ready information about the justification of an author's turn toward new regions.[40]

Schoenberg's next paragraph turns toward the perception of the dialectic *within* the music itself.

> In formulating this justification it seems as if this might be the task of a musicologist. But this is untrue because it is just the audience to whom such recognition is important. And it is the musicologist's duty to guide the audience in order to procure a fair evaluation of one who had the courage to risk his life for an idea . . . Musicologists have failed to act in favour of the truth.[41]

The "justification of an author's turn toward new regions" that Schoenberg speaks of entails a recognition of the dialectical relationships between the works of the precursors and those of the later master, the dialectical opposition of continuity and innovation. It is "untrue" that the justification (through the perceptual recognition of the opposition and its resultant) is "the task of a musicologist" only in the sense that it is untrue that such recognition is *only* of concern to the scholar. On the contrary, it is part of the perception of the music. From Schoenberg's perspective, "musicologists have failed" because they have not equipped audiences with the background necessary for its proper perception. Translated into contemporary terminology, Schoenberg is writing about what we might call his music's "intertextuality." And we might paraphrase his claim by saying that music can be heard well only when it is perceived in opposition to the music which formed the preconditions for the later achievement. In a sense, the music is not a thing in itself. It is the resultant of a relation between itself and its precursors. Of course, Schoenberg is not original here; the essentials of his argument are already found in the hermeneutical dialectics of Schleiermacher.

In addition to the dialectic of innovation and continuity within the works themselves, Schoenberg recognizes an external opposition that propels him through the various stages of his creative life-work. The epigram from William Blake that opened this paper, "Opposition is true Friendship," is particularly apposite toward understanding this dialectical opposition, one recognized by Schoenberg late in his life. The events are nicely summarized by Charles Rosen, and he is worth quoting at length.[42]

> Arnold Schoenberg at the end of his life continued to provoke an enmity, even a hatred, almost unparalleled in the history of music. The elderly artist whose revolutionary works had raised a storm of protest in his youth is a traditional figure, but in old age his fame is generally unquestioned and dissenting voices have been stilled. In Schoenberg's case, the dissent may be said to have grown with the fame . . .
>
> At the end of his life Schoenberg recognized the importance of the hostility that he had faced throughout his career . . . [He] characterized his life in a terrifying and grotesque image: "Personally I had the feeling as if I had fallen into an ocean of boiling waters, and not knowing how to swim or to get out in another manner, I tried with my legs and arms as best I could . . . I never gave up. But how could I give up in the middle of an ocean?"
>
> And he spoke of his opponents with an inimitable combination of genuine sympathy and equally genuine fury: "It might have been the desire to get rid of this nightmare, of this unharmonious torture, of these unintelligible ideas, of this methodical madness – and I must admit these were not bad men who felt this way – though of course I never understood what I had done to make them as malicious, as furious, as cursing, as aggressive . . ." At the end he paid them a superb tribute in speaking of what he had achieved in his life: "Maybe something has been achieved but it was not I who deserves credit for that. The credit must be given to my opponents. They were the ones who really helped me." It was as if he saw that the controversial nature of his work was central to its significance.

That "the credit must be given to my opponents" is a vivid example of Schoenberg recognizing a fruitful dialectical opposition. Schoenberg implies that without opposition, he might have given way to complacency. Opposition along every turn in his path forced him to achieve what otherwise would not have been achieved. In short, it can be argued that for Schoenberg the preconditions for the creative act itself exemplify Heraclitean conflict.

Dialectical aspects of Schoenberg's musical technique

Although dialectical opposition is fundamental to Schoenberg's conception of musical technique, he is generally not explicit to this effect. A striking exception is found in one passage within his *Fundamentals of Musical Composition*. Within the passage Schoenberg discusses the significance of contrasting character and mood, using Beethoven's piano sonata, op. 57 (the *Appassionata*) as his example. He then goes on to say:

> This is not a singular case. All good music consists of many contrasting ideas. An idea achieves its distinctness and validity in contrast with others. Heraclitus called contrast 'the principle of development'. Musical thinking is subject to the same dialectic as all other thinking.[43]

Schoenberg's citation does not correlate exactly with any of the extant fragments from Heraclitus, and it is difficult to say with certainty which Heraclitean fragment Schoenberg had in mind. The most likely source, however, is Aristotle's citation in the *Nicomachean Ethics*.

> And Heraclitus says, "The unlike is joined together, and from differences results the most beautiful harmony, and all things take place by strife."[44]

The choice of the word "contrast" in Schoenberg's paraphrase is interesting. While the terms *strife* (*eris*) and *war* or *contention* (*polemos*) are key words for Heraclitus,[45] "contrast" is not used in any of the English sources that I have checked. Schoenberg's choice of the word *contrast*, as opposed to *conflict* is a softening of the harder edged Heraclitus.[46] This is in great contrast to a passage in the *Harmonielehre* where in his discussion of modulation Schoenberg develops an extended metaphor based on images of war. For example,

> The appetite for independence shown by the two strongest subordinates in the district, the mutiny of more loosely connected elements, the occasional small victories and gains of the competing parties, their final subjection to the sovereign will and their meeting together for a common function – this activity, a reflection of our own human enterprise, is what causes us to perceive as life what we create as art.[47]

While only the passage in *Fundamentals* expressly mentions Heraclitus, the passage in the *Harmonielehre*, where the whole is the resultant of its inner conflict, is much more Heraclitean in its language.

As with Hauptmann and Riemann, Schoenberg's concept of harmony at its very foundation is based on dialectical oppositions. A particularly clear example is found in Schoenberg's description of tonic, dominant and subdominant in the *Harmonielehre*. He describes the dominant and subdominant as two opposing forces with the tonic as a kind of fulcrum or point of equilibrium.[48]

> Now if the C is taken as the midpoint, then its situation can be described by reference to two forces, one of which pulls downward, toward F, the other upward, toward G:

Schoenberg goes on to say that the situation

> . . . may be considered like the force of a man hanging by his hands from a beam and exerting his own force against the force of gravity. He pulls on the beam just as gravity pulls him, and in the same direction. But the effect is that his force *works against* the force of gravity, and so in this way one is justified in speaking of the two opposing forces.[49]

Although the idea of dominant-tonic and tonic-subdominant as opposing force fields is not new with Schoenberg, his depictive analogy, a man hanging from a beam, beautifully captures the idea of energy expended in two contrary directions with a third resultant – gravity pulls down, the man pulls up and as a result the man just hangs there. The resultant, despite its apparent stability or stasis, is achieved through dynamically opposed forces. It is just so, Schoenberg argues, in musical centricity. What is most significant in Schoenberg's adaptation of a dialectical view of harmony is in how Schoenberg subsequently develops this idea. In the larger context of Schoenberg's musical thought, the principle behind the centricity of tonic becomes extended to a wide range of situations that involve what David Lewin in his paper "Inversional Balance as an Organizing Force in Schoenberg's Music and Thought" has named *inversional balance*.[50] Lewin uses the word "force" in this context, and the choice is appropriate: for Schoenberg, opposing centers of balance comprise opposing force fields. As Lewin and others since have shown, inversional balance is among the most basic and highly ramified of Schoenberg's musical techniques.[51]

Among the most well-known of Schoenberg's theoretical formulations is his concept of the *Grundgestalt*, and at the heart of that formulation is another dialectical opposition, that of *centrifugal* and *centripetal* forces.[52] We have already noted that the opposition of these forces exemplified the earlier concept of *counterpoise*. Reaching even further back, Schoenberg's formulation is striking in its relation to the second fragment of Philolaus that was cited earlier: "Nature in the universe was harmonized from unlimiteds and limiters, both the whole universe and things in it." In Schoenberg's context, centrifugal forces are those that require expansion, like Philolaus' *unlimiteds* they constitute the potential for development within a musical idea. Centripetal forces are those that lead to coherence, they hold the idea together and make us perceive it as a unity. They are like Philolaus' *limiters*. In Schoenberg's conception, it is the dialectical opposition of these two forces – successfully realized by the composer who brings them to their full potential – that results in the musical work.[53]

In his paper "Linear Counterpoint" (1931) Schoenberg makes a surprising connection between his principle of the *Grundgestalt* and the bases of musical counterpoint.[54] Schoenberg begins "Linear Counterpoint" with a typically Schoenbergian critique of the linkage implied by the word combination "linear-counterpoint." His argument is basically that while counterpoint entails the *opposition* of two points the concept of a line implies the connection or *joining* of points. As is well known, Schoenberg was fond of word-play, and critiques involving word-play are fairly common in his theoretical and pedagogical writings. In this sense the analysis of "linear counterpoint" as oxymoronic is reminiscent, for example, of Schoenberg's related arguments against the concepts of "non-harmonic tones" (*Harmoniefremde Töne*, literally "tones foreign to the harmony") and "atonality." In both cases Schoenberg's critique hinges on a literal reading of the terms: if tones are "non-harmonic" then they have no place in the study of harmony; "the word 'atonal' could only signify something entirely inconsistent with the nature of tone."[55] There is however a significant difference in the argument against "linear counterpoint" and that difference points out Schoenberg's understanding of counterpoint as dialectical opposition: the contrast between Heraclitean "opposition" and Pythagorean "joining" is at the core of Schoenberg's thought.

In the third paragraph of his paper, after some speculation on the "symbolic and mystical" roots of the word, Schoenberg gives us what is essentially his formal definition of counterpoint.

> But a combination of knowledge and intuition tells me that the masters of counterpoint were very fond of expressing themselves through symbolic and mystical word-play. On this I base the hypothesis that, whatever the origin of the word . . . the deeper sense alone defines the true essence of this art. That is, that counterpoint means an "opposing point" whose *combination with the original point* is needed if the idea is to exist.[56]

I would suggest that the italicized words, *combination with the original*, in the original, distract us from what should be emphasized. A shift in emphasis would better bring out the dialectical aspects of Schoenberg's definition: counterpoint means an "*opposing point*" whose combination with the original point *is needed if the idea is to exist*. In other words, (Schoenbergian) counterpoint denotes a necessary opposition without which the *idea* cannot exist. Unlike the practice of many composers, Schoenberg's counterpoint is never a layering technique whereby a basic melody is enhanced by added musical lines (the practice of Rachmaninov provides a vivid counter-example). In Schoenberg's practice, lines in counterpoint seem locked into a necessary relation – it is the contrapuntal relationship itself that justifies or *requires* its components. Rather than what might be called an "added counterpoint," Schoenberg's practice entails "necessary counterpoint." As in Heraclitus where "cessation of struggle would mean disintegration of the universe," Schoenbergian counterpoint is not something added to create extra interest, it is simply *needed if the idea is to exist.*[57]

Schoenberg immediately follows his definition of counterpoint with three abstract but extremely provocative examples or prototypes for different contrapuntal situations. The first example takes the form of a simple algebraic equation.

> The opposing point may contain the completion: $(a + b)(a - b) = a^2 - b^2$, so that $a^2 - b^2$ means, as it were, the idea represented by the point $(a + b)$ and opposite point $(a - b)$.[58]

The example is interesting in that the "completion" $a^2 - b^2$, while the resultant of the multiplicative relation $(a + b)(a - b)$, takes on a different shape from the components on the left side of the equation. The resultant is a third, other thing. In other words, the "idea" is neither $(a + b)$ nor $(a - b)$ or even $(a + b)(a - b)$, it is the resultant $a^2 - b^2$ achieved through the opposition $(a + b)(a - b)$. The "idea" requires the entire equation for its formulation.

The second prototype is exemplified by analogy with "diophantine equations," i.e. equations having more than one variable and a range of solutions.

> Things may be in the manner of diophantine equations, where there are many solutions, many ways to bring together point and opposing point (polymorphous canons, polymorphous texture) – here point and opposing point are placed as if right and left of the 'equals' sign, hinting at many possible solutions, or sound combinations.[59]

Like a diophantine equation, a polymorphous canon is one capable of multiple solutions.[60] Here Schoenberg suggests that it is in the very nature of some musical ideas that they are predictive of multiple contrapuntal relationships. While the description of "many possible solutions, or sound combinations" no doubt implies successive solutions over the course of a work, Schoenberg's description can be read more radically to suggest the kind of counterpoint explored in the second half of the century by Lutoslawski and others, where the performers have the freedom to realize variable juxtapositions of lines in counterpoint. As in the first example, the resultant is a third thing (here a third and variable thing) achieved through the opposition of the parts. Schoenberg's third prototype suggests the juxtaposition of a musical idea with itself – a kind of musical *Doppelgänger* – to achieve a third resultant.

> Their relationship may be something like that of subject and predicate –
> though in this case, whereas someone wishing to express different things
> without literally 'changing the subject' has, then to change the predicate, in
> music it is enough to change the layout (in space and time).[61]

In interpreting this third prototype, one wonders if Schoenberg may have had non-simultaneous presentations in mind. That is, the counterpoint of subject opposed to itself might involve echoic or canonic imitation, but it might also involve relations that are not temporally contiguous. Of course, similar readings of the first two prototypes are also available. If so, this would extend his conception of counterpoint beyond the juxtaposition of simultaneities, and would include oppositions between successive elements.[62] This reading not only seems reasonable, it is encouraged by the turn that Schoenberg next takes in his paper. Here Schoenberg makes the surprising connection between his prototypical contrapuntal situations and his concept of *Grundgestalt.*

> Anyway, whatever one's views about the pleasure that can lie in conducting
> each part in polyphony independently, melodiously and meaningfully, there
> is a higher level, and it is at this level that one finds the question which needs
> answering in order to arrive at the postulate: 'Whatever happens in a piece of
> music is nothing but the endless reshaping of a basic shape.' Or, in other
> words, there is nothing in a piece of music but what comes from the theme,
> springs from it and can be traced back to it; to put it still more severely,
> nothing but the theme itself. Or, all the shapes appearing in a piece of music
> are *foreseen* in the 'theme'.[63]

To be sure, the passage reads strangely. Why the sudden shifts from abstract contrapuntal prototypes to the implicitly dubious value of "conducting" independent lines, to the "postulate" about thematic unity and thematic generation? It is as though Schoenberg has left out some transitional thoughts, and has made a series of intuitive leaps. To make sense of the passage the reader needs to fill in the gaps. Returning to Schoenberg's first prototype, we can make better sense of his concern about "independent" lines. By analogy with the equation we can imagine $(a + b)$ as one line or group of lines and $(a - b)$ as another. But, as we have seen, the "idea" is not either of these components in isolation or even the recognition of their having a relationship $(a + b)(a - b)$; the "idea" is the resultant of that relationship expressed by the entire equation: $(a + b)(a - b) = a^2 - b^2$. The role, and so the implications of either $(a + b)$ or $(a - b)$ cannot be properly understood outside of their dialectical opposition and its resultant. On this level the entire equation, the "idea," represents a unity that holds conflict within it. The composer, the performer as well as the audience must also grapple with the contrapuntal situation as a complex totality. It would seem therefore that conceptualizing contrapuntal lines "independently" is like trying to define *husband* without taking *wife* into account! This requirement in turn sets the stage for Schoenberg's next intuitive leap. On a higher level, the entire work is the musical "idea." The totality of its dialectical oppositions give rise to a higher unity of imagination. For Schoenberg, the dialectical principle operative in contrapuntal prototypes is the same principle operative in the concept of *Grundgestalt*. At end, the Schoenbergian *Grundgestalt* is a cipher – a mysterious encoding of contraries and unity which can be revealed only through the work's unfolding in time. Contrapuntal oppositions, understood in a most inclusive sense, are the variables in that unfolding.

Given the importance of dialectical oppositions that *are* recognized in Schoenberg's writings, it is remarkable that the most striking aspect of Schoenberg as a latter-day Heraclitean is not really addressed by the composer. With the dissolution of tonality, Schoenberg's post-tonal language develops an aesthetic that brings unresolved opposition or conflict to the forefront of musical language.[64] Indeed, it can be argued that beginning with Schoenberg's middle period, the Pythagorean alternation of discord and concord gives way to the "stricter muse" of Heraclitean conflict.

"Systems" as failed dialectics

Schoenberg begins his *Harmonielehre* with an extended polemic against theorists specifically aimed at those who would restrict or reduce artistic work to a "system."

> And if it were possible to watch composing in the same way that one can watch painting, if composers could have *ateliers* as did painters, then it would be clear how superfluous the music theorist is and how he is just as harmful as the art academies. He senses all this and seeks to create a substitute by replacing the living example with theory, with the system.[65]

Schoenberg returns to similar concerns during his discussion of dissonance in the Chapter on the VIIth degree. At this point Schoenberg describes "the system" as a compromise that we have created in order to deal with the more complex situations that are found in nature. The danger, he warns us, is in subsequently mistaking "the system" for the object itself.

> The passing tone is, then, nothing else but a 'Manier' as it was fixed in the notation. As the notation always lags behind the sound . . . so the notation of these ornaments is of course also imperfect if judged by the sounds [composers surely] imagined. It can be understood, however, as one of those simplifications the human intellect must create if it is to deal with the material. The supposition prevails here, too, that the system that simplified the object was taken to be the system inherent in that object itself; and we can safely assume that our traditional treatment of dissonance, although originally based on a correct intuition, nevertheless proceeded more to develop the system of simplification than really to reach an understanding of the nature of dissonance.[66]

Schoenberg goes on to say that he will train the student in "the system" not in order to enforce rules or an aesthetic, but because our present-day ears have been conditioned by the system so that they accept it as a "second nature."[67] Presumably, if we mistake that second nature for nature herself then we fall into the error of mistaking the system for its "object." He predicts that eventually a new path will be taken, one that will lead "to new secrets of nature." Of course, the reader can anticipate that those "new secrets" themselves might then lead to a new system, which in turn might be mistaken for its object. Schoenberg's later concerns about the systematics of twelve-tone music are found here *in nuce*.

So far Schoenberg's argument has been fairly easy to follow, but what follows is surely among the most strange and difficult passages in the entire *Harmonielehre*. A new paragraph begins with speculation that musical notation may have led to the recognition of dissonance as a separate phenomenon, presumably opposed to consonance. What then follows at first seems to be a startling *non sequitur*. Schoenberg abruptly shifts from the topic of musical dissonance to a discussion of two conflicting human impulses, "the demand for repetition of pleasant stimuli, and the opposing desire for variety, for change, for a new stimulus." The conflict here is a variant of the conflict between continuity and innovation that Schoenberg later describes in his paper "A Self-Analysis." Here, these two conflicting needs give rise to a third impulse, "the impulse to take possession." "To take possession" becomes the surrogate – in Freudian terms, a *sublimation* – for dealing with the psychological conflict which "is for the time being cast aside." Finally, at the end of the paragraph, Schoenberg makes the connection between his apparent *non sequitur* and his ostensibly principal concern, "the system." He does this essentially by claiming that the creation of a system is a mode of taking possession. In other words, the system allows us to take control over what was originally a moment of creative surprise so that it can be reproduced at will. In this sense, the system allows us to take possession of the desired object (the musical effect).

The complete paragraph is as follows. (I have slightly modified Roy Carter's translation here to achieve normative English syntax.)

> The notation of dissonances brought about by passing tones may have led to the confirmation of the phenomenon of dissonance itself. Two impulses struggle with each other within man: the demand for repetition of pleasant stimuli, and the opposing desire for variety, for change, for a new stimulus. These two impulses often unite in one relatively common impulse characteristic of beasts of prey: the impulse to take possession. The question whether then repetition or change shall follow is for the time being cast aside. The more robust satisfaction of the consciousness of possession, with its possibilities for deciding this way or that, is capable of suppressing the subtler considerations and of leading to that conservative repose which is always characteristic of ownership. Faced with the dilemma, whether repetition of the stimuli or innovation be preferable, the human intellect decided here, too, to take possession; it founded a system.[68]

If we think of *pleasure in stability* versus *pleasure in variety* as a dialectical opposition, then we may conceptualize the compromise of *taking possession* either as a failed *Aufhebung* in a Hegelian reading of the passage or as a dissipation of necessary conflict in a Heraclitean reading. The dialectic fails because *taking possession* does not bring the dialectic to a higher level. Instead, the dialectical opposition between the two opposed impulses is temporarily dissipated by compromise. *Taking possession* amounts to reducing the conflict between *pleasure in stability* and *pleasure in variety* to *pleasure in stability* – the object of variety once it is our possession becomes an object of stability. Of course, this does not ultimately satisfy the need to work out the more basic opposition – in a Hegelian reading, we have not achieved a higher synthesis; in a Heraclitean reading we have diffused the necessary opposition or conflict; in either case we have compromised by taking possession – and one can easily imagine a vicious circle of acquisition that can never fulfill the requirements of the dialectical opposition.

The paragraph that follows in Schoenberg's text begins by expanding upon the same idea. The system arises as a compromise so that we can recapture the chance moment of creativity, but ironically, by its own stability, it becomes the impediment to creativity. Halfway through the paragraph, Schoenberg makes another sudden shift of imagery. He moves from "taking possession" through "the system" to a larger moral concern. The conflicting impulses now are "morality" and "immoderate desire," and the resultant amounts to moral compromise.

> Thus it can also be imagined how the chance occurrence of a dissonant
> passing tone, once established by the notation, after its excitement had been
> experienced, called forth the desire for less accidental, less arbitrary
> repetition; how the desire to experience this excitement more often led to
> taking possession of the methods that brought it about. But, should the
> excitement of the forbidden lead to uninhibited indulgence, that essentially
> despicable compromise between morality and immoderate desire had to be
> drawn, that compromise which here consists in a looser conception of the
> prohibition as well as of that which is prohibited. Dissonance was accepted,
> but the door through which it was admitted was bolted whenever excess
> threatened.[69]

Once again, Schoenberg has described a failed dialectical opposition, this
one with "despicable" moral consequences. And once again, immediately
after describing this failed opposition Schoenberg returns to his ostensibly
principal concern, the treatment of dissonance. At this point, however, the
reader cannot be fooled into thinking that it is only dissonance treatment
which is at stake – even though, given the central role of "emancipated
dissonance" in Schoenberg's musical thought, that alone would put much
at stake indeed. As we have seen in several guises, for Schoenberg, conflict
is central to the creative process itself. "Systems" that replace the conflict
between expectation and surprise with "method" undercut the very source
of wonder that they attempt to capture.

Some implications for future analyses

Our readings have been selective. Alone, they give a skewed perspective in
that dialectical oppositions are not as ubiquitous in Schoenberg's prose as
they alone might suggest. Nonetheless, the readings have shown that the
presence of dialectical oppositions in Schoenberg's thought and music does
comprise a significant, indeed central aspect of his imagination. If we are
to go further than close readings of Schoenberg's criticism and pedagogy, it
will be by applying our understanding of dialectical opposition to the study
of his music. If we are to generalize the principles that Schoenberg discusses,
it will be by becoming more sensitive to the various modes of opposition
that are the structural and expressive components of musical composition
over a wide range of styles and historical periods.

We can approach the need to develop a language for aspects of musical
conflict or contrariety in two principal ways, through qualitative descriptions and quantitative models. Although I myself tend to feel more comfortable in the realm of qualitative description, I do recognize the strength of
quantitative models. If we are to develop such models, they will need to focus

on the oppositions among things (timbres, motives, themes, movements, etc.), or within things, as opposed to the naming of things per se.

Apart from quantitative measures of conflict, we can develop a descriptive, qualitative vocabulary that more carefully reflects the role of oppositions in music. The significance of language is often overlooked by music theorists who have a more quantitative or graphic approach toward analysis. Indeed, the suspicion of purely qualitative description is a well entrenched ideology of the field of music theory. Nonetheless, we all recognize that figurative language not only reflects our musical intuitions, it is a factor in the way that we perceive music. If this were not so, we would not bother talking or writing about music. Linguistic recognition feeds into musical cognition, and a vocabulary that is more sensitive to oppositions will surely give rise to an increased awareness of the ways that musical forces can be pitted against one another. For example, we have seen that A. B. Marx conceptualized antecedent and consequent phrases in terms of a dialectical opposition. This way of thinking is alien to most current theory, where antecedent and consequent are neutralized into that which comes first and that which follows. Yet, a performer who thinks of the relationship in terms of an opposition is likely to articulate the phrases in ways subtly different from one who perceives nothing more than an ordinal relationship in a unified field. The same principle applies on a larger structural/dramatic level to contrasting theme groups. The trope of *unity*, unless complemented by a trope of *conflict*, will stress homogenization rather than increased characterization among themes. It has certainly been my experience that the distinctive personalities of themes, for example in sonata forms, are one of the first casualties in many performances. Or, for another example, Classical orchestration often pits the winds against the strings. Hearing the opposition as such is quite different from simply hearing "variety of color" or other relational terms. Recognition (which really is re-cognition in this case) of the ways that phrases and themes, or orchestrational strata can embody conflict in the Classical style, will help us to recognize that it is these same tendencies that are intensified in later music, including that of Schoenberg.

It is also primarily through carefully chosen language that we can address the kinds of concerns that Schoenberg identifies in "A Self-Analysis." Intertextuality, as recognized in Harold Bloom's discussions of *agon*, involves conflict as much as it involves association. If we are to hear the work of Schoenberg, or any significant composer for that matter, in terms of a tradition – and how else shall we hear him well? – then we need to recognize the positive role played by opposition.

3   Dramatic conflict in *Pelleas und Melisande*

It was around 1900 when Maurice Maeterlinck fascinated composers, stimulating them to create music to his dramatic poems. What attracted all was his art of dramatizing eternal problems of humanity in the form of fairy-tales, lending them timelessness without adhering to imitation of ancient styles.

I had first planned to convert *Pelleas and Melisande* into an opera, but I gave up this plan, though I did not know Debussy was working on an opera at the same time. I still regret that I did not carry out my initial intention. It would have differed from Debussy's. I might have missed the wonderful perfume of the poem; but I might have made my characters more singing.

On the other hand the symphonic poem helped me, in that it taught me to express moods and characters in precisely formulated units, a technique which an opera would perhaps not have promoted so well.

Thus my fate evidently guided me with great foresight.

Arnold Schoenberg, February 17, 1950[1]

In December of 1901, Schoenberg moved from Vienna to Berlin having accepted a position as musical director at the relatively new and highly successful Überbrettl cabaret.[2] Schoenberg would stay in Berlin until the summer of 1903. It was during this period that he became acquainted with Richard Strauss, and it was Strauss who suggested that Schoenberg set Maeterlinck's drama.[3] As Schoenberg's later comments indicate, he had originally planned an opera, but changed his mind and settled on the symphonic tone poem that we have today.[4] He also tells us that at the time he was unaware of Debussy's opera on the same subject.[5] The first sketch that we have for the work is from July 1902; the date on the completed score is February 28, 1903.[6]

Maeterlinck's *Pelléas*, Schoenberg's *Pelleas*

Maeterlinck's *Pelléas et Mélisande* had been premiered in Paris, 1892. Influenced by the French Symbolist movement, which in turn had been influenced by Wagnerian aesthetics, *Pelléas* quickly became an international success; it was translated into English in 1894, and into German in 1897.[7] Critics noted the musical qualities of the play from early on, and musicians of the first rank were evidently in agreement; in addition to Schoenberg's symphonic poem and Debussy's opera, both Gabriel Fauré and Jean Sibelius wrote incidental music for productions of the play (Fauré for an 1898 performance in London, and Sibelius for a 1905 performance in Helsinki).[8]

Schoenberg's program notes, written late in life, for a 1949 performance in Los Angeles, recall that *Pelleas und Melisande* "was inspired entirely by Maurice Maeterlinck's wonderful drama. I tried to mirror every detail of it, with only a few omissions and slight changes of the order of the scenes."[9] Schoenberg's "every detail of it," however, cannot be taken literally, and might be read profitably against the grain of Berg's 1920 description of the relation of the music to the text: "Schoenberg's music is inspired by the idea and inner events of this drama and reproduces its exterior action only in very broad terms."[10] To be sure, Schoenberg could have claimed that every detail of his *Pelleas* is infused with ideas suggested by Maeterlinck's drama, but beyond the obvious and profound transformation of images suggested by words and staging into images suggested by music alone, Schoenberg's *reconception* of Maeterlinck (more radical than an interpretation) transforms some basic aspects of the drama, not the least of which is to distill its cast of characters down to the three essential protagonists. And all of this is conditioned by the specifics of Schoenberg's musical *Bildung*, most importantly his reception of a Wagnerian and post-Wagnerian musical language. Schoenberg radically alters basic aspects of the drama and then further "translates" the French symbolist inspired language into a musical language influenced by Wagnerian (and Straussian) compositional practice.[11] Be this as it may, a basic knowledge of the play remains essential to any informed hearing of the musical composition.[12]

Distilled to its essentials, Maeterlinck's play reduces to a love triangle comprising its three main characters: Golaud, a prince, middle-aged and widowed, as we find him at the outset of the play; Mélisande, evidently a princess, but significantly of unknown origins; and Pelléas, Golaud's half-brother. To this essential triad of characters, Maeterlinck adds a relatively small supporting cast: Geneviève, mother of Golaud and Pelléas; Arkël, the king, grandfather of Golaud and Pelléas; Yniold, Golaud's young son by his previous marriage; and some lesser characters – servants, a physician, and some beggars. As we have noted, none of these are depicted by Schoenberg (although Schoenberg's 1949 program notes mention the entrance of the serving women at the death of Mélisande, they function more like props or extras, rather than as active agents in the unfolding drama.)[13]

The tragic relations between Mélisande, Golaud, and Pelléas can easily be outlined in their essentials. Near the beginning of the play, Golaud finds the enigmatic Mélisande who like himself is lost in a wood; in the very next scene we find that they have become married. Mélisande and Golaud's half-brother Pelléas meet and gradually fall in love; from all that we see, it seems to be an innocent, childlike love, yet a loss of innocence clearly underlies and underscores the danger in their mutual attraction. As the love between Pelléas and Mélisande grows, Golaud experiences increasing jealousy followed by rage. As we approach the play's denouement, Golaud finds Pelléas and Mélisande embracing; Golaud kills Pelléas, slightly wounds Mélisande, and then unsuccessfully attempts to take his own life. Although only slight, Mélisande's wound will eventually prove fatal. At the end of the play, Golaud, recovered from his wound, expresses deep remorse for killing Pelléas and for being the cause of Mélisande's imminent death. He agonizes over his jealousy of their innocent love. Meanwhile, Mélisande, who was left comatose following the murder of Pelléas, awakens for a short time. She unexpectedly gives birth to a child whose presence will remain an enigma, and then dies, despite the seeming inconsequence of her wound.[14] This basic overview of Maeterlinck's play also serves as a basic overview of the drama that Schoenberg's music evokes.

The reduction of *Pelleas* to a love triangle is at the core of Schoenberg's conception. The most obvious musical precursor is Wagner's *Tristan und Isolde*, but in *Pelleas* the triangle is much more complexly engaged *as a triangle*. In *Tristan* King Mark is a rather peripheral figure; he is necessary to the premise but of marginal importance in the action. He is introduced well into the opera, and his presence is very much in the background through most of the story (both in terms of staging, and in terms of musical presence through leitmotivic associations). In contrast, Golaud, the figure parallel to King Mark, is central to the drama, especially so in Schoenberg's reconception of Maeterlinck's original scheme. In both play and symphonic poem, we meet Golaud before meeting Pelléas; in both tellings of the tale, Golaud survives the passing of Pelléas and Mélisande. Schoenberg and Maeterlinck depict an undercurrent of increasing suspicion and jealousy from Golaud as the erotic attraction between Mélisande and Pelléas grows, so his presence is palpable even when he is not "on stage," actually or metaphorically.

As with any tragedy (or comedy for that matter), conflict is at the heart of Maeterlinck's play. In *Pelléas* the fatal results of conflict between the protagonists derive from internalized emotional conflicts. Golaud, as he sees the growing affection between Pelléas and Mélisande, is torn between extremes: is theirs a childlike innocence or is he betrayed by a wife and half-brother? After giving way to his murderous rage, Golaud is remorseful, castigating himself for being incited by their innocent, childlike love. Near the beginning of the play, we learn that Pelléas wants to leave the kingdom; a close friend is dying, and he wants to be near him. Had Pelléas left, he would not have met Mélisande. But he was dissuaded. For one reason after another, as the play unfolds, Pelléas delays his departure. Even the fateful event of his final meeting with Mélisande is arranged on the pretext that he is about to depart. Mélisande, oppressed by the gloomy darkness of Arkël's land, also expresses her wish to leave, but her relation to Pelléas is cause to stay. The nascent love between Pelléas and Mélisande is also conflicted and not without a sense of guilt and betrayal. These sources of dramatic conflict, needless to say, find musical analogues in Schoenberg's symphonic poem.

The relationships suggested by the triangle comprise far more than the possibilities of dividing the triad of *personae* into individuals, dyadic and triadic groupings, what might symbolically be represented by {Mélisande}, {Golaud}, {Pelléas}, {Mélisande + Golaud}, {Mélisande + Pelléas}, {Golaud + Pelléas}, {Mélisande + Golaud + Pelléas}, their relations to themselves, to each other as individuals, and to each other as a group of three. The musical implications of portraying the "inner events" of the drama suggest the development of musical means for representing perspectival relationships, ways of associating musical passages with each of the protagonists as they cognitively and emotionally respond to one another (or to the others). For shorthand, let me call this kind of relation a "gazing on." We can tabulate the possibilities of Mélisande "gazing on" as follows:

Mélisande gazing on Mélisande (self-contemplation)
Mélisande gazing on Golaud
Mélisande gazing on Pelléas
Mélisande gazing on the relation of Mélisande and Golaud
Mélisande gazing on the relation of Mélisande and Pelléas
Mélisande gazing on the relation of Golaud and Pelléas
Mélisande gazing on the relation of Mélisande, Golaud and Pelléas

The seven terms of "gazing on" for Mélisande, can then be multiplied by three to include Golaud and Pelléas. The possibilities increase by dyadic or mutual gazing, for example, Mélisande gazing on Pelléas while Pelléas gazes on Mélisande. Moreover, these perspectival relations change and develop over time as the protagonists experience, recollect, and anticipate events. We will return to these ideas in our study of the work's musical motives and themes, their dramatic trajectories over time, and their associations with the three protagonists. For now, let us examine the specifics of Schoenberg's adaptations from the plot and atmosphere of Maeterlinck's play.

The essential documentation of musical correlations to the drama is found in three primary sources: Schoenberg's letter to Alexander Zemlinsky, dated March 20, 1918; Berg's *Short Thematic Analysis* (1920); and Schoenberg's 1949 program notes.[15] Among these, Berg's analysis is the most detailed and explicit. Figure 3.1 summarizes the correlations between Schoenberg and Maeterlinck noted by Berg. (The figure purposely omits Berg's formal

Maeterlinck	Schoenberg	Brief description
I.2	m.1 through Reh. 2	Mélisande lost, weeping
I.2	Reh. 3-4	Golaud finds Mélisande
I.3	Reh. 5-7	Marriage bond, symbolized by the wedding ring
I.4	Reh. 9	Pelléas and Mélisande become acquainted
II.1	Reh. 16	Pelléas and Mélisande at a fountain in the park; Mélisande plays with her wedding ring
II.1, II.2	Reh. 21-22	Mélisande loses her wedding ring, at the same time Golaud falls from his horse
III.2	Reh. 25	Pelléas and Mélisande, by the castle tower, Pelléas plays with Mélisande's hair
III.3	Reh. 30.6	Golaud and Pelléas in the underground castle vaults
IV.4	Reh. 33	Pelléas and Mélisande meet by the spring in the park
IV.4	Reh. 36	Love scene
IV.4	Reh. 48	entry of Golaud, murder of Pelléas, wounding of Mélisande
IV.2	Reh. 56	(memory of) Golaud in rage pulling Mélisande's hair
V.2	Reh. 59	Mélisande's sick room
V.2	Reh. 61	Death of Mélisande

Figure 3.1. Correlations between Schoenberg and Maeterlinck noted by Berg.

descriptions – we will consider those later – and it also omits references to musical passages that are not explicitly linked to specific passages in the drama.)

Schoenberg derives the opening of his *Pelleas* from Act I, scene 2 of the play (I.ii hereafter), where Golaud comes upon the weeping, lost Mélisande. The music begins by focusing solely on Mélisande (along with the lurking presence of fate, personified by its own leitmotiv). We become aware of Golaud's presence only at Reh. 3, after twenty-seven expansive measures of music; once Golaud is introduced, the remainder of the first larger section of music (up until Reh. 5) begins to develop the relationship between Golaud and Mélisande.

The music beginning at Reh. 5 moves us precipitately from their mutual discovery to their wedding scene. In the play (I.iii) we learn of the marriage indirectly, overhearing Geneviève reading a letter to Pelléas from Golaud. By marrying Mélisande, Golaud has disobeyed the wishes of Arkël, and he asks for a signal that will alert him that it is permissible to return to the kingdom. These are the kind of plot details that are alien to Schoenberg's musical procedures. Instead of indirect revelation, Schoenberg places the wedding music as a major structural and dramatic juncture in the work. The marriage bond is depicted first by music clearly stamped with Golaud's personality and perspective and then, more climactically, with music that compositionally weds motives and mannerisms associated with Golaud with those linked to Mélisande. At the end of the music celebrating the wedding bond, we hear the first of three massive intrusions of the FATE motive, each of which is associated with Golaud as agent/patient (if we consider Golaud responsible for his thoughts and actions, then he is an agent; if we consider Fate as the active force, and the musical contexts give much reason for thinking that way, then Golaud is patient). In subsequent descriptions, I will call these three events "catastrophic" intrusions of fate. The third of these signifies the death of Pelléas and sets into motion the events directly leading to Mélisande's death as well.

In I.iv of the play Mélisande is out for a walk with Geneviève when they happen upon Pelléas. He helps Mélisande down a steep path and tells her that he may be leaving tomorrow. Once again, Schoenberg cannot depict specifics of this sort. Instead the music concentrates on two things suggested by the drama: the powerful internal conflicts in Pelléas' character (with fate taking a leading role), and the immediate attraction of Pelléas to Mélisande, the beginnings of their erotic connection. In the larger musical form, the events up until here comprise the first large section of the work.

The second large section incorporates three episodes from the play (II.i, III.ii, III.iii), augmented by music interpolated after the first and second episodes depicting Golaud's growing distrust and jealousy.[16] The first of these is based on Act II.i, in which Pelléas brings Mélisande to a "fountain in the park," actually a deep pool whose bottom cannot be fathomed. Later in the scene, Mélisande plays with her wedding ring, tossing it in the air and catching it over the water's edge. She accidentally drops the ring into the fathomless depths; later we learn that at that same moment Golaud is injured as he falls from his horse (II.ii). Schoenberg's music depicts the pool, Mélisande's playfulness and then the loss of the ring, music that simultaneously portrays Golaud's fall. The two images, the loss of the ring and the fall from the horse, which can only be represented sequentially in the play, are fused into a single moment in the music. The second episode, also involving Pelléas and Mélisande, is based on Act III.ii, the most fairytale-like episode in the play. Mélisande, leaning out of a window in the castle tower, inadvertently lets down her hair, and Pelléas begins to kiss it, and twine it around himself. Although still innocent, this love scene is the most erotic event in the play so far. At the end of the scene, Golaud arrives unexpectedly, and chides them for behaving like children. The third episode, derived from Act III.iii, involves Golaud and Pelléas, the only scene in the play where the two male protagonists are paired. Golaud takes Pelléas to an underground vault beneath the castle. The place is ominous and smells of death. At the end of Schoenberg's depiction of this scene, we hear the second catastrophic intrusion of Fate.

The third large section of Schoenberg's *Pelleas* is derived from a single scene in Maeterlinck's play, Act IV, scene 4. It is nighttime, and Pelléas and Mélisande secretly meet by the fountain in the park, the same fountain where Mélisande lost her ring. The two announce their love for one other, embrace, and kiss. Mélisande sees Golaud approaching and tries to warn Pelléas, but her warning comes too late. They kiss one last time, then Golaud runs Pelléas through with his sword and pursues Mélisande into the darkness. Schoenberg portrays the love scene through a slow building. Its glorious adagio reaches multiple climactic passages, placing the earlier climax heard during the wedding of Golaud and Mélisande into a largely diminished perspective. The adagio is cut off by the third catastrophic intrusion of Fate, signifying the death of Pelléas.

The primary sources, Berg and the composer, list three specific references to the play in the final large section of *Pelleas*. The first of these is remarkable in that Schoenberg presents a scene out of its original sequence. In Act IV.ii, Golaud is gripped by a blind rage over what he perceives as Mélisande's infidelity. In stark contrast to III.ii, where Pelléas entwines himself in Mélisande's flowing hair, in this scene the enraged Golaud drags Mélisande by her hair. By placing this scene after the death of Pelléas, Schoenberg casts it as a vivid memory bound up with Golaud's remorse. The musical means through which Schoenberg prepares this passage are not addressed by Schoenberg or Berg in their commentaries; as we shall see, those means are quite extraordinary. The final two specific references to the play are both taken from the ultimate scene, Act V.ii. These depict Mélisande on her deathbed, and her passing.

While the plot of *Pelléas et Mélisande* carries us through the tragedy, it
is the atmosphere of the play that fascinated audiences around the turn
of the twentieth century; an understanding of this atmosphere is crucial to
Schoenberg's depiction as well. The play has a mythic sense of place and time;
all of its places are strangely no place at all and though the action seems to
unfold over time, in many ways time seems suspended, as if all action belonged in a time out of time. These are the qualities that Schoenberg referred to
in his note cited at the beginning of this chapter: "What attracted all was his
art of dramatizing eternal problems of humanity in the form of fairy-tales,
lending them timelessness without adhering to imitation of ancient styles."
In addition, as our references to fate have indicated, there is a strong sense of
impending doom throughout the play; darkness, in literal and metaphoric
senses, is a recurrent motive present in almost every scene.

In Maeterlinck's text, the exception to the use of darkness that proves the
rule is the very first scene. As the play begins, the servants struggle to open
the massive doors of the castle; when they are finally opened, light streams
in. The servants then work industriously to wash a stain from the doorsill.
Wash as they may, the stain is indelible. Schoenberg, like Debussy, omits this
scene, but its influence is nonetheless pervasive. Maeterlinck's first scene, in
veiled references, foretells what is to come; it initiates the pattern of events
leading to the inescapable destinies of Mélisande, Golaud, and Pelléas. It also
initiates the uncanny representations of time and place that are so salient in
Maeterlinck's play as well as Schoenberg's symphonic poem.

We find out the meaning of Maeterlinck's opening scene only after most
of the plot has unfolded – if we consider the chronology of the play's events,
then the main body of the story takes place in retrospect. All of the events
up until the death of Pelléas have happened before the opening scene.[17]
The stain on the doorsill is from the blood of Golaud and Mélisande; they
were found at the door after Golaud had murdered Pelléas, and wounded
Mélisande and himself. Patrick McGuinness, a Maeterlinck scholar, nicely
captures the significance of the opening.

> It is characteristic of the structure of *Pelléas* that Maeterlinck should
> introduce, from the very start, a motive whose significance remains unknown
> until the end of the play – the servants have come to clean the castle doorstep
> of an unexplained stain . . . The [opening] scene projects itself into the future,
> but also alludes to the play's murky prehistory: something will happen, but
> something has *already* happened.[18]

The "murky prehistory" includes the mystery of Mélisande's origins. When
Golaud finds her, she is unwilling or unable to say who she is. He notices a
crown beside the weeping Mélisande, well within reach in a shallow pool.

He offers to retrieve it, but Mélisande threatens to drown herself if he does so. When he asks if someone has harmed her, Mélisande sobs, "everyone." The reader never discovers how Mélisande came to that place, neither do we find out who Mélisande is.

(The mystery of the fathers is another aspect of "murky prehistory" in the play. Early on we learn that Pelléas' father lies ill within the castle. Much later we hear that he has recuperated, but he is never seen on stage. While we are told that Pelléas and Golaud have different fathers, we never are told any more about this. At the end of the play, Mélisande gives birth to a baby while she is comatose, shortly before she awakens and then expires. If we assume that the love of Pelléas and Mélisande is innocent (and nothing depicted confirms otherwise), then the father is certainly Golaud, a reasonable assumption that is, however, left unconfirmed.)

Of course none of this is directly translatable into musical images, but, as we shall see, the images of darkness, murky prehistory, and the strangeness of time and place, all find analogues in Schoenberg's music.

The reception of Schoenberg's *Pelleas und Melisande*

Schoenberg himself conducted the premiere of the work in Vienna on January 25, 1905.[19] It was not a happy experience for Schoenberg, and unfortunately it set the tone for increasing antagonism yet to come. Over ten years later, in his October 9, 1915 letter to Alexander Zemlinsky, Schoenberg recalls the event as part of a pattern of abuse.

> When I think of how badly my 'Pelleas' was treated here [Vienna] and of the opposition with which even the Songs for Orchestra were received, but above all I remember the uproar about 'Pierrot Lunaire', after which my name was dragged through the mud of all the newspapers at home and abroad . . . surely it isn't cowardly if I now try to avoid that sort of thing.[20]

Late in his life, in his program notes of December 1949, Schoenberg reflects back on the premiere from an even greater distance.

> The first performance, 1905 in Vienna, under my direction, provoked great riots among the audience and even the critics. Reviews were unusually violent and one of the critics suggested putting me in an asylum and keeping music paper out of my reach. Only six years later, under Oscar Fried's direction, it became a great success, and since that time has not caused the anger of the audience.[21]

As Schoenberg remembered, Oscar Fried had conducted an enthusiastically received concert in Berlin on October 31, 1910.[22] However, the historical record shows that the real breakout year for *Pelleas* was 1912, when Schoenberg conducted the work in three important venues. In February of that year Schoenberg was invited by Zemlinsky to conduct the work in Prague. This time *Pelleas* was a success with audience and critics alike. Schoenberg conducted *Pelleas* again in November 1912 as Willem Mengelberg's guest with the Concertgebouw in Amsterdam and The Hague, and then again in December in St. Petersburg with the St. Petersburg Philharmonic as Alexander Siloti's guest. Within a few years, Furtwängler, Scherchen, and Klemperer had all committed to the work.[23] That Schoenberg continued to be identified with *Pelleas* is attested to by his guest appearance conducting *Pelleas* with the Boston Symphony in January and March of 1934 only months after his emigration to the United States.[24]

It is difficult to get a firm sense of Schoenberg's own evaluation of *Pelleas*, and I suspect that it must have varied over the years – the evaluations of past accomplishments were always conditioned by present aspirations, and the work evidently raised deeply conflicted feelings for its composer. Schoenberg mentions *Pelleas* in his sardonic lampoon of music critics, "A Legal Question" (1909), writing of those who are willing and able to critique a work after sleeping through its performance.[25] The first and most substantive critical discussion of *Pelleas* by its composer is found in Schoenberg's long letter to Zemlinsky dated March 20, 1918. The document is interesting on several accounts and worth considering in some detail.

Zemlinsky had proposed some rather drastic cuts in the score (from rehearsal number 50 through rehearsal 59) for an upcoming performance. Schoenberg wrote a rather severe response to the request, defending the organicism of the work and then specifically addressing the passages in question, including some analysis of details in the score.[26] In our present context, however, the most pertinent and interesting aspect of the letter is Schoenberg's conflicted emotional and intellectual response to his own work.

Schoenberg's letter begins by defending the overall form; the composer draws parallels between human and divine creation (a recurrent idea in Schoenberg's writings).

> ... bare survival isn't always important enough to warrant changing something in the programme of the Creator who, on the great rationing day, allotted us so and so many arms, legs, ears and other organs. And so I hold that a work doesn't have to live, i.e., be performed, at all costs either.

Schoenberg's attitude is defensive but understandable; he had experienced incredible abuse from critics and audiences. His insistence that it would be better that the work not be performed at all than performed with cuts, is intensified as he turns to "consideration for the listener."

> . . . he [the audience member] is only a nuisance. In any case, a listener who can dispense with my work or with part of it is free to make use of his more fortunate situation and treat *me* as something he can dispense with *entirely*.

Aside from expressing Schoenberg's bitterness toward abusive audiences, the main thrust of the letter so far is its author's strong belief that *Pelleas* is correct in its original proportions and expressive content. Schoenberg continues by addressing the specific passages that Zemlinsky had suggested for cutting. It is here that Schoenberg's own conflict about the piece begins to emerge.

> I have always told anyone who pays any attention to me that I consider the last part, precisely that from 50 on, the best in the whole work, indeed the only thing in the work, with a few exceptions from what goes before, that is still of interest to me now. Particularly the passage 50–55. I very clearly remember it was here for the first time (while I was composing it) that I realized that many sequences of the preceding parts were only of moderate artistic value and it was here (and I am amazed at your remark about "the peculiar structure of two-measure periods that was at that time still one of your characteristics", which applies to much of the rest of the work, but not at all to this part) for the first time that intuitively and consciously I tried to achieve a more irregular and, indeed, more involved form and, as I can see now, did achieve it.[27]

While we can read Schoenberg's defense of the passages suggested for omission as a variation of the argument "if you think what came before was good, what comes next is even better," it is clear that the passages in question are defended at the expense of earlier parts of the work. Schoenberg's rationale is far from a ringing endorsement of a work requiring large instrumental forces and the surmounting of enormous technical and interpretive difficulties.

After several paragraphs of analysis designed to show the merits of the passages proposed for cutting, Schoenberg returns to the idea of large-scale design.

> . . . this repetition is here [rehearsal 50 and following] more than a recapitulation with variations. Apart from the fact that it follows the lines of the drama (which would no longer strike me as the most essential thing), it seems to me justified (and this is more important to me than justification in light of a formal scheme) by the sense of form and space that has always been the sole factor guiding me in composition, and which was the reason why I felt this group to be necessary. This must be taken on trust, blindly, and it can be taken on trust only by someone who has learnt to have confidence in the rest: I didn't put this part in merely because of the recapitulation, but because I felt it to be *formally necessary*.

> Furthermore, though I think you're right in holding that it isn't formal
> perfection that constitutes the merit of this work, the deficiency appears
> much more obviously in other passages, whereas here it doesn't strike me as
> being particularly apparent. (Frankly, in this respect too I think the passage
> better than what precedes it.)

There are several striking aspects to this part of the letter. First, after mentioning that the work follows the lines of the drama (we recall that Schoenberg
would later write, "It was inspired entirely by Maurice Maeterlinck's wonderful drama. I tried to mirror every detail of it . . ."), Schoenberg tells Zemlinsky
that this no longer strikes him as its most essential attribute. Schoenberg
is clearly distancing himself from an earlier aesthetic, and so alienating
himself from an essential attribute of the work – I will later argue that it is
precisely the correlation of drama and form that comprise the work's central
achievement. Even more striking in the context of the letter is Schoenberg's
insistence that the *formal necessity* of the "recapitulation" – the emphasis is
Schoenberg's – must be taken on faith, and can only be so taken "by someone
who has learnt to have confidence in the rest." But hadn't Schoenberg's previous remarks been designed to shake one's confidence in the rest? And then,
immediately after affirming the formal necessity of the passages in question
in their relation to the whole, Schoenberg casts doubt on the overall formal
design, returning to the strategy of defending rehearsal 50 and following at
the expense of earlier passages.

   After once again arguing against any cuts, this time based on the idea that
"one's first inspiration is almost always the right one," Schoenberg expresses
a final salvo of conflicted assessments.

> I hope you won't be annoyed and won't think I believe in 'infallibility'. On the
> contrary, if I had written more, I shouldn't mind much if this work didn't exist
> at all. True, I can't really think it bad, and even find plenty of very good stuff
> in it, and above all it has a number of features that indicate my subsequent
> development, perhaps even more than my first quartet. But I know exactly
> how far removed it is from perfection and that I have managed to do much
> better things. But I also know that cutting isn't the way to improve a work . . .
>   Anyway, I am sure that while conducting you won't have the feeling it is too
> long. This is a fact I have noticed repeatedly and commented on: whenever I
> conducted it, the work never struck me as too long . . . that faculty of yours
> will, in the end, find this music not too long.

The substantive part of the letter concludes with a description of the dramatic
roles of the work's motives and themes.

> In regard to the program: I have nothing against supplying a program. Only
> I will not write it myself, and cannot, because I have my books in Mödling.

> Therefore, only a few pointers: the motive of the beginning (12/8) refers to
> Melisande. The motive in the second measure (Bass Clar.) is the Fate-Motive.
> At [rehearsal number] 1 in the Oboe: Melisande; at 3 in the horn, Golaud
> (also at 4, 5, etc.); at 9 (E Trumpet), Pelleas; at 16, the Scherzo is the play with
> the ring; 25, the scene with Melisande's hair; 27, Golaud's intervention; six
> measures after 30, in the underground vaults; 33, a fountain in the park; 36 –,
> love scene; 50, the dying Melisande; 55 [56?], Golaud drags Melisande by the
> hair; 59, entrance of the serving women, Melisande's death.[28]

Even here, Schoenberg sends mixed messages. His "few pointers," cannot make any sense without knowledge of Maeterlinck's drama, but he refuses to outline the drama, ostensibly because he does not have his books with him. Is it plausible that Schoenberg would have had to refer to his books to remember the outlines of the drama? Not likely!

In all, ambivalence is not strong enough a word to capture the almost violent shifts from defense – don't change a thing! – to disparagement – "if I had written more, I shouldn't mind much if this work didn't exist at all." And buried just below the surface is a conflict about the work's status – program music or absolute music?[29]

All in all, what are we to make of Schoenberg's letter? An incautious reading would simply indicate that Schoenberg, c. 1918, considered *Pelleas* to be a flawed work, perhaps a deeply flawed work, but that any changes would make it worse! Alternatively, and in a more informed way, one may read the letter in the light of all that had transpired for Schoenberg between 1903 and 1918: the abandonment (or repression) of tonality; the development of a much more condensed style of composition; the intensification of a tendency toward quick, constant, and often radical development of musical material; a growing distrust of descriptive prose and a concomitantly growing commitment to formal descriptions of music; and perhaps less directly (but no less significantly) the profound gulf of before and after opened up by the horrendous events of the Great War. It is not just in the details of Schoenberg's defense of the later part of the work at the expense of what comes before that Schoenberg displays a subordination of early to late. Schoenberg's comment, "above all it has a number of features that indicate my subsequent development," is reminiscent of his assessment of *Gurrelieder*. It values the work primarily in its function as a stepping-stone toward later developments in his life as a composer. In this respect, the letter is part of a larger pattern that Schoenberg followed to a greater or lesser degree throughout his lifetime.

A deeper level of conflict emerges between Schoenberg's tendency to think in terms of a teleological model, and his more radical (in its time) rejection of teleology: when Schoenberg says he does not believe in "infallibility" he might as well say that he does not believe in "determinism," yet the idea of fate or destiny, which we will see to be central in Schoenberg's *Pelleas*, is recurrent in Schoenberg's writings. Schoenberg the Romantic would have understood the free will of the artist, the creator in the image of God, as a given, indeed as significant an attribute as might be imagined. But just as strong, if not stronger, is his tendency to think in terms of destiny and teleological determinism. Despite much in his musical thought that challenges the idea of *telos*, Schoenberg's sense of historical narrative, both personal and otherwise, remains for the most part bound to a teleological perspective. Schoenberg generally thought of his earlier work in the light of where his later works had led him, and he thought of the latter as the fulfillment of his destiny. Take, for example, his 1948 musings on the works of his first period.

> When I had finished my first *Kammersymphonie*, Op.9, I told my friends: 'Now I have established my style. I know now how I have to compose.'
>
> But my next work showed a great deviation from this style; it was a first step toward my present style. My destiny had forced me in this direction – I was not destined to continue in the manner of *Transfigured Night* or *Gurrelieder* or even *Pelleas and Melisande*. The Supreme Commander had ordered me on a harder road.[30]

And so, from the perspective of the atonal period, the rhythmic, melodic, and harmonic language of the tonal works embodies the incipient tendencies of what would come next, and its greatest value is in paving the way. In a similar way, from the perspective of the twelve-tone period, motivic saturation and avoidance of tonal progressions in the atonal period lead to the development of twelve-tone composition. By 1918 Schoenberg's abandonment of tonality meant that the technical means toward tonal expression, apart from nostalgia, were no longer of interest. For the composer, "what interests me now" has to do with technique that is extendible into the present period. Yet that criterion is not necessarily an indicator of the work's success in its own terms nor is it an indicator of the work's continued relevance if judged by other criteria, including the possibility of other historical trajectories unknown to the composer himself.[31]

Schoenberg's later writings on *Pelleas* continue to place it into a historical progression with a teleological bias, even though they emphasize positive aspects of the work seen through this perspective. Schoenberg returns to the problem of sequential writing and the role of *Pelleas* in his overall evolution in "A Self-Analysis" (1948).

> I personally do not find that atonality and dissonance are the outstanding features of my works. They certainly offer obstacles to the understanding of what is really my musical subject. But why then did even the works of my first period always meet resistance at the first few performances, only later to become appreciated?

> It seems that the true cause must be found in my tendency to endow every work with an extravagant abundance of musical themes. In the works of my first period this caused extension to a length that soon began to annoy me. It was of course the tendency of the Wagnerian and post-Wagnerian epoch . . . Much of this length, except in Mahler and Reger, was due to the technique of using numerous little-varied or even unvaried repetitions of short phrases. I became aware of the aesthetic inferiority of this technique when I composed the final section of the symphonic tone poem, *Pelleas and Melisande.* In the greater part of that work, sequences made up a considerable contribution toward achieving the necessary expanse of the presentation, such as is required for easier understanding.
>
> At the very start I knew that restriction could be achieved by two methods, condensation and juxtaposition . . .

Once again, the primary value is found in the ways that it adumbrates things to come. From Schoenberg's late perspective of 1948, the real value of *Pelleas* was in how its contrapuntal presentations of motives prepared the way for later works by opening up the possibilities for "condensation and juxtaposition" that became hallmarks of his atonal works. A similar attitude toward the work is found in his article "My Evolution" (1949) in which he devotes five musical examples to passages from *Pelleas*, this time emphasizing the harmonic advances found within the work.[32]

> Unusual melodic progressions demanding clarification through the harmony . . . may be found in my First String Quartet, Op.7, and in the Six Songs with Orchestra, Op.8, while the earlier symphonic poem *Pelleas and Melisande* suggests a more rapid advance in the direction of extended tonality. Here are many features that have contributed towards building up the style of my maturity, and many of the melodies contain extratonal intervals that demand extravagant movement of the harmony.

While the emphasis (or overemphasis) on forward-looking elements is also present in the early writings of those in Schoenberg's circle, ambivalence toward the stature of *Pelleas* is not found. (As I will argue later, Berg's analysis does show ambivalence about basic aspects of analytic approach.) Anton Webern, in a short article on Schoenberg's music published in 1912, writes enthusiastically of the "vast number" of motivic and thematic elements, the richness of their development and variation, and of the power of the innovative orchestration.[33] Berg wrote his guide to *Pelleas*, the basis of all subsequent analyses, at Schoenberg's request, but his relationship with the work went far beyond the publication.[34] Derrick Puffett has written of Berg's virtual obsession with the piece. After a 1927 performance Berg wrote: "It is truly music that echoes with one week after week, as if one had heard the last note 5 minutes earlier. Gradually the <u>world</u> will also come to feel it."[35] Egon Wellesz, Schoenberg's first biographer, is hardly less enthusiastic.

> On looking back, one sees that after this work a continuation in the same direction was, for Schönberg, impossible. He had reached a summit beyond which he could not go![36]

In 1964 pianist Glenn Gould wrote that Schoenberg's *Pelleas* "is one of the greatest symphonic poems ever written."[37]

In stark contrast to the effusive commentaries by Schoenberg's students, *Pelleas* has not fared so well in recent scholarly criticism. The two most significant studies in English in recent years have been those of Walter Frisch and Derrick Puffett.[38] Frisch approaches the work in the context of his important study of Schoenberg's early period, *The Early Works of Arnold Schoenberg: 1893–1908*. His critical remarks are appended to the main body of a chapter devoted principally to an analysis of thematic and harmonic elements of *Pelleas*.

> Although there are many wonderful moments in *Pelleas und Melisande*, it is probably the least successful of the large-scale works of Schoenberg's early period. That it falls chronologically between *Verklärte Nacht* and the First Quartet seems to have had technical and expressive ramifications. We sense Schoenberg struggling to reconcile programmatic and thematic-formal demands. In the relatively compact dimensions of *Verklärte Nacht*, problems of this kind tended to be swept away by the bold strokes of inspiration. Despite compositional awkwardnesses, the sextet easily convinces us of its status as a masterpiece. *Pelleas und Melisande* fails to do so; it seems bloated, its shortcomings (or long-comings) more exposed.
>
> *Pelleas und Melisande* also shows affinities with *Gurrelieder*, but here too it suffers by comparison . . .[39]

Puffett's journal article, "'Music that Echoes within one' for a Lifetime: Berg's Reception of Schoenberg's 'Pelleas und Melisande'," is principally concerned with Alban Berg's relationship to Schoenberg's *Pelleas*; he provides a well-thought-out critique of Berg's guide to *Pelleas* as well as an informative discussion of the role that Schoenberg's *Pelleas* played in the secret program of Berg's *Kammerkonzert* (1925), a work written to honor Schoenberg's fiftieth birthday. Citing William Austin's influential though dated textbook, *Music in the 20th Century*, as well as the critique provided by Frisch, Puffett echoes and augments their mixed feelings about the piece.

> . . . it is hardly necessary in this stage in the reception of the work to introduce critical qualification. *Pelleas* has long been recognized as one of Schoenberg's most uneven works . . . *Pelleas* as a whole is . . . marvelously crafted, supremely calculated but in the end not quite decided as to what it wants to say.[40]

The following question arises: has historical distance increased our capabilities to hear the work critically? Were the reports of early listeners, listeners as musically sophisticated as Webern and Berg, so beholden to Schoenberg that they were unable to recognize the work's flaws? Alternatively, are our current modes of orientation and appraisal mismatched with the technical and expressive qualities of the work? I will argue for the latter.

The key for a successful reappraisal of *Pelleas* is to be found in an issue astutely formulated by Puffett in his critique of the Berg guide, but not, to my mind, sufficiently developed in his own analysis (and hence hearing) of the piece. Puffett argues that Berg's *Short Thematic Analysis* imposes a bias toward "absolute music" that is not appropriate to *Pelleas*. As Berg says: "Never is it purely descriptive; the symphonic form is always perceived as absolute music."[41] In this aesthetic principle, Berg was certainly influenced by Schoenberg. As we have already seen in Schoenberg's 1918 letter to Zemlinsky, Schoenberg had developed ambivalence toward programmatic description by the late teens. Formalistic analysis was the order of the day. Berg therefore attempts to rescue *Pelleas* by trying to understand it largely in terms of absolute music. But Berg's approach is not quite that clear cut, in fact he seems to share Schoenberg's ambivalence, not about the quality of the piece, but about how to approach its formal and dramatic elements. Berg divides the work into four large parts, subdivided into seventeen smaller sections. Each section is designated by its formal function, its dramatic content, or by both. Figure 3.2 summarizes Berg's designations (the measure numbers are extrapolated from his musical examples and descriptions). The horizontal lines in the figure separate the work into four principal parts.

Of Berg's seventeen sections, eight use both designators – formal function and dramatic content. Two more sections use both designators but have dramatic contents that correlate with only part of the larger section (Reh. 56 and Reh. 62). Four sections are described only by their formal function and three sections are described only by their dramatic contents. From a dramatic perspective, Berg gives no designations or only partial designations for all of the recapitulatory space, so we ask ourselves if the musical recapitulations are necessitated by abstract formal considerations rather than by the requirements of the drama. From a formal perspective (problems inherent in some of the formal designations aside), Berg does not explain the scene by the castle tower, the castle vaults, or the scene depicting Mélisande's death, so we ask if these passages are alien to the "absolute" formal design, instead necessitated only by a dramatic impulse.[42] To the degree that there are places where dramatic events do not sit comfortably within the proposed formal design, that design is either violated or simply not convincing.

Measure	Formal Designation	Dramatic Contents
m. 1	Introduction	Mélisande lost in the forest
Reh. 5	Main Theme	Golaud and Mélisande marry
Reh. 8	Transition	(not specifically ascribed)
Reh. 9	Subordinate Theme	Pelléas, Mélisande and Pelléas meet Mélisande's awakening love
Reh. 12	Codetta	
Reh. 14	Recapitulation	(not specifically ascribed)
Reh. 16	Scherzo-like	Scene by the pool in the park
Reh. 22.4	Postlude	Golaud's growing jealousy and suspicion
Reh. 25	(none given)	Scene by the castle tower
Reh. 30.6	(none given)	Scene in the castle vaults
Reh. 33	Introduction to part 3	The pool in the park Scene of
Reh. 36	Quasi Adagio	farewell (love scene)
Reh. 50	Recap of Introduction	(not specifically ascribed)
Reh. 55	Recap of Main Theme	(not specifically ascribed)
Reh. 56	Recap of Adagio	(includes memory of Golaud's rage)
Reh. 59	(none given)	Mélisande's sickroom
Reh. 62	Epilogue	(includes thoughts that it was not Golaud's fault)

Figure 3.2. Berg's designations for seventeen sections in Schoenberg's *Pelleas.*

And, to the degree that Berg places formal design above dramatic impulse, his analysis subordinates the dramatic impulse to an abstract formal one. Instead of allowing the programmatic elements to drive the work's formal design, Berg reduces them to *a priori* categories of symphonic form; they function as thematic areas, transitions, recapitulations, and the like. While the principal leitmotivs and outlines of the drama are identified by Berg (as supplied by Schoenberg, no doubt), the categories of formal function at Berg's disposal are not sufficient to the task of capturing a sense of the highly complex, drama-generated formal design. As a result, Berg misleads us to underestimate the cogency and complexity of the dramatic associations. Furthermore, we misconstrue formal aspects as well.

As we shall see in some detail, Schoenberg's musical vehicle for dramatic associations is his adaptation of Wagner's leitmotiv technique. While adaptations of Wagnerian leitmotiv technique reappear later in Schoenberg's music, (the associations of specific row partitions in *Moses und Aron* with dramatic characters or events provide many vivid examples), there is no other work by Schoenberg that is as thorough-going in its use of leitmotivs; in *Pelleas* they generate all aspects of dramatic representation and its correlates in formal design. In this respect, *Pelleas* is radically different from *Verklärte Nacht*, *Gurrelieder*, the First String Quartet, and the *Kammersymphonie*, op. 9, the other major works of Schoenberg's first period (we can also include the Second String Quartet, for those who would argue that it too belongs in this group of first period works). It is for this reason that I feel uncomfortable with Frisch's comparison of *Pelleas* with Schoenberg's other early masterworks. I do not think the works are commensurate.

As we have already noted, it was Schoenberg himself who unquestionably set the precedent for viewing the work ambivalently; however, he was steadfast in casting it as absolute music. We recall his comments in the 1918 letter to Zemlinsky: "it follows the lines of the drama (which would no longer strike me as the most essential thing) . . ." The letter emphasizes the formal design over its dramatic genesis, and it is only at the end that Schoenberg adds, almost as an afterthought (and with palpable ambivalence), a description of the dramatic significations of the work's motives and themes. The dramatic identities of these motives and themes are a part of all subsequent commentaries, Schoenberg's own program notes included. But it is the formal description of the arrangement of these elements as they are integrated into a multi-movement symphonic form that Berg and later critics emphasize. (Notably, Schoenberg, in his 1949 program notes, omits any discussion of form.) I propose that we must take Schoenberg's musical adaptation of Maeterlinck's drama, as depicted through the vicissitudes of the leitmotivic and thematic constituents of the work, as first and foremost in our hearing. This is not to say that the formal constituents are without interest; rather I claim that our understanding of form, from the minutiae of leitmotivic design, to large-scale trajectories within the work, must be informed by a sense of dramatic function.

The dramatic function of leitmotivs

The catalogue of leitmotivs and themes shown in Example 3.1 represents what I identify as the eleven primary musical ideas in Schoenberg's *Pelleas*. The example shows each musical idea in its initial presentation and lists them in their order of appearance. As later analysis will show, the conciseness of

Example 3.1. Tabular list of eleven principal leitmotivs and themes, in order of appearance.

some of the examples can be misleading. The examples represent a wide range of musical types; while some, e.g. FATE, comprise short musical ideas that are extended and developed in context by proliferating and juxtaposing multiple transformations of the original, others, e.g. LOVE, are more properly understood as themes rather than motives (defining themes as larger units comprising smaller motivic constituents that cohere into phrases or multiple phrases). It should be noted that Mélisande is unique among the three protagonists in that she is represented solely by motives, MELISANDE LOST and MELISANDE, while both Golaud and Pelléas are represented by motives embedded in (and extracted from) themes. Example 1.4, including the initial presentation of the WEDDING BOND motive, shows that that motive is a constituent of a larger theme whose incipit is the GOLAUD motive; we will call the larger whole and its transformations the "GOLAUD theme," but keep the distinction between "GOLAUD" and "WEDDING BOND" which are also developed as separate motives.

Most of the names that I use in this example and the ones that follow are either derived directly or are easily extrapolated from the descriptions in Berg's analysis and/or Schoenberg's letter and program notes. The designations in the primary sources are summarized in Figure 3.3. From these sources I have adopted the names MELISANDE LOST, FATE, MELISANDE, GOLAUD, WEDDING BOND, PELLEAS, JEALOUSY, and LOVE. There are several leitmotivs found in the primary sources that I omit from my list – Mélisande playing with her wedding-ring, Pelléas playing with Mélisande's hair, the underground vaults, and the portrayal of the fountain in the park. I omit these designations for two reasons: they are restricted to their immediate scenes while the ones on the list have more global implications; even these specific musical passages, as later analysis will show, are largely generated out of the more fundamental motives and themes that are listed.

In three cases I have devised names suggested by dramatic context but not identified as such in the primary sources. Later analysis will more fully show the relevance of these names, but even here we can give some sense of their appropriateness. The name EROS is fairly close to Berg's designation "the awakening of love in Mélisande" (no designation for this motive is given by Schoenberg in either of his primary sources). I find EROS more suggestive than "awakening love" for several reasons. First, there are its obvious connections to Freudian theory as well as to other conceptualizations and depictions of Eros that date back to antiquity, and so connect Schoenberg's musical thought to a richer historical context. The drive, or its evocation through musical means, is one that intensifies over the course of the work during the scenes portraying the evolving relationship of Pelléas and Mélisande; the climactic presentations of EROS are found in the Love scene, just before the death of Pelléas. An awareness of EROS is also forceful in scenes portraying (hence experienced from) Golaud's perspective; his perception of the increasing erotic attraction between Mélisande and Pelléas gives rise to his increasing suspicion, jealousy, and then wrath. While it can be

Schoenberg, March 20, 1918 Letter to Alexander Zemlinsky	Alban Berg *Short Thematic Analysis*, 1920	Schoenberg, *Program Notes*, 1949
Beginning refers to Mélisande lost	as in 1918 letter	does not refer to opening motive
Fate motive first heard in m. 2	as in 1918 letter	as in 1918 letter
Reh. 1: Mélisande	as in 1918 letter	as in 1918 letter
Reh. 3: Golaud	as in 1918 letter, add wedding ring/marriage vow motive	as in 1918 letter
Reh. 9: Pelléas	as in 1918 letter	as in 1918 letter
	Reh. 12.8: awakening love	does not refer to "awakening love" motive
Reh. 16: Scherzo, Play with the ring	as in 1918 letter	as in 1918 letter
	Reh. 23: Golaud's suspicion and jealousy	as in Berg
Reh. 25: scene where Pelléas plays with Mélisande's hair	as in 1918 letter	as in 1918 letter
Reh. 30.6: underground vaults	as in 1918 letter	as in 1918 letter
Reh. 33: fountain in park	as in 1918 letter	does not mention fountain
Reh. 36: love scene	as in 1918 letter	as in 1918 letter
Reh. 50: imminent death of Mélisande	as in 1918 letter; also mentions "new themes" at 50.2 and 50.7	as in 1918 letter; "new motive" at 50.2, associated with death of Mélisande, does not mention new theme at 50.7
Reh. 55 (56?): Golaud dragging Mélisande by her hair	as in 1918 letter	does not mention Golaud dragging Mélisande
Reh. 59: Mélisande's death	as in 1918 letter	as in 1918 letter

Figure 3.3. *Pelleas und Melisande*: Dramatic designations of leitmotivs and themes.

argued that "awakening love" implies an ongoing and intensifying process, "Eros" does the job more efficiently. Moreover, although initially associated with Mélisande, EROS mutually affects Mélisande and Pelléas (as well as their relations to Golaud) so their "awakening love" is mutual. In addition, and perhaps most importantly, I will claim that EROS, along with the JEAL-OUSY motive, participates in a dramatic reversal of fortune of the kind that the ancient Greeks named *peripeteia*. With the death of Pelléas, Mélisande's thoughts move toward her own death, as Golaud's thoughts move toward remorse: the functions of EROS and JEALOUSY are supplanted respectively by DEATH DRIVE and LOST INNOCENCE.

The two musical ideas (displaying more development than motives but less than that of full blown themes) that I call DEATH DRIVE and LOST INNOCENCE are identified by Berg only as formal areas, "new themes" of the recapitulation. Schoenberg does not identify the LOST INNOCENCE motive in either source, but he does characterize what I call DEATH DRIVE as "a new motive [that] appears in the death scene." In the last part of the work, after the death of Pelléas, EROS, recollected by Mélisande and Golaud, loses its momentum and gathering force. In contrast, the DEATH DRIVE idea first appears as Mélisande's death is imminent and reaches its fulfillment in the actual death scene. After the death of Pelléas, the force of EROS gives way to the unyielding DEATH DRIVE.[43]

While Berg does not designate a dramatic role for the idea I call LOST INNOCENCE (the second of his "new themes"), he does identify a later passage that depicts Golaud's recollection of the hair pulling episode derived from Act IV, ii of the play. As Berg shows, that later passage (Berg's examples are from Reh. 57.6–7 and 58.1–2) draws its salient dotted rhythms from LOST INNOCENCE while its pitch content shows kinship to the MELISANDE motive, the LOVE theme, as well as fragments of LOST INNOCENCE (not included in Berg's examples). Among Schoenberg's seminal motives and themes, LOST INNOCENCE is unique in its initial homophonic presentation combined with its strong diatonic implications. This musical representation – evocative of the lost Eden of diatonic tonality famously lamented by Brahms, likely an ongoing source of repressed mourning in Schoenberg – is a powerful means through which Schoenberg conveys the recollective force of the musical idea, here remarkably harkening back to something not found in the previous music.[44] Like the reversal of EROS into DEATH DRIVE, JEALOUSY gives rise to LOST INNOCENCE. Both of these reversals are anticipated by a different sort of reversal as LOVE (between Mélisande and Pelléas) supplants the sanctity of the WEDDING BOND between Mélisande and Golaud.

The themes and motives can be divided into those representing people, those representing drives or basic forces, and those representing emotional complexes: {MELISANDE LOST, MELISANDE, GOLAUD, PELLEAS} + {FATE, EROS, LOVE, DEATH DRIVE} + {WEDDING BOND, JEALOUSY, LOST INNOCENCE}. We can also think of themes and motives in terms of their primary association with one or more of the three protagonists: Mélisande: {MELISANDE LOST + MELISANDE + FATE + EROS + LOVE + DEATH DRIVE + LOST INNOCENCE}, Golaud: {GOLAUD + FATE + WEDDING BOND + JEALOUSY + LOST INNOCENCE}, Pelléas:

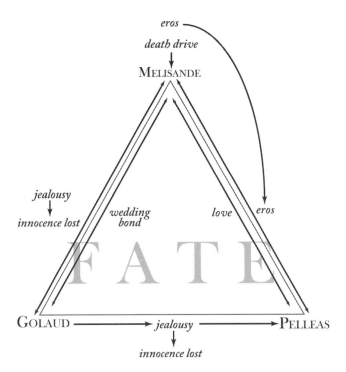

Figure 3.4. Cathexis and the Love Triangle.

{PELLEAS + FATE + EROS +LOVE}. Thus FATE impinges on all three characters, JEALOUSY is uniquely associated with Golaud, the DEATH DRIVE is associated uniquely with Mélisande, while EROS is shared by Pelléas and Mélisande, LOST INNOCENCE is shared by Golaud and Mélisande. A third way to cluster motives and themes is based on changes of perspective in the telling of the story, the shifting of points of view among the protagonists. Thus, for example, we can schematically represent Golaud's reaction to the growing love between Pelléas and Mélisande as {PELLEAS + MELISANDE + EROS + JEALOUSY + FATE}/Golaud. A fourth division views the musical ideas as embodying a directed cathexis, the investment of psychic or emotional energy from one character to another. I show these relations in Figure 3.4.

The figure shows the investment of psychic/emotional energy from each protagonist to the others. EROS arises out of Mélisande (we will later consider the implications of this gendering), but is then mutually cathected between Mélisande and Pelléas. JEALOUSY eventually transformed into LOST INNOCENCE is cathected from Golaud to Pelléas and Mélisande, etc.

Needless to say, the themes and motives are not static entities. Over time, they develop and take on new meanings. They form large-scale trajectories

Example 3.2a. *Hauptstimmen*, mm. 1–11.

of intensification or fulfillment and depletion or exhaustion, and they participate in modes of anticipation, immediacy, and recollection.

Melisande Lost and Fate

Pelleas und Melisande opens with the first of two motives associated with Mélisande, MELISANDE LOST, Schoenberg's musical depiction of Mélisande, lost and weeping. Soon thereafter, in m. 2 and then m. 4, we hear the first intrusions of the FATE motive. Although MELISANDE LOST is most properly understood as a contrapuntal/harmonic complex, there is clearly one voice that is principal (a functional *Hauptstimme*), while the others play subordinate but crucial roles. Example 3.2a shows the principal voices for the first eleven measures, heard in the English horn and muted violas, as well as the punctuated interruptions of FATE, in the bass clarinet. While the inner voices and bass undergo considerable development as the passage unfolds, the principal voice stays closely related to its mimetic source idea. The initial motive, A-Bb-B-F, with its intervallic profile of $<+1+1-6>$, is no doubt meant to suggest sobbing (shallow breaths and then a heaving sigh). The shape of this motive, rhythmic and intervallic, gives rise to the entire passage, and, as earlier critics have noted, its chromatic incipit ($<+1+1>$) becomes a genetic source idea that is imprinted upon

Example 3.2b. Measures 1–6, texture simplified.

subsequent themes and motives. Within the first eleven measures, the four-note melodic contour is modified only minimally, first by truncation, then by the addition of a chromatic lower neighbor (beginning in m. 6), and then by reduction to a single remaining dyad. FATE, perhaps more puzzling than ominous in its initial manifestations, interrupts or intrudes upon the ongoing texture. The major mode triadic descent of its final three notes is at odds with the chromaticisms that surround it. This, with the stark shift in timbre and texture (better seen in Example 3.2b), alerts us to the intrusion of some unanticipated and as yet incomprehensible presence. In m. 2 the interruption results in the breaking off of the melodic line; at the end of m. 3, the analogous place in the phrase, the melody hesitates, as if waiting for the intrusion of FATE. Across the passage, the overall shape of the principal voice (with interruptions by FATE) forms a loose sentence structure: we hear the initial subphrase through m.1, its modified repetition beginning with the upbeat to m. 3, and then a spinning out and liquidation leading into the evanescent half cadence at Reh. 1. Yet the meandering harmonies and spun-out motivic texture do not cohere into a theme. The entire passage sounds as a large-scale *Auftakt*, an anacrusis waiting for a downbeat, although its harmonic vagaries ill define any sense of *telos*. When the first approximation of a cadence appears, at Reh. 1, it can hardly be called a resolution. MELISANDE LOST functions dramatically and formally as an anticipation of something, but from its perspective, we do not know what that something may be.[45]

Example 3.2b shows the first seven measures in more detail; although the texture of the passage is somewhat simplified, the example includes the subordinate voices. The five-part texture comprises the principal voice, a secondary voice with characteristic sixteenth-note, neighbor-tone configurations, two inner subordinate lines, and a bass. While the primary status of the main voice is readily perceived, that status is challenged by other aspects of the passage. Forces combine to create an atmosphere in which the figuration on the foreground always seems at risk of being swallowed up by the music lying symbolically just beneath the surface. These include the restless motion of the secondary voice, its plangent semitone dissonances clashing against the falling tritones of the primary voice, and the dark, murky register of the passage. From the very beginning, the melody, such as it is, is in danger of being overwhelmed by and absorbed into its ground (or underground). As the passage progresses toward the evanescent half cadence at Reh. 1, this tendency is intensified; the inner voices move more and more quickly, gradually overwhelming the previously established harmonic and melodic constituents. In terms of musical technique, the common practice distinction of melody and accompaniment is thrown into partial disarray, as accompaniment threatens to engulf melody. This conflict among the voices

Example 3.2c. Underlying voice leading for the opening.

Chord sequence mm.1-6: ABCDAB[I1]ABCDCDCD[I2]ABAD

plays out a variant of the Dionysian/Apollonian dialectic – the principal voice searches for some semblance of lucidity, while the remaining voices threaten to undo and engulf that lucidity. Or, from a Freudian perspective, the mysterious force of the Unconscious, like a river of magma just below the surface, threatens to erupt, swallow up, and destroy the veneer of order and control at the surface.[46]

The harmony for the first six measures, intrusions of FATE aside, is principally generated by the alternation of two pairs of augmented chords voice-leading to half-diminished seventh chords, each pair a minor third distant from the other. The half-diminished chord, which will play a prevalent role throughout the work, is of course the signature harmony for Wagner's *Tristan und Isolde*. Here it will remain associated with Mélisande. The underlying harmonic sequence of augmented and half-diminished chords ("progression" is too goal-oriented a word for the context), voice-leading simplified, is shown in Example 3.2c.

The "major triad" constituent of the FATE motive, F♯ major in m. 2, and then A major in mm. 4–5, sounds as a *non sequitur*; in both cases it interrupts the meandering alternations of augmented and half-diminished chords but in no way resolves them. If there is any implication of tonal function (a somewhat dubious assertion given the discontinuities involved) then it is as a faintly implied dominant function, first implying B minor, and then D minor; the latter is the key that will eventually bring tonal closure to the work, and the faint dominant implications of FATE in mm. 4–5 may be understood as the first hint in that direction. At the end of each of the two initial presentations of FATE, the final note is folded into the ongoing harmonic sequence; F♯ folds into the B♭ augmented chord in m. 2; in m. 5 A-natural feeds into the A-natural lower neighbor in the melody, voice-leading to B♭. If we hear the initial tone of FATE as being displaced at the octave, so that <+11−3−4> implies <−1−3−4>, the semitone motion mimics the resolution of flat-six to five (e.g. D-C♯-A♯-F♯ as flat-six, five, three, one), playing on the sonorities of the augmented chords that are so basic to the underlying harmonies of the passage. As we shall see, this motion subsequently becomes thematic.

At first, the intermittent bass line composes out a fully diminished arpeggio – the same chord heard played *pizzicato* in clashing discord against the initial FATE motives. Beginning in m. 6 and continuing for the next three bars, the bass line forms an ostinato derived from the FATE motive. Later, Schoenberg will use this same technique in the scene depicting the castle vaults (Reh. 30.6). This initial grounding in FATE is the first hint of the pervasive and overriding force that FATE will achieve over the course of the work. In contrast to its initial presentations, the presentations of FATE in the bass insinuate themselves into the ongoing harmonic alternation between augmented and half-diminished chords; the one tone in the four-note motive that is not consonant with the ongoing harmonic sequence is A-natural; it appears consonant with the initial tone of the melody, but dissonant against the B♭ augmented chord that the melodic A resolves into. This A-natural in the bass, oddly placed a perfect fifth above D, is interesting in several ways. The Fate motive has "right-shifted" so that the first note, instead of being an upbeat as previously, occurs on the written downbeat of the measure. However, the ear interprets the second note of the motive, A-natural, as the metric downbeat (a very Brahmsian use of syncopation). In this sense, the A-natural (the perfect-fifth-making member that sounds like a downbeat) is deceptive.

As we have already noted, the overall harmonic motion through the first eleven measures, at first hesitant and meandering, and then saturated with chromatic inflections, terminates with an evanescent half cadence at Reh. 1. This moment vaguely suggests a D minor tonality, yet to assert that the passage clearly defines a key is to overstate the impact of the cadence, which is hardly prepared and immediately undone, and to understate the significance of the intial harmonic drift, symbolic of Mélisande lost.

Aside from its pervasive function as the genetic source for the $<+1+1>$ ascending semitone idea, MELISANDE LOST plays a small role in the larger composition; literal presentations of the motive are restricted to the beginning of the work and to the beginning of the section that Berg considered a recapitulatory finale, starting at Reh. 50. We will consider aspects of that later passage in due course during our study of the recapitulation's "new themes," DEATH DRIVE and LOST INNOCENCE, both of which are interpolated into the beginning of the recapitulation. For now however, we can approach the question of the dramatic function (as opposed to the obvious formal function) of returning to MELISANDE LOST as we initiate the final phases of the unfolding music drama.

Because Schoenberg did not document the dramatic meaning of the recapitulation, we cannot be certain of his intentions. Nonetheless, there are strong indications that emerge through a close comparison of the symphonic poem with the play. As we have noted, in the Maeterlinck, Mélisande falls into a coma after the death of Pelléas. I interpret the beginning of the "recapitulatory finale," from Reh. 50 to three bars before Reh. 55, as portraying this state – essentially a dream-turned-nightmare experienced from Mélisande's perspective. Based on thematic elements and orchestral color, the association of this music with Mélisande is unmistakable. As the passage continues into Reh. 52, the crowding in of motivic fragments intensifies (e.g. measure 52.1 contains five leitmotivic fragments – MELISANDE, LOST INNOCENCE, WEDDING BOND, DEATH DRIVE, and PELLEAS). To a degree the technique is similar to that employed in *Gurrelieder* during the orchestral interlude of Part I, as discussed in Chapter One. However, here the combination of rhythmic and harmonic language creates a sense of free-floating as the vague metric placement and harmonic indirection of the opening are developed and heightened. I take these as indicators that Schoenberg is portraying Mélisande's coma from her perspective, something impossible for Maeterlinck to have done in the staged version. As such, the passage is the predecessor of dreams and dreamlike states that are portrayed in the Second String Quartet, *Die glückliche Hand*, *Erwartung*, and the String Trio. In its immediate context, the meaning of MELISANDE LOST becomes poignantly transformed – Mélisande, whose death is imminent, is lost.

In contrast to the limited role of MELISANDE LOST (its pervasive genetic traces aside), recurrences of FATE occur at crucial moments throughout the piece. We have seen how Schoenberg's lifelong fascination with the idea of destiny or fate informed his sense of historical *telos*; *Pelleas* is unique in Schoenberg's output in portraying fate with such centrality and specificity. In this regard, as well as in many other aspects of the work, Wagner is the most important musical precursor; however, Schoenberg's deviations from the Wagnerian models are as significant as the parallels.

Three of Wagner's works seem to have specific relevance in understanding *Pelleas. Tristan und Isolde* provides a model of the love triangle as well as some aspects of Schoenberg's harmonic language. *Parsifal*, in its conflicted worlds of chromaticism and diatonicism, also influences Schoenberg's harmony, and may have specifically influenced Schoenberg's portrayal of Eros. First and foremost, it is the elaborate workings of fate in *Der Ring des Nibelungen* that set the precedent for Schoenberg's conception of destiny in *Pelleas. The Ring* depicts fate through two motives: Alberich's curse, first heard in scene four of *Das Rheingold* ("*Wie durch Fluch er mir geriet, verflucht sei dieser Ring!*" "Since by curse it came to be, accursed be this ring!"); and the Fate motive, first heard at the beginning of Act II, scene 4 of *Die Walküre*, the scene in which Brünnhilde will fatefully disobey Wotan's reluctant command that she not protect Siegmund from Hunding's wrath (later, in the first scene of *Götterdämmerung*, this same motive becomes associated with the three Norns). Following their introduction, Wagner's two fate motives play important roles through the remainder of the Ring cycle; the Curse motive forecasts and follows the deadly career of the ring, while the Fate motive portends the fate of Brünnhilde and the destruction of Valhalla. Both motives return in close proximity to one another during the final scene of *Götterdämmerung*. Just before Brünnhilde ignites Siegfried's funeral pyre, she places the cursed ring on her own finger. She then joins Siegfried in the conflagration. Both motives portray inescapable destiny and likewise function within Wagner's drama to foretell, recollect that foretelling, and then confirm it as destiny. In Wagner's presentations, the motives are woven into the harmonic and melodic fabric of the piece. Destiny is inherent in the nature of things. In Schoenberg's case, this technique is modified in a striking way. Akin to Wagner, fate in Schoenberg is inescapable. Unlike Wagner's depictions, Schoenberg's FATE dissonantly intrudes upon the ongoing harmonic fabric. The three catastrophic manifestations of FATE, all associated with Golaud (Reh. 8, Reh. 32, and two measures before Reh. 49), disrupt the larger formal and dramatic continuity as well. In Schoenberg, fate acts as an external force that violently intrudes into the nature of things, tearing apart the continuity of what might otherwise have been. In this respect, his portrayal of fate is more like Kafka than Wagner.

FATE, as an intrusive, disruptive, and ultimately tragic force, impinges upon all three of the work's protagonists but affects each character in distinctive ways. We have already seen how FATE, in its initial presentations, disrupts and then insinuates itself into the ongoing depiction of Mélisande lost. FATE placed within MELISANDE LOST is puzzling, even mysterious. It breaks off immediate continuities (as undirected as they are), but otherwise leaves the portrayal of Mélisande much intact. This is in great contrast with the catastrophic manifestions of FATE associated with Golaud. These exaggerate the intrusive and disruptive aspects of the motive with extraordinary dramatic and formal consequences. The first of these massive intrusions of FATE appears suddenly and unexpectedly as the glorious music depicting the wedding of Golaud and Mélisande (analyzed below) seems headed for its closing cadence in A; we hear an E dominant chord (at Reh. 7.7), but its progress toward A is interrupted by an unprepared move to D in the bass. Then a quick, three-measure crescendo, building up *stretti* presentations of FATE, leads to five measures of a *fff tutti* ironically juxtaposing reiterations of FATE against reiterations of the WEDDING BOND motive. The resultant harmonies alternate first inversion D minor and F augmented which reveals a genetic relation to the alternation of F augmented and B half-diminished in MELISANDE LOST, here with a much intensified, explosive effect. Once the massive intrusion ends (at Reh. 8.6), we return *subito piano* to music that closes off the wedding scene, resolving the E dominant that was left hanging before the intrusion to A major. Now, of course, the cadence comes too late. The mood of the scene has been destroyed, and the meaning of that destructive force remains to be played out. Like its earlier manifestations, the terrifying intrusion of FATE within the wedding scene is a *non sequitur*, but here the impact is more manifold. FATE not only disrupts the immediate harmonic direction of the passage, in a formal sense it radically intrudes into the thematic area, and in a dramatic sense it breaks apart the successful closure of the wedding scene. The passage has no direct analogue in Maeterlinck, and it is unlike anything in Wagner.

This initial explosion of FATE convincingly links up with its subsequent manifestations, each of which rend the fabric of the work, and each of which appear in a more condensed form (four measures at Reh. 32, and then two measures before Reh. 49). The second explosive intrusion of FATE brings the end of the portentous scene in the vaults to an emotional climax as Golaud's wrath toward Pelléas reaches a nearly murderous pitch. At its third catastrophic manifestation, FATE interrupts and terminates the love scene between Pelléas and Mélisande, signaling the death of Pelléas and all that follows.

Perhaps it should not surprise us that Berg does not seem to know what to make of these massive intrusions, especially the first, which cannot be reconciled to the linear narrative of the play or to the formal boundaries of Schoenberg's symphonic form. Berg calls the first intrusion a "transition" (*Überleitung*) between themes (Golaud, then Pelléas), the second a "connecting passage" (*Verbindung*) between the vault scene and the introduction to the love scene, and the third is simply noted as being related to the earlier passages. As Derrick Puffett recognizes, Berg's formal descriptions are wholly inadequate to the events.[47]

We have seen that intrusions of FATE disrupt immediate continuities within MELISANDE LOST, and in so doing portend more significant events to come. In the catastrophic intrusions of FATE associated with Golaud, these same tendencies are augmented and intensified so that they significantly disrupt continuities of formal design and become main determinants in the course of the drama. The disruptive force of FATE is handled in a different, but no less decisive way within Pelléas's theme. We will study that theme and its ramifications more fully below (see Example 3.5), and limit our thoughts here to the immediate role of FATE in shaping Pelléas's character. Pelléas's theme begins with three measures set for trumpet in E that are strikingly different in color and character from anything that we have heard up until this moment. It is this part of the theme that Schoenberg must have had in mind when in his 1950 program notes he characterized Pelléas as "youthful and knightly."[48] The intrusion of FATE effectively bifurcates the theme so that it comprises two conflicting segments with FATE interposed between them. The music after FATE could not be more contrasting with that before. The jaunty trumpet melody (to my ears more Straussian than Wagnerian) cuts off abruptly, and the theme continues with a passionate, chromatic line, doubled at the octave in the upper strings and woodwinds. As we shall see, this bifurcation into conflicting elements is then developed in the music that follows. In contrast to Pelléas, Mélisande's essential character remains unchanged by FATE. In the case of Golaud, the explosive intrusions of FATE affect his actions over large dramatic and formal spans. The impact upon Pelléas is immediate and dramatic, as though he suddenly becomes another person, one who struggles with his former self once FATE intervenes.

The intervention of FATE within the Pelléas theme is also the occasion for the addition of a component to the FATE motive: a two-chord harmonic progression that absorbs and obscures the by now familiar linear constituents of FATE.[49] In its original presentation (Reh. 9.4–9.5), the FATE harmonies are an A♭ dominant seventh in six-five position leading to a B dominant seventh in root position. Given the mysterious and then portentous characterizations of FATE up until this point, this choice of chords is somewhat puzzling. The voice-leading is smooth (inner voices change enharmonically, outer voices move in contrary motion by semitone), and, given the range of chromatic motions that have already been presented, not particularly striking in and of itself. If anything, the progression introduces a degree of sweetness to the FATE motive not encountered before, and representationally that seems to be its point. In short course, FATE, along with its characteristic harmonic progression, becomes associated with EROS (at Reh. 12.12–13). Later, in the music just prior to the love scene, EROS is developed over sequential presentations of the FATE harmonies (Reh. 33.1–10, where the linear FATE motive is absent).[50] Linked to EROS, FATE becomes bittersweet.[51] Perhaps just as important from a representational point of view is the way that the linear constituents of FATE are obscured by being absorbed into the A♭[7]-B[7] progression. Within the Pelléas theme, the pitches of the FATE motive all appear as chord tones; its "triadic" constituents (F♯-D♯-B) are absorbed into the progression, F♯ and D♯ as enharmonic equivalents of G♭ and E♭, and B as the root of the B[7] chord (the specific voicing of FATE, *mf* in the bassoon, in the same register as the sustained chords, is also a factor). Moreover, we are further distracted from recognizing the presence of FATE by the motivic developments in the upper woodwinds (growing out of the Mélisande motive). As a result, the linear FATE motive is virtually swallowed up in the orchestration.[52] Thus FATE is the determinant in changing the course of Pelléas's life, and yet it is presented in a way that obscures its very presence.

Example 3.3a. Rehearsal 1–1.7: *Hauptstimmen* with simplified underlying harmonies.

The MELISANDE enigma

The entry of the MELISANDE motive at the upbeat to Reh.1 precipitates a sudden shift in texture and color. The gathering crescendo that had emerged out of the dark, murky orchestration of the opening breaks off *subito piano* immediately after the first note of the new motive; the accumulation of force as undercurrent threatens to engulf the surface. As in the initial presentation of FATE (upbeat to m.2), the first note of MELISANDE (A♭ upbeat to Reh. 1) is obscured by the ongoing texture, which abruptly terminates only after the new motive has begun. The initial presentation of MELISANDE, in the solo oboe, introduces the treble register for the first time in the work. The motive clearly cuts through the remaining residues of MELISANDE LOST that continue in the subordinate voices (these are not shown in Example 3.3a, which reduces them to their underlying harmonies). The eight-note motive, once completed by the oboe, is handed off to the English horn, transposed a tritone lower, and then transposed down another tritone, to the octave below the original. The motive is liquidated into fragments successively heard in the bass clarinet, bassoon, and then English horn. Like the exposition of MELISANDE LOST, the initial presentations of MELISANDE follow the motivic logic of a musical sentence (statement, modified statement, followed

Example 3.3b. Embedded whole tones in MELISANDE.

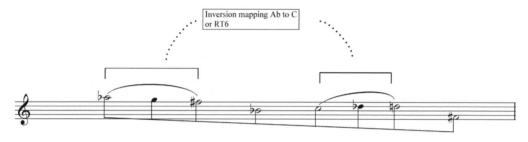

Example 3.3c. MELISANDE at original level and transposed down a tritone.

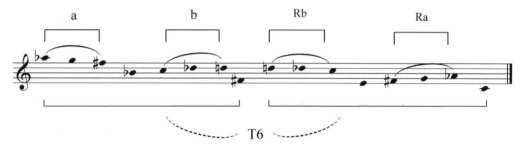

by spinning out to liquidation) without having the kind of harmonic and melodic content that would define a more normative phrase shape, let alone a proper theme. The arrival of A^7 at the downbeat of Reh. 1 is quickly undermined by the chromaticisms that immediately follow. And the hints at tonal directedness, most notably the root motion of a descending perfect fifth across the initial motivic unfolding – from A to D – are vitiated by unstable voicings and by the continual reemergence of the kinds of unstable harmonies – augmented and half-diminished chords – that we have already associated with Mélisande.

In its succinct, quickly recognizable form, in its harmonic and rhythmic flexibility, and in its ability to enter into countless contrapuntal relationships with the work's other motives as well as with transformations of itself, MELISANDE is very much like a Wagnerian leitmotiv. At the same time MELISANDE is also a remarkable precursor to the kinds of motivic properties that Schoenberg would later pursue in his post-tonal music. In its initial presentations, MELISANDE is juxtaposed against transpositions of itself. This gives the music a self-reflective quality and, as we shall see, in this case self-reflection results in a depth of complexity that seems fathomless.

The MELISANDE motive, through juxtapositions with transformations of itself, begins to manifest its enigmatic qualities almost immediately. We begin to explore those properties in Examples 3.3b and 3.3c.

As it is developed throughout the course of the work, the intervallic constituents of MELISANDE will vary according to its tonal contexts. The initial
exposition of the MELISANDE idea, from Reh. 1 to Reh. 3.3, is dominated by
motions through whole-tone space. Much like Debussy, Schoenberg uses the
drift of whole-tone collections to create a suspended or evaded sense of *telos*.
The various whole-tone juxtapositions are generated out of the intervallic
design of the motive itself. As shown in Example 3.3b, MELISANDE, in its
initial presentations, can be understood to comprise a whole-tone penta-
chord embellished by two chromatic passing tones <Ab-(g)-F♯-Bb-C-(db)-
D-F♯>. The two <−8> leaps within the motive delineate an augmented
chord that is embedded in the whole-tone structure <F♯-Bb-D-F♯>; this
is the same augmented chord that had initiated the harmonies underlying
MELISANDE LOST.

The two inversionally related chromatic motions within MELISANDE,
<+1+1> and <−1−1>, are also derived from MELISANDE LOST. In
addition to their genetic association with the opening, these chromatic
trichords give rise to a host of relations between the various transpositions
of MELISANDE.

The initial tritone-related transpositions are particularly striking in this
regard, developing relations that anticipate properties of Schoenberg's
twelve-tone music.[53] The two chromatic trichords of the original, labeled *a*
and *b* in Example 3.3c, become reversed in T_6 so that across the pair we find
the sequence <*a, b,* R*b,* R*a*>, an embedded pitch-class palindrome which
can also be described as a retrograde inversion (RI^D = RI^{Ab}).

The two ways of hearing MELISANDE are at odds with one another.
While the preservation of pitch and rhythmic contour calls attention to the
transpositional relation between the two initial forms of MELISANDE, the
emphases on common-tone D-natural, through agogic accent in the original
and as first pitch in T_6, and on A-flat, first pitch in the original and agogically
accented in T_6, draw our attention to the play on mirror imagery that spans
the pair. If we listen carefully, we become confused by the cross patterns of
reference. The more attentive we become, the less clear (the less fixed) are
the relationships among the prismatic constituents of MELISANDE.

After the liquidation of MELISANDE, completed at Reh. 1.7, Schoenberg composes two measures comprising residues of MELISANDE LOST
before returning to MELISANDE for a more elaborate exploration of its
self-reflective properties set within whole-tone space. Example 3.3d shows
the sequence of MELISANDE motives beginning at Reh. 2 and continuing
through Reh. 3.3. (The tail-end of this passage overlaps with the first appearance of GOLAUD, whose significance we will attend to shortly.) The passage begins with a three-voice *stretto* presenting MELISANDE in its original

Example 3.3d. Rehearsal 2–3.4: MELISANDE in whole tone canon.

Example 3.3e. MELISANDE at original level and transposed up four semitones.

F-sharp 'a quo'   C 'ad quem'   C 'ad quem'   F-sharp 'a quo'

Inversion mapping C to C

Inversion mapping F-sharp to F-sharp

MELISANDE at origin   MELISANDE up 4 semitones

form (and at the lower octave), with each successive entry displaced by two quarter-notes. The arrival of the half note D at the third measure after Reh. 2 coincides with a D^7 harmony. This is followed by the same configuration transposed up a major third (T_4). Halfway through the completion of the second voice at T_4, statements of MELISANDE begin to move through the whole-tone scale (beginning with the transposition starting on D (T_6), on the second beat of Reh. 2.5). This pattern, maintaining the distance of two beats between entries throughout, continues twice through the whole-tone circuit. There is an overall drift into higher and higher tessituras, until the passage is abruptly terminated by a startling C major chord that grows out of Golaud's motive in the French horns.

The close imitation among the voices, with a new motivic entry every two beats, is as disorienting as it is exquisite. While the harmonic arrival at Reh. 2.3 asserts a fairly strong metric downbeat, the ensuing whole-tone canon erodes any sense of metric pulse until the canonical statements of MELISANDE are terminated by the C major chord in the horns.[54] As before, but this time made even more unfathomable by the closeness of the *stretti* and the complexity of the relations among the whole-tone transformations, even the most attentive listener can hold onto only a glimmering of MELISANDE's enigma. Examples 3.3e and 3.3f explore some of those properties.

Example 3.3e shows the basic properties of T_4 relations, those obtaining at the outset of the passage. As shown in the example, the augmented arpeggio, defined by the two $<-8>$ leaps within the motive, is held invariant between T_4 related pairs. (Once the whole-tone canon is established, Schoenberg alters the final note of MELISANDE so that each presentation terminates with a $<-9>$ descent. The shared augmented chord thereafter excludes the final note, but is nonetheless maintained by its initial three members.) The

Example 3.3f. MELISANDE at T4 and T6: The beginning of the whole-tone canon.

C 'ad quem'   F-sharp 'a quo'   B-sharp 'a quo'   F-sharp 'ad quem'

MELISANDE up 4 semitones   MELISANDE down 6 semitones

chromatic trichords (<+1+1> and <−1−1>) share a tritone-related dyad whose members function as *terminus a quo* and *terminus ad quem* across the pairs. For example, in the pair of T_4-related rows shown in the example, we descend chromatically to F♯ in the first member of the pair and ascend chromatically to F♯ in the second member of the pair; as a result the first and last chromatic trichords of the pair form a mirror about F♯ ($I^{F♯}$). This is complemented by a chromatic ascent from C-natural in the first member of the pair, and a chromatic descent from C-natural in the second member of the pair; the center of this mirror image is the same F♯ as before, now mapping C onto C. In addition to the embedded augmented chord and the inversional relations among the chromatic trichords, T_4-related pairs also share other salient properties of pitch-class invariance. In the example, the <−8> dyad F♯-B♭ on the left becomes enharmonically respelled as F♯-A♯ on the right. The span B♭-C-D♭−D on the left (<+2+1+1>), becomes B♭-D (<-8>) on the right. The dyad D-F♯ (<−8>) on the left becomes the span D-e-f-F♯ (<+2+1+1>) on the right.

Once the whole-tone canon begins, T_2 relations hold between every successive voice for the remainder of the passage; the first of these is shown in Example 3.3f. As with T_4-related pairs, we find associations among the *termini* of the chromatic trichords, only now the salient pitches are maintained respectively within the <−1−1> and <+1+1> trichords, switching positions from first to last and last to first. For example, C-natural initiates the chromatic descent on the left, and, respelled as B♯, terminates the chromatic descent on the right. The complementary F♯ terminates the chromatic ascent on the left, and initiates the chromatic ascent on the right. The resultant mirrors are retrograde inversions, reflecting about C and F♯. In addition, the span C-b-b♭-D (<−1−1−8>) on the left is reversed in the span D-C♯-B♯ (<−1−1>) on the right. As the canon progresses, each of these relations is audible in itself (provided we orient our attention toward the so-related elements), but there is too much musical information to allow us to hold them all together. The conflict among meanings gives rise to the instability of changing perceptions that is built into the enigmatic qualities of MELISANDE.

Although subsequent presentations of MELISANDE are too multiple and varied to allow in-depth treatment in our present context, two extraordinary developments should be noted at least in summary form before leaving our discussion of the motive. The first of these, beginning at Reh. 25, develops and intensifies the idea of overlapping presentations of MELISANDE to create a sense of temporal suspension, a technique first explored in the whole-tone canon of Reh. 2–3. The second passage, beginning at Reh. 43, forms a culmination of a sort, where MELISANDE achieves what can be considered its first and only thematic statement.

The musical passage at Reh. 25 depicts the scene at the castle tower where Pelléas wraps himself in Mélisande's flowing hair. The musical depiction, only fifteen measures long, is one of the most exquisite passages in the entire work. We limit our observations here to some basic thoughts on the role of MELISANDE. Example 3.3g shows the first two measures.

The larger passage (from Reh. 25 through 27.4), as might be expected, is composed principally of contrapuntal combinations of MELISANDE, PELLEAS, and EROS. Presumably inspired by the image of Mélisande's flowing hair, Schoenberg immediately establishes a dense contrapuntal web of MELISANDE motives. As the passage continues (at Reh. 26), EROS is added to the ongoing texture whose underlying harmonies are faintly present, *pp* and *ppp*. Superimposed above this texture, a fathomless depth in lieu of a ground, we hear the slow drift of PELLEAS, and MELISANDE as cello and violin solos (doubled at the octave); the whole is a spectacular achievement in leitmotivic polyphony. As with the whole-tone canon after Reh. 2, the densely overlapping iterations of MELISANDE obscure our sense of metric pulse. Instead of whole-tone space as in the exposition of MELISANDE, there is a vaguely perceived diatonicism, as chromaticisms embellish the motion from E minor to $B^{dom\,7}$, but like all else, the harmonies seem to drift.

The sense of temporal suspension here is even more impressive than in the exposition. Now MELISANDE is set in evenly spaced notes in eighth-note triplets, overlapping every two-thirds of the beat. At the opening of the passage, the incessant entries of the <D-C♯> incipit form a kind of slow-trill steady state that hovers within the overlapping presentations of MELISANDE. Even more so than in the exposition, the closeness and equality of overlapping pulses obliterates our sense of meter, and hence our sense of hierarchical groupings of time, an effect that intensifies as the passage continues through Reh. 26. The elaborate clockwork of MELISANDE motives ironically suggests a dilated now-time, the magic space of Eros. The context of this scene as the middle term of three (the scene at the fathomless pool where Mélisande loses her wedding-ring, the erotic scene at the tower, and the menacing scene deep in the castle vaults) is significant in this regard.

Example 3.3g. First two measures of Rehearsal 25.

As I shall argue more fully later, the scenic and musical sequence is unified by an underlying imagistic sequence: *spatial* (watery depth) – *temporal* (depth of time) – and *spatial* (earthly depth).

Schoenberg's musical depiction of erotic now-time finds its poetic correlate in Anne Carson's descriptions of Eros, and in particular in her discussion of the Greek word *deute*, a word that is commonplace in ancient Greek descriptions of Eros.

> *Deute* combines the particle *de* with the adverb *aute*. The particle *de* signifies vividly and dramatically that something is taking place at the moment . . . The adverb *aute* means 'again, once again, over again' . . . *De* places you in time and emphasizes that placement: *now*. *Aute* intercepts 'now' and binds it into a history of '*thens*'.
> (Carson, 1986, 118–19)

In a remarkably similar way, the prismatic, self-reflective statements of MELISANDE beginning at Reh. 25 seem to suggest a history of "thens" contained in an extraordinary "now." In the larger context of Schoenberg's *Pelleas und Melisande*, this dilation and saturation of now-time is situated in the crosscurrents of anticipation, recollection, and now-time that constitute the temporal dimensions of the work. In its rhythmic steady state and sense of uncanny time, the music is a precursor to the technique of time shards that we will study in Chapter Five.

The second extraordinary development of MELISANDE that needs mention in our present discussion occurs at Reh. 43 within the love scene. It is here that MELISANDE, to my ear, achieves thematic status for the first and only time in the work, albeit for only seven measures. I have argued that the initial exposition of MELISANDE – the presentation of tritone related forms, their quick unraveling, and then the polyphonic exploration of whole-tone space – does not have the structure (or feel) of a "theme." The "themes" in the work – GOLAUD, PELLEAS, and LOVE – have tonal orientations, and comprise well-formed sentence structures. To this degree, they are like the musical events that we recognize as themes in Beethoven or Brahms. In contrast, the MELISANDE motive, working principally in contrapuntal combinations with transformations of itself and other motives, does not give rise to this kind of tonal orientation and thematic coherence. I believe this is why Berg considers everything up until the entrance of Golaud's theme as introductory despite its obvious importance. Even in the extraordinary scene by the tower, where MELISANDE arguably plays the leading motivic role, it is MELISANDE's ability to create a contrapuntal texture rather than to spin out a thematic sentence that conditions the structure of the scene.

The presentations of MELISANDE at Reh. 43, are thematic in the sense that they comprise the functional *Hauptstimme* in a well-formed phrase

Example 3.3h. Rehearsal 42–43.9, texture simplified.

(or at least at the outset of that phrase). This ability to shape a developed thematic phrase brings a culminating sense of self-fulfillment to the motive and that which it represents. With hindsight, all of the presentations of MELISANDE prior to this moment seem to have led up to this point, and all of the many presentations of MELISANDE after this passage have a retrospective quality. At Reh. 42, the music just prior to the passage of MELISANDE's fulfillment, we hear the second of four climactic cadences (or near cadences) within the love scene. Example 3.3h begins with this music (texture greatly simplified).

At Reh. 42 we arrive on a B pedal tone over which MELISANDE, in octaves, embellishes the dominant harmony. The tonic E major is avoided at Reh. 43 (tonic closure is strongly suggested and avoided throughout the love scene),

Example 3.3h. (*cont.*)

and the harmony moves deceptively to a C minor chord in first inversion. C minor in turn embellishes an E♭-dominant which touches on A♭ minor at Reh. 43.8. Once the MELISANDE part of the phrase has moved from E♭ to A♭, the FATE progression (here A♭ to B), modified to accommodate the modal shift from minor to major, returns us to an evanescent B-dominant as MELISANDE dovetails with PELLEAS in the bass, and as EROS emerges in the clarinet. As the phrase continues, we move to a C-dominant (just before Reh. 44), which resolves deceptively to D minor in first inversion, to begin the third statement of the LOVE theme. That statement gradually builds to the highest climax of LOVE as we reach a B-half-diminished chord beginning at Reh. 46. In the larger context, the development of MELISANDE at Reh. 43 functions as a lull between the more ecstatic culminations of LOVE that surround it. In this context MELISANDE takes on a particular sweetness.[55] We move through three statements in treble mid-range (woodwinds and viola), each a step higher than the last, and then elaborate and extend the final statement in *stretto* with a modified statement of MELISANDE in the bass (beginning at 43.5). The functional *Nebenstimmen* are composed of fragments from LOVE and the PELLEAS motive, both beautifully supporting MELISANDE as functional *Hauptstimme*, but easily missed as the sweep of MELISANDE statements carries us through to the arrivals of A♭ at 43.7 and 43.8.

The Golaud theme and the Wedding Bond

Like the first appearances of FATE and MELISANDE, the first appearance of GOLAUD, beginning with the upbeat to Reh. 3, shown in Example 3.3d, is a stark intrusion upon the ongoing musical fabric. Unlike FATE and MELISANDE which interrupt and terminate (or temporarily terminate) the ongoing music, the initial presentation of GOLAUD is juxtaposed against the continuing whole-tone canon of MELISANDE motives. It is as though at first Mélisande is oblivious to Golaud's presence. The MELISANDE canon terminates with the arrival of the startling C major triad at Reh. 3.4. It is only after this that the motives seem to interact.

The initial presentation of GOLAUD is strikingly at odds with MELISANDE's ongoing textures, colors, and intervallic content. Indeed, the initial juxtaposition of MELISANDE and GOLAUD approaches the limit of incommensurability described by Harold Bloom "in which absolutely incommensurate realities collide and cannot be resolved."[56] The first emergence of GOLAUD can be described as a three-stage compositional and dramatic process spanning from Reh. 3 to Reh. 4.3. It is an imperfect process of wresting control over the MELISANDE derived materials and of attempting to "fit" GOLAUD with MELISANDE, a fit most fully achieved during the second large phrase of the GOLAUD theme, after Reh. 6.

As GOLAUD is about to be heard for the first time, the principal lines in the ongoing MELISANDE canon are all in the woodwinds, and these are supported by muted lower strings as a series of whole-tone transpositions of augmented chords from Reh. 2.6 to Reh. 3.2. In contrast, GOLAUD first appears as a unison in the first, second, and third horns, *weich, aber bestimmt, hervortreten* ("delicately, but resolutely, to the fore"), which opens at 3.4 into a startling C major triad. The GOLAUD fragment embeds a partial circle of fifths, F♯-B-E-A-D (Reh. 3.1 to 3.3 in Example 3.3d), before veering off into C major, the proleptic and misplaced dominant of the F major GOLAUD theme that will begin at Reh. 5. It is as though the vague tendency of MELISANDE to resolve into D, the ultimate tonic for the entire work, is given tonal direction and then precipitately negated or resisted. GOLAUD's initial harmonies are directed, even if they take surprising turns of direction, while MELISANDE's harmonies drift. The rhythmic juxtaposition is as striking as those of timbre and harmony. GOLAUD has a strong but shifting metric sense. It is notated so that at first it lies against the grain of the written meter (a beat "early"), yet as an aural "fact," any perceived sense of meter has been dissolved by the MELISANDE canon. The perceived meter of GOLAUD shifts at Reh. 3.3 to coincide with the written meter, and this shift is achieved even more emphatically at Reh. 3.4 with the surprising C major triad.

The second stage of GOLAUD's emergence begins at Reh. 3.7 after two measures of connective music generated out of fragments of MELISANDE derived ideas. This connective music is understood as reacting to what has just taken place, the disruption of Mélisande's solitude brought about by an awareness of Golaud's presence, an awareness signified by the C major chord at Reh. 3.4 and the concomitant termination of the whole-tone canon. The following passage, shown in Example 3.4a, has two primary constituents: a series of three partially overlapping statements of MELISANDE, beginning respectively on A, B♭, and B; this is juxtaposed against a reiteration of the first six notes of GOLAUD. At this stage, the <−8> leaps in the MELISANDE motive project the written meter, the downward leap always coinciding with the metric downbeat; unlike before, the meter is not obscured by the canon because there is no close *stretto*. At cross-purposes with MELISANDE, GOLAUD projects a consistent 2/4 meter, "left-shifted" by one beat. The change from whole-tone to chromatic space is noteworthy and may be understood to indicate some impact of GOLAUD on MELISANDE, but the new chromatic canon, in and of itself, maintains the sense of harmonic drift that has been associated with Mélisande all along. The GOLAUD fragment includes the F♯-B-E-A span of the fifths cycle, and remarkably

Example 3.4a. Rehearsal 3.7–4.3, texture simplified.

Example 3.4a. (*cont.*)

(astoundingly!) the coincidence of the chromatic MELISANDE canon with the GOLAUD fragment produces combined harmonies that support the motion by fifths. Understood in isolation, the chromatic canon maintains the consistency of MELISANDE's tonal ambiguity. However, in combination with GOLAUD the MELISANDE material has willy-nilly been brought into the tonal sphere of GOLAUD's thought.

The third stage of emerging GOLAUD begins with the upbeat to Reh. 4 just after the English horn completes the chromatic canon by spinning out the third and final statement of MELISANDE. GOLAUD is transposed down a fourth and motivically has begun to take on the characteristics of its thematic statement to come; the sequential repetition of the opening dotted eighth, sixteenth, dotted quarter rhythm, an ascending third and descending fifth, absent in previous GOLAUD fragments, will be conspicuous in the GOLAUD theme. The presence of MELISANDE is effaced in that there is no intact statement of the MELISANDE motive. The horns, associated with Golaud, expand into three voices, the principal voice doubled. The harmonic motions at the outset and termination of the phrase are particularly noteworthy. The motion from F to A, and then A to C (applied dominant of F), bridge the contradictory harmonic tendencies between MELISANDE and GOLAUD. This same conflict and bridging will be played out more fully across the first two statements of the GOLAUD theme.

The initial part of *Pelleas und Melisande* is brought to a close by two measures of transitional material derived from MELISANDE, functioning much like a quick-dissolve in cinema. These measures lead directly into the depiction of the wedding with the GOLAUD theme beginning at Reh. 5. Example 3.4b shows the principal voice for the theme and also provides a reduction of the underlying harmonies.

The GOLAUD theme is composed of two principal phrases (beginning at Reh. 5 and 6 respectively), their extension and dissolution (to 7.9) at the end of which the second phrase merges into the first catastrophic intrusion of FATE (through 8.5). The theme concludes in the measures immediately after the explosive force of FATE is spent (through 8.10). The final measure of GOLAUD dovetails with the music that prepares the PELLEAS theme that will follow.

Both principal phrases of GOLAUD are structured as musical sentences – a subphrase, its modified reiteration, and then a spinning-out to a cadence. The first phrase, at least the outset, is clearly grounded in F major, and the metric and hypermetric framework is also clearly projected. This contrasts with the rhythmic and harmonic ambiguity of the Mélisande centered material that has preceded. The phrase is subdivided somewhat lopsidedly into 4+4+3 measures. The WEDDING BOND motive (beginning with the E at 5.2), embedded in the theme, grows out of the ascending third,

Example 3.4b. Rehearsal 5–7.4: Golaud theme, with simplified harmony and figured bass.

descending fifth motive reiterated at the beginning of the phrase. In its anticipation of the metric downbeat, the WEDDING BOND motive adds a touch
of composed-out rubato to the phrase rhythms, but not enough, however, to
challenge the clear metric design. The fourth measure of the theme is a con-
textually salient ascending major triad, extended chromatically to the major
sixth, <+4+3+1+1>. This idea is reiterated in the eighth measure, and then
forms the principal constituents of the three-measure spinning-out at the
end of the phrase. Major triads in either linear or vertical dispositions have
been relatively rare thus far, and the disposition of this ascending arpeggio is
the retrograde of the triadic descent embedded in FATE. Hard on the heels
of the motive that Schoenberg (or Schoenberg through Berg) identified with
the wedding vow, this retrograde of FATE seems to express an "unconscious"
or repressed awareness of the role of FATE to come. The "FATE-repressed"
motive is conspicuously absent in the second phrase, and the catastrophic
intrusion of FATE that dovetails with the end of that phrase has the force of
a Freudian "return of the repressed."

If the role of FATE is repressed through its veiled presence in the first
phrase, MELISANDE is noticeably absent. This too is in great contrast to
the second phrase where transformations of MELISANDE form luxuriant
Nebenstimmen throughout. Also in great contrast to the second phrase, the
dense orchestration of the first phrase is primarily in the lower registers;
the phrase avoids the higher treble until its final measures, and this along
with the considerable amount of close motion in the inner voices (not shown
in the example) gives the phrase a constrained quality which is greatly
relieved as the orchestration opens up and "breathes" in the second phrase.

The tonal direction of the harmonies becomes less clear as chromatic
motion in the bass intensifies toward the end of the first phrase and the
final harmony, a misspelled F-dominant in four-two position, voice-leads
into A major to begin the second phrase of the GOLAUD theme. As we have
already noted, this motion recollects and intensifies the progression that had
led into Reh. 4. With the omission of the "FATE- repressed" motive, the 4+4
grouping at the outset of the phrase is reduced to 3+3. In lieu of "FATE-
repressed," transformations of the WEDDING BOND motive comprise
the spinning-out part of the phrase, now expanded to six measures leading to the cadence on A at Reh. 7.4. While the four-measure groupings of
the first phrase would seem to be more normative, the 3+3 of the second
phrase has more grace and an easier sense of flow. At least in retrospect, the
"FATE-repressed" part of the original phrase now sounds like an extension
within the first two subphrases, having expanded the more graceful 3+3
into a troubled 4+4.

The music leading up to the arrival of A at 7.4 is the most ecstatic that
we have heard so far. Although we are still early in the piece, this will be *the*

climactic moment for the GOLAUD theme; all subsequent returns to GOLAUD will have the force of recollection and, more important, the sense of loss. The too early climax of GOLAUD is in striking contrast to the slow progress toward fulfillment of MELISANDE. The unraveling of the theme once A is achieved is precipitous. In only four measures, the harmony falls back to an E-dominant, essentially undoing the tonic arrival. Then after two more measures, we proceed to the D bass and build-up to the catastrophic intrusion of FATE. The iterations of WEDDING BOND continue to be transformed throughout the process from the ecstatic climax of the second phrase to the already retrospective dissolution of that phrase and then, in horrific visage, juxtaposed against the iterations of FATE. After the fury of FATE is spent, we hear one final iteration of the WEDDING BOND motive, *piano, espressivo*, before transformations of MELISANDE carry us into the PELLEAS theme. The contrapuntal conflict between FATE and the WEDDING BOND will be played out in each of the remaining catastrophic intrusions.

As we have said, all further references to the GOLAUD theme and the WEDDING BOND motive in some way recall and react to their originating moments, their glorious presentation beginning at Reh. 6 in particular. We close our discussion of GOLAUD by briefly considering the dramatic content and formal function of those musical recollections. The first of these occurs at Reh. 14. Berg described this moment as a *Reprise* of the principal theme. Of course, there is some truth to this, but the description is misleading nonetheless. We can best understand the dramatic and formal function of the return of GOLAUD by considering its placement in the music that surrounds it. The music just prior, the passage beginning at Reh. 12.4, is the first development of EROS, which forms a kind of coda-space to the PELLEAS theme (this much is in agreement with Berg's analysis). However, in distinction to the typical retrospective function of coda-space, a retrospective function that the GOLAUD reprise at Reh. 14 will express, the space of developing EROS signifies desire whose fulfillment is projected into the future. The music at Reh. 15, immediately following the return of GOLAUD, resumes the coda-space of the PELLEAS area by returning to the contrapuntal play of PELLEAS, MELISANDE, and EROS (Berg, rather awkwardly, subsumes this music into the space of his "Reprise.")

It is in this context that we hear the return of the GOLAUD theme, sandwiched in between the two sections of developing EROS. The theme is a foreshortened version heard in contrapuntal combination with statements of MELISANDE. The affect is passionate, but the ecstatic play of orchestration and counterpoint heard previously is gone. The theme, in F major like the first phrase of the original, is now only one phrase long. The opening of the thematic statement is modified to begin with a transposition of first GOLAUD motive with its embedded circle of fifths. This particular motivic contour had been suppressed or abandoned in the principal thematic statement, and in this sense the return of GOLAUD reaches further back than the GOLAUD theme and the associated event of the wedding. The phrase builds to its climax in its sixth and seventh measures, spinning out sequential variants of the WEDDING BOND motive. The remainder of the phrase is its gradual liquation, as the WEDDING BOND motive is gradually dissolved up until the downbeat of Reh. 15. It here that the coda-space devoted to EROS, PELLEAS, and MELISANDE continues.

What are we to make of the return of GOLAUD, recollected and further developed in the dramatic context of the growing love between Pelléas and Mélisande, embedded within the formal context of the PELLEAS thematic area? I would suggest that the only way to make sense of this recollection of GOLAUD (and specifically of the WEDDING BOND) is to hear it as from Mélisande's perspective. The usage, someone remembered by another through the invocation of the former's music, is one commonplace in Wagner; however, the earlier master can rely on characters and staging to make his meaning clear. For Schoenberg, it is a bold move, easily misconstrued, but vivid and potent in its dramatic force once the listener realizes the orientation. Mélisande's episode of turning inward and remembering Golaud and the vow between them in the context of her growing attraction toward Pelléas makes dramatic and psychological sense. Through dramatic and psychological meaning, the "return of GOLAUD" in the midst of "awakening love" makes formal sense as well. As we shall later see, this procedure is inverted at the end of *Pelleas* where Golaud, in the larger context of remembering his love for Mélisande, recalls the mutual love of Mélisande and Pelléas.

The next development of GOLAUD-derived material takes place in the context of the first emergence of the JEALOUSY motive (after Reh. 22). We will defer discussion of this passage until we turn to a treatment of JEALOUSY. After this, GOLAUD returns just before the death of Pelléas. Golaud's lurking presence is announced by a momentary intrusion of the GOLAUD motive at Reh. 47.8. At Reh. 48, fragments of GOLAUD menacingly contribute to the musical intensification before the third catastrophic intrusion of FATE.

Another significant development of GOLAUD and the WEDDING BOND is in the music beginning at Reh. 55, the passage leading into Golaud's recollection of the hair-pulling incident, a bitter retrospective episode placed just before the death of Mélisande. Here GOLAUD and WEDDING BOND are combined with transformations of JEALOUSY THAT have taken on the rhythmic characteristics of LOST INNOCENCE.

After the death of Mélisande, all of the remaining music functions as a coda to the entire work. Eighty measures in length, the coda is shaped by three principal sections or episodes. The first and last of these are developmental recollections of the GOLAUD theme with particular emphasis on transformations of the WEDDING BOND motive. The middle episode itself flows seamlessly through three smaller passages: a remarkably free-flowing contrapuntal web of MELISANDE and PELLEAS motives; a climactic build-up that integrates MELISANDE and PELLEAS with EROS; and a recollection of the LOVE theme. During the first part of the middle episode (Reh. 64–65), the motives seem suspended in time, and the textures of the music are reminiscent of the passages that had depicted the initial attraction between Pelléas and Mélisande. We recall that this music, in the context of the coda to PELLEAS, had preceded and followed Mélisande's recollection of GOLAUD (Reh. 14). The final coda-space inverts the contents and perspectives. Now GOLAUD precedes and follows, and the middle MELISANDE and PELLEAS space is understood from Golaud's perspective; he, and we the spectators present only through dramatic irony, are the only ones left. We have named the development of Mélisande's character at the opening of MELISANDE LOST. Golaud's final recollections might just as aptly be named GOLAUD LOST. Placing the reminiscences of Pelléas and Mélisande "inside" the memories of the wedding of Golaud and Mélisande, Golaud mourns their passing as part of his own loss. There are compelling reasons, dramatically and formally, for the repetitions of the GOLAUD theme. Schoenberg was right, not just stubborn, to resist Zemlinsky's suggestions for cuts. As the work comes to its close, a fragment of the GOLAUD motive, now in the bass, is the very last thing that we hear. Wavering between D and F, perhaps signifying the key that is and the key that might have been, the minor third is generated out of the GOLAUD head-motive, a D-F♯ ascent at its origin, fallen to D-F-natural at its close.

Conflicted Pelleas

Example 3.5 shows the first phrase of the PELLEAS theme area (texture simplified), and the two bars that precede it. In our discussion of the FATE motive we considered some basic aspects of the PELLEAS theme. Pelléas's conflicted character is depicted by bifurcating the phrase into two opposed halves separated by the FATE motive (and the first appearance of the FATE harmonies). The first part of the phrase has its principal voice in the E trumpet, a particularly brilliant color that captures, in Schoenberg's words, Pelléas's "youthful and knightly" character. The jaunty rhythms of the principal motive are complemented by the equally exuberant counter-melody in the first horn, as well as by fleet figuration in the clarinets (not shown in the example). The sudden burst of rhythmic activity, the abrupt and striking change of color, and the sense of plunging into a harmonic progression

Example 3.5. Two measures before Rehearsal 9 to Rehearsal 10: PELLEAS theme, texture simplified.

already under way, all contribute to a sense that PELLEAS emerges *in medias res*. The interruption by FATE, whose linear motive lies hidden in an inner voice, is covered by transformations of MELISANDE that grow directly out of the two measures that precede Reh. 9 (transforming <E♭-F-G> into <E♭-F-G♭>). The dramatic meaning, Pelléas gazing upon Mélisande for the first time, is fairly transparent. The second part of the phrase shows Pelléas's passionate and lyrical side; in great contrast to the solo trumpet melody that preceded, its sweeping, expressive principal line is set in the octave doublings using the combined color of flutes, oboes, English horn, French horn, violins, violas and celli. We will later discover that the genetic traces of this part of PELLEAS form a central constituent of LOVE. The color and affect between the two halves of the phrase could hardly be more contrasting.

The PELLEAS theme is set in a never-quite-fulfilled E major; the arrival of E with a suspended seventh at Reh. 10 is as close as we come to a tonic cadence, and even apart from the suspended seventh, the arrival on E, after one erratic phrase, comes "too soon" in the larger thematic area to suggest closure. Later in *Pelleas*, E will be the tonic of the LOVE theme. As that theme finally unravels, a penultimate E appears conspicuously in the bass, depicting the death of Pelléas (at 49.4); the arrival of E is tellingly prepared by F, not B. Before the LOVE theme terminates, the E, having never achieved a full triad, gives way to a D♯ half-diminished chord, as the theme is dissolved without tonal closure. Whereas the GOLAUD theme began on a solid tonic (F major) and then drifted, the bass line in the first phrase of PELLEAS targets E, approaching it chromatically, first descending from the subdominant (A) and then ascending from the dominant (B). One brother starts with a tonal anchor, a *terminus a quo*, which cannot be maintained, the other strives toward a goal, a *terminus ad quem*, that cannot be achieved, except through death.[57]

The sense of entering the theme *in medias res* is complemented by the precipitate move to its development section after one short, bifurcated phrase. The conflict between PELLEAS(α), the motive "to the left" of FATE, and PELLEAS(β), comprising the second part of the phrase, after the intervention of FATE, remains central. We begin the development at Reh. 10 with the material and affect of PELLEAS(α), Pelléas's cavalier nature. The initial brilliance of the trumpet is softened somewhat by placing the theme in the horns, but the counter-theme and figuration "to the left" of FATE seem, for the moment, to have negated the music "to the right." This mode and matter abruptly terminate with the arrival of Reh. 11, where we return to the music and affect of PELLEAS(β). Its sweeping line and rich doublings are now in the clarinets, horns, and lower strings. At Reh. 11.4, PELLEAS(α) returns, taking on a new affect as it enters into its first duet with MELISANDE. The rhythmic aspects of the music embody the kind of free-float that we have associated with MELISANDE, and the passage, at least in retrospect, starts to take on the qualities that later become associated with the emergence of EROS. Before that happens, however, the duet is abruptly terminated at Reh. 12 where the cavalier side of Pelléas, once again developing PELLEAS(α), returns for a brief three measures only to be supplanted by the emergence of EROS. That along with Mélisande's recollection of the GOLAUD theme will dominate the remainder of the PELLEAS theme area.

In discussing the role of the GOLAUD reprise, we have already considered some aspects of this coda-like extension of PELLEAS: the emergence of EROS which combines with motivic fragments of PELLEAS and MELISANDE and the reprise of the GOLAUD theme, heard in this context from Mélisande's perspective. Here I would add two significant points: first, that the juxtaposition of EROS, which is prospective and anticipatory, with memories of GOLAUD, which is recollective and retrospective, forms another kind conflict that by its placement becomes associated with PELLEAS; and second, that the predominance of EROS, GOLAUD, and MELISANDE within the coda to PELLEAS effectively undermines the role of PELLEAS as the principal source of formal and expressive coherence for this part of the work.

The emergence of EROS in particular, and the subsequent effacing of PELLEAS-derived material during the coda to PELLEAS, sets up a pattern that has long-range as well as immediate consequences. In contrast to the almost obsessive recollections of the GOLAUD theme, first by Mélisande and then by Golaud himself, PELLEAS never returns as a thematic area. Although PELLEAS(α) will play a continuing role in the piece, that role will occur only in the context of various contrapuntal combinations with other motives, principally MELISANDE and EROS. PELLEAS(β) will play a major role, but only insofar as its genetic traces are integrated into LOVE. From a dramatic perspective, it is the essentially retrospective character of Golaud that demands that his theme be recollected; it is the essentially unstable, forward-looking character of Pelléas that disallows the recollection of his theme as theme.

Returning to Berg's formal analysis (Figure 3.2), we may note that one of the interesting features (or inconsistencies, depending on your point of view) of his formal overview is that the recapitulation of the Adagio (what we are calling the LOVE theme) stands in lieu of a recapitulation of the Subordinate theme (PELLEAS). In that LOVE embeds transformations of PELLEAS(β), and like the PELLEAS theme aspires toward an E tonic (never satisfactorily fulfilled), the substitution of LOVE for PELLEAS is formally attractive. As we shall see, Schoenberg imbues the LOVE theme with multiple characteristics derived from P E L L E A S. A number of interesting arguments for the musical associations can be made in terms of the drama. The initial emergence of P E L L E A S, like G O L A U D in this respect, asserts the individuality of the male protagonist by vividly distinguishing his musical materials from their immediate environment. Soon thereafter, the inescapable intertwining of Pelléas's (and Golaud's) destiny with that of Mélisande is depicted through contrapuntal combinations of P E L L E A S/M E L I S A N D E and G O L A U D/M E L I S A N D E. The bond that cements the relation of Golaud with Mélisande is portrayed in the G O L A U D theme; in a similar way the L O V E theme culminates the bond between Pelléas and Mélisande, hence the dramatic plausibility of substituting L O V E for P E L L E A S and for relating the recapitulatory spaces of L O V E and G O L A U D. Given the mutual cathexis of Golaud/Mélisande and Pelléas/Mélisande within their respective thematic areas, the contrasting play of perspectives is remarkable in the ways that it complements the erosion of P E L L E A S-derived material (or through L O V E, its displacement into a theme mutually defining Pelléas and Mélisande). The G O L A U D theme is primarily processed as coming from Golaud's perspective. Even the recollection of G O L A U D by Mélisande can be understood as Mélisande remembering Golaud remembering the vows between them, which is to say Mélisande imagining Golaud's perspective. In contrast, the perspective of L O V E is a mutual gazing of Mélisande on Pelléas and Pelléas on Mélisande.[58] It is as though apart from his relation to Mélisande, Pelléas no longer has a perspective of his own. In the one place within the larger L O V E theme where the individuality of one or the other predominates (Reh. 43), it is M E L I S A N D E that provides the functional *Haupstimme* supported by iterations of P E L L E A S (α), which function as a subordinate voice. I have characterized this passage as M E L I S A N D E fulfilled (N.B. not as P E L L E A S fulfilled), the brief moment at which M E L I S A N D E is able to achieve true thematic substance. The P E L L E A S theme is like a promissory note that cannot be fulfilled.[59] The degree to which Schoenberg has drained Pelléas of separate existence, prior to his death, is remarkable, and the musical means that deny Pelléas's separate existence are bound up with those that make Mélisande's death inevitable after the passing of Pelléas.

Eros

> Eros once again limb-loosener whirls me
> sweetbitter, impossible to fight off, creature stealing up
> > > fragment from Sappho, translated by Anne Carson[60]

The fragment from Sappho that serves as the epigraph for our discussion of Schoenberg's portrayal of E R O S is remarkably apposite in all of its particulars. Eros personified as "impossible to fight off, creature stealing up" captures a sense of being gradually overwhelmed by something unexpected and impossible to anticipate, resisted but irresistible. The epithet "limb-loosener," captures the emotional sense of being "knocked silly," and the physical sense of sexual release. And "sweetbitter," Carson's order-preserving translation of *glukupikron*, normatively "bittersweet," captures a sense of erotic sweetness inevitably followed, sooner or later, by a bitter sense of loss. All of these senses have direct analogues in Schoenberg's musical portrayal.

Example 3.6a shows the passage in which we hear the first appearance of Eros. The larger context of this passage is the extended coda to Pelleas, whose formal and dramatic functions we have already begun to discuss. At this point (Reh. 12.4), we have just heard the series of mutually contradictory passages that develop out of the original bifurcation within Pelleas. The *Langsamer* tempo indication has been preceded by a similar *Langsamer* (at 11.7) that had introduced the contrapuntal combination of Melisande and Pelleas(α), and that had functioned as a precursor to the emergence of the Eros motive before us. The first *Langsamer* has been interrupted by a return of Pelleas(α) at Reh. 12 (marked *Wieder lebhafter* – lively once again), and now that is broken off as the tempo and mood of the first *Langsamer* return (notated as *sehr zart* – very tenderly – at 11.7, an affect that returns in our present context).

The passage opens with a transposition of the Fate progression (A six-five to C^7) that we had first heard within Pelleas. The subordinate ascending line, <E-F♯-G, G-A-B♭>, is derived from Melisande Lost, and the principal opening motive is Melisande. Eros emerges out of the sustained D♯ in the clarinet beginning at 12.8 ("creature stealing up") to gradually dominate the texture over the next three measures ("impossible to fight off"). The clarinet soars to its upper register and is then doubled at the octave by a solo violin before trailing off. The rhythmic contour is fluid ("limb-loosener"), gently tugging against the also subtle counter-rhythms suggested by the contrapuntal entries of Pelleas below. The motive outlines a half-diminished arpeggio, Mélisande's signature harmony, but also a sonority found in the progressions attendant to Pelleas, both before and after the intervention of Fate. Fate returns at Reh. 12.12 in counterpoint with Melisande: Fate is now heard in both of its guises, linear and chordal, at the same transpositional level as in the original Pelleas theme. As the passage continues (beyond the Musical Example) we hear a second unfolding of Eros in counterpoint with Pelleas(α), and then the juxtaposition of Melisande and Pelleas(α). This is followed by the reprise of Golaud that we have already discussed and then by further developments of Melisande, Pelleas(α), and Eros, all of which

Example 3.6a. Rehearsal 12.4–12.13: the emergence of EROS.

Example 3.6b. Flute melody at Rehearsal 16 and emergent EROS.

segues into the depiction of the fathomless pool, the first of three episodes in the second large section of *Pelleas und Melisande*.

EROS plays a significant role in all three of the "second movement" episodes. Transformed versions of the motive suffuse the "scherzo-like" scene by the pool. Example 3.6b shows the first of these transformations within the flute melody that begins the episode.

The playful figuration hides the underlying EROS that emerges at the tail end of the flute's line. EROS-derived material continues as the *giocoso* mood intensifies (through Reh. 19) and then transforms into darkening grotesquerie by its climax at Reh. 22, the music depicting the loss of the wedding-ring and Golaud's simultaneous fall. Soon after this, in combination with the first development of JEALOUSY (to be discussed below), the perception of augmenting EROS between Pelléas and Mélisande is experienced from Golaud's perspective.

EROS, heard once again in combination with MELISANDE and PELLEAS, returns at Reh. 26 within the glorious second episode, the scene by the tower. As before, the scene breaks off as we return to Golaud's perspective (at 27.5), where further developments of JEALOUSY embed wrathful presentations of EROS and MELISANDE (marked *fff* and *schreiend* – screaming – at Reh. 29). Another wrathful manifestation of EROS occurs toward the end of the episode at the castle vaults (at Reh. 31) shortly before the second catastrophic intrusion of FATE. Through all of this, EROS has been gathering force through the depth of its recollected occurrences, rapturous from the perspectives of Mélisande and Pelléas, loathsome from the perspective of Golaud.

The next context for the continuing development of EROS is the music from Reh. 33 through Reh. 35, the span that Berg characterized as an introduction to the third part of the symphony.[61] This music sets the stage for the grand Adagio that will follow, where ever-augmenting EROS is a significant constituent. It should come as no surprise that EROS reaches its climactic transformations in the context of the LOVE theme. We will defer discussion of those developments until we analyze that theme.

With the termination of LOVE, the cathexis of Eros quickly ebbs, and the motive we are calling DEATH DRIVE takes its place for Mélisande. From Mélisande's perspective, we hear EROS only once more. This is during Mélisande's death scene (Reh. 59 through the end of Reh. 61). At Reh. 61, a solo violin plays a single statement of EROS (beginning with the upbeat to Reh. 61) while the cortège-like ostinato in the harps continues beneath. The ostinato pauses for a moment as the motive concludes, and then the ostinato resumes in counterpoint with DEATH DRIVE, closing off the scene and signifying Mélisande's death. The final statement of EROS from Mélisande's perspective expresses her final memory of love lost, just before her passing; the transformation of the sweet into the bitter is complete. The final statements of EROS are all from Golaud's perspective, entwined with his memories of the LOVE theme (at Reh. 65), sandwiched between memories of the GOLAUD theme, his recollections of love lost.

EROS and its transformation into a constituent of LOVE cannot achieve cadential closure. As such it participates in the musical imagery of "imperfection," one of the chief tropes in our larger inquiry. To close our discussion of Eros, I return to Anne Carson's splendid commentaries on Sappho. Carson cites a fragment on the subject of desire attributed to the poet.[62]

> As a sweet apple turns red on a high branch,
> high on the highest branch and the applepickers forgot –
> well, no they didn't forget – were not able to reach . . .

Carson then goes on to discuss the imagery (I have added the clarifications placed in square brackets):

> The poem is incomplete perfectly [imperfectly!!] . . . It is one simile, whose point remains elusive since the *comparandum* never appears . . . As an object of comparison suspended in line 1 [the apple as metaphor for the bride] it exerts a powerful attraction, both grammatical and erotic, on all that follows; but completion is not achieved – grammatical or erotic.
>
> (Carson, 1986, 26–7)

Carson's larger point is that Eros, by its very nature, cannot achieve "completion." The insight holds as true for Schoenberg's setting as it does for the originating poet of the erotic.

Jealousy

The JEALOUSY motive is introduced and developed almost exclusively in what Berg calls the second large part of the symphony – the scenes by

Example 3.7a.   Rehearsal 22–24: Golaud's fall, emergence of JEALOUSY.

Example 3.7a. (*cont.*)

the fathomless pool, the castle tower, and the castle vaults. We recall that Schoenberg interpolates Golaud-space in between the first two scenes that develop Pelléas/Mélisande-space. JEALOUSY first appears in this context. JEALOUSY reaches its third and ultimate climax at the end of the scene in the vaults just after the second catastrophic intrusion of FATE (respectively, Reh. 32 and Reh. 32.5). The only other emergence of JEALOUSY occurs prior to and during the passage where Golaud recalls the hair-pulling episode (beginning just before Reh. 55); in this singular development JEALOUSY is infused with the rhythmic surface of LOST INNOCENCE so that the original emotion and its reversal through *peripeteia* are fused.

Example 3.7a places the first appearance of JEALOUSY into a somewhat larger context. The downbeat of Reh. 22 marks the tragic climax of the scene where Mélisande loses her wedding-ring, which is simultaneous with Golaud's fall from his horse. The moment is a remarkable "seam" in the work, essentially a cross-cut from the mutual perspectives of Mélisande and Pelléas to that of Golaud as we move from the scene by the fathomless pool to Golaud's fall, and then to an internal landscape of Golaud's brooding and rising suspicions. It is a moment of maximal dissonance, a massive stacking of *fff* thirds over a Bb bass. The elusive local tonic is A, and the harmonic tension between A and Bb developed earlier in the scene (Reh. 17 and following) reaches its climax here. The conflict between the "flat side" and the "sharp side" has been a harmonic signifier of the conflicted relationship between Golaud and Mélisande from the beginning, and it returns to that sense here. The "fall" music, scored for trombones and tuba, is generated out of a transformation of GOLAUD. It begins with Golaud's characteristic dotted rhythm, lowering the major third ascent of the original to a minor third. The implied Bb minor at the head of the falling motive notably comes to rest (or exhaustion) on A, liquidating any sense of meter on the way. At this point (22.4) we hear a radical change in color, texture and register as an ascending series of thirds and sixths in the woodwinds, with prevalent diminished harmonies, is vaguely associated with Mélisande's motives. The ascent, which further diffuses any sense of metric orientation, is crowned by the first of two statements of MELISANDE that unfold over the next four measures. The extraordinary counterpoint weaves a fragment of GOLAUD (once again asserting Bb minor), and then the WEDDING BOND motive (asserting Eb minor) into the texture. The metric disorientation continues as the overlapping motives assert contradictory downbeats. At the end of the second MELISANDE unfolding, the first part of the passage comes to rest over an extended E dominant function. The first entrance of JEALOUSY appears after the fermata to begin a musical sentence that extends from Reh. 23 until the measure before Reh. 25 (eleven measures beyond the end of Example 3.7a).

As already recognized by Berg, the JEALOUSY motive is genetically related to both MELISANDE and FATE; indeed, it can reasonably be argued that it is a fusion of the two. If the octave displacement is removed and the first note omitted, JEALOUSY takes on a $<-1-1-7+1+1>$ contour, very closely related to the original shape of MELISANDE. The primary genetic relation of JEALOUSY to FATE is its ascending major seventh followed by two descending notes, $<+11-3-4>$ in FATE and $<+11-1-7>$ in JEALOUSY. As the passage continues, Schoenberg explores the connections to both motives through contrapuntal juxtapositions.

The order of leitmotivic presentations is a significant constituent of the sentence structure, and we can begin to approach the formal design by noting those relations. The first part of the sentence, 23.1–23.4, comprises overlapping statements of $<$JEALOUSY-EROS-PELLEAS-MELISANDE-FATE$>$; this sequence is repeated up a perfect fourth (modified once FATE returns in three part *stretto*) to comprise the second part of the sentence, Reh. 23.5–23.9. The final part of the sentence (not shown in Example 3.7a) brings the passage to a climax and then gradually liquidates the entire episode as we approach Reh. 25, the beginning of the next episode, the scene by the tower. As in the first two subphrases, the final, climactic part of the sentence begins with JEALOUSY, now heard in contrapuntal combination with WEDDING BOND. This combination is a variant of the FATE/WEDDING BOND counterpoint heard during each of the three catastrophic intrusions of FATE; it is fraught with psychic tension as one impulse binds the marriage together while the second tears it apart. The climax of the phrase is extended as the JEALOUSY incipit strains toward a statement a perfect fifth higher than before (with the E-F dyads of 24.2) and then falls to a dissonant statement of GOLAUD (beginning D♯-F♯ over an E bass) to form a secondary peak in register and the dynamic peak of the sentence (all voices *ff*); we then segue, *subito piano*, to the liquidation of the sentence beginning with <MELISANDE-PELLEAS-MELISANDE>. The process continues as the texture is pared down to a series of block chords that transition into the return of Mélisande-Pelléas space as we begin the next episode, the scene at the tower.[63]

Volatile shifts of orchestral color and dynamics and harmonic and rhythmic instability all work in concert to express the emotional conflict that drives the music. In all of this it is as though the "centripetal" force of the sentence structure counterbalances the "centrifugal" of its antithetical constituents. At the beginning of the sentence, Schoenberg orchestrates the first emergence of JEALOUSY in the string basses, *piano*, but doubled at the octave, calling our attention to the line by stripping away all other voices. The overlapping sequence of <EROS-PELLEAS-MELISANDE-FATE> that follows shifts color for each of its constituents. The entire sequence is played *forte* (EROS, in the violas, is marked *ff*) and *Heftig* (violently). JEALOUSY has conditioned their perception so that love has been changed into hate. The second iteration of JEALOUSY, still in the basses (and now in counterpoint with another iteration of FATE), returns the dynamic level to *piano*. Once again the remaining sequence of motives is marked *forte* and *Heftig*, with shifting colors much as before. The third part of the sentence begins with JEALOUSY transposed four octaves above the original, now fully emerged, *ff* doubled in the flutes, clarinets, and *forte* in the violins (who continue their crescendo into the following GOLAUD), and, as already noted, now heard in counterpoint to the WEDDING BOND motive, also *ff*, doubled in the bass clarinet, third bassoon, lower horns and lower strings. In its small-scale trajectory, from quiet brooding to violent paroxysm, the progression of JEALOUSY motives within the sentence forms a microcosm of the larger trajectory of JEALOUSY within the work.

The second development of JEALOUSY terminates the scene at the tower; we recall that the analogous place in Maeterlinck's play is when Golaud comes

Example 3.7b. Rehearsal 28–28.4: *Hauptstimme*, GOLAUD/JEALOUSY.

upon Pelléas and Mélisande, Pelléas wrapped in her hair, and scolds both for their childish behavior. In the music, the return of Golaud-space at Reh. 27.5 is marked by GOLAUD breaking off the previous motion toward a cadence on E, the always-denied "perfection" associated with the love between Pelléas and Mélisande. GOLAUD gives way to JEALOUSY as the music, functioning as an extended *Auftakt*, builds to the downbeat of Reh. 28. As before, the crescendo of jealousy is contained (barely) in a musical sentence. The opening of the sentence is marked by a head-motive that fuses the GOLAUD incipit with a continuation derived from JEALOUSY (shown in Example 3.7b) in counterpoint with the WEDDING BOND motive and transformations of MELISANDE.

The orchestration is much more massive than in the previous Golaud-space as the motives already named, along with EROS and plummeting chromatic motions combine to form a tumultuous passage that borders on chaos. The sentence culminates with a *ff* climax of JEALOUSY, doubled in octaves in the lower strings, lower brass, and bassoons, and this is followed immediately by a transformation of PELLEAS, then FATE (both linear and chordal), leading into the scene at the vaults.

As we have already noted, the third and ultimate climax of JEALOUSY (Reh. 32.3) appears at the end of the vault scene, appended to the second catastrophic intrusion of FATE. The statement, *fff* in the strings, terminates with the FATE progression, which in turn leads directly into the development of EROS that sets the stage for the Adagio (*Langsam*) that follows.

Love

Example 3.8 shows the first phrase of the LOVE theme. The example includes the principal voice along with a simplification of the supporting voices and harmonic setting. The phrase comprises a misshapen sentence structure. Its subphrase constituents divide the seventeen-measure whole into: *a* $(4)+(1)+b$, $b^2(3+3)+b^3$-*cadence*$(4+2)$. Instead of repeating or varying the first four-measure subphrase, as would be normative in sentence structure, Schoenberg moves directly into the spinning out or "continuation" section of the sentence, but not before inserting an ambiguous single measure poised

Example 3.8. Rehearsal 36–37: first phrase of LOVE.

between the *a* and *b* sections. After this hesitation, the sentence spins out through a three-measure idea (*b*), its intensified reiteration (*b* up a step $= b^2$), and its further development and intensification (b^3) leading into the half cadence just before Reh. 37.

Within our discussion of the PELLEAS theme we noted that LOVE in some ways, both formal and dramatic, becomes a substitute for PELLEAS.[64] The odd fifth measure of the phrase bifurcates the sentence into two uneven halves (*a* and b^{1-2-3}); in this respect its rhetorical function is much like the intervention of FATE within the PELLEAS theme. Here the moment of hesitation is marked by rhythmic uncertainty – the E-natural in the melody at 36.5 seems inexplicably long – and by harmonic interruption, as the C minor of 36.4 moves precipitately to E dominant (prolonged into 36.6). The embellishment of E in the melody, through its lower chromatic neighbor, is reminiscent of the similar neighboring motion over the FATE progression in PELLEAS (<Ab-A-G♯-A>, first violins, Reh. 9.4–9.6). As in PELLEAS, although less markedly, the affects "to the left" and "to the right" of the divider are different. The *a* section of the phrase, with its slow-moving bass, consonant melodic leaps, and relative stability of rhythmic patterning, has a settling affect (all the more noticeable after the turbulence of the introduction that precedes it), while the *b* section, derived from PELLEAS(β), is more restless and energized. Because the *b* sections are more restless than *a*, the omitted repetition gives the phrase a sense of lurching forward, or leaping ahead of itself in anticipation. Subsequent developments of the theme, more normative in this respect, will make the omission conspicuous. The original PELLEAS(β) contour <+1+10−1−1+4+2−8−1+1> is modified into <+1+9−1−1+4−2−9+3>, somewhat softening the <+1+10> incipit of the original, before presenting it in a heightened form the third time around (<+1+13> in 38.12). The climax of the phrase at the beginning of b^3, a B7 – Mélisande's signature harmony – is the first of a series of increasingly intensified climaxes that form a trajectory through the entire scene.

To be fully understood, the phrase beginning at Reh. 36 needs to be placed into its larger context, emerging from the music beginning at Reh. 33, and continuing its formal and dramatic unfolding until the music at Reh. 49 signifies the death of Pelléas. One of the remarkable properties of this entire span is the development of the conflict between tonal space and whole-tone and/or chromatic space, the former associated with Pelléas (and elsewhere with Golaud), the latter with Mélisande.[65]

Before we step back and view the larger section as a whole, we should focus on some of the ways that this conflict is worked out at Reh. 36. The overall tonal arc of the phrase results from reining in its expansive chromaticisms through diatonic scalar motion and, more important, through fifth motion across the phrase. The most fundamental progression in the bass is E-A-B-B-F♯-B (at Reh. 36, 36.6, 36.9, 36.12, 36.15, and 36.16); each of these notes (with the exception of F♯, which leads into the cadence) supports the beginning of a structural unit in the phrase: *a b b² b³ cadence*. In addition to the structural fifths in the bass, the opening four measures of the melody are rich in perfect fourths and perfect fifths as well. In contrast, the opening bass motion moves through an augmented chord (E-G♯-C), a sonority associated with Mélisande from the very opening of the piece. Here it is a salient detail, but over the larger span of the LOVE scene, motion through augmented arpeggios takes on extraordinary significance.

Figure 3.5 provides a sketch of the formal and expressive elements of the entire LOVE scene, the third of Berg's four large parts comprising the whole of *Pelleas und Melisande*. The figure is divided into seven horizontal strata: 1) rehearsal numbers and tempi; 2) formal units, describing phrase structures, their constituents, and their place within the whole; 3) measure groupings; 4) motivic constituents; 5) dramatic and rhetorical function, describing dramatic imagery as well as the expression of intensifications and dissipations of emotional (and sexual) energy over the course of the whole; 6) dynamics and mass, describing the most basic fluctuations in orchestrational mass and dynamic levels; and 7) bass progression, showing the principal harmonic motions, motivic unfoldings, and transformational relations projected through the bass. Bass notes in bold print are either members of structural augmented arpeggios or cadential; structural fifth motions are shown through curved arrows.

The large-scale structure of the LOVE scene is composed of four main parts: an introductory sentence spanning from Reh. 33 through Reh. 35; the initial principal sentence, comprising Reh. 36; an expanded second principal sentence spanning from Reh. 37 through Reh. 42; and an even more greatly expanded third principal sentence preceded by contrasting material (called "secondary sentence" in Figure 3.5) and extended and liquidated by the music that portrays the intervention of Golaud and the death of Pelléas. Remarkably salient throughout the scene are its intensifications and dissipations of dynamic energy. The build-up and discharge of psychic and sexual energy are expressed through changes in mass, dynamics, rhythm, and harmony. Indeed, the scene as a whole can be understood in terms of its huge waves of motion/emotion, virtual flood tides and ebb tides of psychic/sexual cathexis. The sustained climactic plateaus at Reh. 40, 42, and 46, are all associated with prolongations of B, the dominant of E, which finally arrives at 49.4, after the death of Pelléas.

The introduction to the LOVE theme comprises a single elaborate musical sentence. Middle-ground structuring through whole-tone and augmented progressions begins immediately. The initial bass progression, from Reh. 33

Rehearsal Number	33 *Ein wenig bewegt*	34 *steigernd*	35 *rit.*	36 *Langsam* *rit.* *rit.*
Formal Unit	Introductory Sentence, Large-scale *Auftakt* to **36**		cadential ext.	First Principal Sentence
	a a′ a″ b			a b b^2 b^3
Measure Groupings	(4 + 4 + 2)	(2 + 2)(2+2)(1+1)	(2 + 2 + 3)	(4) (1) (3 + 3) (4 + 2)
Motivic Constituents	FATE, EROS, WEDDING BOND, PELLEAS(b), MELISANDE	PELLEAS(a), MELISANDE, WEDDING BOND <-5+2>, <-2+5>	MELISANDE, PELLEAS(α)	LOVE theme
Dramatic/ Rhetorical Function	Conflicted counterpoint and unsettled tonal space express emotional conflict and set the scene for the LOVE theme. Build to a climax at 35, which quickly dissipates, simplifying the counterpoint, "zooming in" to PELLEAS and MELISANDE.			Relaxation of harmonic tension as B-dominant resolves to E. Love theme builds to an emotional high point through the sequence of b^1 – b^2 – b^3, climaxing at the B-half-diminished 7th, and then relaxing through the fifth motion F# - B. This climax is the first of a series that intensifies to a highest point at 46.
Dynamics and Mass	Highly contrapuntal *tutti* with predominantly soft dynamic range. *p-mp* *p-sf* *p-sf* *mf* *cresc.* *f* *dim.* *p*			Begin predominantly in the strings; gradually build to *tutti* at climax of phrase (full orch. minus brass). *p* *cresc.* *f* *ff* *dim.* *p*
Bass Progression	D E F# A# B C D♭ F# G# E C# B A F B $^{\varnothing}7$ $^{\circ}7$ $^{\circ}6/5$. $^{\circ}7$. $^{\circ}7$ $^{\varnothing}7$ I$^{D\text{-}C\#}$ I$^{D\text{-}C\#}$ v^7			E G# C♭ G#A A#B B EF# B $^{\circ}7$ (v^7) V

Figure 3.5. Overview of the Love Scene: Rehearsal 33–49.

Rehearsal Number	37 *Im Zeitmass*	38 *Ein wenig bewegter*	39 *steigernd*	40 *Breit*	41 *Nach u nach beschleunigend Breit*	42 *Breit*
Formal Unit	upbeat to 38	Second Principal Sentence	a a′ b¹ b²	cadential ext.	pull-back and build-up between cadence/climax at 40 and cadence/climax at 42	second cadential extension
Measure Groupings	(4 + 5)	(4 +	4) (2+2) (3)	(2) (5)	(5 + 2)	(6)
Motivic Constituents	LOVE (a, b)	LOVE (a)	LOVE(a+b)	LOVE(b) LOVE(a)		(MELISANDE LOST) MELISANDE PELLEAS($\alpha+\beta$)
Dramatic/Rhetorical Function	quieting of affect then intensify toward 38	Expansive presentation of LOVE theme. Awkwardness of first principal sentence is remedied by 4+4 expansion of a-a′. The first cadential extension at 40 brings the thematic area to its highest climax up until this point. The lessening of intensity at 41 and then build-up to 42 brings the phrase to a higher climax yet.				
Dynamics and Mass	gradual cresc. and increase in mass	Begin with horns, lower strings and woodwinds, gradually adding upper voices as the music approaches 40		*Tutti*, broad overlapping statements of motive.	*Subito p-pp*, then *ostinati* build up to 42	*Tutti*, with doubling of all motives at the octave, harp runs, etc.
	mp - f	*mf - ff*	*f - ff*	*ff*	*p cresc - ff*	*ff - dim. p*
Bass Progression	**E G#** D♭ A**B C**	**E♭** BC#**D** E♭FG♭ **E♭**FG♭ (chromatic)	F E E♭DD♭C**B**	C#D**G** F#E#E**D#** G# C# **B**		

Bass progression figures: ø7   ø7   °7   V7

Figure 3.5. (*cont.*)

	43	44	45	46
Rehearsal Number	*Ein wenig bewegter*	*Etwas bewegter*	*steigernd*	
Formal Unit	Secondary Sentence (B section of LOVE theme) a – a´ b extend/transform	Third principal sentence (44-44.8 is T₄ of 38-38.8) a a´ b cadential ext./climax		
Measure Groupings	(2+2) (2 + 2) (4) (2.5 + 1.5)	(4 + 4) (4 + 7) (2+2)+(2+2+3) overlapping *stretti* override metric groupings		
Motivic Constituents	MELISANDE LOVE(b), PELLEAS(α),	PELLEAS(α), EROS, FATE LOVE(a) LOVE(a) EROS, LOVE(b) GOLAUD fragment		
Dramatic/Rhetorical Function	Fulfillment of MELISANDE, sweeten affect and lessen energy after climax of 42	Modified FATE prog. moves Ab to B, bringing PELLEAS and EROS to the fore Building intensification of erotic energy toward the highest climax of the LOVE scene beginning at 46	Sustained climax of EROS/LOVE(b)	First indication of Golaud's presence; ominous foreshadowing
Dynamics and Mass	blended colors of woodwinds, strings, and horns p- mf –f subito pp-p	full, blended orchestration p-mf	mf-f f	ff
Bass Progression	Eb E FGAb Eb Ab A B EDC	F E G F# Gb6-5 A-A# BB#C#DGG#AA#D#EF DFB ω₇ T₁		

Figure 3.5. (*cont.*)

Rehearsal Number	46.9	47 *steigernd*	*sehr breit*	48 *Viel rascher*	49 *Nach und nach langsamer*
Formal Unit	continue cad. ext. and climax of 3rd principal sentence	liquidation of LOVE(b), builds to final climax	continue cadential extension: final climax/dissolution	phrase unravels as motifs cresc. to third and fatal intrusion of FATE	phrase dissolves as bass moves from F to E to D, ending without closure
Measure Groupings	overlapping *stretti*	(3)	(1.5) (3.5 + 1)	(1) (2+2) (2)	(3) (4) (3)
Motivic Constituents	EROS, LOVE(b)		EROS / MELISANDE GOLAUD PELLEAS(α) / LOVE(b)	GOLAUD, MELISANDE, WEDDING BOND / FATE, WEDDING BOND	falling motif / PELLEAS FATE / MELISANDE
Dramatic/Rhetorical Function	continue sustained and highest climax of EROS, LOVE(b)	pull-back and then intensify toward final climax	final climax of Eros, pull-back to PELLEAS(α) and MELISANDE in conflict with GOLAUD, final climax of LOVE(b)	build-up to third catastrophic intrusion of FATE	death of Pelléas
Dynamics and Mass	*ff*	continue *tutti*, blended orchestration — *mf cresc.*	*ff fp cresc. fff*	*ff-fff fff*	precipitate thinning of orchestral texture — *ff-f-mf-mp-p f p*
Bass Progression	C C# D D# G G# °7 ... I^{C-F}	AA# B E FF# G G# C D# E# F F E E♭ D A D♭ D		= C# F	E E E♭ D °7

Figure 3.5. (*cont.*)

Measure	33.1	33.2	33.3	33.4	33.5	33.6	33.7	33.8 38.9
Bass	**D** C$^\#$ C B D C$^\#$ C B				**E** E$^\flat$ D D$^\flat$ E E$^\flat$ D D$^\flat$ F$^\#$ F			

T_2 T_2

| Chords | B$^{\flat\,6/5}$ C$^{\#\,7}$ C^0 B^7 B$^{\flat\,6/5}$ C$^{\#\,7}$ C^0 B^7 | | | | C$^{6/5}$ E$^{\flat7}$ D^0 D$^{\flat7}$ C$^{6/5}$ E$^{\flat7}$ D^0 D$^{\flat7}$ D$^{6/5}$F^7 | | | |

FATE   FATE   FATE   FATE   FATE   FATE   FATE   FATE   FATE
(sub.)   (sub.)   (sub.)   (sub.)

Figure 3.6. Bass motion and Fate motive: Rehearsal 33.1–33.8.

to Reh. 34, composes out an augmented arpeggiation filled in with a whole-tone between its first two members, D-E-F$^\#$-A$^\#$. The next series of bass tones fills out a chromatic space, A$^\#$-B and C-D$^\flat$, emphasizing the first of each pair and thereby extending the bass projection of the "D" whole-tone scale. The whole-tones continue with F$^\#$-(G$^\#$)-E, forming a complementary pair to A$^\#$-C, symmetrically disposed about D. The arrival of C$^\#$ just before Reh. 35 breaks the "D" whole-tone sequence, and sets up the motion to B that will end the phrase. Instead of leading directly into the B half cadence, however, C$^\#$-B is strikingly subsumed into a falling motion that immediately ensues in the bass. The resulting progression, C$^\#$-B-A-F (marked by horizontal brackets in the figure), forms a mirror image of the initial motion D-E-F$^\#$-A$^\#$, reflecting about the initial tones of each sequence, I$^{C\#-D}$. Remarkably, the motion from B to E that initiates the LOVE theme at Reh. 36 can be subsumed into the same center of inversional balance: I$^{C\#-D}$ = I^{B-E}. The technique is reminiscent of the subsumption of the MELISANDE-generated, chromatic canon to GOLAUD-generated fifth motion prior to Reh. 4.

As can be seen by interrelating the bass progression with the formal description in the second stratum of the figure, the motion through whole-tone space embedded in an augmented arpeggio supports the initiation of phrase constituents: D initiates the *a* subphrase, E initiates *a'*, F$^\#$ initiates *a''*, and A$^\#$, concluding the augmented arpeggio, initiates the spinning out of the sentence (*b*). Some details of harmony and voice leading within the sentence are shown in Figures 3.6 and 3.7.

The progressions at the surface of the music are explicitly derived from the FATE progression, as first heard in the PELLEAS theme. Figure 3.6 schematizes the chord motions at the outset of the phrase. As can be seen in the figure, the bass line descends chromatically D-B (twice) and then E-D$^\flat$ (twice),

Measure	34.1	34.2	34.3	34.4
Bass	A♯ - B ⌞___⌟	A♯ - B ⌞___⌟	C - D♭ ⌞___⌟	C - D♭ ⌞___⌟
Chords	ᵒ⁄₇ – [0248]	ᵒ⁄₇ – [0248]	ᵒ⁄₇ – [0248]	ᵒ⁄₇ – [0248]

Figure 3.7. Rehearsal 34.1–34.4: Schematic of bass and harmonic progression.

with each chromatic dyad supporting alternately the FATE progression or a close substitute where a diminished chord serves in lieu of the initiating six-five chord. As the music continues, the pattern is truncated to a two-note figure F♯-F (repeated), still supporting the FATE progression.

The *b* section of the phrase, which begins with the arrival of A♯ in the bass, coincides with an abrupt shift in figuration, voice leading, and harmonic motion. Figure 3.7 schematizes the bass line and harmonies for its first four measures. The chromatic bass motion now ascends, with each dyad supporting a half-diminished seventh and then a whole-tone structure derived from the linear progression that had initiated the phrase. (The transformation of the linear progression into chord-type, similar in this respect to the third measure of the LOVE theme, anticipates Schoenberg's post-tonal procedures.)

A proper understanding of the motivic constituents of the phrase requires close score study, and here we can only address the most general aspects of Schoenberg's counterpoint and its concomitant dramatic affects. As Figure 3.5 indicates, the music at Reh. 33 comprises a dense contrapuntal web; FATE controls the harmonic progressions, and the linear constituents include juxtapositions of EROS, WEDDING BOND, PELLEAS(β), and MELISANDE. The passage embodies an extraordinary aspect of Schoenberg's expressive use of complex counterpoint: his ability to simultaneously portray conflicting emotions. The motives crowd each other out, rising to the surface and submerging as other constituents overwhelm them in turn. The distinctive rhythms and pitches comprising the individual motives interact in varied combinations of conflict (the ironic juxtapositions and contradictory imperatives of WEDDING BOND and ever-augmenting EROS) and complementation (paired couplings of MELISANDE and PELLEAS(α)). At 34.5, Schoenberg introduces a new motive denoted in Figure 3.5 by its basic intervallic shape <−5+2> and by the retrograde of that shape <−2+5>, both of which are used in the passage. Berg identifies this motive, salient and unique to this place, with the spring in the park, the fathomless pool where Mélisande lost her wedding-ring. Its development (beginning at 34.6 in the horns) is heard in juxtaposition with transformations of MELISANDE and a series of sweeping arpeggios in the high woodwinds. As before, the pitch and rhythmic conflict among the constituents expresses a heightened, conflicted emotional state. At the end of the phrase, after the striking C♯-B-A-F motion in the bass and coincident with the arrival of the B-dominant, Schoenberg pares down the motivic content to PELLEAS(α) and MELISANDE. There is a tremendous sense of sweetening and settling of affect and an almost cinematic "zooming in" on the two. This short "love duet" beautifully prepares the *Langsam* that follows.

Rather than provide detailed commentary for the remainder of Figure 3.5, we will limit remarks to a few salient points. The dialectic between augmented arpeggios, often incorporating whole-tone scales, and motion by fifths remains important through the whole LOVE theme. The series of ever-heightening climaxes (five measures before Reh. 37, at Reh. 40, at Reh. 42, and at Reh. 46) is an extraordinary aspect of the theme: the fading memory of the climax to GOLAUD pales in comparison. Yet, what might have been a final erotic climax is supplanted by the catastrophic intrusion of FATE before Reh. 49. As we have earlier noted, when the long delayed tonic E does finally arrive after Reh. 49, signaling the death of Pelléas, it is not preceded by its dominant. E instead is a falling away from F, the note that terminates the final augmented arpeggio in the bass after Reh. 48. We recall that F was the tonic that had initiated the GOLAUD theme.

Reversal of fortune: Death Drive and Lost Innocence

The music immediately following the death of Pelléas and the dissolution of the LOVE theme begins what Berg called the recapitulatory finale. Its opening passage is shown in Example 3.9a. We have already made several important interpretive claims regarding this music: it is to be heard from Mélisande's perspective; following Maeterlinck, Schoenberg portrays Mélisande as comatose at this stage of the drama, so the music represents a dream-like consciousness; and the new motives emerging here represent reversals of fortune, dramatic *peripeteia*, converting EROS into DEATH DRIVE, and innocence (and later, JEALOUSY) into LOST INNOCENCE. Although initiated by Mélisande, LOST INNOCENCE reaches its climax of despair in a passage associated with Golaud where the transformation of JEALOUSY into LOST INNOCENCE becomes thematic.

As the passage begins, MELISANDE LOST has returned, down a half-step from its origin. Although it has been the genetic source for many of the work's motivic constituents, this is the first time that MELISANDE LOST has appeared intact since the beginning of the piece. The orchestration, more lucid than before, begins solely in the woodwinds (except for three *pizzicato* chords in the lower strings), providing a striking contrast to the murky

Example 3.9a. Rehearsal 50: return of MELISANDE LOST, emergence of
DEATH DRIVE and LOST INNOCENCE.

Example 3.9b. Diatonic framework of LOST INNOCENCE.

combination of strings and lower woodwinds heard at the beginning. At the second beat of Reh. 50.2, MELISANDE LOST merges with (or is transformed into) MELISANDE, and at the end of the next measure we hear the first of the two new motives, DEATH DRIVE. DEATH DRIVE, broken into four short segments, continues to spin out over the next four measures in counterpoint with PELLEAS(α) at 50.4, with MELISANDE and JEALOUSY at 50.5, and overlapping with the beginning of the WEDDING BOND motive at 50.6. At 50.8 we hear the second new motive, LOST INNOCENCE. Conspicuous by their absence are the interpolated FATE motives from the original. Perhaps of most importance, the rhythmic sense of phrase has been greatly altered. Whereas at the beginning of the piece we are able to hear an underlying sentence structure, now the overwhelmingly contrapuntal fabric suspends any normative sense of phrase.

Although distinctive in terms of rhythm and contour from their precursors, the new motives do show some genetic relations to previous material. The rhythmic shape of DEATH DRIVE's opening segment is a variant of the opening segment of MELISANDE LOST. More tellingly, its intervallic content <+2+1+4+4> is very close to that which opens EROS, <+2+1+3+4>. Its embedded augmented arpeggio is familiar from MELISANDE and FATE and has been a pervasive aspect of the LOVE scene. LOST INNOCENCE, in its rhythmic shape, tonal directness, and homophonic presentation, is strikingly different from anything before, yet it too has genetic relations to previous material. The contour of its opening – descending conjunct motion, a leap downward, and then an ascent – shares qualities with MELISANDE, a correspondence noted by Berg. Berg also comments that the sixteenth-note triplet figure (on the third beat of its first measure) alludes to the music of the "quasi-scherzo" (at Reh. 16), the scene in which Mélisande eventually loses her wedding-ring. As Puffett has recognized, that music itself is derived from MELISANDE.[66]

In contrast to MELISANDE, LOST INNOCENCE has a diatonic framework, a middleground structure of a descending E major scale embellished by a series of lower neighbors as sketched in Example 3.9b. This diatonic frame, as well as its homophonic setting and its salient dotted rhythms, distinguish LOST INNOCENCE from its surroundings. Heard in contrast to the prevailing tendencies of harmonic and metric drift, LOST INNOCENCE has a quality that seems to reach back beyond the confines of the work. As I have previously suggested, LOST INNOCENCE may be understood to refer to the lost Eden of diatonic tonality. Yet, even here there is a tension between whole-tone and diatonic space as a descending whole-tone scale is projected by agogic accent (shown in Example 3.9b). Another level of tension is supplied by the highly chromatic harmonies that underlie the melody; these are at odds with its descending diatonic scale.

The original presentations of both DEATH DRIVE and LOST INNOCENCE sound like fragments. We easily hear the first three segments of DEATH DRIVE as progressive expansions of one another; their size accrues across the sequence from five notes, to six, then eight, and their contour develops from an ascending figure that terminates in an augmented arpeggio through the addition of a descending semitone (another variant on the $^\flat$6–5 motive) into an expanded contour of rise and fall. The fourth segment, however, is a departure; it returns to the five notes of the first while foreshortening and inverting the last part of the contour of the third from $<+ +- ->$ to $<- - + +>$. The affiliation of the first three segments and the departure of the fourth, which forms a kind of new beginning, calls for two more segments to complete the process. To apply one of the central tropes of this study, the compositional embodiment of the DEATH DRIVE implies an ongoing state of imperfection.

Although it is too late in the piece for a new, full-blown theme to emerge, LOST INNOCENCE has all the hallmarks of a thematic fragment; ironically, it sounds like a fragment of a theme that is not actually heard within the confines of the piece. The salient dotted rhythm that is iterated twice at the opening of LOST INNOCENCE is an interesting detail of construction. Despite all of the rhythmic diversity that has preceded, this dotted rhythm has not been heard before. Because of this, we will recognize later developments of the rhythm as being derived from this motive. The music that follows will take advantage of this property in surprising ways.

The music that portrays Mélisande's dream space spans from Reh. 50 until three measures before Reh. 55, 41 measures in total. (Recall that this includes the passage that Schoenberg praised in his letter to Zemlinsky.) The larger passage divides into two distinct parts, roughly equivalent in length. The first of these, comprising the music from Reh. 50 up until the downbeat of Reh. 53, develops its musical techniques out of the passage we have just considered. At Reh. 51, we hear further development of MELISANDE LOST in contrapuntal combinations with DEATH DRIVE. The contrapuntal texture thickens as we approach Reh. 52, and the leitmotivic vocabulary starts to augment. Within a few measures we hear JEALOUSY, MELISANDE, and PELLEAS(α) added to the ongoing developments of LOST INNOCENCE and DEATH DRIVE. The sense of tonal drift and metric disorientation is

Example 3.9c. Celli and basses, 3 mm. before Rehearsal 55: Fusion of GOLAUD, JEALOUSY, LOST INNOCENCE.

maintained and even intensified, as is the suspension of sentence structures. Subsumed into this texture, the ongoing statements of LOST INNOCENCE lose their sense of tonal anchoring. As the passage approaches its liquidation, we hear overlapping statements of LOST INNOCENCE and then a final sequence based on the tail of the motive (beginning with the triplet figure) accompanied by a descending scale in parallel thirds. The scale, a small detail of the contrapuntal working out in its immediate context, gives rise to a chromatic variant that forms an ostinato at Reh. 53, and later to a cortège-like ostinato that is heard throughout Mélisande's death scene.

The music that spans Reh. 53 up until three measures before 55 is a premonition of the death scene. The entire passage develops and greatly intensifies the DEATH DRIVE motive. One of its striking features is a C♯ pedal tone in the bass whose reiterated eighth-note pulses gradually crescendo from pp to f as the contrapuntal texture of DEATH DRIVE-derived material swells toward its dissonant climax. At Reh. 54, the pedal tone is abandoned for the moment as a sequence of JEALOUSY-derived motives trace an augmented arpeggio in the bass (D-F♯-A♯). C♯ returns (at 54.4) at the episode's ff climax and then gives way to an F-natural bass (Golaud's key) as the FATE motive recalls the death of Pelléas. The C♯ returns, ppp, accompanied by fragments of the DEATH DRIVE motive, to conclude the dream become nightmare.

Example 3.9c shows the music that immediately follows. The change in orchestration and the introduction of the GOLAUD head-motive signal that we have shifted perspectives. The short statement in the celli and string basses is a remarkable synthesis of motives; it emerges from what has just been developed in Mélisande-space, and anticipates what is shortly to come. After the opening two notes signal Golaud's presence, the next three notes derive from the JEALOUSY head-motive ($<+1+11>$); JEALOUSY segues immediately to figuration derived from LOST INNOCENCE, and then LOST INNOCENCE leads into the head-motive from PELLEAS.[67]

Berg identified Reh. 55 as the recapitulation of the principal theme (GOLAUD), and Reh. 56–58 as the recapitulation of the Adagio (LOVE). Within the space of the latter, Berg identifies Golaud's remorseful recollection of the hair-pulling episode, the scene that precedes the death of Pelléas in Maeterlinck's play. In Schoenberg's presentation, the scene is not

Rehearsal No.	55			
Bar Groupings	(2)	(3)	(2)	(3)
Motivic Content	GOLAUD head-motive fusion of JEALOUSY/ LOST INNOCENCE	WEDDING BOND	GOLAUD head-motive fusion of JEALOUSY/ LOST INNOCENCE	WEDDING BOND
Dynamic Level	*mf*	*f*	*mf*	*f*

56				57
(2)	(1)	(3)	(2)	(1)
fusion of LOVE/ LOST INNOCENCE	WEDDING BOND	GOLAUD head-motive LOVE/LOST INNOCENCE JEALOUSY/LOST INNOCENCE	WEDDING BOND LOST INNOCENCE	WEDDING BOND JEALOUSY/ LOST INNOCENCE
f	*cresc-dim.* *f*		*ff*	*ff*

57.2		58				
(1)	(6)	(1.5)	(1.5)	(2)	(1)	(4)
JEALOUSY/LOST INNOC. LOST INNOCENCE	LOST INNOCENCE (fragments) JEALOUSY (fragments)	continue as before	MELISANDE	LOST INNOC.	PELLEAS	MELISANDE
ff	*ff* *f dim.*	*dim.... p*	*mp*	*p*	*p*	*p*

Figure 3.8. Leitmotivs and measure groupings: Rehearsal 55–58.

placed in its chronological sequence, but rather remembered in anguish as Mélisande's death approaches. Berg's term, "recapitulation" (*Reprise* in the original German), is somewhat misleading. To be sure, material associated with the earlier themes does return; however, those materials are not only further developed, they are heard in juxtaposition with new material. Moreover, there is thematic and textural consistency between the two "recapitulations" that binds them together as a larger whole, which creates a remarkable tension between recollective and anticipatory impulses. Figure 3.8 begins to explore these relations by tabulating the leitmotivic content and measure groupings.

One striking aspect of the dual "recapitulation" is that rhythms derived from LOST INNOCENCE infuse the whole, first conditioning JEALOUSY then LOVE. Another striking aspect is in how the WEDDING BOND motive alternates with the other motives in both sections, an alternation emphasized by the terraced dynamics of Reh. 55. Indeed, the entire passage forms an expanded sentence structure, with Reh. 55 comprising *a* + *a'* and Reh. 56 through the first measure-and-a-half of 58 comprising the spinning out and liquidation. The climax of the larger passage, as we have characterized it, a climax of despair, begins at Reh. 57. At this point the obsessive iterations of WEDDING BOND and the fusion of JEALOUSY and LOST INNOCENCE reach a *ff tutti* (including a full complement of brass) that is sustained over the next five bars as JEALOUSY and LOST INNOCENCE break down into overlapping fragments, the LOST INNOCENCE fragments creating a shrill *ff* in the orchestra's highest registers. In the context of this climax of despair, the gathering force of LOST INNOCENCE realizes its potential as the dramatic reversal of JEALOUSY. All its fury spent, the music forms a *diminuendo* over the next two-and-a-half measures, and then breaks off as the orchestral texture is reduced to a single voice: MELISANDE played by a solo clarinet. The shift in color, texture, and motive, signals a short return to Mélisande-space, and this is spun out over the next measures through a series of motivic fragments: LOST INNOCENCE; then PELLEAS; then MELISANDE, first the entire six-note motive and then breaking off after the first three notes of another statement. In the Maeterlinck play, Mélisande regains consciousness before dying. It seems reasonable to interpret this short passage as depicting that event, reduced to a short moment in Schoenberg's version. Mélisande's death scene follows.

A sweeping harp glissando (omitted from Example 3.9d), projecting $E^\flat$ minor and played at a hushed *ppp*, brings us into the death scene. Simplified to its most basic structure, the entire scene comprises a prolonged plagal cadence.[68] Aside from a brief move to $A^\flat$ minor (to be considered shortly), the entire scene, up until its final measure, is heard over a sustained $E^\flat$-$B^\flat$ pedal scored in the lower strings and bassoons and later in the bass trombone and tuba as well. The upper voices project $E^\flat$ minor but avoid resolution into an $E^\flat$ minor triad until the penultimate measure; once achieved, the $E^\flat$ minor triad, an unembellished *pp tutti*, is sustained for one measure before the plagal cadence into an open $B^\flat$-F fifth, the last measure of the scene.

In terms of phrase structure, Mélisande's death scene can be thought of as comprising two sentences plus the start of a third, which is prematurely terminated by the plagal cadence. Example 3.9d shows the first sentence. At its outset, the orchestral texture is composed of five primary constituents: 1) scalar motion in parallel thirds form the cortège-like ostinato noted earlier – scored for flutes and piccolos, the ostinato seems to grow out of the MELISANDE motive that precedes the scene; 2) overlapping DEATH DRIVE fragments spin out in the clarinets; 3) rhythmically augmented statements of DEATH DRIVE are scored for horn and violas; 4) the harp plays incessant eight-note pulses alternating $E^\flat$ and $B^\flat$; 5) the lower strings sustain the $E^\flat$- $B^\flat$ pedal. The rhythmically augmented statements of DEATH DRIVE in the horn and violas comprise the *a-a'* sections of the sentence. Heard against the $E^\flat$-$B^\flat$ pedal, the first four pitches of the

Example 3.9d. Rehearsal 59–60.4: Death of Mélisande, Death Drive (texture simplified).

augmented Death Drive motive project E♭ minor (with F heard as a passing tone). The final pitch, D, combining with G♭ and B♭ to form an augmented arpeggio, is heard as a major seventh dissonance above the bass. In contrast to the ♭6–5 resolution associated with the augmented triad through most of the piece, in this context the dissonant tone points to an upward

Example 3.9d. (*cont.*)

resolution, another aspect of dramatic reversal. At the end of the fourth measure, the augmented statements of DEATH DRIVE give way to a figure played by solo trumpet and trombone. The contour of this figure can be heard as a distorted augmentation of MELISANDE or as a variant on the inverted contour of DEATH DRIVE discussed in the context of Example 3.9a. It begins the spinning out part of the sentence. At Reh. 60, the MELISANDE/DEATH DRIVE variant gives rise to an ascending whole-tone sequence of DEATH DRIVE motives, and this in turn leads into the overlapping close of the first sentence and beginning of the second.

The second sentence begins as the first. After introducing a new variant of MELISANDE/DEATH DRIVE, a statement of EROS emerges as a violin solo just before Reh. 61. This poignant recollection terminates with a brief suspension of the eighth-note ostinato in the harp and the $E^\flat$-$B^\flat$ pedal in the lower voices as we move to an $A^\flat$ minor triad in the horns. The latter, heard in dissonant tension with the final note of EROS, a high $F^\flat$ suspended against the $A^\flat$ minor triad, is articulated by a fermata. The regular pulse of uncanny time is stopped for a moment and then goes on. The third sentence begins as the first two, but we hear the augmented DEATH DRIVE motive only again once before the orchestral *tutti* articulates the penultimate $E^\flat$ minor triad. The closing plagal cadence follows as a final harp arpeggio rounds out the death scene.

Final thoughts

With the death of Mélisande, the last of the motives with a sense of forward momentum has been spent. EROS-turned-to-its-opposite had given way to Mélisande's DEATH DRIVE, and that motive had fulfilled its function with her death. All that remains is from Golaud's perspective, and all of that is retrospective. Retrospection has been characteristic of Golaud all along. The exquisite coda-space of *Pelleas und Melisande* brings that quality to its highest intensity and fullest realization.

The work's final tonality, D minor, begins to be strongly projected at Reh. 62 with the return of GOLAUD. It is undermined at Reh. 64, touching on E major as GOLAUD gives way to MELISANDE, and PELLEAS-becoming-LOST INNOCENCE. The tonality is further destabilized as recollections of EROS, PELLEAS, MELISANDE, and LOVE unfold at Reh. 65. GOLAUD re-emerges after Reh. 66, first in the bass and then in the upper voices as the work once again points toward its final goal. As we approach Reh. 69, the bass descends F-E♭-D; the arrival of D coincides with a statement of the head-motive of GOLAUD (played by the oboes) and an underlying octave descent in the basses and celli, further solidifying D minor as we enter the final twelve measure of the piece. The bass returns for its penultimate statement of F and makes its final descent from F through $E^\flat$ to D five measures before the end of the piece. D then reaches up to F, falls back again, and the motion is repeated one last time before the music settles into its final D minor triad.

The close in D minor expresses the conflict between something achieved, the tragic fulfillment of the work, and something long resisted that can no longer be avoided. At its close D minor seems inevitable, but that inevitability has not always been so clear. To be sure, there have been hints of D minor as early as the fleeting half cadence on A at Reh. 1, the initiation of the MELISANDE motive. Most tellingly, the original statement of GOLAUD, in F major (at Reh. 5), is prepared by an A major triad that is immediately followed by a C major triad (at three measures before Reh. 5). The A major triad functions as a dominant implying a move toward D minor. The C major triad negates A major as dominant, and helps to prepare the move toward F instead. As we have seen, GOLAUD never achieves a closing cadence in F, just as LOVE never achieves a closing cadence in E. Adding to this complex of keys, we recall that Mélisande's death scene is grounded by an $E^\flat$ pedal. The reiterated approach toward the final grounding in D, from F through E♭, associates with those prior events, and convincingly tells us that they have led inexorably to this ending.

Troubled by Schoenberg's deep ambivalence about program music, and placed into skewed perspective by Schoenberg's teleological historicism, the reception of *Pelleas und Melisande* has suffered in the concert hall and in the scholarly literature. And perhaps its luster has been dimmed by the magnificent company that it keeps: our long meditation on *Pelleas* is not meant to devalue *Verklärte Nacht*, *Gurrelieder*, the First String Quartet, op. 7, or the Chamber Symphony, op. 9, all astounding accomplishments of Schoenberg's first period. Still *Pelleas* inhabits a special place because of its own achievements. It is where Schoenberg explores the limits of composing with *Leitmotivs*; it is the locus of an extraordinary play of temporal orientations – retrospection, prolepsis, and a sense of suspended now-time, all subject to eruptions of an ever mysterious, and inexorable Fate; and above all, its fusion of dramatic and formal design, using *Leitmotivic* development *and* conflicting temporal perspectives to realize its ends, is its central and most radical achievement, an "emancipation of discourse" that is the hallmark of musical greatness.

4 Motive and memory in Schoenberg's First String Quartet

For David Lewin[1]

As would be true of any enduring piece of music, there are multiple ways to think about what matters most in Schoenberg's First Quartet: the genesis of the work's themes as the Quartet unfolds, the ways they form familial relations as well as the conflicts and contrarieties that any family must have; the work's prodigious use of counterpoint, the technical and expressive solutions to problems that lesser composers dare not even attempt; the complex and elusive sense of harmony and voice leading, an aspect of early Schoenberg that after nearly a century still confounds theorists; the question or questions about the work's relations to a larger tradition of string quartet composition; the many different voices that emerge out of Schoenberg's unifying voice, shadows of Beethoven, Schumann, Liszt, Wagner, Brahms, Mahler, and Reger; the place and force of this work in Schoenberg's creative evolution. All of these questions, and more, provide substantial and fertile ways to focus on Schoenberg's Op. 7. Although this chapter will touch on some of these topics, its primary focus is on the work's musical form. Or perhaps I should say, its musical *forms*, for Op. 7 is not a static, singular object; its formal unfolding is full of wonder and surprise, and surprise precludes and undermines the kind of stasis that the singular "form" seems to indicate.

To state the obvious, Schoenberg's music is grounded, from beginning to end, in the craft and many of the assumptions of his precursors. In particular, the embedding of multiple movements in a single movement form is a dramatic possibility and formal challenge that is inherited from Beethoven, Liszt and others. Every one of his early large-scale compositions provides another solution to the same compositional problem, and long abandoned it notably returns at end of his life in the String Trio and the Phantasy for violin and piano.

An interrelated set of problems or challenges that Schoenberg also inherits from the nineteenth century might be characterized as the problematics of *memory*. Concerns with the nature and impact of memory are particularly significant among the multiple changes in perspective and focus that distinguish the Romantic world-view from that of the Enlightenment. This is as true of Romantic poetry as it is of music, as it is of historical narratives. Even more forcefully, it can be argued that Romantic music, especially in

Germany and Austria, is an encoding of memory and consciousness itself. As we have already seen in our analyses of *Gurrelieder* and *Pelleas und Melisande*, the forms of Romantic music mimic the processes of coming to know, the processes of anticipation and recollection that form consciousness, or self-consciousness. It's no wonder that Schopenhauer thought that music was a direct representation of the *Will*.

The generation that fills the first half of the twentieth century inherits its fascination with human psychology, and specifically with the construction of human memory from the Romantics. In a sense, *all* of the writings of Sigmund Freud are about the problematics of memory. In literature, the play of memory is central for Franz Kafka, James Joyce, Marcel Proust and Thomas Mann. And the music of Schoenberg, his students, as well as Stravinsky and his, each in his own very different way, uses new forms and processes that find new ways to play on our sense of musical memory, both within works *and* as those works participate in larger traditions. Of course, the perception of musical form, *any* musical form, is bound up with the musical memory. Schoenberg recognizes this in his essay, "Brahms the Progressive": "*Form in Music* serves to bring about comprehensibility through memorability."[2] Musical themes and their generative constituents, musical motives, are the primary means through which musical memory is forged.

The title for this chapter is a pun on the title of a book by the philosopher Henri Bergson, in its English translation, *Matter and Memory*.[3] Bergson, who had his heyday in the early part of the twentieth century, was a philosopher well known to the Second Viennese composers; yet, although Schoenberg had the German edition of *Matter and Memory* as well as four other books by Bergson in his library, the fact that not all of the pages in his copy of *Matter and Memory* are cut seems to indicate that the book was not exactly at the top of his reading list.[4] And so, I am not about to present a Bergsonian reading of Schoenberg. Nonetheless, I do think that a distinction that Bergson makes about two types of memory is useful in coming to terms with the form of Op. 7. Bergson's categories are useful because they are inherently musical, not because Schoenberg was a Bergsonian.

At one point in *Matter and Memory* Bergson describes the process of memorizing a passage.[5] The student reads the material over the course of several occasions, and at the end has committed the passage to memory. The final "knowing by memory" is the result of a cumulative effect. To recall the passage, the student need not explicitly recall the several study sessions that led to the passage being memorized. On the other hand, there *are* the memories of having studied the passage, the specific memories of having come to know it. The one type of memory is the accumulation of the past that informs the present, as it is oriented toward the future. The other type of memory self-consciously and selectively reflects back on the past, and brings it into the context of the present, sometimes to anticipate a future. The second type of memory brings a particular kind of focus to information presumably available but not consciously recollected in the first.

In the temporal unfolding of a musical composition, there is generally a sense that the ongoing present is informed and motivated by the cumulative past. This is like Bergson's first type of memory (and this is an attitude implicit in David Lewin's development of his *interval function*).[6] In addition, music also has the ability to make us recollect specific passages within the work. In doing so we remember their original place and impact, and self-consciously relate what *is happening* to what *has happened*.[7] This is like Bergson's second type of memory. It is through the variables of projecting an ongoing, cumulative past which in turn stimulates selective recollections of that past, both recent and remote, that composers create our sense of musical form. I find the play of these two types of memory to be particularly apposite in understanding the form of Schoenberg's Op. 7.

For Bergson, time and space are radically different kinds of things. His title, *Matter and Memory*, is meant to suggest a disjunction, rather than a conjunction of the two. He claimed that our understanding of time is sullied by conceptualizing time spatially, as something extended. In contrast, *Schoenberg's* discussions of form and function in music are often spatial in their orientation; his concept of tonal regions, and his discussions of phrase shapes provide clear examples.[8] And though he writes about memory here and there, for example in the passage from "Brahms the Progressive" that I have already cited, the role of memory is not particularly well addressed in Schoenberg's pedagogy.

In the course of this chapter, our approach will try to mediate between spatial and temporal aspects of musical form. To insist that music unfolds in time, not space, is like insisting that bachelors are unmarried men. It doesn't tell us much. In fact we do experience the time of music as suggesting musical spaces; aspects of our common parlance, such as references to thematic *areas*, or even to pitch as *high* or *low*, indicate as much. On the other hand, composition can contain thematic or motivic references that leap over established musical spaces, and that function to evoke recollective memories that cut across boundaries of time and space. Ultimately, I will suggest that the perception of musical form, and the form of Op. 7 in particular, is based on the interaction of memories that define musical spaces, and memories that challenge and in some sense redefine those spaces.

Schoenberg's program notes of 1906 and their revision in 1936 are a good place to start our consideration of the work's form. The program notes provide an overview of the formal design and a catalogue of principal themes. Table 4.1 outlines Schoenberg's presentation, omitting musical examples and adding measure numbers.[9] Schoenberg begins his 1906 analysis with a caveat:

> The following analysis distinguishes between four parts; they are not, however, four separate movements, but rather connected sections which blend into one another. To be sure, the thematic types are those of the traditional four movements, but their intricate structure is an attempt to create a single unified, uninterrupted movement.[10]

The paragraph stands in opposition to the rest of the essay as a warning that the formal overview which Schoenberg will be able to provide cannot sufficiently address the most central aspect of the work's formal design, the integration of multiple movements into a single movement form. Nonetheless, the program notes are useful in getting a general orientation toward the piece.

Schoenberg's outline divides the work into four principal sections. In sum these correspond to the movements that might have comprised a string quartet by Haydn or Mozart: sonata, scherzo, adagio and rondo. While the division of the whole into four parts is central to Schoenberg's formal overview, even in this bare-bones outline there are aspects that modify or even disrupt what might have been a more typical four-movement design. Most noticeably, the Sonata movement does not recapitulate its principal and subordinate theme groups after its development section. Instead, Schoenberg places the recapitulation of the Sonata's principal theme group at the end of the Scherzo, and the recapitulation of the Sonata's subordinate group at the end of the Adagio. In this respect, primary articulators of musical form are displaced so that they interpenetrate the embedded movements. Moreover, even a cursory examination of Schoenberg's themes reveals that the first theme of the Scherzo is introduced in the transition between the two theme groups of the Sonata and that the Rondo derives its themes from the Adagio, and then goes on to include the principal Scherzo theme, and to close with material derived from the opening of the Sonata.

In short, even the basic thematic catalogue of Schoenberg's program notes can give us some indication of the ways that the composer has associated the quasi-independent movements to create a larger dramatic and structural design. Nonetheless, the most salient aspects of Schoenberg's outline remain the division of the whole into four parts and the division of those parts into thematic areas that correspond with traditional forms. Part One contains the two opposed thematic areas of a sonata. Part Two is a scherzo

Table 4.1 *Analytic Outline of the First String Quartet based on Schoenberg's program notes of 1936 and 1906.*

PART ONE – Sonata
  I. Principal Theme Group
    A)   Opening Measures
    B)   Mm. 14 and following
    C)   Mm. 24 and following
  Transitional
    Rehearsal A and following
  II. Subsidiary Themes (2ND Theme Group)
    A)   57 after A…
    B)   71 after A…
    C)   reformulations of II.A at 82 after A and at B
  Development and Transition
    Rehearsal B to E

PART TWO – Scherzo
  Scherzo: Rehearsal E
  Trio: Rehearsal F
  Concluding Section: Rehearsal G
  Development: 34 after G to 38 after I
  Recapitulation of the Principal Theme group 38 after I

PART THREE – Adagio
  Main Theme: Rehearsal K
  Middle Section: 52 after K
  Repetition of first Adagio theme: Rehearsal L*
    (*Note: actually a contrapuntal combination of both themes, which functions as a development)
  Transition: 24 after L
  Recapitulation of the Subsidiary theme Group and
    Transition: 52 after L, 78 after L

PART FOUR – Rondo Finale [Description from 1906 analysis]
  Reformulation of first Adagio theme: Rehearsal M
  Reformulation of Second Adagio Theme: 26 after M
  Reformulation of Principal Scherzo Theme: Rehearsal N
  Small Development of rondo themes, 35 after N
    Closing Group
      Using the opening theme its companions and the
  Scherzo theme:
      Rehearsal O to the end

Table 4.2 *Analytic Outline of the First String Quartet based on Webern's notes of 1912.*

A main Sonata Movement [Schoenberg's Part One], with a long fugato [A to A.56] separating the Principal and Subsidiary themes*
[* Note: Webern does not mention the development section of Reh B to E in this context but assumes this first development later in his analysis]
    Scherzo and Trio [E to G.34]
    Large-scale development [G.34 to I.38]
Recapitulation of Principal Theme [I.38 to I.80]
    Extension: Adagio [K to L.38]
Recapitulation of the Subsidiary Theme [L.52]
    Coda: Rondo Finale [M to end]

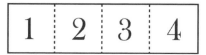

Figure 4.1. Schematic of the form extrapolated from Schoenberg's program notes.

including a trio section and a modified *da capo*. Part Three, the Adagio, is constructed as an ABA form. And Part Four is a concluding Rondo.

Figure 4.1 is a schematic of the form extrapolated from Schoenberg's program notes, purposely disregarding the important interpenetration of thematic content that we have already noted. As Schoenberg's warning predicted, the schematic does not capture the formal complexity or the formal unity of the whole.

The dotted lines between the principal sections are a clumsy attempt to show that the sections "blend into one another." Assuming that this blending is done through transitional material, and we shall subsequently see that this assumption is quite inadequate to the form, the figure shows the four movements connected like box cars in a freight train, with only their couplers to keep them from drifting apart. Figure 4.1 clearly fails as a model for the kind of form that Schoenberg has achieved.

In contrast to Schoenberg's notes, Anton Webern's program notes of 1912 make a concerted effort to describe the single movement form.[11] An outline based on Webern's notes is shown in Table 4.2.

It is a fair assumption that Webern had noticed that the unity of the single movement form was not well addressed in Schoenberg's notes. His comments on this crucial aspect of the piece are particularly interesting:

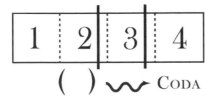

Figure 4.2. Schematic of the form based on Webern's analysis.

> At bottom the form of the Quartet is that of a single enormous sonata movement. The Scherzo and the big development are interpolated between the first development [B to E] and the Recapitulation, while the recapitulation itself is extended by the Adagio between the principal and Secondary Themes. In this scheme the Rondo-Finale can be considered as a greatly expanded Coda.

In order to characterize the entire work as a large-scale sonata movement, Webern's analysis highlights the recapitulations of the Sonata's Principal and then Subordinate theme groups, that we have noted as being embedded respectively in Schoenberg's Scherzo and Adagio, giving them a structural emphasis that is not explicit in Schoenberg's thematic catalogue. Then, in order to make sense of all the intervening and subsequent material, Webern characterizes the Scherzo as an interpolation, the Adagio as a cadential extension, and the Rondo as coda. Figure 4.2 reduces Webern's view to a schematic drawing.

While Figure 4.2 addresses aspects of a single movement form not well addressed in the schematic of Figure 4.1, for most listeners, it is at the cost of intuitive plausibility. The Scherzo, Adagio and Rondo simply comprise too much musical matter to be relegated to the status of parenthesis, cadential extension and coda. Yet, Webern was on to something. The work does have the unity that Schoenberg claimed for it. And, moreover, that unity *is* based on principles that Schoenberg had learnt from studying the dynamics of sonata form.

Early in the nineteenth century, the premier expositor of sonata form, Adolph Bernhard Marx, had viewed the form as a dialectical unfolding wherein the Principal and Subordinate Themes were conceptualized as the basis for opposition as well as higher unity.[12] I would suggest that principles not so very different from the ones described by Marx underlie the dynamics of form in Schoenberg's Op. 7. But Schoenberg's basic opposition is not between the Principal and Subordinate themes of the Sonata; it is between the work's two halves. Figure 4.3 is a schematic of this opposition and higher unity.

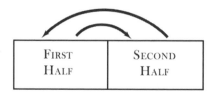

Figure 4.3. Schematic of the basic opposition and higher unity.

Figure 4.3 is stimulated by David Lewin's work on transformational networks.[13] In conceptualizing the figure, I reduce musical functions in the work into two broad categories, each of which contains two opposed forces. The first category of functions is spatially oriented; it opposes functions that lead to individuation and closure versus those that assert the interconnectedness of the parts and the unity of the whole. While the comparison with Bergson's two memory types is inexact, we might say that space forming corresponds most closely with Bergson's cumulative memory. Within Figure 4.3, functions that lead to individuation are shown by the vertical lines that create boundaries. The horizontal lines show functions that create unity. A second category of functions is concerned with leaping over boundaries, and with an explicit orientation toward time. Within this category, one set of functions is engendering and anticipatory. It is denoted by the arrow moving left to right. An opposed set of functions is recollective and integrative. It is denoted by the arrow moving right to left. Both arrows reflect aspects of Bergson's recollective memory.

We can begin to fill in the schematic with content by considering the ways that Schoenberg articulates the formal divisions of the quartet. Toward these ends, I find three principal techniques. First, unity is created through thematic continuity, and formal disjunction by thematic differentiation. Second, various levels of closure within the work are articulated by the varying size and force of motivic liquidations of the kind that Schoenberg describes in his pedagogy. Third, despite the harmonic ambiguity and instability that dominates this work, Schoenberg uses clear and strong points of harmonic arrival as major structural downbeats.

By all of these criteria, the strongest articulation internal to the piece is the arrival of the Adagio at Rehearsal K. As we have already noted, the first two movements are thematically bound together by the anticipation of the principal Scherzo theme within the Sonata's transition. We have also noted that the Rondo derives its main themes from the Adagio. Here we can add that the Adagio themes, in mood, as well as intervallic and rhythmic structure, are the single greatest departure from the opening material within the work. On thematic grounds alone, the Quartet divides most basically into two halves. Moreover, the liquidation at the end of the Scherzo, just before the Adagio begins, is the largest liquidation of the piece, both in terms of sheer size and in terms of dramatic impact as the ensemble grinds its way down to the repeated Ds and then to the sustained cello solo that gives way to the Adagio. Finally, the beginning of the Adagio articulates A minor, the minor dominant for the piece, distinctively if fleetingly, in a way that sets it apart from previous points of arrival.

On the other hand, the need to go on at the end of the first half is signaled by several principal means. There is the incompleteness of the initial Sonata emphasized in Webern's analysis. There is no sense of harmonic closure. And moreover, given a Sonata followed by a Scherzo, Schoenberg trusts, I assume, that we will have the expectation of a slow movement and finale. The boundary of the first half necessitates the second half. The recollective memory that leaps over the boundary of the first half into the second is largely based on our knowledge of tonal forms, the forms used by Schoenberg's precursors. The single anticipatory and engendering arrow of Figure 4.3 indicates the need to go on at the juncture between the two halves. In dialectical terms, Schoenberg has engendered a first that needs a second.

At the end of the work, the final statement of the opening theme, radically transformed, but instantly recognizable, has a recollective and integrative function. This, depicted by our right to left arrow, is the primary means through which the articulated or divided sections are brought back together into a larger unity. The recollective and integrative function embodied in the final statement sums up and in a sense remembers all of the recollective functions throughout the work. These functions operate in two basic forms. First, a series of recapitulations of the opening theme (and other themes as well) reflects back on successively larger and larger spans of unfolding formal design, perceived through cumulative musical memory. Second, Schoenberg intertwines contrapuntal reminiscences of earlier themes within the ongoing exposition or development of subsequent musical themes. Thus, concurrent and concomitant with the opening of new thematic space, Schoenberg is able to reach back into the work's past, integrating that past into the music's present. The remembering of the first theme at the very end is the last in a series of restatements, the passages Schoenberg characterized as recapitulations included. Each of these functions to recollect, through the perspectives of all that has happened in between, the entire work's unfolding, up until that point. The sublimity of the final recapitulation, at Rehearsal O, owes much of its power to the perception of the huge gulf of time and experience that separates it from the original statement. It carries the weight of the most fundamental recollective and integrative function in the piece; it gets its force from all that has happened remembered through it.

In sum, I believe that Webern was right to recognize sonata principles at work in the larger form of Op. 7, but that he is not convincing in his

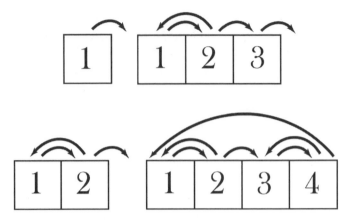

Figure 4.4. Four staged schematic of the form.

assertion that the primary opposition lies between the Principal and Subordinate groups of Schoenberg's first movement Sonata. The synoptic opposition is between the two halves, and the most far-reaching recapitulation is achieved in the stability of D major only at the very end of the work. In this sense, the work as a whole can be viewed as a larger sonata form.

Figure 4.4, constructed along the lines of Figure 4.3, depicts the work in four different stages corresponding to Schoenberg's four parts. The first stage is from the perspective at the end of the Sonata. Although there are recollective and integrative functions within the movement, the schematic shows only the most basic engendering and anticipatory arrow, pointing into the space that will be filled by the Scherzo. This left to right arrow is the resultant of several combined forces: the recapitulation of the Sonata is incomplete, the Scherzo theme has been anticipated but has not yet been given thematic status, and the liquidation of the Sonata, at Rehearsal C to C30, is without harmonic closure.

The second stage of Figure 4.4 is located at the end of the Scherzo. The principal constituent of the recollective and integrative arrow, right to left, is the recapitulation of the Principal theme group of the Sonata at I38. Like the final statement of the opening theme at the very end of the work, this recapitulation reflects back on the source of all that we have experienced within the piece up until this time. Reaching back through the Scherzo to the beginning of the Sonata, this arrow creates the larger unity of the first two quarters. In addition, stage two includes the anticipatory and engendering arrow that is carried over from the first stage, and also the arrow anticipating the second half, as in Figure 4.3.

The third stage of Figure 4.4 is located at the end of the Adagio. The figure omits the reflective and integrative arrow that is suggested by the recapitulation of the Sonata's Subordinate theme group, as well as other recollective functions within the Adagio, and instead emphasizes the most basic function of the Adagio as engendering and anticipating the Rondo.

The fourth stage reintroduces the overarching arrow, right to left, that we have already seen in Figure 4.3. In addition, a new recollective arrow connects the Rondo to the Adagio. This function is expressed generally through the relatedness of the Rondo themes to those in the Adagio, and more specifically through the double recapitulation of the Adagio/Rondo themes at N68, just before the final restatement of the work's opening theme at it close. The final stage of Figure 4.4 shows that the two halves are isomorphic with each other, as well as with the most fundamental dialectic, as shown in Figure 4.3.

The combination of spatial and temporal aspects in Figures 4.3 and 4.4 is suggestive of two approaches toward understanding musical form. The arrows, anticipatory and recollective, suggest a phenomenological account of the piece. This is from the vantage of traveling within the form, and experiencing its various perspectives through a succession of now-times. On the other hand, the boxes, which denote the work's four parts, suggest an overview of the work, perceived in spatial terms, as an object outside of time or at least aside from its temporal unfolding. Whereas the formal overview tends toward the fixed and hierarchical, a phenomenological account will be based on changing perspectives of boundaries, both anticipated and recollected.[14]

The kind of contrast between the fixed and hierarchical versus the unfixed and changing nicely corresponds with distinctions between two kinds of space, both conceptual and literal, that were defined by the philosopher Gilles Deleuze, and then further developed in his collaboration with Félix Guattari.[15] In the formulation found in his book *Difference and Repetition*, Deleuze names his spaces *agrarian* and *nomadic* and associates the two spaces respectively with the ancient Greek ideas of *logos* and *nomos*, logos denoting fixity and order in the cosmos, and nomos, associated with the Greek word *nemo* (to pasture), denoting unfixed boundaries.

> A distribution of this type [i.e. agrarian space] proceeds by fixed and proportional determinations which may be assimilated to 'properties' or limited territories within representation. The agrarian question may well have been very important for this organization of judgment as the faculty which distinguishes parts ('on the one hand and on the other hand'). Even among the gods, each has its domain, his category, his attributes, and all distribute limits and lots to mortals in accordance with destiny. Then there is a completely other distribution which must be called nomadic, a nomad *nomos*, without property, enclosure or measure. Here, there is no longer a division of that which is distributed but rather a division among those who distribute *themselves* in an open space – a space which is unlimited, or at least

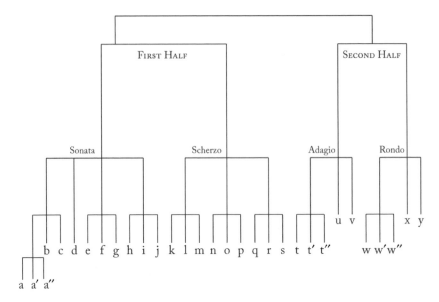

Figure 4.5. Opus 7 overview.

without precise limits. . . . To fill a space, to be distributed within it, is very different from distributing space. It is an errant and even 'delirious' distribution, in which things are deployed across the entire extensity of a univocal and undistributed Being. It is not a matter of being which is distributed according to the requirements of representation, but of all things being divided up within being in the univocity of simple presence (the One – All). Such a distribution is demonic rather than divine, since it is a peculiarity of demons to operate in the intervals between the gods' fields of action, as it is to leap over the barriers or the enclosures, thereby confounding the boundaries between properties.[16]

While the two kinds of space can be used to distinguish among composers, for example Bruckner strikes me as "agrarian" while Mahler's forms are more 'nomadic' in tendency, for our present purposes I am interested in thinking of the perception of musical form as a dialectic between the two kinds of space.

Figure 4.5, in the form of a branching diagram, provides an "agrarian" overview of the entire work. A phenomenological orientation will subsequently provide a complementary and antithetical "nomadic" perspective. The Key to Figure 4.5 provides the reader with content for each branch. My discussion here will concentrate only on the most fundamental and far-reaching aspects of the diagram. The trunk in Figure 4.5 bifurcates into the work's two halves, and then again into its four movements. Each of these trifurcates into a three-part form, and the process of trifurcation occurs

Key to Figure 4.5

BRANCH, MEASURES	FORMAL FUNCTION	SALIENT FEATURES
a, 1-13	First Principal theme, and "liquidation theme"	establishes D minor tonic
a/, 14-23	Second Principal theme	B^b minor
a//, 24-29	Close of Principal group	V/E^b
b, 30-64	development of P	tonicize E^b and $C^\sharp$
c, 65-Reh. A	recap and liquidation of P	return to D minor
d, A-A55	transition to Subordinate theme group	anticipates Scherzo as well as First Subordinate theme
e, A56-A70	First Subordinate theme	begins in E^b
f, A71-A81	Second Subordinate theme	begins in F, ends in A^b
g, A82-A103	Close of S group	modulatory, cadences on A^b and E^b
h, Rehearsal B	Development, first part	waltz in e, based on S1
i, C-C30	Development, second part	restate P1 in $C^\sharp$
j, C30-E	end Development and transition to Scherzo	cadences on E^b and D, includes transformations of P and S
k, E-E50	main Scherzo theme	in G^b
l, E50-E105	lyric Scherzo theme	unstable, homage to Brahms
m, E106-E133	Close of Scherzo	to G^b
n, F-F79	Trio, first section	unstable
o, F80-F141	Lyric Trio Theme	to E, includes transformations of P_2 unstable, includes cadences on E and $C^\sharp$
p, G-G33	Transition based on Scherzo theme	begins in $C^\sharp$
q, G34-G111	Development of Scherzo	unstable, includes transformations of P_1
r, H-I37	2nd part of Scherzo Dev., liquidation of Scherzo	return of D minor tonic
s, I38-I80	Recap of P and liquidation of the first half	A minor, includes transformations of S
t, K-K51	First Adagio theme	E major, include transformations of P_1
t/, K52-K79	Second Adagio theme	F minor
t//, L-L23	combine Adagio themes	unstable to V/B^b, includes transformations of P_1
u, L24-L51	transition to recap of S	unstable
v, L52-L91	recap S group, transition to Rondo	A major, transforms 1st Adagio includes transformations of P_1
w, M-M25	First Rondo theme	unstable, transforms 2nd Adagio includes transformations of P_1
w/, M26-M47	Second Rondo theme	A major, return of 1st Adagio
w//, M48-M59	return of first Rondo theme	F major, A major, includes transformations of Scherzo theme
x, N1-N89	development and liquidation of Rondo	D major, transforms P_1
y, O1-O51	Close of entire quartet	

again for all branches of the Sonata and Scherzo, as well as for the leftmost branches of the Adagio and Rondo. At the lowest level, the leftmost branch of the Sonata trifurcates once again.

The patterns of branching, bifurcation at the highest levels, and trifurcation at lower levels of structure, suggest nested symmetries, smaller forms embedded within the larger forms. In discussing Figures 4.3 and 4.4, we have already considered some aspects of the primary bifurcations. The trifurcation of the leftmost branch within each of the four movements is particularly salient; in each case the resultant is a miniature version of the larger three-part form.

The lowest three branches at the bottom left, labeled a through a″, form a miniature sonata exposition where branch a is the first theme (mm. 1–13), branch a′ the contrasting lyric theme (mm. 14–23), and a″ the closing theme (mm. 24–9). A larger sonata form comprises branches a through c. Here, branches a through a″ comprise the exposition, branch b is the development, and branch c is the recapitulation. At the next higher level of structure, branches a through c comprise the Principal Theme Group, branches e through g are the Subordinate Group, and branches h through j represent the Sonata's development.

Similar kinds of nesting take place within the other movements as well. The leftmost branches of the Scherzo, k through m, form a miniature Scherzo-Trio-Scherzo, and the leftmost branches of the Adagio and Rondo each compose a smaller ABA form in the context of the larger ABA that constitutes the movement. In sum, the overview of a branching diagram suggests an orderly disposition of nested forms. Figure 4.5 presents a stable, hierarchical and geometric conception of formal design.

A phenomenological perspective will result in a very different account. Here a space that has been traversed or anticipated is reconsidered in the context of a subsequent and larger frame of reference so that old boundaries are eroded or given new meaning as the piece unfolds. This aspect of experiencing musical form is somewhat analogous to experiencing architectural space, not through the overview of a floor plan, but through the changing perspectives that we experience as we inhabit or walk through that space. The resultant is something in between Deleuzian agrarian and nomadic spaces. Perception centers on defining and delimiting space, but the boundaries are not stable and secure.

Needless to say, this kind of spatial revision affects the details of phrase design as well as larger aspects of form. Here I will concentrate on large-scale revisions. We recall that the opening of the work creates the initial space of a miniature sonata form. The rapid unfolding of the miniature sonata exposition suggests the kind of condensation that we associate with Schoenberg's music beginning with his next major work, the Chamber Symphony, op. 9. The entire initial exposition, comprising the first theme, its liquidation and transition to the second theme, the second theme's liquidation and then the closing theme, all takes place within twenty-nine measures – about a single minute's worth of music. Even adding the first development, and then the recapitulation of the first theme along with its liquidation, we still have heard less than three and a half minutes of music altogether.

The experience of the opening exposition suggests a highly compact musical form, and the condensed development and initial recapitulation does little, if anything, to alter that perception. To all of this, the music that functions in our overview as the transition to the Subordinate group – branch d of Figure 4.5 – stands in stark contrast. We can consider this transition as the initial passage of formal aporia. As I enter its space, through a last moment twist in the shape of the liquidation motive, I experience a sense of formal disorientation. This is the place at which I come to doubt the force of my initial perceptions of space and place. The transition unfolds at a more leisurely pace than all that preceded it, in fact it is nearly twice as long as the initial exposition; yet the passage is perceived as a transition nonetheless, and as such it is our first indication of the larger dimensions of the work to come. What had the force of the main hall, gradually comes into focus as an anteroom, a status that will be revised again and again as ramifications and recollections of the opening material embrace larger and larger spans as the piece unfolds.

The other left-branch nestings, at the outset of each larger movement, result in similar kinds of formal revision. For example, in traversing the leftmost branches of the Scherzo, the second branch has the force of a contrasting Trio. The subsequent space of the larger Trio, branches n through p, forces a perceptual revision that negates our initial perception of functions and boundaries, by placing the nested form into a larger, more comprehensive space.

A technique with implications similar to those involving nested forms occurs at branch h, the beginning of the larger Sonata development. Here Schoenberg gives us eighty-six measures of an unmistakable waltz. Granted, its motivic materials evolve directly out of the Subordinate group. Nonetheless, it is as though we have leapt directly into the dance movement. When the restatement of the first theme of the Principal group occurs, in C♯, at rehearsal C, it undercuts the status of the waltz, and brings it convincingly back into the space of Sonata development. As with our initial perceptions of a condensed sonata form and of a condensed scherzo, the force of this initial waltz at first suggests a radical foreshortening of space, which is negated by subsequent perceptions.

In sum, while the nesting of forms in our overview is suggestive of symmetry, hierarchy and stability, the phenomenological resultants are asymmetrical and destabilizing. Yet there is another aspect of form that is even more "nomadic" in its implications, and that is far less recognized by the branchings of Figure 4.5. This aspect of form derives from the inter-penetration of themes across the formal boundaries of the movements. An early example of this technique within the work is the anticipation of the Scherzo within the transition between theme groups in the Sonata.

The transition introduces two new themes albeit in incipient forms: the first theme of the Subordinate group, and more emphatically, the principal theme of the Scherzo. Anticipating the Subordinate group in the context of a transition to that group is more in line with the Deleuzian concept of agrarian form. This aspect paves a smooth transition into the next section of the larger Sonata. The incipient Scherzo theme however is more nomadic in its force. And although it has transitory reappearances during the development of the Subordinate group and in the transition to the Scherzo, it is only at the Scherzo proper where the transition's principal motive finally takes on the solidity of a true thematic statement. In anticipating its "realization" as the Scherzo theme, the Scherzo motive of the Sonata transition leaps over the boundaries that separate the two movements, and suggests the larger opposition and unity of the Sonata and Scherzo.

The most profound aspects of this kind of thematic displacement involve transformations and recapitulations of the Sonata themes outside of the "Sonata Movement." The passages that involve this technique are summarized in Table 4.3. Recalling Bergson's two kinds of memory, cumulative versus self-consciously recollective, we can say that the placement of these Sonata references outside of the initial "Sonata space" allows and requires them to function as musical recollections. These are the functions that we began to study in Figures 4.3 and 4.4 through our left to right arrows. Here we can add that such recollections are particularly nomadic in their implications. They override and disregard the boundaries of formal subdivisions, and, especially in those passages where Sonata recollections intertwine with the unfolding of new thematic space, rather than dividing space in the agrarian manner, they range through the space of a unified whole that resists being divided into parcels.

We have already considered the most basic aspect of this technique in discussing the recollective and integrative arrow of Figure 4.3. I have characterized the successive restatements of the first principal theme as summations that take us back to the beginning of the piece to recollect all that has transpired in between; the ultimate closing of the work is a sublime reaching-over of its entire span. To close this chapter, I would like to turn

Table 4.3 *Thematic Recollections of Sonata themes outside of "Sonata space".*

Measures	Place in Formal Overview	Themes Recollected
C30-E	transition to Scherzo	$P_{1,2}$ and $S_{1,2}$ in counterpoint with anticipations of the Scherzo theme
F80-F141	middle section of Trio	P_2 in counterpoint with *dolce* theme
H-I37	second part of Scherzo development	$P_{1,2,3}$ in counterpoint with Scherzo material
I38-I81	recapitulation of Principal group	P_1
K-K51	first Adagio theme	$S_{1,2}$ in counterpoint with first Adagio theme
K52-K79	second Adagio theme	$P_{1,2}$ in counterpoint with second Adagio theme
L24-L51	transition to recap of the Subordinate group	P_1 transformations fill L38-L51 and lead directly to the recap of S
L52-L91	recapitulation of the Subordinate group	$S_{1,2}$ in counterpoint with second Adagio theme
M-M25	first Rondo theme	P_1 in counterpoint with first Rondo theme
M26-M46	second Rondo theme	P_1 in counterpoint with second Rondo theme
O	Close of the work	P_1 transformations

to the related technique, where thematic recollections intertwine with the ongoing exposition of new thematic material.

The first set of recollections in Table 4.3, the transition to the Scherzo, allows that passage to reach forward as transition to the Scherzo, and reflect back in a quasi-coda-like way on the Sonata that has just past. At rehearsal D, the transformation of the first Principal theme, marked *langsam* and *ausdrucksvoll*, not only recollects the motives of the work's opening, in temperament it anticipates the final recollective statement at the end of the quartet. Like the final statement, we can consider this a *sublimation* of the opening. The same technique is used during the Trio and Scherzo development. In each instance sublimated references to the opening reach back to the beginning and anticipate the close.

The order of recollections is particularly interesting during the Adagio. As the Adagio's first theme unfolds, the counterpoint recollects the Subordinate group of the Sonata. And then as the Adagio's second theme unfolds, the counterpoint reaches further back to the Principal group. In sum, as the Adagio goes on, the recollective memories within it reach further and further back to the work's origin.

Toward the end of the Adagio, the passage just before the recapitulation of the Subordinate group remembers the first Principal theme. Once again, this recollection is a sublimation of the opening. In its immediate proximity to the recapitulation of the Subordinate group, it enlarges the space of recollecting beyond that of the recapitulation proper.

Although it is not included in Table 4.3, the Rondo can be understood as a recollection of the Adagio. Like the recollections of the Sonata throughout the quartet, it is as though the Rondo sees the Adagio in a new light. In this case, the Rondo as a whole performs the traditional role of "comic" reconciliation. In counterpoint with its comic recollections of the Adagio, the Rondo continues the series of sublimated references to the Principal theme group of the Sonata. Finally the close at rehearsal O completes the series of sublimated recollections, as I have said, by reaching back over the entire work. Indeed, by achieving a tonal stability nowhere else achieved within the work, we may say that the end reaches back beyond the work's frame to a tonic stability that Schoenberg's world, like that of Brahms before him, could only imagine in nostalgia through the recollections of sublimated memories.

Coda

I have come to recognize the two kinds of space developed by Deleuze and Guattari as variants and refinements of the ancient Greek distinction between things Dionysian and Apollonian. Like nomadic space, Dionysian space erodes divisions and hierarchies and, like agrarian space, Apollonian space creates division and hierarchy. The dialectic between the two kinds of space/memory is a variant on our trope of conflict, and a concomitant of its correlate flux. Here, the sense of flux that is necessary to any musical work is augmented by the instability that results from our changing perceptions of boundaries, those in turn the resultant of the interpenetration of our two kinds of time-space. Finally, the reaching-over at the end creates a tension between the tonic as something achieved and the tonic as something recollected, suggesting a space outside of the work's positivistic boundaries. The longing for this Edenic space brings us to the realization of the third constituent of our tropical nexus, imperfection.

5 Uncanny expressions of time in the music of Arnold Schoenberg

the clock ticked on and on, happy about being apprenticed to eternity . . .

John Ashbery: "Wakefulness"

Die Uhren stimmen nicht überein [The clocks are not in unison]

from the Diaries of Franz Kafka

Introduction

Schoenberg's generation inherits its fascination with things uncanny from the Romantics. One need not look far to find examples in German literature from the nineteenth century: the poetry of Goethe, Hölderlin, and Heine, and the prose of E. T. A. Hoffmann and the Grimm brothers provide the most conspicuous and celebrated examples, as do August Schlegel's German translations of Shakespeare (*Hamlet*, *Macbeth*, *A Midsummer Night's Dream*, and *The Tempest* all feed into Romantic visions of the uncanny). Within Schoenberg's generation, Freud becomes the supreme analyst of the uncanny, while Kafka invents its most profound examples, so much so that his name becomes synonymous with the uncanny. Schubert and Wagner must top the list of musical precursors to Schoenberg's depictions of things uncanny, but examples also can be found in Mozart, *Don Giovanni* in particular, Beethoven, and others.

The principal focus of this chapter will be on one particular development of Schoenberg's rhythmic practice. It involves the use of a steady pulse-stream, set in contrast to its immediate musical environment, and expressing a sense of altered, "uncanny" time. The practice has antecedents in Schoenberg's tonal music, in Wagner before him, and even earlier, in the music of Schubert. It reaches maturity in the atonal works beginning around 1908, developing into what we will call *time shards*; time shards continue to play a role in the twelve-tone music, though necessarily transformed by their new compositional and expressive contexts.[1] Although there are identifying markers that will allow us to trace the technique across stylistic boundaries, like all else in Schoenberg's musical language, the technique changes over time, modified in each instance to fulfill the conceptual and expressive requirements of the moment.

Within Schoenberg's musical development, uncanny time participates in the overlap of two conceptually distinct domains: his rhythmic practice writ large and his fascination with various ways of expressing or evoking the uncanny. Needless to say, uncanny time exhausts neither domain. To my knowledge, there has been no extended treatment of Schoenberg's rhythmic practice as of yet; such would be an enormously difficult undertaking, one necessarily cognizant of changes from work to work, and of the manner and degree of Schoenberg's adaptations of and departures from the rhythmic practices of his precursors and contemporaries.[2] Some general observations, however, can be made, and these will help to place the development of time shards into a larger context.

It is clear that rhythm in the early works develops principally out of the practices of Brahms and Wagner,[3] that most connections with tonal rhythms become highly attenuated during the atonal period, and that the twelve-tone works, beginning in the mid-1920s, often use rhythmic patterns that are reminiscent of earlier music. The role of the written meter in organizing the music as a perceptible constituent of musical form, varies greatly even within any given work. Nonetheless, it is safe to say that meter and its concomitant sense of regular rhythmic periodicity is generally least perceptible during the atonal period (with many clear exceptions), and that it returns as an organizing force with the advent of Schoenberg's twelve-tone technique. The emergence of time shards as an expressive constituent of the atonal works is made vivid by the general attenuation of rhythmic periodicity during that phase of Schoenberg's career. The regular pulse-stream associated with time shards stands in sharp contrast to the more elastic sense of subjective time that had become the norm.

The strangeness of passing time

Music is a temporal art whose technical vocabulary is overwhelmingly descriptive of objects extended in space. This paradox is not music's alone; difficulties attendant to musical description are shared by all modes of temporal experience. Although the elusive nature of experiential time has captured human imagination since antiquity, at the very least since Augustine's famous musings on the nature of time in his *Confessions*,[4] discourse concerned with the experience of time takes on an unprecedented centrality around the turn of the twentieth century.

Schoenberg belonged to a generation of artists and thinkers that was virtually fixated on the nature of passing time.[5] Advances in theoretical physics might be at the top of the list of a changing world-view. Einstein's theories of relativity demolished the temporal constants of a Newtonian universe. But the concepts of theoretical physics are remote from the quirks of human experience. For Schoenberg's generation, the arts and humanities defined one's sense of self. Creative literature, always a good indicator of our changing sense of self, vividly exemplified a new fascination with temporal experience. The narratives of James Joyce, Marcel Proust, Franz Kafka, and Thomas Mann are all concerned with the nature of experiential time: Joyce gives us multiple and overlapping temporal perspectives; Proust, unforeseeable infusions of things past into a fleeting present; Kafka, dream-like sequences of an ever-mysterious sense of being; and Mann, in *The Magic Mountain*, a sense of perceived time's utter relativity as temporal experience dilates or contracts the passing of the seasons, days, or even moments. The strangeness of passing time becomes important in theater as well as the novel. As we have seen, the characters in Maurice Maeterlinck's *Pelléas et Mélisande* inhabit a strangely timeless realm. August Strindberg's *Ein Traumspiel*, which explores the temporal and spatial disjunctions suggested by its title, may have had a direct influence on Schoenberg's own dream play, *Die glückliche Hand*.[6] In the visual arts we find a prismatic fracturing of time and space in the cubism of Georges Braque, Pablo Picasso, and others. Developments in cinema use editing techniques to juxtapose events that were otherwise spatially and temporally disjunct. In philosophy, the nature of experiential time becomes a central and essential aspect of the discipline's discourse. Although more abstract ideas about time had been formulated from the very beginnings of philosophy and had been in the philosophical mainstream as an *a priori* condition of human consciousness since Kant, the actual experience of passing time becomes central in the writings of Henri Bergson, Edmund Husserl, and William James.[7]

In large part, these developments in the arts and humanities are stimulated by, or at least interact with, advances in science and technology, cinema being perhaps the most vivid example. Advances in transportation and communication change our perspectives of time and space, and for the first time in human history, recordings, photographs, and motion pictures allow images and sounds to have a permanence inconceivable for earlier generations.[8]

Music too participates in this larger picture. The capacity of music for retrospection and anticipation embedded in its ongoing "now-time" had already been well developed in the nineteenth century. Time's arrow, overwhelmingly teleological in the goal-oriented harmonies of common practice tonality, had already begun to drift or seem suspended in extended passages by Wagner. Debussy takes this tendency even further as he develops "non-functional" harmonies.[9] The non-linear disruptions of psychological time, breaking off ideas without completion along with intrusion of apparent *non sequiturs,* already pervasive in Mahler, become hallmarks of early Stravinsky. And the perspectivism of Joycean narrative finds precursors in the contrapuntal juxtapositions of Stravinsky and Ives, whch fold together musical perspectives that in earlier music would necessarily have been separated by time. Needless to say, the impact of musical thought is no more self-contained than the speculations of philosophy or the narratives of fiction. Music, as the model of temporal experience *par excellence,* had a profound influence on the thought of Bergson and Husserl, as on the story-telling of Proust, Joyce, and Mann.

And so it should come as no surprise that Schoenberg's musical imagination participates in the larger concerns of his generation, to include its questioning of the nature and perception of time, time's uncanny, paradoxical attributes, and the altered senses of time that are the concomitants of altered perception in general. Musical passages that suggest an altered or uncanny sense of time range through Schoenberg's entire life's work.

Three types of uncanny musical time

My use of the word "uncanny" is adopted from the standard English translation of that untranslatable German word, *unheimlich.* I am influenced in particular by Freud's celebrated essay on the topic.[10] The essay explores a range of meanings, from benign to horrific, through which the word *heimlich* is transformed into its opposite, *unheimlich.* Things "homey" and so habitual, comfortable and safe, give rise to things private, hidden, secretive, merging *heimlich* and *unheimlich,* and then darken more and more as we move toward the *unheimlich* side of the spectrum, to the bizarre, strange, and disturbing. For Freud, the *unheimlich* emerges through the repression of events that once had been *heimlich,* either in personal or cultural memory. The repressed returns with an alienated strangeness, transformed from one side of the spectrum of meanings to the other.

By this way of understanding things *unheimlich,* time shards participate in a more encompassing context of uncanny elements within Schoenberg's works. Time shards are uncanny, at least in large part, because their regular pulse-streams evoke a ghostly presence of the way that time "used to go." As we shall see, in addition to time shards, there are two other basic techniques for producing an uncanny temporal effect. Moreover, there are ways to evoke the uncanny in music that are not strictly temporal (apart from the obvious property that all events in sounding music are temporal). In post-tonal music, musical rhetoric, motivic development, even orchestration can invoke the ghostly presence of tonal precursors. For listeners who recognize the suppressed and re-emergent ghosts, the music becomes uncanny. To one steeped in the tradition, Schoenberg's music is suffused with uncanny voices of the Austro-German tradition. It is not just a matter of influence; it is more like someone, long out of mind, coming into mind in an unexpected way. Chapter Seven will explore such effects in Schoenberg's String Trio.

Schoenberg's sense of musical time, like all else, is rooted in tonality. The homey time-keeping device of common-practice tonality is a regular pulse-stream, the underlying *tactus*, embedded in and organized by meter. Just so, the Newtonian clock of the Enlightenment can be imagined as a regular underlying pulse-stream that coordinates the temporal happenings of the universe. Whether it was consciously Newtonian or not, the temporal unfoldings of common-practice tonality are overwhelmingly controlled by an underlying *tactus*. The pulse-stream, through meter and hypermeter, is arranged into hierarchically disposed congruencies, and in that guise it anchors phrase rhythms and their constituent harmonic progressions.[11] In common practice, the disruption of the pulse-stream is one way to create a sense of the uncanny, but it is not the only way. The passage of time can also become uncanny when the sequence of temporal events contradicts normal expectations of continuity. A third means for expressing the uncanny occurs when the pulse-stream, instead of being perceived as the underlying conveyor of musical thought, draws attention to itself as signifier; although the parallel is imperfect, it is as though the cadence of speech were to become that to which we attend, rather than its semantic content. This last technique is the precursor to Schoenbergian time shards.

Before turning to a more extended discussion of time shards and their musical antecedents, it will be worthwhile to briefly consider the first two techniques in Schoenberg's precursors and in his own practice. The first technique, disruption of the pulse-stream, creates an uncanny effect in some of Beethoven's late works, as in the opening of the first movement of the String Quartet, op. 132, with its abrupt shifts of tempo and affect, or the opening of the final movement of the *Hammerklavier*, where the music seems to grope its way toward the formulation of the fugue subject, or the opening of the finale of the Ninth Symphony, in which a series of musical fragments ultimately gives way to the main theme. Such disruptions are heard as musical *aporia*, as formed by thoughts considered and then rejected. They mimic Beethoven's compositional process itself, a process of spontaneous self-censoring, of thoughts cut off midstream, of assertion and then denial. The uncanny effect is in large part due to the illusion of watching (hearing) Beethoven's musical thoughts take form before our very ears. Instead of hearing "the work composed," we hear, or have the illusion of hearing the work as it is being composed. That which should have been concealed is revealed to uncanny effect. Closer to Schoenberg's generation, Gustav

Mahler often used similar shifts of tempo and affect as basic elements of his musical rhetoric; ideas are aborted without conclusion as other ideas intrude into consciousness.

The second technique, the disruption of temporal sequence to create an uncanny effect, finds a striking example in the opening of Mozart's overture to *Don Giovanni*. Mozart begins the work by quoting music from the damnation scene, so that we hear the ghostly presence of the Commendatore's voice calling out the name "Don Giovanni" (the flutes, mm. 3–6, are derived from scene xv of the second act, the setting of the words "Don Giovanni" and "m'invitasti") *before* the Commendatore's death, and long before the series of events that ultimately lead to the damnation scene.[12] More common is the use of a musical fragment, or fragments, to recollect the past, as in the opening of the last movement of Beethoven's Ninth Symphony where the first three movements are recollected through musical fragments. Echoic recollections are a basic constituent of Schubert's songs; motives often shift from the voice to piano as the textual utterance is symbolically internalized. The technique of fragmentary recollection becomes a central aspect of Wagner's composition with leitmotivs; time and again Wagner will recollect an earlier passage through a leitmotivic fragment. One example among many in *Der Ring des Nibelungen* is the curse motive, the music that Alberich sings in the fourth scene of *Das Rheingold* as he curses the magic ring that he has stolen from the Rhinemaidens and that he has been forced to relinquish to Wotan. This music returns at critical moments throughout the Ring cycle, always recalling Alberich's curse.[13] At each recurrence, the curse not only further fulfills its promise, it also recollects its own deepening history. The technique of recollecting a whole through a fragment is important to Brahms as well; the endings of his Third Symphony and of his Clarinet Quintet use the technique to stunning effect, each recollecting and finally resolving ideas from the opening of their respective first movements – as though those thoughts, seemingly long forgotten, have remained, repressed and unsettled behind all that has since transpired.

Schoenberg's music has rhythmic aspects that develop out of both of these forms of temporal displacement. Disruptions of the pulse-stream are basic to Schoenberg's musical vocabulary in many works, often to uncanny effect. The wonderful slow movement to his Fourth String Quartet abounds with examples and the String Trio is particularly remarkable in this respect. Fragmentary recollection is also a basic technique for Schoenberg. The third movement of his Second String Quartet uses flashbacks from the first two movements that take on new meaning with the addition of the voice and Stefan George's poem about suffering, burning fever, and a longing for the release of death.[14] In the hallucinatory imagery of *Erwartung*, the ghostly emergence of Schoenberg's setting of Joseph Henry Mackay's poem *Am Wegrand*, op. 6/6, comprises an uncanny flashback to a tonal work in the context of Schoenberg's most extreme exploration of atonal flux.[15] Schoenberg's use of fragmentary recollection is fundamental to many of his works. We have already considered their force in passages from *Gurrelieder*, *Pelleas und Melisande*, and the First String Quartet (respectively in Chapters One, Three, and Four). One of Schoenberg's most powerful developments of fragmentary recollection depicts a series of flashbacks at the end of the Golden Calf scene of *Moses und Aron*, Act II, scene 3, mm. 928–66. Here Schoenberg contrapuntally combines recollections of four distinct episodes: the song of jubilation that the *Volk* sing at the prospect of building the Golden Calf (originally at II.3, m.191 and following); the young woman's motive (first heard in Act I, scene 2, as she exuberantly expresses the anticipation of Moses' arrival with news of the new God, and later leading up to the sacrifice of the virgins, Act II.3, after m. 759 and following); the music associated with the orgy of drunkenness and dancing (originally from II.3, m. 606 and following); and the music associated with abusive military might and murder (originally II.3, m. 526 and following). Through the combination of these fragmentary flashbacks, after the orgies of animal sacrifice, sexual abandon, drunkenness, murder, and human sacrifice, in the dissipation and exhaustion of the final moments of the scene, we experience a highly condensed reliving of the whole.

Precursors to time shards

Having considered temporal disruption and displacement (through anticipation or recollection), we can move on to the precursors for uncanny time shards: when a steady-state pulse-stream, instead of being perceived as the underlying conveyor of musical thought, draws attention to itself as signifier. The tonal technique that is closest to that which evolves into Schoenbergian time shards is one used by Schubert in many of his songs. "Erlkönig" provides a striking example. There the frenetic pulse-stream simultaneously mimics hoofbeats, and the anxiety of the father and his son, as time is running out. Schubert abruptly breaks off the stream in the song's final bars to signify the death of the child; only then do we hear the final line of Goethe's poem, "in seinen Armen das Kind war todt" (in his arms, the child was dead). The closing cadence, like that in so many of Schubert's songs, is not something positively achieved, as it had been from Bach through Beethoven, but something resisted that ultimately could not be avoided.[16] "Gretchen am Spinnrade" provides another superb example. There the pulse-stream simultaneously mimics the spinning-wheel and

Gretchen's emotional entrapment; Schubert disrupts the relentless pulse at key junctures within the song as Gretchen's musings distract her from her spinning; despair increases each time we fall back into the relentless spinning. Schubert's cycle *Winterreise* uses obsessive pulse-streams in many of its songs to signify restless footfall and inescapable emotional conflict. The relentless pulse of the final song, "Der Leiermann," is particularly devastating, combining mimesis of the organ grinding, of wandering without goal or termination, and of inescapable emotional entrapment.

Some of Mahler's movements capture this sense of an uncanny, signifying pulse-stream. His setting of "des Antonius von Padua Fischpredigt" ("St. Anthony of Padua's sermon to the fish") from *Des Knaben Wunderhorn*, later to become the source for the scherzo to the Second Symphony, comes to mind. Here the steady pulse-stream signifies the ongoingness of the water, the fish, and nature's relentless spinning out of time, irrespective of human concerns. The futility of the sermon, if ambiguous in the text, is made vivid by the irony of the music.

Schoenbergian time shards

Regular pulse or cadence (a word originally derived from speech patterns, but one still used to denote the rate of footfall in military music) can mimic verbal expression, and hence thought, bodily rhythms, and hence emotion, as well as the motion of physical transport, a way of getting from one place to another. The perfect cadence is a "perfected" cadence, a cadence or pulse-stream that has reached its goal; and of course, all tonal music is goal oriented; sooner or later, directed motion takes us to tonality's inevitable singularity, its final goal.

Schoenberg's time shards maintain or revert to a regular pulse-stream while suspending or altogether negating the possibility of closure (perfection). We have characterized Schubert's uncanny pulse-streams as resisting but ultimately leading to cadences that could not be avoided. In Schoenberg's uncanny time shards, the regular pulse-stream no longer anchoring the music and no longer leading to closure, becomes *unheimlich* in its new environment.

Verklärte Nacht

Passages in *Verklärte Nacht* (1899) are among the significant precursors to time shards within Schoenberg's works. The expression of altered time that emerges in the second half of the work (see Example 5.1) stands in contrast to the lyrical writing that has dominated until this point.

Example 5.1. *Verklärte Nacht*, mm. 251–4.

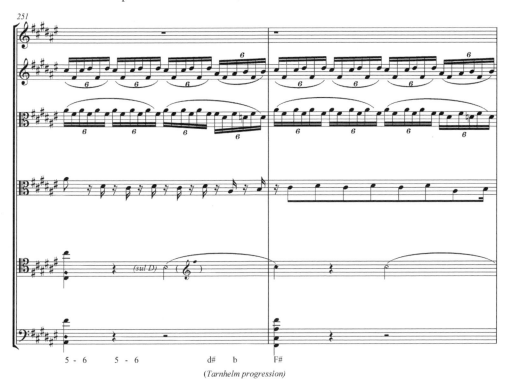

The altered sense of time and space, symbolic of *Verklärung* (transfiguration, radiance, ecstasy), is expressed through figuration whose polyphony comprises a rhythmic steady state, an intricate clockwork suspended over an F♯ pedal. The 6–5 voice leadings (in the violin II shadowed by viola II) recollect and transform the 6–5s in the work's opening motive while the continuation of the measure integrates the uncanny voice leadings of Wagner's *Tarnhelm* motive[17] – symbolically, things once seen become invisible, things invisible become seen. Once the magical space has been established, Schoenberg continues the passage by juxtaposing against this frame his lyrical themes from the first part of the work – symbolically, all that has transpired is seen in the new light of *Verklärung*. The importance of this moment is underscored at the work's ending, which recollects and further transforms this passage over a D pedal, the work's final tonic.

The expression of magical time/space in *Verklärte Nacht* is clearly indebted to Wagner, both in its general properties, and, as we have noted, in some of its specifics as well (one clear precursor is the magic fire music at the end of *Die Walküre*). Traces of a Wagnerian prototype will ramify throughout Schoenberg's expressions of uncanny time, although the branchings will become ghostlier as Schoenberg continues to evolve as a composer. From a psychological point of view, the Wagnerian trace becomes suppressed over time. In *Verklärte Nacht* however, the adaptation of Wagner is right at the surface; rather than being repressed, Wagnerian technique is utilized in a dialectic with other elements, some Brahmsian, and some distinctly Schoenbergian.

Entrückung

Schoenberg's 1903 tone poem, *Pelleas und Melisande*, is an important stage in the evolution of the composer's concerns with temporal orientations. The analysis in Chapter Three described how the compositional techniques of *Pelleas* explore the three basic temporal orientations: retrospection assigned to Golaud, anticipation to Pelléas, and an uncanny sense of dilated now-time, identified with Eros and assigned to Mélisande.

At the cusp of his second period, Schoenberg uses regularly pulsed time to express the famous *Entrückung* (transport, rapture) that opens the fourth movement of his Second String Quartet (Example 5.2a).

The global moves of the initial eight-note *Gestalt* are clear and consistent; it is transposed up a series of perfect fifths (themselves uncanny remnants of their tonal functions) moving up through the voices from lowest to highest and then hovering "at the ceiling" by alternating the final five notes of violin I (handed off to violin II) with the final five notes of the viola transposition,

Example 5.2a. Second String Quartet, *Entrückung*, mm. 1–3.

Example 5.2b. Two partitions of the *Entrückung* motive.

Example 5.2c. *Entrückung* motive, underlying whole tones, and tonal implications.

g# 7 = iv7/d#   Vb5/d#   d#7 = iv7/bb   Vb5/bb

bb7 = iv7/f   Vb5/f   f7 = iv7/c   Vb5/c

now up an octave in the first violin. As Example 5.2b shows, the motive suggests two partitions: 4 + 4, both halves sharing the same contour, <++−>, as well as 3 + 5, suggested by the first recurrent third (as G♯−B begins the initial three-note space, so F♯−A♯ begins the conclusive five-note space); the latter partition is the one developed by Schoenberg beginning at the end of m. 1.

I find that the perceptual alternation of these two partitions is a principal aspect of the passage's uncanny sense. Example 5.2c shows how the 4 + 4 partition embeds a chromatically embellished whole tone tetrachord, articulated by the first and last note of each four-note subsegment. Without the octave displacements, each whole tone tetrachord would define an overall descent − <G♯-F♯-(A♯)-E> in the first. Each whole tone tetrachord is linked to the next by a descending semitone (displaced down one octave). Thus the octave displacements transform an underlying whole tone/semitone descent into an ascent by the octave displacements within each *Entrückung* motive (the disorienting paradox, down is up, is part of the uncanny affect).[18]

Example 5.2d. *Entrückung* motive, voice-leading implications of the 3+5 partition.

to e7-b5   to b7-b5   to f#7-b5   to c#7-b5

Example 5.2c also notates the tonal implications of the 4 + 4 partitioning – functions that are made ghostly by the perceptual "interference" supplied by the opposing 3 + 5 partition.

Example 5.2d, based on the 3+5 partition, makes its underlying voice leading more explicit. The 3 + 5 voice leading reveals a chordal sequence that is at odds with the 4 + 4 reading; not only is it more Wagnerian in its syntax, most remarkably, it switches the goal harmony in each motivic statement from the beginning (successive *termini ad quem*) to the end (successive *termini a quo*), further developing ideas that spring from Schoenberg's earlier characterizations in *Pelleas und Melisande*. The flickering between the two perceptual models, 5.2c and 5.2d, is much like the well-known *Gestalt* switches in visual images like the duck-rabbit or the Necker cube. What we hear is altered by subtle changes in perceptual focus, each claiming our attention.[19] The contrasting examples also point out a methodological problem in voice-leading graphs that settle on one singular reading.

The Book of the Hanging Gardens

In choosing the fifteen poems from Stefan George's *Buch der hängenden Gärten* that he eventually set, Schoenberg omitted sixteen poems out of the complete thirty-one-poem sequence.[20] The omitted poems, the first ten and the final six, are those with the most explicit narratives. The poems that remain convey only a vague sense of the protagonist's identity and his loss of kingdom and love. A sense of veiled memory and profound loss infuses the entire cycle. I also find a curious sense of distancing, as though all of the memories are of long ago; this distancing is intensified, for me, by the purposeful choice of a woman's voice to tell a man's tale. As a result, we always stand at least one voice removed from the protagonist.

Along with the contemporaneous *Drei Klavierstücke*, op. 11, *Das Buch der hängenden Gärten* comprises Schoenberg's first exploration of atonality – Schoenberg's "pan-tonality." To be sure, a new world of expressive possibilities emerges as tonality is abandoned, but one does not abandon a language

Example 5.3a. Opening of *Unterm Schutz von dichten Blättergründen.*

that has given rise to one's entire tradition without some sense of loss. Musically speaking, Schoenberg was leaving his entire world behind. And so, it is not far-fetched to imagine that George's text had particular salience for Schoenberg in these terms alone.

The abandonment or repression of tonal functions was concomitant with the loss of the *raison d'être* of tonal rhythms. Schoenberg's post-tonal rhythmic practice(s) has been the subject of much controversy, especially in the period of the mid-1920s and beyond when Schoenberg coupled his emergent twelve-tone technique with phrase rhythms that seemed to be a throwback to those of tonality. Suffice it to say that the works beginning with *Das Buch* and continuing until World War I forged new rhythmic possibilities at the same time as they opened new ways of composing with the tones.

A consistent underlying *tactus* is largely abandoned throughout the Op. 15 cycle; in this context, those places that create a consistent pulse-stream draw attention to themselves. The first song opens as the piano, left hand alone, sets up a regular *tactus* for its first five notes, disrupting the regular stream after the second F♯. The same F♯ disrupts a tonal motion that might have led the E down to D, setting up a D major-minor tonality. We will return to this consideration shortly.

The interruption of the initial pulse-stream is heightened by the disruption of registral and contour space as the piano completes measure two with its G♯–G-natural. We begin the motive again in m. 2, and this time the breaking-off happens even earlier, the disruption of registral and contour space being further heightened. The continuation, still in the left hand alone, regains the *tactus* (at least until it dissolves in m. 6) at the expense of the original contour and grounding in D. At the end of the opening passage, the original F♯-D-F-natural motive is recollected once again, now doubled in duration, dilated in memory, and musically reinforced by doubling at the octave below.

The poem for the first song places us within a memory of the gardens, soft voices murmuring in the darkness, the play of starlight strangely taking on the visage of falling snow, the sound of fountains seeming like the expression of sorrow uttered by fabulous beasts. The climax of the poem and song, really more catastrophe than climax, happens in the final two lines. George's text understates the moment that Schoenberg takes to be the moment of catastrophe:

Kamen kerzen das gesträuch entzünden,	Candles came, illuminating (igniting) the bushes,
Weisse formen das gewässer teilen.	White forms, dividing the waters.

The word "entzünden" can be translated either as "illuminating" or as "igniting." The white forms, dividing the waters, reflect the light. The dividing of the waters is a somewhat veiled creation myth; the poetic imagery, reaching back to pre-Babylonian texts, is even older than its familiar place in the Torah. The role of creation by catastrophe has many variants; it lies at the heart of various Gnostic traditions, and is central to developments in Jewish Kabbalah as well. Within the Bible, both Jewish and Christian, catastrophic exile is the story of Adam and Eve. *The Book of the Hanging Gardens* as a whole is a story of exile and loss.

The ending of the first song, shown in Example 5.3b, integrates the fiery imagery of catastrophe into the final transformation of the opening motive. Once the singer expresses the word "Kerzen" (candles) with the descending third G♯-E♯ (itself an enharmonic repelling of A♭-F that had earlier set the words "Leiden künden" (proclaiming sorrow), the two-note motive is taken over in the piano right hand, which obsesses on the figure over the next three bars. Coincident with the marking *etwas drängend* (somewhat urgently), the piano left hand initiates a series of chords that, except for the first and last, return to the pulse-stream of the very opening.[21] The effect of these reiterated chords is like a tolling of time, itself an old trope often associated with doom.[22] As the voice utters its final text, *weisse formen das gewässer teilen*, the left hand resumes the pulse stream as it reiterates the opening motive. Now the point of disruption is revised to become the catastrophic *Kerzen* motive. This is transferred to the bass register, and the song comes to a close (or to the impossibility of closure) with the final, enigmatic right-hand chords. Are they transformed dominants pointing to the impossibility of closure in D?

The beginning of the song had broken off a progression that pointed toward D, a tonal center about which Schoenberg obsessed over his entire career. Within the imagery of Op. 15, the avoidance of closure on D is

Example 5.3b. Ending of *Unterm Schutz von dichten Blättergründen.*

symbolic of a break in what had been the rounds of nature's normal course, a rupture that had caused loss of a kingdom and of love. Understood within a larger frame of reference, D major-minor recollects the key that had been *the* central tonality for Schoenberg. D minor/major had been a highly significant key for Schoenberg: *Verklärte Nacht, Pelleas und Melisande,* and the First String Quartet had all been in D. Of course, D was a key with precedents, Beethoven's Ninth Symphony among them! D in uncanny contexts would continue to resonate throughout Schoenberg's lifetime. We will consider the emergence of this tonal center in *Vergangenes,* the second movement of the Five Orchestral Pieces, op.16 and in *Erwartung* later in this chapter, as well as in the String Trio, in Chapter Seven.

The impossibility of a cadence on D, expressed through implication and denial, remains a strong aspect of the entire Op. 15 cycle. Nowhere is this more true than at the very end of the last song. This is shown in Example 5.3c.

Schoenberg prepares the "imperfect" ending through a passage for piano alone that extends seventeen measures beyond the final vocal phrase. The final bass ascent, A to D, is concomitant with an A–B♭ voice leading, mimicking a 5–6 motion in D minor. The other chord tones fade away and we are

Example 5.3c. End of *Wir bevölkerten die adbenddüstern Lauben* (with added tonal closure).

left with only B♭ still sounding at the end of the song. I have added in brackets the resolution that is expected and denied. The bracketed B♭ returns to A via a double neighbor, bringing in the G♯ leading tone, and then all resolves to a D minor triad. The ending that is repressed, or impossible, helps to express the sense of loss that the song and cycle have been about – *"nun ist wahr das sie für immer geht"* (now it is true – that she is gone for ever).

Vergangenes

Several beautiful developments of the time shard technique are found in the second movement of the Five Orchestral Pieces, op. 16, a movement tellingly entitled "Vergangenes" (times past).[23] The movement opens with a contrapuntal motive, or motto, that is extended until the end of the third measure by the moving figure in the bass clarinet and third horn, terminating on F-natural. Heard over a D pedal, the motto suggests but does not fully confirm D minor: the harmony at the end of m. 3, D minor with added sixth and ninth, is as close to a D minor triad as we will get. As in some of the Op. 15 songs, as well as in many of Schoenberg's later works, the key of D remains a ghostly presence, never fully realized.

After the completion of the motto, a sweeping lyrical line moves through changing combinations of woodwinds. The line drifts away from D but keeps D minor-major in our ears through conspicuously placed chord tones: F and

Example 5.4a. *Vergangenes*, mm. 1–9 (texture simplified).

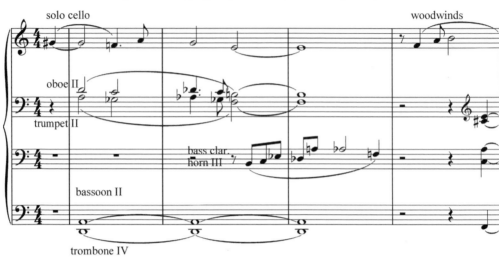

G♭ (enharmonically F♯) are the first and last notes for the initial gesture, and D is its high point; D and A are the first and last notes for the second half, and F♯ is its high point. Although the opening music has a fairly consistent underlying eighth-note pulse, the smaller gestures and color shifts are quite elastic, so the overall effect is fluid and lyrical. The first larger gesture, ten measures in all, is terminated with a fermata followed by a grand pause. The harmony sustained just before the grand pause has C♭ as its bass (in the low trombone) and A-natural in the upper line (doubled by the English horn, bassoon, and clarinet); this augmented 6th suggests a move to B♭, VI of D minor. Example 5.4b shows the music that immediately follows.

Example 5.4b. *Vergangenes*, mm. 10–19.

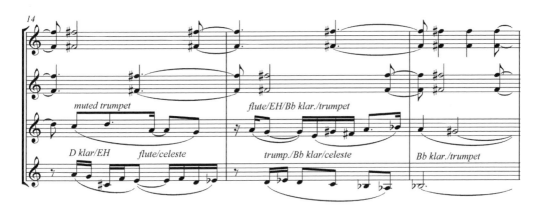

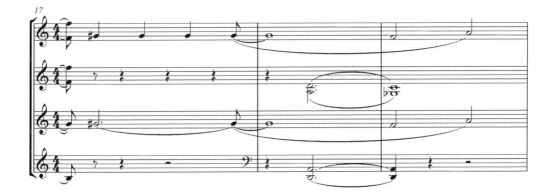

The music after the fermata is radically different from that which had preceded it. The bass register is gone; an F♯ pedal in octaves (an enharmonic fifth away from the preceding C♭ bass) is iterated through a regular pulse-stream with offset quarter-note pulses resulting from the alternation of flute/piccolo and celesta. The remaining voices, all in the higher woodwinds, are composed of short fragments of rapidly changing colors that dovetail with one another to form a *Klangfarbenmelodie* of two contrapuntal lines.[24] The opening four-note gesture in the D clarinet, reflected in mirror image by the flute, is the motivic source for many of the subsequent figures. Later in the movement, it will be significantly recollected in its exact contour, in semitones <+1–3–2>. Locally its contour is generalized <+ – –> to give rise to a surprising number of variants including the clarinet figures in mm. 12–13, the trumpet in m. 14, and the beginning of the lower line in m. 15. The combined lines convey a sense of drift, in part due to intermittent whole-tone collections, both chordal and linear, that incorporate the F♯ pedal. The most salient whole-tone line is initiated by the agogically accented notes in the D clarinet, mm. 12–13, and continued in the muted trumpet in m. 14 (G♭, E, D, C, D). After being interrupted by the continuation of m. 14, a variant of the <+ – –> contour, the whole-tone motion resumes to close the lower contrapuntal line (D, C, B♭, A♭, B♭). The sonority at the end of the shard (m. 16–17) is a whole-tone chord symmetrically disposed about G♯; G♯ continues past the end of the shard to emerge as the first note of the return of the opening motto.

The F♯ pedal, in addition to chiming time, functions like a permeable upper and lower boundary for the *Klangfarbenmelodie*; the high overtones of the flute/piccolo/flute create a kind of sound halo, a bright light that will be intensified later in the movement. A high proportion of the *Klangfarben* pitches skirt the upper and lower F♯ boundaries, coming in and out of heightened conflict with the tolling F♯s. The *Klangfarben* G-naturals in m. 10 and elsewhere are particularly salient in this respect.

The effect of the whole passage, up until the return of the motto, is a suspension, both temporal and pitch-wise. The F♯ chiming ironically doesn't seem to carry time forward: indeed it is only when the chiming breaks off and the G♯ *Hauptstimme* emerges that we sense the ongoingness of the musical narrative.

A second, even more extraordinary time shard occurs beginning at m. 47. It too forms an elaborate clockwork that spins in suspended time. As would be true of virtually any passage taken out of its context, this remarkable clockwork gains much of its power from the ways that it is prepared and subsequently developed. But even within the artificially limiting constraints of an excerpted passage from the middle of the movement, we can

Example 5.4c. *Vergangenes*, mm. 47–56.

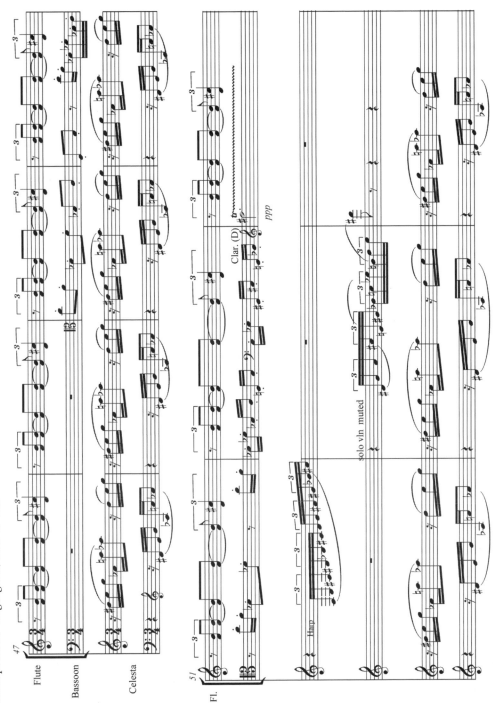

observe some of the properties that make this episode so remarkable. At its outset, the music juxtaposes two circular ostinati, one in the flutes and the other in the celesta. Each has a mechanical precision of its own, and each sustains the same rhythmic ratios and pitch relations to the other as the passage continues. And yet the drift is anything but settled. In the flutes the alternation of triplets and duples, blurred by the ligatures connecting each to each, gives the figure a slightly wobbly feel despite its mechanical regularity. The close stretto in the celesta, each loop ending with a three-note fragment from its own beginning, vaguely suggests E minor-major, but this is at odds with the flutes, especially their D-C♯ non-resolution of the F-B tritone. In the third measure, the bassoon enters with a percolating figure reminiscent of the kinds of bassoon figuration one might find in Mozart, but now wonderfully strange in its new pitch and rhythmic environment. Unlike the ongoing flute and celesta ostinati, the bassoon figure is immediately fragmented and accelerated and eventually liquidated. The harp whole-tone scale (with an added C♯, the C♯-D dyad shared with the flutes) adds another layer, one easily imagined in extension below and above its actual tones. As the passage moves towards its ultimate liquidation, Schoenberg saturates the space with a quick, successive build-up of constant sixteenth notes derived from the bassoon figure and then a layering of duples and triples at eighth-note, sixteenth-note, and thirty-second-note diminutions. The uncanny cyclical time that goes nowhere has been saturated at its interstices. Like the earlier shard, this uncanny clockwork seems in radical discontinuity with what had come before. After its moment of maximal saturation, the clockwork abruptly disappears except for fragments of the percolating bassoon motive which continue to thread through the texture, now dominated by the return of lyrical material from earlier in the movement.

Erwartung

Passages expressing uncanny time proliferate in Schoenberg's middle period, nowhere more so than in *Erwartung*. At Schoenberg's request, Marie Pappenheim created a text that was full of broken phrases, elipses, and sudden shifts, one that was well suited for the composer's musical vision.[25] *Erwartung* alternates passages of fluid, lyrical writing with segments that parse time into metronomic pulses. All of the music, both lyrical and metronomic, is broken into short fragments. The fragments overlap, intertwine, and sometimes interrelate, but more often there is a sense of intrusion or distraction. Quantitatively, the lyrical fragments dominate, but the uncanniest moments occur when time shards break in and out of the ongoing texture.

Example 5.5a. *Erwartung*, mm. 1–3, *Hauptstimmen* and "time shard" only.

At the crux of the drama is the confusion of perception and projection. We are never sure how much is hallucinated nor do we know how much, if anything, is "real."[26] The intermittent time shards play a crucial role in expressing this confusion. We hear the first glimmerings of the technique in m. 3. The passage is contrapuntal, like most in *Erwartung*.

The harp *Nebenstimme*, marked *deutlich* (clearly), along with the flute and bassoon, form one band of steady state, while the cello weakly asserts another, liminal, like something barely perceived, or overheard at a great distance. The top line of the shard participates in the voice leading that forms a vaguely heard connective thread through the first four measures. The bassoon B (m. 1) connects to the oboe's first and last pitches C♯, B♯ (mm. 2–3), and then to the flute B- B♭, harp B-C, and into the singer's chromatic neighbors about C. C is then handed to the basses to bring us to the downbeat of m. 5. A secondary voice-leading thread can be traced from the very first note in the bassoon, G♯, through the inner voice in the oboe and into the *deutlich* harp of m. 3. While the voice leading connects the shard to its environment, the sharply articulated pulse separates it. We notice the intrusion of a new kind of rhythmic space, set off from and opposed to that which has been predominant up until this moment. But at this stage of the work, the fragmentary time shard has not yet taken on a clear dramatic function.

The first prolonged time shard occurs in m. 9. Bassoons, harp, and middle strings provide the sixteenth-note ostinato while the flute *Hauptstimme* plays

Example 5.5b. *Erwartung*, mm. 6–10.

an opposed melody, one that falls into synchronicity with the ostinato just before it is cut off. The mechanical rhythm of the ostinato is vividly set off from its surroundings, an effect heightened by the overlapping pause in the voice. Pitchwise, the flute, prepared by the oboe then horn in mm. 6–8, floats about Bb/A♮ before handing its line off to the viola in m. 10. The strange pulsating sixteenth notes, however, are more of an intrusion. Just before the shard begins, the texture of m. 8 is composed of two opposing strata: the horn and trumpets versus the cellos and basses. The terminal harmony in the brass, A♯-E-A, a chordal structure that is virtually Schoenberg's musical signature,[27] remains suspended as the string stratum moves to a C minor triad in second inversion. The vocal phrase, overall, resists resolution to C minor until its final Eb, (*verwelkt*) coincides with the beginning of the shard. The shard itself is a fracturing of components of the counterpoint that has preceded it, a kind of broken mirror (a crazy surface) that oddly combines in its reflection a composite of pieces broken off from the preceding. The harp ostinato, D-G♯, forming the bass, is derived from Ab-D, the outer voices of the string sonority that lead into the C minor triad. The ostinato in the cello, F♯-G, which begins just prior to the fully-comprised shard, mirrors the G-Ab-G motion that precedes it in the bass. The first and last notes of the first trumpet line, F♯-G♯-A, give rise to the bassoon ostinato, A-F♯. The viola ostinato, C♯-E, has the most far-fetched antecedents, the composite C♯ to E across trumpet and horn. In sum, the strangely mechanical clock time of the shard transforms the living experience of all up until this point into a kind of soulless automaton. The shard, which is a true shattering, quickly liquidates in m. 10 without any sense of resolution. The text helps us to understand another aspect of its representational meaning.

Hier hinein?. . Man sieht den Weg nicht.	Here, inside? One can't see the path. .
Wie silbern die Stämme schimmern . . . wie	How silvery the tree trunks glisten. . like
Birken! . . . oh unser Garten . . . Die Blumen	birches!. . Oh, our garden . . . the flowers for
für ihn sind sicher verwelkt	him have surely withered. .

In the first part of the text, the woman seems to gaze outward toward the darkened path and the shimmering tree trunks. She then turns inward; the imagined garden whose flowers wilt represents an absence strongly felt. With the shift to internal experience, her first words, "hier hinein?," take on a secondary meaning – inside the forest, inside the fractured psyche. Just so, the time shard that interrupts the ongoing text can be heard to correlate with either the external shimmering of the birch or with some

Example 5.5c. *Erwartung*, mm. 16–19.

kind of sensation projected from within. In either case, the shard mimics a trope that Schoenberg had learned from Wagner to depict the glimmering of light. The uncanny shard is related to the transfigured moonlight of *Verklärte Nacht* as well as the setting of twilight at the opening of *Gurrelieder*. What is different here is that this glimmering is a broken off piece of time, a

Example 5.5c. (*cont.*)

shard of moonlight that has momentarily shattered the already fragmentary thoughts of a predominantly subjective space.

A similar technique gives rise to another shard in mm. 16–17.

Aber hier ist es wenigstens hell . . der Mond	But here at least it is bright . . earlier, the moon
war früher so hell . . O noch immer die Grille mit ihrem Liebeslied . .	was so bright . . Oh, as always the cricket . . . with its love song . .

The lyrical *Hauptstimme* in the violin is composed of two whole-tone dyads separated by eleven semitones: FG + EF♯. The time shard comprising the celesta ostinato (marked *sehr deutlich*) alternates major thirds at the distance of eleven semitones, CE + BD♯, and their contraction to major thirds at the perfect fifth, DF♯ + AC♯, as the upper and lower thirds move by whole tones in contrary motion. The ostinato integrates the E-F♯ dyad from the violin into an uncanny clockwork that breaks into the texture, spins going nowhere, and then, just as abruptly, breaks off. The harp *Hauptstimme*, which takes over the principal line from the violin, derives its pitch-classes from the celesta ostinato except for G and F; those had been the first dyad in the violin. The text that overlaps with the beginning of the ostinato equivocates between an outward gaze and the psychological space of recollection: "earlier the moon was so bright." As before, the shimmering time shard equivocates: is it the present brightness or the recollected moonlight?

Example 5.5d. *Erwartung*, mm. 24–6.

The shimmering in m. 17 gives way to another steady state, depicting the cricket – "oh, as always the cricket . . . with its love song" – who provides an uncanny measuring of external time, tinged by the recollection of love lost. The cricket ostinato, still in the celesta, can be conceived as a collapsed version of the preceding ostinato. The space implodes into a chromatic cluster, F-Ab alternating with F♯-G, as the whole-tone voice leading of the previous shard collapses into the semitone voice leading of the "cricket."

The first mention of the murdered beloved, imagined or otherwise, is immediately followed by the first mention of death. This in turn gives rise to the first shard that seems to depict anxiety itself.

willst du ihn nicht suchen?. . So stirb   will you not look for him?. . So die right
  doch
hier . . Wie drohend die Stille ist . .   here . . How menacing the stillness is . .

The shard is composed of two strata. The *Hauptstimme* in the flutes alternates
its recurrent G♯-B dyad with moving major sevenths (the D-E♭ at the bottom
of the first two sevenths echoes the voice's "doch hier") – is the recurrent
dyad meant as an echo of the first two notes of the piece? Flutter-tonguing
associates the flute sonority with the tremolo *am Steg* in the lower strings, the
second stratum. The strings go through their eleven-note sequence twice;
because of color, register, and density of the chords, this layer is heard as
a ghostly presence of vaguely perceived contours. A similar color sounded
briefly in m. 2 – there a naturalistic hearing would assume that the figure
paints the rustling of leaves. The ascending semitone figures so prevalent in
the upper line give rise to the vocal response, "how menacing the stillness
is." The "menace" seems most convincingly projected from within.

    Part Three of *Erwartung* begins and ends with extended time shards. The
first, mm. 91–4, once again portrays the uncanny moonlight using figuration
reminiscent of that which we have already considered. The later passage,
extending from mm. 112–23, is clearly meant to portray a state of emotional
anxiety. Just prior to this moment, the woman reaches a crisis, fearful of being
attacked by a wild beast, presumably imagined. She cries, "Kein Tier, lieber
Gott, kein Tier. ." (no beast, beloved God, no beast . . .) and then "ich habe
solche Angst . . . Liebster, mein Liebster, hilf mir. ." (I have such fear . . .
beloved, my beloved, help me . .) The shard, whose beginning overlaps with
"Liebster, hilf mir," adds layers until the passage finally comprises four strata
by the end of m. 116. Three of these strata compose the clockwork of the shard
(flute, bassoon, and strings), and the fourth, the *Hauptstimme*, more fluid
and detached by register, is heard in opposition to the rest. The *Nebenstimme*,
flutes in octaves, forms a salient and obsessive pattern that strongly projects
D minor, briefly tonicizing the dominant and then moving to the tonic; it is
supported by the sustained D in the oboes. The constant sixteenth notes in
the strings comprise a foundational layer whose beginnings are generated
out of the trills that end m. 112. Its steady state fluctuates by whole steps; of
its total ten pitches, five belong to the D minor diatonic collection and five
do not (assuming we choose either C or C♯/D♭ as diatonic but not both).
The combination of the sixteenth-note steady state and flute *Nebenstimme*
comprises the full chromatic aggregate. The bassoons add another layer,
G♭-E♭, obsessively iterating two pitch-classes shared with the sixteenth-note
ostinato, but dissonant to the D minor collection in flutes. The *Hauptstimme*,
in three octaves (piccolo, D clarinet, and B♭ trumpet) is the last voice to enter.

Example 5.5e. *Erwartung*, mm. 112–23.

Example 5.5e. (*cont.*)

Example 5.5e. (cont.)

Its first and last notes tug against the D minor collection; the initial G♯/A♭ (notated as a sharp in the upper voices and as a flat in the trumpet) enters as a blaring *ff* at odds with the prevalent As in the *Nebenstimme*; the final F♯ veers away from D minor, its pitch-class in agreement with the G♭ in the bassoon ostinato. The second and third pitches of the five-note *Hauptstimme* agree with the *Nebenstimme*'s D minor, while the penultimate C rubs against the raised leading tone of the *Nebenstimme*. Overall the passage crescendos from *pp* to *ff* and then decrescendos, dying out to *ppp*, fading to virtual silence before it is liquidated. The sum total effect is a sustained and unresolved dissonance composed of forces that assert D minor and those that deny it.

We have already noted the importance of D major/minor for Schoenberg a number of times. Within *Erwartung*, the most salient emergence of D minor through an uncanny fragment occurs at m. 411.

The passage is not a time shard, but it is an uncanny recollection of Schoenberg's song *Am Wegrand*, op. 6/6.[28] The *Erwartung* text, "Tausend Menschen ziehn vorüber . . . ich erkenne dich nicht" (A thousand people pass by . . . I don't recognize you), is a close paraphrase of the John Henry Mackay text that opens "Am Wegrand": "Tausend Menschen ziehen vorüber, den ich ersehne, er ist nicht dabei!" (A thousand people pass by, the one I long for is not among them). Apart from the text, the line that the woman sings in *Erwartung* does not recall the earlier setting. However, the orchestra, blurring her inner and outer landscape, does remember and develop music from a later passage in the song, mm. 22–3. This part of "Am Wegrand" is shown in Example 5.5g.

In *Erwartung*, the lines in the clarinet and English horn (m. 411) are derived from the vocal line of the song, whose original text was "Sehnsucht erfüllt die Bezirke des Lebens" (Longing fills life's domain). The bass clarinet and bassoons play the song's bass line, itself derived from the opening melody in the voice (op. 6/6, mm. 3–4), that which had set "Tausend Menschen ziehen vorüber . . ." Thus the remembering of "Am Wegrand" is simultaneously a misremembering, as the woman provides a countermelody not heard in the original set to a text heard elsewhere and surrounded by a sonic environment generated out of yet another passage in the lied. The uncanny and mistaken memory of "Am Wegrand" in *Erwartung* compresses, adds accretions to, and transforms the recollection.

I take our closing example from *Erwartung* from the work's last two measures, an interpenetration of chromatic and whole-tone space that forms the final liquidation of the work. If the music up until this point had comprised a crazed network of fragments – some loosely connected, others clearly disruptive – the closing measures express an ultimate dissolution. Most of the

Example 5.5f. *Erwartung*, mm. 411–13 (texture simplified).

Example 5.5f. *(cont.)*

Example 5.5g. *Am Wegrund*, mm. 22–4.

orchestra plays a sweep of chromatic scales in contrary motion, at an extremely soft dynamic level, effectively vanishing upwards and downwards simultaneously. The bassoon, bass clarinet, and string basses play a ghostly descending whole-tone scale in thirds, a pattern that had been significant in "Am Wegrand." In sum, the final shard atomizes the whole as though to capture a nightmare variant on Prospero's "Our revels now are ended: these our actors – as I foretold you – were all spirits and are melted into air, into thin air." The meaning of the last words is open ended: "Ich suchte . . .", variously translated as "I searched," "I longed for," "I tried." The verb is in the imperfect past, indicating that the seeking, longing, and struggle continue as all vanishes into nothing. What are we to make of this ultimate vanishing? Transforming the plenum of *Erwartung* into a vacuum, the final liquidation itself is perhaps the uncanniest event of all.[29]

Mondestrunken

It is difficult to speak about the rhythmic language of *Pierrot lunaire* in general terms because the twenty-one songs embody a wide diversity of rhythmic practices.[30] Some of the songs are clearly parodies – *Valse de Chopin*, *Parodie*, *Serenade*, *Heimfahrt* – and while most seem to be *sui generis*, they nonetheless integrate bits and pieces reminiscent of various tonal practices. Regular pulse-streams are used in a variety of ways, and in many cases the conceptual distinction between time shards and meter is slippery. Many of the songs nonetheless contain passages that clearly fit the criteria we have developed for discerning time shards. Nowhere is this more evident than in the first song, *Mondestrunken* (Moon-drunk).

Mondestrunken opens with a two-part ostinato in the piano and violin which will be the source for most of the musical ideas that compose the song. The violin line accompanies the more elaborate seven-note idea in the piano

Example 5.5h. *Erwartung*, final two measures (texture simplified).

Example 5.5h. (*cont.*)

Example 5.6a. Opening of *Mondestrunken*.

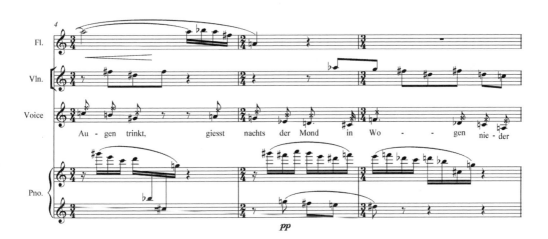

with a simple alternation of F♯ and D♯ *pizzicato*. The piano more directly expresses the imagery of the text – cascades of intoxicating moonbeams – while the violin clicks off the tick-tock of time that goes nowhere.

Den Wein, den man mit Augen trinkt,	The wine that one drinks with one's eyes,
giesst nachts der Mond in Wogen nieder	pours nightly down in waves from the moon.

As shown in Example 5.6b the underlying voice leading in the piano moves from an augmented triad, through French augmented 6th, to a fully-diminished chord. Perhaps not uncoincidentally, the underlying voice

Example 5.6b. *Mondestrunken,* implicit voice leading of the piano ostinato.

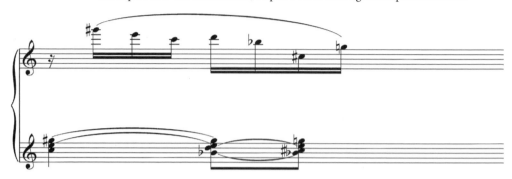

leading is quite close to a progression that occurs on the surface at the very opening of Schoenberg's *Pelleas und Melisande.* As we shall later see, this is not the only correspondence between *Mondestrunken* and *Pelleas.* The voice-leading connections to Wagner are still present, but displaced from the surface. It is interesting to compare the imagistic aspects of the *Pierrot* ostinato with the *Entrückung* motive from the Second String Quartet. In the earlier work, upward octave displacements of downward scalar motion contributed to the uncanny sense of ascent, there symbolic of the soul leaving its earthly body at the moment of death. In contrast, the *Pierrot* ostinato uses downward octave displacements to depict the wine that pours down from the moon.

The placement of the ostinato within the meter is somewhat disorienting; at first it is easy to hear the second pitch, E, as the metric downbeat, a hearing supported by the violin (the distinctive dissonances, between the piano and violin are another matter, to which we shall return). The misheard downbeats are corrected as the *Sprechstimme* accent on "Wein" reorients us. The regular eighth notes in the voice and the subsequent accent on "Augen" reconfirms the metric downbeat only to initiate an alternation of triple meter and duple meter, from m. 4 until m. 11 in which each metric downbeat is aurally recognizable. The pitch language contradicts the rhythmic fit between the piano and violin. The two parts of the ostinato share no pitch-classes, and the rhythmic coincidence between the parts of E/F♯, D/D♯, along with the closeness of F♯/G at the end of each figure, adds to the oddness of the juxtaposition. The uncanny clockwork is one whose gears mesh in strange ways, a technique we have already seen developed in *Vergangenes.*[31]

After being established through literal repetition over the first four bars, patterns recognizably derived from the ostinato dominate the texture for the rest of the song with relatively few abatements of its characteristic sixteenth-note rhythms. These brief abatements, along with the reemergence of the

Example 5.6c. *Mondestrunken*, mm. 23–8.

ostinato that inevitably follows, are among the most magical moments in the
song. The passage beginning in m. 23 is of particular interest in this respect;
mm. 23–4 comprise a time shard set off from its surrounding texture by
characteristic rhythms and pitch configurations. The ostinato reemerges
in m. 25 and then undergoes an extraordinary development over the next
measures leading up to and into the third and final stanza of the text.

  Some consideration of the structure and imagery of the poem will place
all of this into context. The Otto Erich Hartleben text (based on the French
of Albert Giraud) is divided into three four-line stanzas in all twenty-one
of the poems. And, characteristic of all of the poems, the first two lines of

the first stanza are reiterated to become the last two lines of the second; the third stanza in every text closes with another iteration of the first line. (Given these constraints the diversity among the twenty-one songs is all the more impressive.) In *Mondestrunken* the ostinato that opens the song returns intact at its original pitch level at three places: the music between the first two stanzas (with a single altered note in mm. 11,15 and 16, and a literal repetition at m. 17); the close of the second stanza (m. 25); and at the end of the song (piano, left hand m. 35–6, and in the final measure, piano, echoed by the flute). These recurrences of the ostinato thus help to articulate the poetic structure by bringing back the musical imagery of the opening at or near the end of each stanza.

The return of the opening couplet at the end of the second stanza allows us to add elements to its already fantastic imagery.[32] The wine that Pierrot drinks through his eyes is suffused with lusts, thrilling and sweet.

Gelüste, schauerlich und süss,	Lusts, thrilling and sweet,
Durchschwimmen ohne Zahl die Fluten!	Float numberless through the floodwaters!
Den Wein den man mit Augen trinkt,	The wine that one drinks with one's eyes
Giesst nachts der Mond in Wogen nieder.	Pours nightly down in waves from the moon.

The music that accompanies the first half of the stanza (not in the example) includes piano figuration very loosely adapted from the ostinato figure, exaggerated faux-lyrical gestures in the drunken violin, and an eccentric combination of fantastic trills and running figures in the flute. Setting off the return of the opening lines of text, the texture changes radically at m. 23. The duples in the piano and violin (*am Steg*) combine with the triplets in the flute to form a fantastic clockwork. The strangeness of fit that we have heard between the parts in the opening ostinato is developed and intensified here; the outer voices of the clockwork comprise a stream of intervals of either thirteen or eleven semitones. The inner voice runs through the gamut of intervals contained within.[33] It is as though the moonlight is being strangely refracted as time clicks away, yet curiously stands still. The voice, in contrast to the regularly pulsed, meter-defining eighth notes that had characterized the first setting of this text, is offset, and any aural sense of meter is suspended despite the quirky though regular pulse-stream in the instruments. Again we encounter the old trope of uncanny time, by moonlight, as Pierrot gazes in wonderment at the titillating, intoxicating moonbeams!

The reemergence of the ostinato and its subsequent development is an amazing display of compositional virtuosity. The minor thirds of the original violin figure emerge out of the violin line, at first hidden within the time shard (second half of m. 23), then set off and transposed up a semitone in the final fragment of the shard (m. 24). The figure returns to its original pitch-classes (once again *pizzicato*) in coordination with the return of the piano ostinato at m. 25. The flute echoes the piano, and the echoic pairing continues as the ostinato is transposed down through an augmented triad (based on the first three pitches of the original, and painting "*in Wogen nieder*") into m. 27. After descending through the augmented triad, the piano ostinato splits into halves, the final four notes in the piano answered by the first three in the flute as the music continues to develop the augmented triadic descent through the end of m. 28. At the same time, the violin figure also moves through an augmented triad, returning to its original pitch level in m. 27 before liquidating into the faux-arpeggio that leads into the third stanza. The juxtaposition of violin and piano at mm. 27–8 reveals a remote property of the ostinato, one that is concealed within its original strangeness of fit: an augmented triad extended from the first pitch in the violin, F-sharp, will be the same as one extended from the first pitch in the second half of the piano ostinato, originally D. Thus the compression in the piano, beginning in m. 27, traces the same augmented arpeggio as that in the violin, <F♯, D, B♭>, all of this a whole tone away from the descent of the original augmented arpeggio <G♯, E, C> and its condensation in the descent of head-motives in the flute, mm. 27–8. The two augmented arpeggios that combine to control the motion over mm. 25–8 comprise the "even" whole-tone scale. We may recall that the opening development of the *Melisande Enigma* (as discussed in Chapter Three) had used the same device.

An excursus: motivations for twelve-tone serialism

Our next series of examples will study aspects of Schoenberg's Third String Quartet, a twelve-tone work composed in 1927. We will argue that the time shard idea underlies the rhythmic language of the entire first movement of the Third Quartet, and more tentatively that the rhythmic language of all four movements develops out of a reconceptualization of time shards as they enter into an uneasy relationship with meter: cognizant of metric function in common-practice tonality, but twice removed from the earlier practice (by way of contextual atonality's turn toward serialism). That reconceptualization of time is a concomitant of the techniques of twelve-tone serialism, and a brief excursus on the cultural-historical contexts that underlie that momentous change in Schoenberg's musical technique will be apposite. For our present purposes, we will not be concerned with technical aspects of twelve-tone serialism but with historical factors that may have motivated

Schoenberg's move in that direction.[34] We will return to a more technical discussion of Schoenberg's twelve-tone serialism in Chapter Six.

The evolution of twelve-tone serialism happens precisely during the years between the two World Wars. It is a fair assumption that the ideas that transformed Schoenberg's compositional language emerged, at least in large part, in response to the pressures of the times. Schoenberg, engaged essayist that he was, gives us few clues in this direction. His claims of "greater comprehensibility" conceal much more than they reveal.[35] We will posit five interrelated factors that contributed to the new developments in compositional technique:

1. A sense of loss, compensated by a more self-conscious need to engage the tradition from which he sprung.
2. A rejection of the intuitive, quasi-mystical approach toward art that had dominated the years prior to the war.
3. A need for sure footing in turbulent times.
4. A heightened sense of craft as a core value for the artist.
5. Fulfillment of a spiritual need in the face of rising anti-Semitism.

To state the obvious, the Great War had left Europe devastated; Germany was much diminished, humiliated by the Treaty of Versailles, and the Austro-Hungarian Empire was dismantled.[36] If Europe as a whole had lost her moorings, the impact on Austria and Germany was all the more profound. An old world had been lost, and the shape of the new world to come was up for grabs. To many it was painfully apparent that the war had violently ended the great age of Viennese culture. In some fundamental ways, the Vienna of Haydn, Mozart, Beethoven, Schubert, and Brahms no longer existed. For Schoenberg, a product of cultural *Bildung* if ever there was one, this lineage had always been basic to his sense of self. The post-war period evidently made Schoenberg all the more insistent on developing connections to the past as if to compensate for this loss. Schoenberg's new approach would attempt solidarity with tradition across the gulf of an utter break with that tradition. Schoenberg rejected simple nostalgia: something new would have to be made, connected to the past, but looking toward the future. The evolution of twelve-tone serialism is grounded in this context.

The twelve-tone method was in large part a rejection of the intuitive approach that dominated the period before the war. In these years Schoenberg, along with many of his contemporaries, believed that the unconscious mind was the source of all human creativity.[37] Composition, once grounded in a strong sense of craft, could turn to a visionary mode, bypassing rational thought to access the unconscious. Among Schoenberg's works, *Erwartung* is the most extreme example of this orientation, but an introspective visionary stance is at the heart of all of his works from 1908 until the World War. The experience of the War and its aftermath might have been enough to cause Schoenberg to reconsider this stance; however, there are other factors that must have motivated him as well. The years after the Great War saw a rise in what historian Peter Gay has called "vulgar mysticism"; irrationality had taken on a darkening aspect.[38] Schoenberg was not the only intellectual to react against this threatening wave. The twelve-tone method allowed Schoenberg to veer away from cheapened mysticism and to move toward better balance of reason and intuition.

Twelve-tone serialism also allowed Schoenberg to find a way toward sure footing in turbulent times. The interwar period was notoriously volatile. The Weimar Republic in particular was a cauldron of hotly contested ideas, murderous political turmoil, Utopian hopes, hyperinflation, and fears of Armageddon. Intellectuals fiercely sought for some Archimedean point. In a period so adrift, the twelve-tone method allowed Schoenberg to have some well-defined, central idea to hold fast. The reaffirmation of compositional craft can be thought of as a partial response to this same need, a response paralleled in the visual arts most famously by the *Bauhaus* movement.[39] As with his self-conscious identification with a musical lineage, the composer's craft had always been important to Schoenberg. Yet twelve-tone composition brought the reasoned development of craft to the forefront in ways that had been sidestepped by the more intuitive approach of the pre-War years.

Anti-Semitism, which had long been part of Austro-Germanic culture (as with most of the rest of Europe as well), took a vicious turn in the years after the Great War. Germany and Austria had lost the war, it was said by anti-Semites, not because its armies had been defeated but because they had been "stabbed in the back" by the Jews.[40] Schoenberg and his family intimately experienced the hatred directed at Jews as early as 1921.[41] The year of Schoenberg's Third Quartet, 1927, also saw the publication of Hitler's *Mein Kampf*. It is impossible to untangle Schoenberg's turn toward Judaism, and toward a new sense of spirituality, from the events of those times.[42] It is not unreasonable to think that the evolution of the twelve-tone method is inseparable from Schoenberg's spiritual quest. Indeed, there are aspects of the new musical language that might be specifically identified as "Jewish." Twelve-tone serialism allowed endless permutations of one single idea to underlie all the individual ideas within a work. From a cultural-historical perspective, one could hardly imagine a better technical basis for expressing deeply held monotheism. In fact, although it is doubtful that Schoenberg ever thought of twelve-tone serialism this way, there are striking parallels between twelve-tone music and aspects of medieval Kabbalah.[43]

Third String Quartet

Schoenberg begins his program notes for the Third Quartet, op. 30, with a recollection.

> As a little boy I was tormented by a picture of a scene of a fairytale "Das Gespensterschiff," (The Ghostship) whose captain had been nailed through the head to the topmast by his rebellious crew. I am sure this was not the *program* of the first movement of the third string quartet. But it might have been, subconsciously, a very gruesome premonition which caused me to write this work, because as often as I thought about this movement, that picture came to mind.[44]

The work opens with an obsessive, even feverish sounding ostinato; on the one hand, the ostinato consistently divides the measure into equal eighth-note pulses, while on the other, its palindromic symmetry of pitch iterations (1-2-2-2-1) contradicts the normal divisions of *alla breve*.[45] Although color and registral shifts (alternating at the octave between the second violin and viola) demarcate the *alla breve* time signature, pitch associations across the measure contradict it. For example, the final C of each group wraps around to the G-E-E that follows to form a scarcely concealed C major arpeggio.[46] There is more than one way to hear the implicit voice leading which is obscured by the octave displacement of the D♯. Example 5.7b shows one possible model. An alternative hearing would emphasize the embedding of C major/C minor (D♯ as misspelled E♭); as we shall see, this hearing is attractive for several reasons. One could also posit an A minor seventh arpeggio embellished by the wayward D♯. Tonal sonorities are never too far away, but they neither coalesce nor solidify.

To better understand the role of the furtive major and minor arpeggios embedded within the ostinato, a brief consideration of the recapitulation of the principal theme at m. 239 will be useful.

Among other changes, the ostinato has been inverted, I^{G-C}, so that the earlier embedded C major arpeggio has become an embedded C minor arpeggio; as before, a modal shift is also embedded, now C minor-major rather than C major-minor.[47]

The ostinato that opens the movement is iterated twelve times before the pattern is finally altered, pitch-wise, but not rhythmically, at m. 13. The attack pattern is then maintained for another six measures, before beginning to transform. As we traverse the movement, ostinato-derived figures sometimes mitigate and other times intensify their harshness. For example, slurs and a soft dynamic level notably mollify its biting edge at the outset of the second theme group beginning at m. 62 (as at its recapitulation at m. 174).[48]

Example 5.7a. Third String Quartet, first movement, mm. 1–12.

There is an even greater relaxation of affect at the beginning of the coda; however, the uneasy undercurrent never fully dissipates until a brief but very striking passage beginning at m. 311, a point to which we shall return.

The first violin *Hauptstimme* enters in measure five. Over the next eight measures, it is composed of short, fragmentary sounding gestures of variable durations; these interact with the two-note gestures in the cello. The

Example 5.7b. A model for the implicit voice leading.

Example 5.7c. Third Quartet, first movement, mm. 239–44.

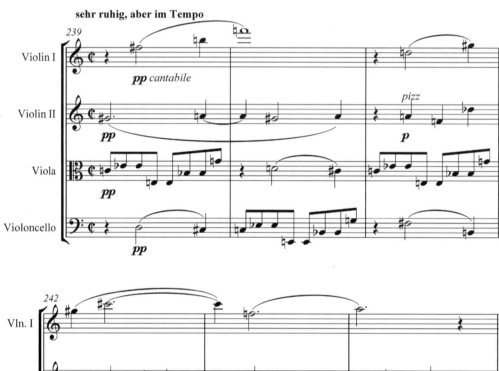

perceived *Hauptstimme* downbeats at measures 5, 7, 9 and 11 contradict the written meter, while the arrivals at measures 6, 8, 10, and 12, are in accord with the written meter. The violin gestures combine to form two four-measure phrases, while the first gesture in the cello, contradicting those symmetries, overlaps the end of the first four-measure group and the beginning of the next. Pitch and rhythm conspire to make the slow moving voices sound in conflict with the ostinato as well as with each other. The vessel of the metric unit can hardly contain its contents. After the first eighteen measures, the vessels break; there are few places in the remainder of the movement where the shards seem to coalesce into their metric frame. We should not need Schoenberg's prompting to hear this music as uncanny!

Schoenberg's short analysis of the movement emphasizes the role of the ostinato; his brief musical examples include six transformations of the ostinato and three examples of the slower moving "main voices." Although he mentions variety of "mood or character," having recollected the image from his childhood at the outset, he avoids returning to that theme. After the initial recollection, the descriptive language concentrates solely on form: intervals, transitions, main voices, subordinate themes, and the like. In light of Schoenberg's misgivings about program music – at the very least an ambivalence – we should not be surprised by his emphasis on form over content. More curious, however, is that Schoenberg omits any mention of basing the Quartet on a model, Schubert's String Quartet in A minor, D804.[49] There are so many points of contact between the two works that it would be all the more uncanny if Schoenberg was not consciously aware of the connections. He does discuss the Schubert A minor Quartet at three separate points in his *Structural Functions of Harmony* (never mentioning his own Quartet).[50] The Schoenberg Quartet is uncanny in both its internal workings, and in its relationship to the Schubert A minor Quartet. We will return to the former before considering the latter.

An insightful study of rhythmic conflict in the Third Quartet by Jeff Nichols emphasizes the opposition between perceived duple and triple groupings, one that is pervasive through the entire first movement.[51] As Nichols recognizes, the duple versus triple conflict can be heard almost as soon as the *Hauptstimme* enters the texture; measures 9 through 12 are particularly apposite in this regard.[52] Nichols' commentary on layers of triple versus duple groupings is very apt, and very much in the spirit of time shards that we have developed here.

> The stark contrast between those layers, each unyieldingly projecting its own grouping of the underlying pulse streams, subsumes the complex accents of the surface rhythms not into an ensemble meter, but into an idea: duple and triple pulse-groupings struggling for priority. The culmination of the passage shown in [the musical example] (corresponding to m. 277) does not resolve this conflict.[53]

I would only add that the evanescent shards of triple and duple meter, juxtaposed in overlapping, short-lived fragments, never really solidify into

Example 5.7d. Third String Quartet, first movement, mm. 311–23.

polymetric "layers"; the conflicted duple and triple beat groups emerge and break off in such profusion that even the conflict of triple versus duple is itself always on the verge and never fully solidified, at least not until the two potential meters are separated out forming a remarkable moment of metric clarity with the turn toward 9/4 (three threes) at m. 311.[54]

The larger context for that moment of metric clarity is the expansive coda beginning at m. 278 and continuing until the end of the movement at m. 341. Martha Hyde has noted that in composing this extended coda space, Schoenberg conspicuously departs from the Schubert model, a point to which we shall return.[55] The first thirty-eight measures of the coda (mm. 278–316) are a remarkable *Entspannung*, a palpable release of tension after all that has led up to the wrenching climax of m. 277. The climactic *ff fermata* of 277 is immediately followed by a *pp* marked *etwas langsamer*. Over the next thirteen measures (approaching the passage that begins in 9/4) the markings indicate a continual lessening of tension: *calando* at 282, *sehr ruhig* at 292, and *calando* again at 305. The coda leading up to the 9/4, all at a subdued dynamic level, also contains the movement's first markings of *dolce* beginning at m. 297.

Coda space is traditionally the place for retrospection. Examples of retrospective codas abound in Schoenberg's earlier works – the codas for *Pelleas und Melisande* and the First String Quartet are remarkable examples that we have already studied in the confines of this book. The coda for the Third Quartet is retrospective in a very particular sense in that we hear the *Entspannung* as (temporary) relief from whatever had caused the irresolvable conflict up until this point. The affect of the coda is like catching one's breath after a bout with excruciating pain. As such, it anticipates a technique that will be further developed in the String Trio where pain and relief alternate. The Third Quartet anticipates developments in the Trio in another way as well. The culmination of the *Entspannung*, the passage that begins in 9/4, is recognizably a waltz parody. The waltz is introduced by two introductory phrases, each comprising four measures of 3/4, mm. 311–12.5, and 312.5–14, mimicking the opening of countless Viennese waltzes. The waltz "proper" begins with the upbeat to 315 but then quickly unravels as the overlapping triples proliferate, *steigernd, accelerando*, intensifying and accelerating. The waltz is then negated more fully with the return of the obsessive ostinato fragments beginning with the upbeat to 321. *Tempo I* indicated at 324 returns us to the conflicts that had been relieved up until this point by the great *Entspannung* of the coda. We may recall that the coda to the First Quartet achieves a tonal clarity without precedent in the work, so suggesting a lost world antecedent to the body of the Quartet itself. The waltz fragment in the Third Quartet likewise recollects something beyond the frame of the work. The waltz fragment never settles tonally – the strictures of twelve-tone technique "forbid" that. It does settle metrically, if only for a brief while, recollecting the grounding in metric clarity from a world lost as it remembers (or evokes a memory of) the "gay Vienna" of Schoenberg's youth. The return of the ostinato negates the sustainability of that grounding and of that genre. In a very salient way, by undoing the recollective function of the coda, the close of the coda negates the viability of the coda itself.

Musical negation, the musical rhetoric of expressing something and then immediately negating that expression, had been a hallmark of Beethoven. The opening of the finale of the Ninth Symphony provides a vivid example (*Nicht diese Töne!*) as does the opening of the finale for his final String Quartet, op. 135, *Muss es sein . . . Es muss sein*. In both of these examples, the thoughts rejected lead to an affirmative conclusion. Musical negation was also basic to Schubert; however, his rejected thoughts are usually something positive, something yearned for that cannot be sustained or finally achieved. Schubert is famous for moving to idyllic key areas that are contradicted by some more pervasive "reality." For example, "Gute Nacht," the first song in *Winterreise*, set in D minor, moves to a hopeful D major as Schubert begins the final octave of Müller's text, "Will dich in Traum nicht stören . . ." (I will not disturb your dreaming . . .). D major is sustained until the repetition of the final text, "an dich hab ich gedacht" (I have thought of you), where the false F♯ in the melody – expressive of false hope – is poignantly moved down to F-natural, moving us back to the gloomy and inescapable "reality" of D minor.

Related techniques are used in Schubert's A minor Quartet. The principal theme of the first movement is composed of three phrases. The first two phrases end on a dominant (at measures 10 and 22) with the expectation of a subsequent phrase that will achieve tonic closure. The upbeat to the third phrase introduces C♯, and the phrase that follows prolongs A major until the very last moment. The cadence at m. 32 precipitately returns to A minor, a return emphasized by the *subito ff*. At its recapitulation the principal theme is foreshortened to two phrases; now the second phrase is in A major, but once again the theme precipitately returns to minor at the cadence. The work then recapitulates its subordinate theme in A major (originally in C major) and even cadences in A major before the coda restates the cadence three measures later, now in the "correct" key of A minor. At the end of the coda, we hear a final statement of the principal theme. This time there is no A major phrase. To be sure, the reintroduction of C♯, three measures before the end, hints at A major for a last time, but the final cadence is definitively in A minor. We had earlier noted the shifts of C major-minor that are embedded in Schoenberg's ostinato and its recapitulation. Within Schoenberg's Quartet, the unsustainable *Entspannung* of the coda, most deeply felt as we achieve the metric clarity of the waltz, is an even deeper connection to things Schubertian.

But the most salient connection to the Schubert is in the crucial role played by ostinati in both works. The principal theme of Schubert's Quartet

Example 5.7e. Third String Quartet, Adagio, mm. 1–3.

is gorgeous, but the most memorable aspect of the opening is the haunt-
ing ostinato itself. When it disappears we long to hear it again; when it
returns time and again, Schubert achieves the most poignant moments in
the movement. In one respect, Schoenberg gives us the negative image of
Schubert. Schubert's ostinato is bittersweet; its undercurrent gives the theme
its poignancy. Schoenberg's ostinato is biting, disruptive, and inescapable.

An undercurrent of undulating eighth notes continues to play a conspicuous role in Schubert's second and third movements, an *Andante* in C
major, and an A minor *Menuetto*. It is only with the sprightly A major finale
that the after-effects of the first movement ostinato are finally dispelled.
Schoenberg's uncanny ostinato ramifies through all four movements; sometimes it is so radically transformed that the recollected ostinato is vaguely
perceived at best, and sometimes it is more easily recognizable. The most
radical effacement of the ostinato takes place in the *Adagio* second movement. If the coda to the first movement was the most sustained *Entspannung*
within that movement, the entire slow movement functions as the *Entspannung* for the Quartet as a whole. The obsessive relentlessness of the first
movement plays no role here. The ghostly presence of the first movement
ostinato is discernible, however, in the opening statement of the movement's
principal theme.[56] The violins incorporate the ostinato pitch-classes, rear-
ranging the consecutive dyads of the ostinato into vertical harmonies; the
viola responds with a linear idea whose first five notes are the ostinato
transformed.

The opening pitches of the principal theme to the third movement (*Intermezzo*) are likewise derived from the first movement ostinato (or from the
second movement *Hauptthema*, itself derived from the ostinato).

Example 5.7f. Third String Quartet, Intermezzo, mm. 1–2.

Example 5.7g. Third String Quartet, Intermezzo, mm. 23–6.

Example 5.7h. Third String Quartet, Rondo, mm. 1–2.

Example 5.7i. Third String Quartet, Rondo, mm. 206–end.

More striking, however, are the explicit recollections of the ostinato within the movement, still ghostly perhaps, but more clearly associative with the earlier obsessive function. The passage from m. 23 to m. 26 is a case in point. The first violin of mm. 23–4 is derived from the ostinato at the recapitulation of the principal theme in the first movement. The continuation of mm. 25–6 is derived from the original ostinato.

A more remote transformation is used to generate the Rondo theme of the final movement. The five notes of the original ostinato compose the opening harmony and melody. The salient alternation of E and D♯ in the melody, separated by eleven semitones, replicates the displacement that we recall from the ostinato.

But even more so than in the *Intermezzo*, passages reminiscent of the ostinato emerge and disappear within the movement's texture. The very closing idea is extraordinary in this regard.

The violins alternate a transformation of the original ostinato with a transformation of the ostinato from the first movement recapitulation; we recognize the transformed ostinato, inflected by the shape of the finale's principal theme from which it emerges, as *unheimlich*; the problem of the first movement, signified first and foremost by the ostinato, had never been resolved. The uncanny clockwork softly runs out of time through the *ritardando* of the final measures.

Some closing thoughts

Chapters Six and Seven, centering respectively on *Moses und Aron* and the String Trio, will provide more examples of time shards, but the reader by now has a good sense of kinds of music that might apply. Our discussions of Schoenberg's time shard technique have reached back to his precursors – Schubert, Wagner, Beethoven, and others – but they have ignored his contemporaries. There are clear parallels and distinctions to be made between Schoenberg's "shards" and the motoric rhythms of Stravinsky and Bartók. Of particular interest are the ways that Schoenberg's practice interacts with that of his students, especially Webern and Berg. The time shard technique is pervasive in Webern's "atonal" music dating from 1909 until the First World War. During that period Webern makes extensive use of techniques very similar to the ones that we have described in Schoenberg's music from those years. Webern's Six Pieces for Orchestra, op. 6, Four Pieces for Violin and Piano, op. 7, Six Bagatelles for String Quartet, op. 9, and his Five Pieces for Orchestra, op. 10, all make conspicuous use of the time shard technique through juxtapositions of lyric, fluid writing with uncanny, clockwork ostinati. Alban Berg conspicuously uses his own adaptation of the technique as early as his 1912 work Five Orchestral Songs, op. 4 based on picture postcard texts of Peter Altenberg. Berg's *Wozzeck*, written after the First World War, also makes extensive use of time shards.

There remains the necessity of mapping the ramifications of time shards beyond the generations of Schoenberg and his students. The technique, either through the influence of Schoenberg directly, or indirectly through the influence of Webern, continues to evolve in the generation of composers that emerges after World War II. Passages of strange clockwork in the music of Boulez, Ligeti and others owe much to the rhythmic practices of Schoenberg (and Webern). With notable exceptions, Schoenberg scholarship over the past fifty years or so has tended to concentrate on innovations in the realm of pitch, although this neglect is beginning to be remedied. Our development of time shards is not designed to be the last word on the subject. Hopefully this discussion, like all else in this book, opens a space.

6   The tone row as the source of dramatic conflict in *Moses und Aron*

> Unsere Gesetze sind nicht allgemein bekannt, sie sind Geheimnis der kleinen
> Adelsgruppe, welche uns beherrscht. [Our laws are not generally known; they
> are the secret of the small group of nobles who rule us.]
>
> Franz Kafka, "Zur Frage der Gesetze"

> Vor dem Gesetz steht ein Türhüter. [Before the law stands a doorkeeper.]
>
> Franze Kafka, "Vor dem Gesetz"

> Nah sind wir, Herr,
> nahe und greifbar.
> [We are near, Lord,
> near and at hand.]
>
> Paul Celan, "Tenebrae"
> [translated by Michael Hamburger]

Introduction

Schoenberg's opera *Moses und Aron* constitutes one of the composer's central achievements. It is a work of great dramatic impact, rich sonic complexity, and profound spiritual and philosophical inquiry. It is also the locus for Schoenberg's most extended exploration of twelve-tone composition. After the Introduction to this chapter places the work into an historical context, our primary focus will be on the ways that conflict is built into the twelve-tone row as it induces mutually exclusive partitions of itself and then generates derived partitions that develop and interact with those primary partitions. The partitioned row forms are used to portray individuation and conflict among the opera's protagonists. They also raise questions about cognition and perception that are at the core of Schoenberg's musical expressivity. Having developed an extensive, although by no means exhaustive study of the row's properties, the penultimate section of the chapter inquires more deeply about Schoenberg's portrayal of God, Moses, and the music of the covenant within the opera's first scene.

   The roots that fed into the making of *Moses und Aron* run deep. Questions of self-knowing and spirituality are entangled in Schoenberg's musical thought from early on. *Verklärte Nacht* and *Gurrelieder* are both works about spiritual renewal, even though neither is thematically "religious." The final

movement of the Second String Quartet, setting Stefan George's text, is
explicitly about merging with the divine source of being at the moment of
death – *Ich bin ein funke nur vom heiligen feuer* (I am only a spark from the
holy fire). Indeed, it would not be far-fetched to argue that Schoenberg's
musical evolution parallels changes in his ways of grappling with matters
that are religious and philosophical in nature.[1] Schoenberg's unfinished
oratorio, *Die Jakobsleiter* (1915–17) and his play *Der biblische Weg* (1926–7)
both foreshadow and inform the religious-philosophical ideas of *Moses und
Aron*, the concerns of the play leading most directly into those of the opera.[2]
And although *Moses und Aron* reaches a summit of sorts, Schoenberg's
works explicitly concerned with Judaism or with spirituality more generally
continue up until his death – *A Survivor from Warsaw*, *Kol Nidre*, *Modern
Psalms*.

Although he was born into a Jewish family, we have no evidence that
Schoenberg received religious training. His interest in the Bible is documented in an 1891 letter to a cousin. In the letter the teenage Schoenberg
announces that while he considers himself "an unbeliever" he finds "that
nowhere in the Bible is there any nonsense . . ." on the contrary, "the Bible
gives us the foundation of all our state institutions (except the telephone
and railway)."[3] Schoenberg's 1898 conversion to Protestantism in Catholic
Austria seems not to have been based on opening up career opportunities;
although there is no evidence that he was active in the church, Schoenberg's
deep reverence for the biblical Jesus would never leave him.[4] One of the texts
that Schoenberg composed near the end of his life for his *Modern Psalms*
centers on Jesus: *Jesus war zweifellos das reinste, unschuldigste, selbstloseste,
idealistischeste Wesen, das je auf dieser Erde gewandelt hat* (Jesus was doubt-
less the purest, most innocent, most unselfish, most idealistic being that this
earth has yet produced).[5] And yet it would be a mistake to think of Schoenberg's spiritual life wholly in terms of any normative religious affiliation. His
changing religious-philosophical perspectives are influenced by an amalgam
of influences, including poets, philosophers, musicians, and others. In his
return to Judaism, one cannot overemphasize the impact of rising anti-
Semitism during the Weimar years. Even if Schoenberg had wanted to reject
his ancestral roots, the directions taken by society would have prohibited it
nonetheless.

The main work on the libretto was done in 1928, although Schoenberg had
already been thinking about the topic for some years. Schoenberg worked
on the music intermittently, from May 1930 until the completion of Act II
on March 10, 1932. Schoenberg also completed a libretto for what was to
be the opera's Act III, one final scene. Although there are some sketches for

Act III, the music was never completed. As we shall see, the status of the libretto for the final act has remained controversial.

On one level *Moses und Aron* is the retelling of a biblical story selected from events described in the book of Exodus and fancifully re-imagined by Schoenberg. In this respect, the opera participates in a long tradition of works based on biblical stories and religious themes in general. To be sure, Schoenberg's retelling of a story from the Bible is more audacious than most, yet the characters and events are all clearly recognizable variants of the biblical account. In setting a biblical topic, Schoenberg asserts or reasserts his place as a composer within a continuing compositional tradition, one that requires that it be re-formed for each successive generation.

From another perspective, *Moses und Aron*, composed on the eve of World War II, is Schoenberg's personal response to his own historical moment, a moment tempered by the growing anti-Semitism and pathological nationalism that was soon to consume so much of European civilization. The *Mattsee* incident – he and his family were asked to leave the Austrian lake resort in the summer of 1921 because Jews were no longer welcome – had very much brought the problems of anti-Semitism home for Schoenberg; it had forced him to re-evaluate his own sense of self. Much of what Schoenberg does in the years that followed is at least in part the result of this experience. Of course being required to leave a summer resort can hardly be compared to the horrors that fell to millions. Yet that experience arguably forced Schoenberg to turn outward, to recognize the growing crisis at hand, and to turn inward, to re-evaluate his religious, political, and aesthetic senses of self. As Schoenberg works out the relationships between God, Moses, Aron, and the *Volk* within the confines of his opera, he concomitantly works out his own personal relationship to events in Europe, to the religion of his birth, and most important, to the paradoxes and irresolvable conflicts of his own spiritual life, his role as a musician, and his role as a member of a community whose identity was radically redefined by the trauma of the Weimar years and those that followed. *Moses und Aron* is an opera about a people who leave behind oppression and slavery, only to stumble and suffer as they forge a new sense of self; it is no small irony that the work immediately precedes Schoenberg's emigration from Germany and Austria, a time when he, like so many emigrants, was forced to forge a new sense of self. Of course, those who were able to leave, Schoenberg included, were the luckiest remnants of Europe's Jewry.

There is yet another perspective on the work: in a sense, the whole of *Moses und Aron* is a prolonged meditation on symbolic thought – language, music, image, all the means through which we humans interact – on the power of

symbols, our need to use them, and on the inevitable misunderstandings and
even bitter conflicts that arise whenever we confront new symbolic thought
that is incommensurable with world as we have known it. *Moses und Aron*
makes thematic the paradox of communicating something new through art
or language when the perpetual tendency of art and language is to harden
into a deadening settling of the world as it already is.

The story that the opera tells, at least in its bare outlines, is summarized
easily enough. Moses, chosen by God, is compelled to be His prophet. Aron
will speak for Moses, who resists his mandate by telling God that he can think
but not speak (*Ich kann denken, aber nicht reden*). Moses meets Aron in the
desert and it immediately becomes clear that their visions are at odds. On
hearing news of this new God, the mercurial *Volk* express waves of jubilant
expectation that turn again and again to cynical mockery. Aron intercedes
for an ineffectual Moses and the first Act closes with the Israelites confirming
their new status with a triumphant march. A short interlude sings of Moses'
long absence. As Act II opens, Moses has been gone for forty days, and the
people speculate that he is dead. The Israelites lose faith; they rebel, and
build the golden calf. The long Golden Calf scene, the centerpiece of Act II,
degenerates into suicides, rapes, and murder. When Moses descends from
the mountain, the calf disappears at his wrathful command. Moses and Aron
argue at length, Moses claiming that Aron has betrayed the Idea, and Aron
insisting that the *Volk* require images to understand, indeed that Moses too
must use images: the tablets of law themselves are an image. At the end of
Act II, Moses stands alone, defeated, as he utters *O Wort, du Wort, das mir
fehlst* (O word, you word that fails me).

We have noted that although Schoenberg composed a libretto for the
work's third act, aside from some fragmentary sketches he never completed
the music. As before, the story line is easily summarized. Aron is brought on
stage in chains, and Moses, after arguing for the primacy of his idea, directs
the chains to be removed: Aron can be free if he can live, having betrayed
the idea of God. Once the chains are removed, Aron stands up and falls dead
(*Aron frei, steht auf und fällt tot um*). Just before Aron dies, Moses warns
that when the people abandon the fighting for the idea of God – *um für
den Gottesgedanken zu kämpfen* – they will always be thrown back into the
wilderness – *immer werdet ihr wieder heruntergestüzt werden . . . zurück in
die Wüste*. After Aron dies, Moses speaks his final sentence, addressed to the
Volk: *Aber in der Wüste seid ihr unüberwindlich und werdet das Ziel erreichen:
Vereinigt mit Gott* (But in the wilderness you will be insurmountable and
will reach the goal: united with God).

In his own mind Schoenberg was long convinced that he could compose
the music for the final scene. Yet despite living for almost another twenty

years after the composition of Act II, and despite composing numerous works of great scope and complexity during those years, Schoenberg was never able to compose Act III. As it became clear that the final scene would never be completed, Schoenberg considered allowing the opera to be produced without its final scene, but near the end of his life he suggested that the final scene be spoken, without music.[6]

There are essentially two schools of thought on the status of Act III. One, that Schoenberg could not complete the third act because he was at an impasse that would not permit him to go further after the close of Act II. From this point of view, Moses' final words at the end of Act II permit no continuation. A second perspective holds that the libretto for the final scene does bring some needed closure, and that it is appropriate, or even necessary for it to be spoken, with all music stripped away.[7] I myself fall into the first camp. I do not find Schoenberg's libretto for Act III to be dramatically convincing or emotionally satisfying. I believe that Schoenberg had composed himself into an impasse that would not allow continuation.

The opera has essentially four protagonists, God, Moses, Aron, and the *Volk*. The *Oxford English Dictionary* entry on "protagonist" (derived from the Greek for "first" + "actor" or "combatant") cites controversy over the appropriateness of the word being used in the plural. In *Moses und Aron*, each of the four personae has claims to be considered "first." At the end, I interpret the work as a tragedy, and place Moses as the central protagonist, but the dramatic tension among the four personae, each vying for dramatic first place, should not be underestimated.

God (actually two distinct divine emanations that stand in lieu of God, who does not appear directly) appears in only two scenes, Act I.i, and to a much more limited extent in Act I.iv. Yet God, or God's choosing of Moses, Aron, and Israel, precipitates and colors every aspect of the drama that follows. From a sonic point of view, the divine Voices comprise the first sounds that we hear, and they so form the primal versions of the twelve-tone material whose genetic traces suffuse the entire opera.

In other ways, Moses is the central and most tragic agonist, one who takes on all comers, and always ends on the losing side (Schoenberg's libretto for the third Act aside). He resists the Divine imperative in Act 1.i, only to be overwhelmed and compelled to prophecy. He resists Aron's image-laden fantasy and cannot share Aron's love for the *Volk*. His words and thoughts cannot reach the Israelites, and for Moses his incommunicable vision *is* God's promise. At the end of Act II, he is overwhelmed by both Aron and the Israelites. Schoenberg's Moses is a heroic figure, larger than life, but still a flawed human being, one who has been given a task that can neither be achieved nor abandoned. Moses' failure is inevitable and somehow necessary. The libretto for Act III contradicts all of this, and as I have said, I find that it remains unconvincing. For me, a short final scene cannot displace the dramatic weight of two full Acts.

I feel that Aron too has claims of being first among agonists, although many interpreters of the opera might not agree. Aron is Moses' link to the people, and after all, the divine covenant is not with Moses, it is with the people. Like Moses, Aron is a heroic figure who is overcome by forces beyond his control. In the long fourth scene of Act I, Aron withstands multiple waves of onslaught by the volatile Israelites, sometimes mocking, and sometime threatening. Yet, by the end of the Act, he leads them in triumph. In Schoenberg's version of the story, it is not Moses who leads the people out of bondage, it is Aron. At the beginning of Act II, with Moses gone for forty days at the mountain of revelation, and the Israelites in mounting fear, anger, and disbelief, Aron can no longer withstand the deluge of the people. In a brilliant substitution for the drowning of Pharaoh and his army by the Red Sea, Schoenberg portrays an Aron who is finally overwhelmed by the sea of people. And so he finally relents so that they may build the golden calf. When the wrathful Moses descends from the mountain, his powers augmented, he destroys the golden calf with a word. Yet Aron defends the people, and in his compassion understands not only their need of images but Moses' reliance on image as well. In Schoenberg's telling, this is what precipitates Moses' smashing of the tablets. In Act II, Aron's love for the people trumps Moses' love for his idea of God. By the end of the Act the Israelites reconfirm the covenant, as they understand it; they once again leave the stage in triumph, while Moses is left alone. Given Schoenberg's libretto for Act III, or his attempt at a libretto, it might seem patently clear that Schoenberg himself did not think of Aron as heroic, indeed, he is shown to be not worthy of life. For me, this is a principal reason why the libretto for the final scene does not ring true. At the risk of hubris, I would claim that Schoenberg misreads his own character.[8]

The Israelites too have a claim on being "protagonist," for it is they, not Moses or Aron, who must fulfill the divine prophecy. It may be uncomfortable for modern day liberal thought, but Schoenberg's *Volk* are "chosen." To be sure, they are profoundly flawed, but their collective voice is most similar to the Voice of divinity, in polyphonic richness, in overwhelming force, and in fecundity of musical invention.

Theodor Adorno raises some interesting issues concerned with the paradoxes that inhere in the making of *Moses und Aron*, and these have been central in some recent scholarship on the work. Before turning to analysis of the twelve-tone row and its principal transformations, we will consider some of Adorno's arguments.

Given its religious-philosophical theme, Adorno saw the derivation of the entire opera from a single twelve-tone row as problematic.

> The undifferentiated unity from which the ruthless process of the integration allows nothing to be exempted comes into collision with the idea of the One itself. Moses and the Dance round the Golden Calf actually speak the same language in the opera, although the latter must aim to distinguish between them. This brings us close to the source of traditionalism in Schönberg . . . In his eyes the idea of musical vocabulary as the organ of meaning was still instinctive and unquestioned.[9]

While it is true that all of the music in the opera is genetically derived from a single source, that source is neither Moses nor the Israelites: God, or God's emanation(s) begins the work and sets its musical vocabulary into motion. And yet to claim that "Moses and the Dance round the Golden Calf actually speak the same language," is more abstract than heard. The row derivations, and hence melodic and harmonic languages of the Israelites are radically different from the language of Moses – for though he speaks throughout the opera (excepting twelve notes that we will attend to later), Moses still has characteristic music that accompanies his spoken words. The Israelites embody a wealth of musical invention, and none of their principal themes are shared with Moses. On the other hand, the Israelites are able to sing the divine song of the covenant, having the polyphony that Moses necessarily lacks. We will later consider this music in some depth.

Adorno also finds problematic "the inadequate sense of authority, the shadow-side of modern individuation."

> The desire to outdo every form of subjectivity meant that he had to create a powerful, dominant self amidst all the feeble ones. An immense gulf opens up between the trans-subjective, the transcendentally valid that is linked to the Torah, on the one hand, and the free aesthetic act which created the work on the other.[10]

Gary Tomlinson, citing Adorno along similar lines, adds some supportive commentary:

> "By conjuring up the Absolute and hence making it dependent on the conjuror, Schoenberg ensured that the work could not make it real." By virtue of the attempt to represent it, the divine is brought under the aegis of the post-Enlightenment subject and thereby rendered mundane.[11]

Is the conjuror Schoenberg, Moses, Aron, or the *Volk*? Schoenberg himself is conflicted, and quite aware of the paradox in Moses' uttering *unvorstellbarer Gott* (unrepresentable God) in a context where divinity is presumably being represented. But we need to be cognizant of several factors: first, although Schoenberg identifies a composite *Voice from the Thornbush* and another composite *Six Solo Voices*, that represent divinity, there is no direct representation of *God*.[12] God is not listed in Schoenberg's *Dramatis Personae*. Second, there is a major strand of Kabbalistic thinking wherein the creation itself is a falling away from God's Absolute nature, the *Ein Sof*. And so, any knowing of God is necessarily a shattered knowing of God in exile from God's Absolute; this the famous "breaking of the vessels" of Lurianic Kabbalah, a topic to which we shall later return. It would be foolish to think that Schoenberg was learned in Jewish mysticism, his library is devoid of anything that we would recognize as Jewish studies. But it would be even more foolish to think that Schoenberg's Moses has divine consciousness. Moses in all Jewish tradition is still a man, and subject to human frailty and limitation. Schoenberg's Moses exemplifies this in spades. Moses experiences the glimmering of a light whose full intensity even he could not bear. Aron experiences a complementary glimmering – not the direct revelation of Moses, but not simply a weakened lesser light either. And we recall, once again, that the Israelites, so full of contradictions as a whole, are also the only protagonist who can sing the Divine polyphony. *Moses und Aron* does not portray the Absolute, although it arguably portrays a quest toward the absolute that by its very nature cannot succeed, nor, within the Jewish tradition, can it be abandoned. Adorno understood this.

> God, the Absolute, eludes finite beings. Where they desire to name him, because they must, they betray him. But if they keep silent about him, they acquiesce their own impotence and sin against the other, no less binding, commandment to name him.[13]

The twelve-tone row: basic properties

The entire opera is based on the standard 48 transformations of a single source row: $<A,B^\flat,E,D,E^\flat,C^\sharp,G,F,F^\sharp,G^\sharp,B,C>$.[14] Among its many structural properties, the row possesses *hexachordal inversional combinatoriality*, in other words, there is an inversion that exchanges the unordered content of the first six notes with that of the last six, a property common to most of Schoenberg's mature twelve-tone works, first named and systematically theorized by Milton Babbitt.[15] As a result, the correlated hexachords will sound like close variants of one another, providing a basis for continuity and contrast that is built into the row structure. Example 6.1 shows the pair comprising the source row and its combinatorial inversion. The combinatorial pair along with its retrogrades forms a quartet of row forms and this row-quartet, along with its twelve transpositions, constitutes the basic

Example 6.1. The source row and its combinatorial inversion.

Example 6.2. Three partitions of the source row.

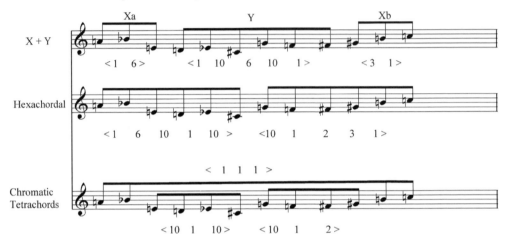

fabric of the work. David Lewin named such row-quartets "areas" and we will follow him in this, naming the source area A_0.[16] The area transpositions will range from A_0 through A_{11}; each area will be composed of four rows, each labeled with the same number as the area: for example A_0 will comprise S_0, I_0, R_0, and RI_0.[17]

Example 6.2 shows the source row partitioned in three ways, each of which is used in the opera, the first two extensively, the third, far less so, but at crucial junctures. The example also notates the ordered pitch-class intervals within the components of each partition.[18]

We can begin our discussion of the partitioned row by noting that the term itself – *partition* – is problematic, at least in describing Schoenberg's practice, despite being universally adopted in twelve-tone theory.[19] Taken from mathematics, the colloquial as well as technical meaning of the word suggests dividing a space or a collection of elements that in itself is indifferent to its divisions. We can partition a room in any way that suites our fancy or needs. Or, using the numbers 1 through 3 for an example, we can partition the set {1,2,3} into any grouping that exhausts the set without redundancies: {1}+{2,3}, or {2}+{1,3}, or {3} + {1,2}, or {1}+{2}+{3}. Without further desiderata, none of these partitions is more natural or better than any other. In the abstract, Schoenberg's twelve-tone rows can be partitioned in just the same way: the twelve elements (pitch-classes in Schoenberg's practice) in the abstract are indifferent to the ways that they might be grouped. In more concrete terms however, the intervallic sequence of a Schoenbergian row induces associations among the tones and so forms natural groupings among them; rather than being indifferent to its partitions, we can say that the order of the row suggests or generates its own internal groupings, and so induces its own natural partitions. In this sense a twelve-tone row is roughly analogous to a geological space. To be sure, geological space can be partitioned by an abstract grid, say square kilometers, but a more natural partitioning would use naturally induced criteria: oceans, mountains, rivers, changes in soil type, and the like. Differing criteria, say changes in rock or soil type versus changes in altitude, might induce mutually incompatible partitions. Just so, the tendency toward natural partitionings in Schoenberg's twelve-tone rows is complicated by mutually incompatible tendencies that inhere within the row. In this sense, Schoenberg's twelve-tone rows are "conflicted": their natural tendencies contradict one another. And yet another layer of complication arises when row forms are musically compared to one another, through counterpoint, successive placement, or by other means. Associative tendencies, hence natural partitions that might not be readily apparent in an isolated row form, can be induced by comparing two or more partitioned rows. To begin to understand these tendencies within the *Moses und Aron* row, let us consider the three partitions of Example 6.2.

The musical cogency of these partitions will become more apparent once we compare row forms that associate through the partitionings (one such association is the combinatorial property shown in Example 6.1), but we can begin by noting inducements that are more readily perceived without comparing row forms. The first partition, identified as "X+Y" after David Lewin, is the first to be developed by Schoenberg in the context of the opera.[20] X+Y divides the row into an "inner" hexachord, comprising an ordered pitch-class interval palindrome $<1–10–6–10–1>$, and two "outer" trichords, which have distinct intervallic profiles, but which share interval $<1>$. The second partition divides the row into two hexachords, comprising the first six and the last six notes of the row. Each ordered hexachord contains a chromatic dyad plus a chromatic tetrachord; the ordering, dyad-tetrachord-tetrachord-dyad suggests another palindrome induced by intervallic content: $<<A B^\flat> <E,D,E^\flat,C^\sharp> <G,F,F^\sharp,G^\sharp> <B,C>>$, in ordered pitch-class intervals, $<<1><10,1,10><10,1,10><1>>$. The third partitioning divides the row into three chromatic tetrachords, associating the first and last dyads, as X+Y had associated the first and last trichords. It too

Example 6.3. X+Y partitions of the source row and the retrograde of its combinatorial inversion.

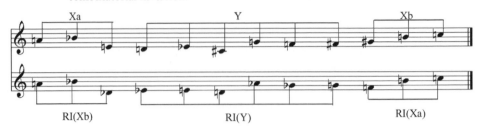

has palindromic implications. The three partitionings are mutually exclusive in that each violates the inducements of the others. For example, one cannot maintain X+Y while asserting either of the other partitions.

X + Y

Having noted the three basic partitions, we can begin to understand how they engage row forms comparatively and how those row associations become expressive constituents of the opera. Example 6.3 shows two rows, the source row in the X+Y partition, and the retrograde of its combinatorial inversion, also partitioned X+Y. The labels, <Xa, Y, Xb> and <RI(Xb), RI(Y), RI(Xa)>, reflect the twelve-tone operation that moves one form onto the other, but these labels are rather remote from a perceptual point of view.[21]

Comparing the two rows, we note that the ordered X-components have a very close fit. We can easily hear the first three notes of the bottom row <A,B♭, D♭> as a variant of the first three of the top row <A,B♭,E>; the same can be said of the last three notes in each row. The abstract labels – Xa compared to RI(Xb) and Xb compared to RI(Xa) do not capture this quality, in fact they contradict it, asserting that the first trichord in the top row associates with the last trichord in the bottom row, etc. The confusion of labels, which parallels a confusion of cognition and perception, is even more apparent when comparing the two Y-components. The transpositional relationship between the two is readily heard, while the (transposed) retrograde inversional relationship is extraordinarily difficult to perceive, a difficulty compounded by the readily recognized transposition. However, it is not so much that either choice, "retrograde inversion" or "transposition," is wrong, but rather that neither is an adequate name for the musical relationship. We might paraphrase the musical conundrum to claim "that which cannot be adequately named cannot be adequately conveyed (through language)," a thought that brings us into the realm of musical signification, representation, and the role of the X+Y partition in the opera.

Example 6.4. Mm. 11–13 (texture simplified).

Moses und Aron begins with a scene loosely based on the story of the burning bush (Exodus, Chapter 3). We will consider dramatic import of the scene more carefully later. For now we need only recognize two crucial aspects: first, that it is the moment of Moses' revelation, his direct confrontation with Divinity and the altered, augmented consciousness that goes along with that experience; and second, that this leads directly to Moses' call to prophecy. These two aspects of the scene give rise to the central dramatic idea of the entire opera, an irresolvable dilemma centering on Moses. On the one hand, Moses cannot deny his call to prophecy: it is a Divine imperative that he cannot resist. On the other hand, Moses cannot communicate his vision to Aron, and through Aron to the people – the final words of the second act that we have already noted (*O Wort, du Wort, das mir fehlt!*) summarize his tragic situation.[22]

Schoenberg portrays the mystery of Divinity at the very opening of the opera through music derived from the row forms shown in Example 6.3. We will study that passage in due course, but for our present purposes it will be helpful to go a short way into the first scene, where things clarify a bit, and where the music more closely parallels the row relations that we have studied in Example 6.3. This is the passage where the Divine Voice speaks and sings in *words* for the first time in the opera.[23] The music is shown in Example 6.4.

The musical texture is divided into two primary strata: harmonic trichords that are sung, and linear ideas that are instrumental. The example omits a third stratum, the speaking choir, which adds another layer of complexity; we will address this aspect later (in Example 6.29) so that for now we might concentrate on aspects of the partitioning. The two linear ideas form a miniature canon, the *comes* imitating the *dux* one measure later and two octaves, plus a semitone higher. Both lines share the same rhythmic shape and pitch-contour. As a result, an attendant listener, Moses we may presume, will surely hear the transpositional relationship. As in our abstract example, we can reasonably say that without a deeper understanding of the passage, the retrograde inversional relationship will elude us (of course, a tone-deaf response, based on matrix study rather than listening, might argue otherwise). Perhaps the complexity eludes Moses as well – this we cannot know for sure. The strata of vocal trichords is also divided into two voices, the women's and men's trichords: *Lege die Schuhe ab: Bist weit genug gegang(en)* . . . (lay your shoes aside: you have gone far enough . . .). Each vocal layer comprises two chords; using Example 6.3 as our reference, we can note that the women's chords are derived from Xa-Xb, and the men's chords from RI(Xa-Xb). All four chords are bounded by an eleven-semitone interval (a major seventh); both progressions share the same voice leading in their lowest and highest notes: the upper line goes A to B, and the lower, B♭ to C. The inner voices for the vocal chords are distinct however, E to G♯ in the women's voices, and D♭ to F in the men's voices. As a result, the two-chord progression in the men's voices sounds like a close variant of the two-chord progression in the women's voices; we associate the first chord of each with first of the other, and the same is true for second chords. The inversional palindrome, *Schuhe ab* mirrored by *Bist weit ge-*, and *Lege die* mirrored by *–nug gengan-*, is not only much more difficult to perceive, but as is the case with the linear ideas (the Y-components), the more difficult perception is efficiently blocked by the more ready one. One more aspect of the X+Y partition is worth noting: the X-chords are suitable for laconic statements while the linear Y-component has the potential for a more lyrical style. This distinction within the Divine Voice is further developed over the first scene. It may also be applied to Moses and Aron, the former more laconic, the latter more lyrical in his nature. A similar distinction gives rise to separable attributes of the folk.

Hexachordal partition

Having considered some basic aspects of the X+Y partition, we can move on to the second of our "naturally induced" partitions, the division of the row into ordered hexachords. Example 6.5 compares the same row pair that we studied in Example 6.3, only now partitioned into conjunct hexachords.

As before, we can note that the first two notes and last two notes of the compared rows are identical. The hexachordal partition undermines the interval palindrome of the Y-component, while revealing a new set of relationships

Example 6.5. Hexachordal partition of source row and the retrograde of its combinatorial inversion.

Example 6.6. The *Hauptstimmen*, Act I, scene 1, mm. 71–8.

among the "inner" tetrachords. The pitch-classes $<$E,D,E$^\flat$,D$^\flat>$ in the source row, and $<$D$^\flat$, E$^\flat$, E, D$>$ in the retrograde inverted row are permutations of one another. The same ordinal permutation relates the remaining inner tetrachords, $<$G,F,F$^\sharp$,G$^\sharp>$ and $<$A$^\flat$,F$^\sharp$,G,F$>$. In both cases, if we number the ordinal positions in the source tetrachord $<1,2,3,4>$, the related tetrachord in the retrograde inversion becomes $<4,3,1,2>$. Thought of in terms of an anagram (with no relation to the drama at hand!), we can name the transformation STOP-POST, moving the inner tetrachords of S to RI, or POST-STOP, moving the inner tetrachords of RI to S.[24] As a whole, each ordered hexachord sounds like a close variant of its associate. As in the rows in comparative X+Y relations, the aurally cogent relationships are not well addressed by the twelve-tone operation, transposed retrograde inversion; indeed, once again the aurally cogent relationships distract us from hearing the retrograde inversion.

Example 6.6 shows the *Hauptstimmen* for the passage beginning in m. 71 of the first scene, the first extensive and consistent development of the hexachordal partition. The full contrapuntal texture of this passage comprises one of the most complex passages in the entire opera. It is fair to say that an attentive listener will be overwhelmed by its musical and textual density; in terms of the drama, we may assume that the same holds true for Moses. Moses remains silent throughout the passage and for the rest of the first scene. The words set through this music essentially comprise Schoenberg's version of the convenant between God and Israel. They are omitted in the example because the textual underlay requires the passage's polyphony to be fully represented. The *Hauptstimmen*, shared by instruments and voices begins with the words *Dieses Volk ist auserwählt vor allen Völkern, das Volk des einzigen Gottes zu sein* . . . (These people are chosen above all peoples, to be the people of the one God . . .). The same music with a closely related text is uniquely recapitulated three times in the course of the opera, although it is never again sung by the Divine Voice.[25] We will return to these aspects later; for now, it will suffice to say that the passage has substantial dramatic and structural weight.

The hexachords in Example 6.6, one per measure, are labeled according to their row derivation: Sa and Sb are respectively the first and second hexachord in the source row, Ia and Ib the first and second hexachord in the combinatorial inversion, and so forth. Over the eight-measure passage, we hear all eight hexachords of the combinatorial quartet – Sa-Sb, Ia-Ib, RSa-RSb, and RIa-RIb – but no two row segments are presented successively. Instead Schoenberg juxtaposes hexachordal pairs that share the relations we have studied in Example 6.5. The first four measures use the hexachord pairs that share opening dyads – first C-B, then A-B$^\flat$. The last four measures use the hexachord pairs that share closing dyads, B-C and B$^\flat$-A. The remaining notes undergo a series of POST-STOP or STOP-POST permutations, the tetrachordal relations that we noted more abstractly in Example 6.5. The whole eight-measure passage is articulated into two symmetrical halves by a registral shift, coincident with the change of clef. This aspect of the symmetry is reinforced by the two by two measure construction of each half (all of this is obscured, however, when we hear the full contrapuntal texture). Much more obscure is the inversional pitch-class palindrome that extends over the whole passage: put another way, the pitch-classes that comprise the final four measures of the passage are the (combinatorial) retrograde inversion of those that comprise the first half. Extended palindromes of any sort are difficult to perceive, and this rather abstract inversional pitch-class palindrome is further obscured by rhythms and registral dispositions that contradict the large-scale mirror. Nonetheless, the eight-measure passage comprises an elaboration on the palindromic structures that have been pervasive, if elusive, throughout the scene. All in all, the music of the covenant continues to develop and intensify the perceptual difficulties between "appearance and reality" (in musical terms, the difference between more readily perceived relations and underlying twelve-tone structure) that have been inherent throughout the scene. The hexachordal partition, as used in the covenant music, portrays a more lyrical aspect of Divinity, along the lines of our observations about the laconic and lyrical in X+Y.

Chromatic tetrachord partition

The third of our "naturally induced" partitions in Example 6.2 divides the row into three chromatic tetrachords by coupling the "outer" dyads, $<<A,B^\flat><B,C>>$ in the source row, and by maintaining the "inner" tetrachords that we have studied in the hexachordal partition. The chromatic tetrachord partition is used very sparingly in *Moses und Aron*, but it does signal a series of crucial events within the opera. The partition first emerges during the massive fourth scene of Act I, in conjunction with the three signs that God has shown Moses so that Moses may persuade the elders of Israel and lead them out of Egypt (Exodus, Chapter 4): the transformation of Moses' staff into a serpent; of his hand into a leprous hand; and of water into blood. In the biblical narrative Moses, as instructed by God, instructs Aaron, and then Aaron speaking for Moses performs the signs, thus convincing the people (Exodus, 4.28–31). Schoenberg's version of these events departs substantially from the Bible. During the first part of the scene, Moses and Aron try to communicate Moses' vision without the signs; the people react with volatile emotional swings from celebration, to fear, to ridicule. Through all of this Moses is particularly ineffectual and by m. 623, almost two hundred measures into the scene, he is ready to admit defeat – *Allmächtiger, meine Kraft ist zu Ende: mein Gedanke ist machtlos in Arons Wort!* (Almighty, my strength is at end: my thought is powerless in Aron's word!). In response, the Divine Voice, absent since the end of the first scene, returns. The Voice sings one word, *Aron!*, after which Aron takes command, performing the first of the three signs.[26] (The music, which we will consider later, is shown in Example 6.17.) Although the chromatic tetrachord partition is not fully realized until the third sign, the transformation of water into blood, there are glimmerings of the partition associated with the first two signs. Example 6.7 shows the music just prior to the manifestation of the first sign, the transformation of the staff into a serpent: *Dieser Stab führt euch* (This staff leads you).

The music, set in A_{11}, is a hybrid of the X+Y partition and the chromatic tetrachord partition. The upper woodwinds and strings play the chromatic tetrachord derived from the first and last dyads of the row, Aron sings the Y-component of S_{11}, and the lower woodwinds play the remaining pitches

Example 6.7. Act I, scene 4, mm. 642–4.

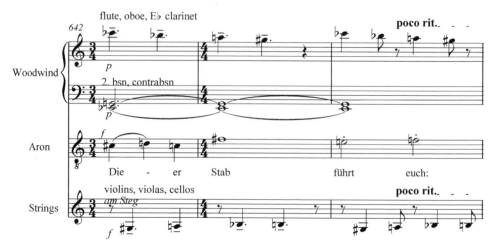

Example 6.8. Chromatic tetrachordal partition of Area 8.

in the aggregate. Because we have heard X+Y in many instances before this moment, and because the chromatic tetrachord partition has not yet been fully formed, the Y-component, along with its musical associations, is most salient. It expresses the Divine source of the sign, and Aron's connection, however imperfect, with that source.

Glimmerings of the chromatic tetrachordal partition emerge and submerge as the scene continues until the partition is fully realized in the portrayal of the third sign. The music that depicts the transformation of water into blood begins in A_8. Example 6.8 shows the chromatic tetrachord partition applied to RS_8 and its combinatorial inversion, I_8. Example 6.9 shows the beginning of the musical passage that portrays the pouring of water transformed into blood.

The partition divides A_8 into three chromatic tetrachords: if placed into descending order, $\{A^\flat \ldots F\}+\{E \ldots D^\flat\}+\{C \ldots A\}$. These are labeled respectively a, b, and c in Example 6.8. As noted in our discussion of the hexachordal partition, the order of the inner tetrachords, "b" and "c," maps STOP-POST. The pitch relations work in conjunction with extraordinary orchestration – combining string harmonics with piano, celesta, harp, and upper woodwinds – to depict the transformation of water-into-blood. In

Example 6.9. Act I, mm. 870–2.

their overall descent, the high, bright colors mimic the flowing liquid, glistening in the sunlight. The chromatic tetrachords are voiced as consecutive harmonic dyads. The "a" component, in the flutes (doubled by the harp), alternates A♭/G and G♭/F. The "b" and then "c" components are at first shared between the high strings (doubled by piano) and oboe and clarinet (doubled

Example 6.10. Chromatic tetrachord partition of Areas 10, 6, and 2.

by celesta), E/D to E$^\flat$/D$^\flat$ and then C/B$^\flat$ to B/A. The second iteration of "b" then "c" – piano to celesta, then celesta to harp – takes advantage of the STOP-POST property, in reversing the order of dyads. The closing piano dyads G$^\flat$/F to A$^\flat$/G (mm. 871–2) form another "a" component, this rhythmically divided by the harp-harp "c" component. Schoenberg continues to develop the chromatic tetrachord partition over the next seven measures, all depicting the imagery of water-into-blood.

The most extraordinary development of the chromatic tetrachord partition occurs during Act II in the music that depicts the elders imploring Aron to relent and allow the people to construct the golden calf. The passage takes advantage of an abstract property which assures that any twelve-tone row partitioned into chromatic tetrachords will hold those tetrachords invariant (in varied ordinal permutations) as the row is transposed by four or eight semitones, or when it is inverted and transposed by four or eight semitones. Thus, the chromatic tetrachord partition can be used to interrelate A_{0-4-8}, A_{1-5-9}, A_{2-6-10}, and A_{3-7-11}, partitioning the forty-eight row forms into four trios of combinatorial quartets. Schoenberg does not systematically explore all of these relations, but he does conspicuously apply the partition to A_{2-6-10} in a passage (Act II.ii, mm. 167–71) that depicts the climax of the crisis that directly precipitates the building of the golden calf. Moses' failure aside, this is the central calamity of the opera. The entire first part of Act II, builds up until this moment, depicting the gathering anxiety and discontent surrounding Moses' long absence. Within the passage the elders plead with Aron "*Aron, hilf uns, gib nach!*" (Aron, help us, relent!). Example 6.10 shows the partition applied to A_{10-6-2}, comparing RS and I forms. Example 6.11 shows the musical passage.

Example 6.11. Act II, scene 2, mm. 166–70.

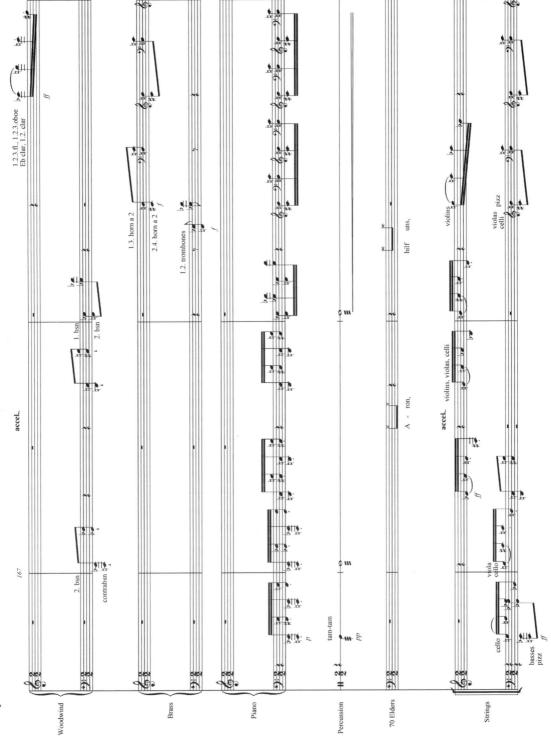

Example 6.11. (*cont.*)

Before moving on to the musical passage, we should note some of the most salient aspects of the A_{2-6-10} partitioning. The partition permutes the three (unordered) tetrachords labeled a, b, and c, as noted in Example 6.11. As before, moving from RS to I within each area holds the outer dyads invariant, and permutes the inner tetrachords by the POST-STOP transformation. An additional property, one that is highlighted in the actual passage, induces each RS-form to share one *ordered* "inner tetrachord" with one I-form. Thus, "a" within RS_6 has the same order as "a" within I_2, "b" within RS_2 has the same order as "b" within I_{10}, and "c" within RS_{10} has the same order as "c" within I_6 (all of which is equivalent to saying that those comparative S and I forms map their first inner tetrachords onto their retrogrades, yet another interesting palindromic property of the row).

As row forms break down into aggregate-forming shards of chromatic tetrachords, Schoenberg uses the dizzying profusion of relations combined with a shattering of row integrity to depict the societal breakdown that precipitates the creation of the golden calf. The functional *Hauptstimme* for the beginning of the passage is in the strings, first in the celli and then adding higher strings over mm. 167–8. At the end of m. 168, the sequence is continued in the upper woodwinds, and then completed by the violins in the first beat of m. 169. The ordered tetrachords for the entire sequence are precisely those three that are shared between an RS and I form: in the order of their appearance, $RS_6a=I_2a$, $RS_{10}c=I_6c$, and $RS_2b=I_{10}b$. The piano over the same measures, doubled by the basses and bassoons, voices the tetrachords as pairs of harmonic dyads. The first tetrachord is $RS_2b=I_{10}b$; the second piano tetrachord uses another property where $RS_6c=I_{10}$;[27] the music continues with $RS_2b=I_{10}b$, and $RS_{10}c=I_6c$. Although all three tetrachord types are present (a, b, and c), thus assuring a twelve-tone aggregate, and though each ordered tetrachord equivocates between two row forms, no complete row is to be found. Of course, it would be far-fetched to assert that this profusion of quickly unfolding relationships is perceptually available; this as well as the continuation of the passage is more readily heard as an extraordinary breakdown in the fabric of the work.

The second half of the passage begins with the second beat of m. 169. The brass (trumpets and horns at first) descends through chromatic tetrachords, $<B^\flat$-A-$A^\flat$-G$>$ in the upper voice, $<G^\flat$-F-E-$E^\flat>$ in the inner voice, and $<$D-$C^\sharp$-C-B$>$ in the lower voice, each tetrachord derived from the "outer dyads" of the A_{10-6-2} group. This pattern is reiterated five times, with octave shifts, taking us through the third beat of m. 171. The resultant cascade of augmented triads forms a distinctive harmonic color found nowhere else in the opera (although compare the benediction to the convenant music as discussed in Examples 6.32 and 6.33). The remaining voices, piano doubled

by upper woodwinds and violins, also form harmonies of augmented triads. These are voiced so that each group of four sixteenth notes comprises
the alternation of augmented trichords at thirteen semitones, with each
four-note sequence moving onto the adjacent group by inversion across the
combinatorial axis. As in the cascades of brass chords, the pitches in the
remaining voices are derived from the outer dyads of the A_{10-6-2} group; only
here they are arranged so that the first two notes of S_{10-6-2} or RI_{10-6-2} invert
onto the first two notes of I_{10-6-2} or RS_{10-6-2}. It is interesting to note that the
resultant hexachords, are of type [014589], the hexachord that Schoenberg
would "discover" only much later in his career, the so-called *Wunderreihe*.[28]
Broader augmented chords in the woodwinds, strings, and piano, sound
along with the final chromatic cascade to bring the passage to its conclusion. As we have seen, Schoenberg uses the chromatic tetrachord partition
in the first act to portray the three transformational signs. Those signs are
symbolic of the people's need for things visible. In the second act, the more
fully realized potential of the chromatic tetrachord partition is used to signal
the building of the golden calf, a degraded version of things visible.

Odd/even partition

Moses introduces a new partition in the second scene that will be adapted and
developed by Aron to become the source of the music most characteristic of
him. We will name that partition "odd/even." Given an ordinal numbering
of 1 through 12 for any row, the odd/even partition divides the row into
"odd" and "even" numbers.[29] The odd/even partition is an example of a
partition whose musical interest is derived in large part from its comparative
relations with a more primary partition, in this case X+Y. Odd/even emerges
in the second part of the second scene, in conjunction with the first dialogue
between Moses and Aron. As before, we will begin with an abstract example
and then move on to the musical passage.

Example 6.12 shows the odd/even partition applied to I_4, the first row-
form to be so partitioned in the opera. The odd and even hexachords are
divided into odd and even trichords, labeled "o_4a," "o_4b," "e_4a," and "e_4b."
The example compares the odd/even partitioning of I_4 to its combinatorial
inversion, S_4, as well as to the source row, S_0, both of which are partitioned
into X+Y.

We will first compare the odd/even components of I_4 with the X+Y
components of S_0. The comparison includes a strongly induced relation
between X-components of S_0 and o_4a and e_4a: o_4a is a circular permutation
of Xa, while e_4a shares <B-C> with Xb. The comparison of Y-components is
weaker because there is only one held adjacency, although the combination

Example 6.12. Comparison of odd/even partition of I4 with X+Y partitions of S0 and S4.

of o_4b and e_4b (equivalent to the second hexachord of I_4) holds five notes of its six notes in common with Y_0. We can also note in passing that e_4b could be spelled as a $C^\sharp$ major triad; this property is not initially emphasized, but it becomes salient once Aron usurps the odd/even partition. The comparison of odd/even (I_4) with X+Y (S_4) reveals a different set of relations. o_4a shares $<\text{A-B}^\flat>$ with Yb, o_4b shares $<\text{F}^\sharp\text{-G}>$ with Ya; in a similar way, the even trichords each share two pitch-classes with an X-chord, e_4a with Xb and e_4b with Xa. In sum, the odd/even partition relates I_4 to X+Y of S_0 or S_4 by inducing structures that can be recognized as compositional variants of the X+Y components.

Example 6.13 shows Act I, scene 2, mm. 124–9, the first usage of odd/even. Aron sings the text, *Du Sohn meiner Väter, schickt dich mir der grosse Gott?* (You, son of my fathers, does great God send you to me?), while Moses speaks, *Du Sohn meines Vaters, Bruder des Geistes, aus dem der Einzige sprechen will: Vernimm mich und ihn; und sage was du verstehst* (You, son of my father, brother of spirit, through whom the One will speak: hear me and Him, and say what you understand). The opening dialogue, more a confrontation than a dialogue, sets the tone for the whole scene, indeed for the relationship between the brothers throughout the opera. Aron sings of "fathers" in the plural; he is thinking of the patriarchs, and so of their lineage, folk Israel. Moses uses the singular genitive, which can be paraphrased in English as "my father's son." Since the two are biological brothers, I take his primary meaning to refer to their natural father, although it is also possible to imagine that Moses refers to a heavenly Father (an image more at home in the Christian

Example 6.13. Act I, scene 2, mm. 124–9.

Example 6.13. (*cont.*)

tradition than in Judaism). In either case, the folk, implicit in Aron's formulation, are not implied by Moses. Moses cares for God and his mandate;
to be sure, this involves the folk, but they are not his central concern. Aron
cares for the folk, and for God because He will care for the folk. The brothers
seem to care for each other only in that each needs the other to fulfill his
own destiny. The brothers are opposed in their ideas and the musical texture
vividly reflects this conflict.

The passage is composed of three contrapuntal networks. Moses is represented by the trombone, basses, and, of course, by his speaking voice.
Aron is represented by his lyrical singing voice. A third stratum, composed
of the piccolo, flutes, and harp, is derived from the "desert music" of the
first part of the scene.[30] The fragments of desert music use a hexachordal
subpartition, first in A_0 and then in A_4. For our present purposes it will
suffice to say that its texture and color are at odds with the other voices.
Aron sings a linear row-form, S_4. Linear presentations of the row are relatively rare in *Moses und Aron* and it is even more extraordinary in that Aron
continues, beyond the excerpt in Example 6.13, to sing a linear presentation
of the entire combinatorial row-quartet (A_4), $<S_4\text{-}I_4\text{-}RS_4\text{-}I_4>$ comprising
mm. 124–45.[31] Aron's song is phrased so that the Y-component of the row

is articulated as such: the first trichord of Y sets *Väter*, and the second sets *schickt dich mir*. The only variant from the original Y-contour is that the central tritone (or six-semitone interval) descends where as in the original it ascended. The entrance of the trombone and basses at the upbeat to m. 124 is a striking change in timbre, register and dynamic level. Although trombones and basses had played a significant role in the first scene, the twenty-five measures of music that precede this moment in the second scene are predominantly in the treble register, with flute and violins dominating the orchestral timbre; the dynamic levels are *piano* and *pianissimo*. The *forte* trombone and basses at m. 124 use an odd/even partition of the first hexachord of I_4: o_4a in the trombone, and e_4a in the basses. As we have seen in Example 6.12, o_4a is a circular permutation of Xa in S_0, while e_4a is a close variant of X_0b.[32] Thus, the Moses-associated instruments effectively recall the events of scene 1, but do so through a row area (A_4) that will almost immediately become associated with Aron. The odd/even partition of I_4 is interrupted by Aron's entrance, and by the desert music of mm. 125–6. Odd/even of I_4 continues when the trombone and basses return at the end of m. 126, the trombone playing o_4b, and the basses e_4b. This is the music that accompanies Moses' text beginning with *Du Sohn meines Vaters*. Now the musical associations are with Aron's ongoing tone row, and in particular with the Y-component that sets Aron's *Väter*. The $F^\sharp$-G in the trombone echoes the first pitches of *Väter*, and the low F in the basses (127) associates with the trombone's register to complete the mimesis of Aron's Yb. The initial order of attacks in the trombone and basses, $<F^\sharp$-$A^\flat$-$G>$, cutting across the odd/even components, comprise Yb in I_4, and this too interacts with Aron's Y-component. After Moses says *Vernimm mich und ihn*, the opening odd/even components of I_4 return, now in the tuba and basses. Once again, the associations harken back to the opening of the first scene.

Aron's first development of the odd/even partition begins at m. 148, after Aron has completed his linear presentation of the combinatorial quartet. After some transitional developments of the desert music, Aron's new theme modulates to A_7, beginning with statements of S_7 and I_7. Example 6.14 shows the partitioned rows. Example 6.15 shows the actual passage, where Aron transforms Moses' terse ideas into a lyrical outpouring.

Aron: Gebilde der höchsten Phantasie,wie dankt sie dir's dass du sie reizest zu bilden.	*Aron*: Creation of highest fantasy, how grateful it is that you rouse it to form.
Moses: Kein Bild kann dir ein Bild geben vom Unvorstellbaren.	*Moses*: No image can give you an image of the inconceivable.

Example 6.14. Odd/even partitions of S7 and RI7.

Example 6.15. Act I, scene 2, mm. 148–52.

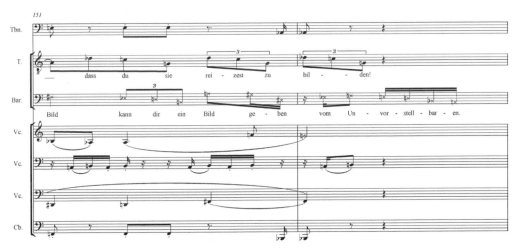

The passage is composed of three interacting strata. The odd/even partition of S_7 and RI_7 is shared between Aron (who sings the "even" notes) and the third celli (who play the "odd" notes). A second stratum, not partitioned by odd/even, divides row forms between the first and second celli, first I_7 then R_7. A third stratum comprises Moses' reaction to Aron and includes instruments associated with Moses, the trombone and basses. For our purposes we will concentrate mainly on Aron's odd/even partition.

Aron's melody takes advantage of several aspects of the abstract partitioning that become salient in the passage. Four out of the six odd/even components derived from the two row forms contain adjacencies of ordered pitch-class interval 11, and so have the potential to be voiced as descending minor seconds; in the actual music these will sound like appoggiaturas, chromatic upper neighbors embellishing a more fundamental structure. The two remaining components – e_7b and o_7a – can be spelled as triads, respectively minor and major. The source row, as well as its hexachordal and X+Y partitions, is without contiguous triads; triadic structures derived from odd/even become salient aspects of the music associated with Aron.

Aron's song, using the "even" components, takes advantage of the close fit between the partition and the gestures of chromatic tonality. His singing of *Gebilde der höchsten Phantasie* outlines an F minor triad (inflected by an A-natural appoggiatura) and then a C minor triad. To be sure, the contrapuntal voices complicate the situation: tonal gestures are virtually always contradicted by other elements in Schoenberg's quirky musical textures. As the melody continues, each descending semitone is voiced to sound like an appoggiatura, a potential we noted in the abstract case. Aron's song is never far away from Wagnerian chromaticisms: *wie dankt sie dir's* inflects F major as *Gebilde der* had inflected F minor, and the remainder of the melody inflects the C-G fifth, which eventually gets its third in the cello at m. 152. Each of the "even" trichords in Aron's song is recognizable as a variant of a single *Gestalt*. The shape of *Gebilde der . . .* undergoes variation in *höchsten Phantasie, wie dankt sie dir's*, and the thrice-iterated *Gestalt* of *dass du sie reizest zu bilden!* It is as though the transforming *Gestalt* itself spins out the idea of *Gebilde der höchsten Phantasie*. The even components, in the lowest cello line, comprise the outlines of a theme that Aron will make more explicit beginning at m. 163, *Auserwähltes Volk* (Chosen people), the most highly ramified of all of Aron's themes.

Moses' reaction, *Kein Bild kann dir ein Bild geben vom Unvorstellbaren*, continues the confrontational dialogue that has been an ongoing development since Moses' entry at m. 126. The confrontation continues through m. 162 as Aron develops his theme of *höchsten Phantasie*, and Moses counters each of Aron's ideas with his own, more severe vision. Aron's singing of

Auserwähltes Volk opens a new thematic area, while continuing to develop the odd/even partition; this is the first time where Moses does not interrupt Aron. The music that opens this section is shown in Example 6.16.

Auserwähltes Volk, einen einzigen Gott   Chosen people, one single God, to love
    ewig zu lieben . . .   eternally

Aron's melody, doubled in the celli and lower woodwinds, is composed of the "odd" components of S_7 (*Auserwähltes Volk*), then RI_7 (*einen einzigen Gott*), and then I_7 (*ewig zu lieben*). The upper woodwinds complement the melody, playing the "even" components of those rows. The remaining strings add another layer, primarily based on the hexachordal partition, subdivided into conjunct trichords. These voices play the combinatorial inversions of the principal voices, thus forming the sequence I_7-R_7-S_7 over the excerpted passage. The exception to this is in mm.164–5, where the basses, doubled by piano and harp, play the "even" partition of RI_7; this is derived from the melody that had set *wie dankt sie dir's dass du sie reizest zu bilden* (mm. 151–3).

    Aron's melody is beautifully crafted, once again interweaving reminiscences of chromatic tonality throughout. The ascent through *Auserwähltes* traces a half-diminished chord (B inflecting B♭), which collapses into a full diminished chord as D moves down to C♯. As we have seen in our analysis of Schoenberg's *Pelleas und Melisande*, in an earlier period Schoenberg had borrowed these sonorities from Wagner to express longing and sexual desire. Here the love is of another sort, although Aron's word choice in a previous phrase, *reizest zu bilden* (you rouse it to form), implies a sensual aspect – the verb *reizen* can be variously translated as to stimulate, excite, lure, entice, or tempt. Of course, the power of *Eros* will become fully manifest in the second act's scene centering around the golden calf.

    The first vocal ascent in Aron's melody targets the F♯ that sets *Volk*, moving the opening E up a whole step (plus an octave). The next vocal phrase, *einen einzigen Gott*, uses the same boundary of pitch-classes, now E in the upper register, and F♯ as before, associating *Gott* with *Volk*. The melody for *einen einzigen Gott* traces an E major arpeggio, and then B minor (inflected by B major). *Ewig zu lieben* begins with a pitch inversion of *Auserwählt* and then changes register, moving into Aron's highest tessitura for the setting of *lieben*. The reversal of the semitone motion, from descending *appoggiature* to ascending, leading tone-like structures, beautifully expresses a sense of longing, once again incorporating an old semiotic code into Aron's newly evolving musical language.

    The *Auserwähltes Volk* melody becomes a central theme as the opera progresses. Its first remarkable return is at the moment when Aron, summoned

Example 6.16. Act I, scene 2, mm. 163–8.

Example 6.17. Act I, scene 4, mm. 630–3.

by the Divine Voice, takes command from a faltering Moses to produce the three signs that will convince the people of Moses' call to prophecy. We had briefly noted this passage in our discussion of the chromatic tetrachord partition.

The Divine Voice, singing the single word *Aron!*, is derived from m. 59 in the first scene where the original text is *Aron soll dein Mund sein!* (Aron will be your mouth!). The Voice (six solo voices with orchestral doublings) sings the X-chords in S_8 and I_8, set in the women's and men's voices respectively. The Y-components are fractured, or incomplete and shared among the basses, celli, timpani and tuba.[33] Aron's exclamation "*Schweige!*" (Silence!) is not addressed to the Divine Voice, but to Moses, who has just admitted defeat. During the music immediately leading up to the Divine utterance, the score indicates that Aron is to move menacingly toward Moses, arms raised and fists clenched. The pitches that set "*Schweige!*" are contiguous in either R_8 or RI_8, but they do not fit into the surrounding partitions; they are thus disruptive from a serial perspective, and they certainly have that impact, irrespective of recognizing the underlying serial procedures. Aron's next words, "*Das Wort bin ich und die Tat!*" (I am the word and the deed!), modulate to S_{11}, using the "odd" hexachord in the *Auserwähltes Volk* contour. The complementary S_{11} "even" hexachord is in the violins. A_{11} will remain stable over the next thirteen measures, concluding with the passage where Aron sings "*Dieser Stab führt euch*" set to Y_{11}, in conjunction with the first glimmerings of the chromatic tetrachord partition, the music that we considered in Example 6.7. Thus, the shattering of Y at m. 630 and its reemergence just as the staff is about to be transformed into a serpent (m. 642–4) is part of a dramatic process. One might assert a local continuity between the Y-fragments in 630–1 <E^b-D-E>-<E^b-$C^\sharp$-D> and the E^b-D motion in Aron's *Wort bin ich*, however, juxtaposed against the X-chords and Y-fragments of A_8, the odd/even partition of S_{11} seems more to disrupt than to continue the Divine partition. On the other hand, the new row area allows Aron's high note to be B^b, the same pitch that had previously been the highpoint of "*ewig zu lieben.*" Toward the end of the excerpt, the horns play the ordered trichords of S_{11}, a partitioning that is further developed in the following measures.

Fragments of the *Auserwähltes Volk* melody return several additional times during the remainder of the first Act, becoming particularly conspicuous toward the end of the Act where they form an orchestral ostinato in accompaniment to the final chorus of the *Volk*.[34] The final chorus is set in A_7, the same "key" as Aron's original formulation of *Auserwähltes Volk*. The first Act ends with the *Auserwähltes Volk* hexachord as *Hauptstimme* in the trombones and tuba, so that it is the last thing we hear just before the curtain goes down. The most poignant development of *Auserwähltes Volk* takes place in the fifth and final scene of Act II, after Moses has descended from the mountain, and after he made the golden calf vanish, showing magical powers far beyond the sort that failed him in Act I.[35]

Ordered tetrachord partition

We now turn to another partition initiated by Moses, dividing the row into its contiguous tetrachords. The ordered tetrachord partition is clearly secondary in the opera: there are very few passages that it controls and these are short-lived. The partition, although not without structural integrity, is weaker in its natural inducement than X+Y or the hexachordal partition, and its relative scarcity within the work combines with its weaker natural inducement so that it is perceived as a disruption of the more naturally induced partitions rather than a generating source for musical developments. Yet the partition structures two very conspicuous events within the opera, both associated with Moses. Its first appearance coincides with Moses' first words in scene 1, the first words that we hear in the opera. Its second

Example 6.18. Ordered tetrachord partition of RI1 and S10 and embedded Y-component of S0.

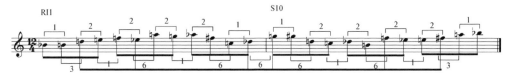

conspicuous appearance is in scene two, coincident with the first and only time in the entire opera that Moses is given the option to sing.

Example 6.18 shows the abstract structure underlying mm. 8–10 of the first scene, the ordered tetrachord partition applied to RI_1 and S_{10}. The partitioning into 4+4+4 is arithmetically simple and so arguably induced on those grounds alone. While the inducement through the intervallic structure of the series is not as strong as X+Y or the hexachordal partition, there are, nonetheless, some associative properties worth noting. The example divides each tetrachord into two dyads, and by the upper brackets shows the interval class palindrome that is induced between the pitch-classes internal to those dyads: $<<1><2>><<2><2>><<2><1>>$. The lower series of brackets shows the interval classes that connect the dyads one to another. Here there is an overall palindrome across the two forms, as would be true of any RI+S, but there is no palindrome within a single row. The example also shows an embedded Y_0 across the two rows.[36] The embedded Y_0 is far-fetched in the abstract but, as we shall see, it is quite salient in Schoenberg's realization. On the other hand, the remaining palindromic interval structures are obscured in the actual music. No reasonable perceptual modeling of the passage could assert that these properties are heard, even by the most attentive listener. The passage is shown in Example 6.19.

As we have already noted, Moses' words here are the first words to be spoken or sung in the opera.[37] The words *Einziger, ewiger, allgegenwärtige, unsichtbarer und unvorstellbarer Gott!* ("One, eternal, omnipresent, invisible, and unrepresentable God!") comprise a list of attributes that characterize Moses' perception of Divinity, at least so far as words can characterize that which cannot be characterized (*unvorstellbarer Gott!*). We will consider this list of attributes more fully later in our study of Moses' unfolding character. For now, we will concentrate on the voicing of the partitioned row forms, and their interaction with the spoken words.

Moses' words interact with an unlikely quartet of English horn, tuba, viola, and cello. Their four-part harmony punctuates the list of attributes, coinciding with the first syllable of the first three, and then offset as the list concludes, *unsichtbarer und unvorstellbarer Gott!* The tetrachords are

Example 6.19. Act I, scene 1, mm. 8–10.

derived from the partitioned rows that we considered in Example 6.18. However, the connections among the tetrachords are based on voice leading rather than on the interval class symmetries that underlie the abstract example; as a result, the conjunct dyads, which are the basis of the $<<1><2>><<2><2>><<2><1>>$ interval class palindrome in the abstract, are not consistently voiced in the actual passage. Thus, the underlying potential for symmetry is negated by Moses' formulation. The most salient voice, aside from Moses' speaking voice, is the English horn, whose line is equivalent to Y_0. Its pitch contour, $<+1,-2,+6,-2,+1>$, is the same

Example 6.20. Ordered tetrachord partition of I2 and S2.

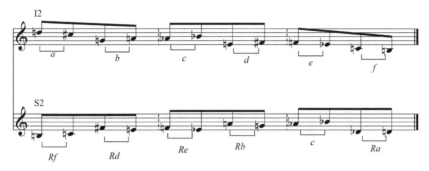

as that which accompanies the Divine Voice X-chords in the music that immediately follows, the passage we studied in Example 6.4. The bars that precede as well as those that immediately follow Moses' words are in A_0 partitioned almost exclusively by X+Y. In this sense, the music that accompanies Moses' words is disruptive: the tetrachords are a "misfit" that disrupt the musical textures that surround them. On the other hand, the Y_0 motive as presented in the music *prior* to Moses' words has not yet achieved the contour that will become its most characteristic contour throughout the opera. Moses speaks the first words, and his music forms the first normative Y-contour, even though it is extracted from row forms that are not equivalent to the serial quartet associated with the composite Divine Voice (henceforth Voice), A_0. The Voice responds in turn with more words, and with the continuation and further development of that Y-contour, now "properly" placed within the X+Y partition of A_0.

Moses returns to the ordered tetrachord partition in scene 2 to form the only passage in the entire opera where he is permitted to sing. Example 6.20 shows the serial derivation.

Moses, doubled by the string basses, will sing a linear form of I_2 partitioned into ordered tetrachords. His accompaniment will be composed of harmonies derived from an ordered tetrachord partition of the combinatorial inversion, S_2. Example 6.20 labels the dyadic components of I_2, *a* through *f*, and shows how those dyads are permuted in S_2. We can note that in contrast to the inner tetrachords of the hexachordal partition (or the chromatic tetrachord partition) with their characteristic POST-STOP or STOP-POST mappings, the ordered tetrachords distribute the dyadic components among them so that while the conjunct dyads are preserved, no dyadic coupling is preserved within an ordered tetrachord. So, for example, the first tetrachord of I_2 shares one dyad with the second tetrachord of S_2 and one with the third tetrachord of S_2. Moreover, the inversionally related tetrachords, those that will be directly juxtaposed in the music, share no

Example 6.21a. Act I, scene 2, mm. 208–14.

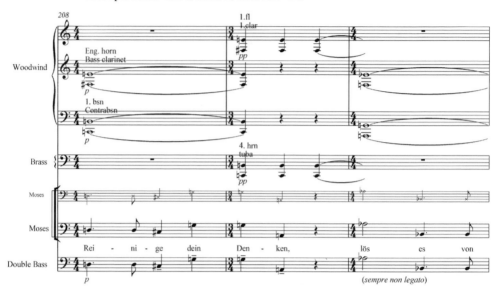

Example 6.21b. *Reinige dein Denken* contour, intervals, and embedded interval palindromes.

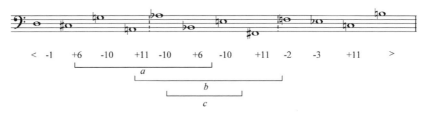

pitch-classes; this is not trivial in that the second ordered tetrachord cuts across the hexachordal division.

Example 6.21a shows the musical passage derived from the abstractions of Example 6.20.

Apart from the interludes of "desert music," the scene has been textured up until this point either by music and text initiated by Aron, to which Moses responds, speaking over and against Aron, or by music that Aron sings alone, uninterrupted. The passage beginning at m. 208 breaks the pattern; now Moses initiates the idea. Of course, the most salient disruption in the ongoing texture is that Moses *sings*. Moses' words are a stern correction to Aron's sensibility: *Reinige dein Denken, lös es von Wertlosem, weihe es Wahrem . . .* ("Purify your thought, sever it from worthless things, consecrate it to truth . . ."). The partition into ordered tetrachords is strongly projected. Each I_2 tetrachord sets a syntactic unit separated by a comma, and each S_2 tetrachord, in the woodwinds and brass, coincides with its combinatorial inversion. The dyadic permutations, salient in the abstract, are not particularly emphasized, although some are used to create continuities between the chords and the vocal line. For example, the G-A dyad of *dein Denken* becomes the lower part of the chord that follows in m. 210, while the upper dyad of that same chord, F-E♭, connects with the setting of *weihe* that follows it. On the other hand, connections among the remaining dyads are weakly projected. For example, although the D-C♯ dyad of *Reinige* is embedded in the chord of mm. 213–14, it would be dubious at best to assert that that relationship is musically cogent.

The conflict that is central to Moses' character is embedded in his melody in interesting ways. Example 6.21b extracts Moses' line from its context, supplies pitch intervals, and brackets three embedded palindromes, two of which contradict one another as well as the tetrachordal partitioning (*a* and *b*), while the third (*c*, a subsegment of *b*) coincides with the partitioning, which we have seen to be textual as well as chordal. The *a* palindrome might have been extended back to the first note, D, and continued past E by adding a descending semitone, E♭: $<-1,+6,-10,+11,-10,+6,(-1)>$. This of course

Example 6.21c. *Reinige dein Denken* pitches arranged in ascending order, with intervals.

would have disrupted the linear row-form. The actual continuation, F♯-F, induces the *b* palindrome, whose pitch-class contents coincide with an inverted Y-component, at the expense of negating the *a* palindrome, and in conflict with the ongoing tetrachordal partition. Finally, the continuation of the closing tetrachord supplies the "missing" E♭ that might have extended the first palindrome but which breaks off the second palindrome, and undercuts palindromic structuring for the remainder of the line. Thus, the partition and voicing of Moses' line highlight tensions that are built into the twelve-tone source row. There is yet another hidden symmetry in the registral placement of the notes.

Example 6.21c arranges the pitches of Moses' tone row into an ascending order so that the whole inverts about D/E♭, its pitch center. As with the other concealed symmetries, only a glimmering of this is perceptually available: the G-A dyad of *dein Denken* is symmetrically disposed against the A♭-B♭ dyad of *lös es*, properties that are obscured and contradicted by the partition and textual syntax. In sum, Moses' ordered tetrachord partition is fraught with internal contradictions, it conceals at least as much as it reveals, and it disrupts more than it connects.

Partitions of the *Volk*: *Bringt ihr Erhöhrung*

So far, we have described three "naturally induced" partitions (X+Y, hexachordal, and chromatic tetrachordal), plus two partitions that derive their musical integrity through comparison with naturally induced partitions (odd/even, and ordered tetrachords). X+Y is first associated with Divinity and then transferred variously to Moses, Aron, and the Israelites. The hexachordal partition is also initiated by the Voice and then transferred to Aron and the Israelites. The ordered tetrachord partition is rarely used and strongly associated with Moses. The odd/even partition is first associated with Moses and then becomes typical of Aron. And the chromatic tetrachord partition is first associated with Aron and then with the Israelites. We have not yet studied a partition that first emerges out of the *Volk*. Because of the extraordinary diversity of partitions that they initiate, the music of the *Volk* cannot be easily characterized, apart from its volatility, diversity, and seemingly inexhaustible inventiveness.

Example 6.22. *Bringt/Bleib* partition applied to members of A2.

The Israelites as portrayed by Schoenberg are extremely variable in mass, and unstable in temperament. At times we know them as individuals, each of whom has his or her own characteristic musical rhythms, textures, colors, and row partitionings. Examples include the idealistic young woman and young man of Act I.iii, both of whom return to die tragically in Act II.iii; the nay-saying Priest of Act I.iv; and individuals who come to the fore in Act II.iii: the pathetic invalid, and the powerful and murderous Ephraimite. At other times the Israelites form smaller groups of varying sizes and temperaments: examples include the beggars, twelve to sixteen in number, the twelve tribal leaders who follow the Ephraimite, and the four sacrificial virgins, all part of Act II.iii; as with individuals, each group has its own characteristic music, and hence characteristic partitionings. And yet at other times the folk react as a whole, seeming like a force of nature, capable of forming a deluge of overwhelming power in their collective mass. The emotional range of the folk as a whole is matched by an astonishing range of row partitions that interact with the other musical variables.

A comprehensive catalogue of *Volk* partitions would be out of place in the context of this study, and we will make no attempt here at developing a comprehensive list.[38] Instead we will limit this part of our study to two partitions, with a passing nod to a third which interacts with the second. Both of our partitions involve the larger mass of the folk. The first of these is associated with the music that begins Act I, scene 4. The opening word of the text, *Bringt ihr Erhöhrung* (Do you bring exaltation), will supply us with a name for the underlying partition.

Unlike the other partitions that we have studied so far, *Bringt* cuts across two row forms from the same combinatorial quartet: S+RI, RI+S, I+RS, or RS+I. Example 6.22 shows *Bringt* applied to $I_2 + R_2$, $S_2 + RI_2$ and $R_2 + I_2$, the row pairs that the Israelites will sing at the beginning of Act I.iv. We can conceptualize the respective partitioned rows as comprising an antecedent and consequent. *Bringt* antecedent partitions its row into ordinal numbers <1,2,6,8,9,12> and its complement. *Bringt* consequent partitions its row into ordinal numbers <1,2,3,8,10,12> and its complement. In Example 6.22 the *Bringt* hexachords are denoted by stem direction, and each hexachord is divided into its beamed trichordal components.

The I_2+R_2 pair is shown in the top staff. The trichords in the antecedent are labeled $a + b$ and $c + d$. All four of the I_2 *Bringt* trichords share their ordered pitch-class segment with either an X-chord (*a*, *b*, and *d*) or a trichord comprising half of a Y-component (*c*): *a*, <D,D♭,B♭> is the opening X-chord in R_2; *b*, <G♭,F,C♭> is the opening X-chord in I_6; *c*, <G,A,G♯>, is the second Y-trichord in I_5 or R_6; and *d*, <E,E♭,C>, is the opening X-chord in R_4. Thus, the I_2 *Bringt* antecedent is a fanciful recombining of X and Y-components into two, new linear hexachords. The R_2 *Bringt* consequent permutes and recombines the same trichords: *a* is repeated literally; *b* and *d* undergo the same ordinal permutation as they move to *b′* and *d′* (<123> to <213>)[39]; and *c* undergoes a circular permutation as it moves to *c′* (<123> to <312>). In sum, the consequent is readily heard as a close variant of the antecedent, holding all of its trichord-types, but reordering them in ways that are no longer contiguous in any linear row form.

The S_2+RI_2 pair, on the second staff, is the combinatorial inversion of the first pair. With appropriate substitutions for row identities, all of the properties that apply in the first *Bringt* antecedent-consequent will apply in its inversion.

The third pair, R_2+I_2, reverses the row order of the first pair, to form a close variant of that pair, a kind of ABA′ structure through the three phrases. The properties that associate any combinatorial pairing of I and R are distributed through the *Bringt* antecedents composed of I_2 compared to R_2. I_2 *a* is transformed into R_2 *w* by moving <D-D♭-B♭> onto <D-D♭-A>; I_2 *b* is transformed into R_2 *x*, <G♭-F-C♭> into <F-E-C♭>, and so forth. The move from R_2 antecedent to I_2 consequent does not preserve and permute the trichords as in the first two pairs; instead the trichords undergo different sorts of transformations: *w* to *w′* preserves the opening dyad and moves A to G; *y* to *y′* also involves a substitution, now G to A, and permutes the remaining dyad; *x* to *x′* and *z* to *z′* both maintain their final pitch-class, while moving the remaining pitches in a semitone *wedge* outward (in *x* to *x′*) or in a semitone *wedge* inward (in *z* to *z′*).[40] We have earlier studied a passage where Aron sets the words *Gebilde der höchsten Phantasie* using the odd/even partition (Example 6.15). Aron's words might well have described the fanciful transformations of the source row that characterize the *Bringt* pairs as developed by the *Volk*. As we shall see, later developments of the *Bringt* partition make that association more vivid.

Bringt ihr Erhöhrung,	Do you bring exultation,
Botschaft des neuen Gottes?	tidings of the new God?
Schickt er als Führer euch	Does He send you to us
uns zu neuer Hoffnung?	to bring us new hope?
Gern wollen wir ihm Geld, Gut	Gladly will we offer Him
und Leben opfern!	money, goodness, and life!

Act I.iii depicts the hopes and fears of the Israelites as they anticipate the arrival of Moses and Aron, who cross the desert toward them. Scene 4 opens with a song of jubilation just as they arrive. Set beginning in I_2, the row that had earlier set *Reinige dein Denken*, Schoenberg most likely thought of the reference (perceptually obscure) with great irony. Example 6.23 shows the vocal parts for the passage – the omitted orchestra parts add some doublings, and also some fragmented strands of X+Y that will later be developed by the chorus. The passage is built upon the abstract relations that we studied in Example 6.22, and Example 6.23 labels the row forms just as in the previous example. Unlike the abstract partition, the *Bringt* "antecedents" attach each first note to the *Nebenstimme* (for example, the altos, initial D-natural), while the consequent phrases are partitioned just as in the abstract. As a result, the *Hauptstimme* (first in the sopranos) begins with a dyad that is embellished in the "consequent." Thus, the soprano *Bringt ihr*, $<D^\flat\text{-}B^\flat>$, becomes *Botschaft des*, $<D\text{-}D^\flat\text{-}B^\flat>$. The subsequent inversion in the basses works the same way, $<C\text{-}E^\flat>$ becoming $<B\text{-}C\text{-}E^\flat>$. The dyadic reversals within the *b* to *b′*, *c* to *c′*, and *d* to *d′* permutations of Example 6.22, become particularly salient in the actual music. Some examples include the setting of *Erhöhrung* in the sopranos (mm. 443–4), $<G^\flat\text{-}F\text{-}C^\flat>$, transforming into *neuen Gottes*, $<(B^\flat)\text{-}F\text{-}G^\flat\text{-}C^\flat>$, the analogous places in the bass inversion (*Erhöhrung* at mm. 448–9, and *neuen Gottes* at mm. 451–2) and similar reversals in the *Nebenstimme*. The dyadic reversals have interesting voice leading implications, as do the invariant pitches. Within the soprano *Hauptstimme* the voice leading from $B^\flat$ to $C^\flat$ controls both phrase halves, as does the voice leading from $E^\flat$ to D within the bass inversion. Another feature is how the internal repetitions within the *Nebenstimme* induce patterns that are not available in the abstract mappings of trichords. For example, the alternation of $G^\sharp$-E in the altos (m. 443) cuts across trichords to elaborate on the pattern of descending thirds initiated by *Bringt ihr* in the sopranos. The song also has evanescent references to tonality that contribute to its lyrical effect. For example, the reiterated $G^\sharp$-E of the *Nebenstimme* in 443 combines with

Example 6.23. Act I, scene 4, mm. 443–57.

the initial D♭-B♭ of the *Hauptstimme* to form a (misspelled) half-diminished chord. Within the soprano *Hauptstimme* the play of B♭ major-minor is quite salient, as is the play of C minor and A♭ major in the bass inversion, a sleight of hand available because the soprano G♭ of m. 443 is heard as ♭6, leading to F, while the analogous G in the basses, m. 448, is part of a C minor arpeggio, leading into A^b, and so mimicking a leading tone exchange, the *Leittonwechsel* of chromatic tonality. The reader may recall the similarly striking role of the C minor arpeggio in Aron's setting of *höchsten Phantasie* (see Example 6.15).

Once the first phrase pair is completed additional voices – the soprano mm. 448–52 and the alto and tenor mm. 453–7 – weave fragments of X or Y from A_2. For example, the altos in mm. 455–6 sing $<E,F,E^b>$ and tenors continue in mm. 456–7 with $<A,G,A^b>$, the two combining to form the Y-component of S_2. Thus, the additional counterpoint further elaborates on the free associations of X+Y that characterize the *Bringt* components.

As we have already noted, at first Moses and Aron are ineffectual in conveying their message to the people. This precipitates Moses' capitulation and Aron's seizing of control, the music we studied in Example 6.17. The music that directly precedes Moses' capitulation is based on the *Bringt* partition, but what was before a song of hope and jubilation now becomes a taunting song of ridicule. The music that begins this extended song (mm. 566–620) is shown in Example 6.24.

Bleib uns fern mit deinem Gott,   Keep us far with your God,
    mit dem Allmächtigen!   with the Almighty!

At the outset, the altos and celli share the *Bringt* partition of S_2 while the upper strings and tenors share a secondary partitioning of I_2. Instead of following S_2 with its RI_2 consequent, the violins and choral basses share a *Bringt* partition of I_2 while the remaining voices sing and play a modified version of *Bringt* S_2. The changes in contour bring out the C minor arpeggio in the altos (566–7) and its inversion G^b major in the basses (569–70); these structures override the trichordal partitions that we studied in Example 6.22. Once again, the C minor arpeggio recalls Aron's setting of *höchsten Phantasie* (see Example 6.15). Fantasy degraded remains one of the opera's central themes.

The triumphant march

Although the *Bringt* partition plays an important role in Act I.iv, it is nonetheless limited to that scene alone. The folk's triumphant march plays an even bigger role in scene 4, and it returns near the end of the opera to compose the last music that the folk will sing in Act II. The march is always associated with the folk in an affirmative, celebratory mood. Its first appearance is right after Aron's successful demonstration of the first sign, the transformation of Moses' staff into a snake. The march returns, in variation, after

Example 6.24. Act I, scene 4, mm. 566–71.

Example 6.25. March partition and its ordered interval permutations.

the second sign, the transformation of Moses' hand from healthy to leprous and back. After the third sign, water-into-blood, the covenant music returns for a double reprise, first Aron and then the folk, and this is followed by the march in a third variation. The last scene of the opera (II.5) begins with the final confrontation of Moses and Aron (assuming that the sketches for the third act are rejected). The extraordinary confrontation lasts almost 100 bars and ends with Aron affirming his love for the people as well as his own role in God's mandate. The folk respond with a final reprise of the covenant music, this time overlaid with music derived from the march. The covenant music is then liquidated and followed by a truncated version of the march that leads the folk off stage and leaves Moses alone to end the act.

The march and its reprises use a variety of partitions. The one that we will define as *March* is recurrent through all of the statements, but always as one element among many. As we shall see, there is a marked disparity between the rich inventiveness of the *March* partition and the way that it is flung out and swallowed up by competing textures within the march. Example 6.25 shows *March* as it structures mm. 687–9.

Like *Bringt*, *March* cuts across two row forms, in this case dividing them respectively into 5+7 and 7+5. Whereas *Bringt* permutes pitch-classes within trichordal segments, *March* permutes ordered pitch-class intervals among the pentachords and septachords. Example 6.25 labels the components of the partition *Q*, *R*, *S*, and *T*, along with their inversions I*Q*, I*R*, I*S*, and I*T*. It also notates the ordered pitch-class intervals within each *March*-component. *Q* permutes and inverts ordered pitch-class intervals onto *T*, and so *Q* permutes onto I*T*. *R* permutes and inverts onto *S*, and so *R* permutes onto I*S*. I*Q* permutes and inverts onto I*T*, and so I*Q* permutes onto *T*. And, I*R* permutes and inverts onto I*S*, and so I*R* permutes onto *S*. Moreover, every four-element permutation (four ordered pitch-class intervals) moves ordinals <1234> to <2341>, moving first to last, while every six-element (six ordered pc intervals) permutation moves ordinals <123,456> onto <312,645>, moving last to first with each three-interval grouping. *March* seems designed to negate X+Y and the hexachordal partition, replacing their abundant cross-relations with a new abundance. The fantasy of the folk is far afield from the Divine, but no less fecund, ramified, and mind-boggling!

Ein Wunder erfüllt uns mit Schrecken	A wonder fills us with fear
Der Stab, der sich wandelt zur Schlange	The staff, that transforms into a serpent
zeigt Aron als Herrn dieses Volkes.	Shows Aron the lord of this folk.
Ist Aron der Knecht dieses Moses,	Is Aron the servant of this Moses,
Und Moses der Knecht dieses Gottes . . .	And Moses the servant of this God . . .

The march is an onrush of creativity, multi-form and interpenetrating among the groups that comprise the *Volk*. The passage shown in Example 6.26 takes us from the beginning of the march and just into its first full *tutti*. The passage builds its texture by adding one new element at a time. We begin with a steady pulse in the percussion, a rare moment of utterly even pulses, *unheimlich* simplicity in the context of the opera. The polyphony of women's speaking voices then adds a new layer of timbre inflected by the march's characteristic rhythmic motives. Next, horn, mirrored by the celli, and basses mirrored by bassoon, add the element of pitch controlled by the *March* partition, just as in the abstract of Example 6.25. Given the richness and complexity of *March* associations, the actual setting, at least at the outset, is most extraordinary in the extravagance of its understatement. Despite being notated as *Hauptstimme*, the horn and the other voices that combine to form the *March* complex are perceived as hardly more than an accompanying rhythmic layer. This structural extravagance is a kind of spilling of seeds before the facts of the golden calf scene. The passage reaches its first *tutti* with the addition of the men's voices.[41] This introduces yet another partitioning, which we will touch on only briefly. It is shown in the abstract in Example 6.27.

The men's voices sing a "deceptive" partitioning of I_9. In contrast to *March* which avoids X and Y segments, the deceptive partition mimics the first X-trichord in R_9 (the harmony that opens the men's singing) and then the second Y-trichord in I_0 (or its R_1 equivalent).[42] As it continues, the march develops ever new combinations built primarily out of the three strata that compose the opening: women's speaking choir, deceptive partitions of the men's singing choir, and instrumental variants on the *March* partition.

Example 6.26. Act I, scene 4, mm. 684–90.

Example 6.27. I9 partitioned as in the men's voices, Act I scene 4, mm. 690–1.

God, Moses, and the music of the covenant

Within Jewish tradition there is an injunction against speaking the name of God, except in prayer, and even then that which is uttered is never equivalent to the Hebrew Tetragrammaton, which remains ineffable. The composing of *Moses und Aron* was self-consciously part of Schoenberg's return to the faith of his ancestors and though Schoenberg was neither a learned or "observant" Jew (as the unfortunate phrase goes) he proved to be extraordinarily sensitive to aspects of the tradition, despite his audacious retelling of the biblical story.

In the *dramatis personae* of the score, there is no voice or ensemble named "God." Instead Schoenberg designates a speaking choir as *Stimme aus dem Dornbusch* (voice from the thornbush) and a separate choir of *6 Solostimmen* (six solo voices), each with an orchestral double.[43] The *Stimme aus dem Dornbusch* is restricted to the first scene; it is associated with something visible, the burning bush, through which it is manifest, although certainly not embodied in any normal sense of the word. The solo voices, what we have been calling the Voice, represent some fully disembodied manifestation or emanation. The Voice is heard again, twice during Act I.iv, and in neither case is there anything visible that is connected with the Voice. On the other hand, the manifold Voice, in summoning Aron, precipitates the signs through which Aron reveals the Divine presence; without visible signs the folk cannot embrace Divinity.

Irrespective of the designations in the score, Moses does address Divinity through the name "Gott." Yet, there are clues in the drama that might suggest that Moses' name for Divinity, "Gott," as well as his list of attributes, though well-conceived as can be conceived, still falls far short of that which cannot be conceived. The opening music of the first scene is shown in Example 6.28a.

The opera begins with the moment that Moses first perceives Divinity, the moment just before his call to prophecy at the burning bush. It is important to recognize that the initiating visionary moment happens just before Moses uses *words* to characterize the Divine attributes (shown in Example 6.19), after which the voices from the bush respond in kind, proclaiming Moses' calling through their polyphony of speaking and singing choirs.

At the initial moment, perception of the world as Moses had known it is utterly shattered. Without warning, Moses is suddenly thrown out of his

Example 6.28a. Act I, scene 1, mm. 1–7.

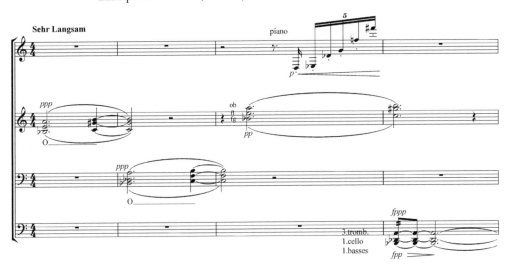

old world of knowing and being into a mental and spiritual landscape that could not have been imagined a moment earlier, the moment before the work begins. In the Introduction to this book we had noted that Kafka sometimes places a world-changing calamity antecedent to the story, so that our first experience of the protagonist finds him already plunged into an altered reality. It is just so here, as it will later be at the outset of the String Trio.

The shattering is first manifest as a prismatic fracturing of temporal continuities whose sum result is a remarkable development of the time shard technique. Within the first seven measures we hear seven discrete pulse streams, each at odds with the others. The initial tactus, equivalent to the written dotted half note, is established by the female Solo Voices, along with their orchestral doubles. They sing the vowel "O." The first disruption occurs when the male voices enter at the written downbeat of m. 2, two-thirds of a beat "too soon." After a rest that maintains the duration of the written dotted half note, the woodwinds reestablish the tactus of the female voices in m. 3. The sixteenth-note quintuplet plus pick-up provides a strongly contrasting pulse stream: a ratio of 15:1 in relation to the original tactus, it is the first of a series of fragments derived from the inner six notes of the tone row, which have not yet taken on their characteristic Y-contour. Had the tactus stream of the male voices followed the lead of the female voices, their next entry would have been on the written second beat of m. 4. Instead, the low brass enter one third of their tactus too soon, now coinciding with the second woodwind chord and so in temporary alignment with the original tactus. The low brass chord seems to rebound after impact and is then joined by the male voices in m. 5; their combined pulse-stream coincides with the notated barline for two pulses, and then dissolves. New time shards emerge and disappear: the eighth-note quintuplet in m. 5 doubles the durations of the previous quintuplet, now 15:2 in relation to the original tactus; the quintuplet then merges with and transforms into the figure in the upper winds and strings (at m. 6) with longer durations surrounding the two-note core of quarter notes within triplets, a ratio of 4 $\frac{1}{2}$:1 in relation to the original tactus. The triplets at the end of m. 6 arrive a third of a written beat too soon in relation to the preceding figure: they form a 9:1 ratio with the original tactus, 2:1 in relation to their immediate precursor. That pulse stream is dilated in the bass at m. 7 to form a 3:1 ratio against the original tactus, as a single pulse of that tactus (along with its original chord) returns. And finally the sixteenth notes in the second half of m. 7, broken into three-note gestures, establish a 12:1 relationship to the opening tactus. Each fragment is a shard of time broken off from a temporal continuum and broken off from its context in what will subsequently emerge as the work's twelve-tone row.

As noted in Chapter Five, our metaphor of time shards was inspired in part by the "breaking of the vessels" in Lurianic Kabbalah.[44] That image seems particularly apposite toward understanding the opening of *Moses und Aron* as a creation-catastrophe of a sort. As noted in Chapter Five, Harold Bloom has used the "breaking of the vessels" as a metaphor for the "revisionary ratios" through which strong poets clear creative space by strongly "misreading" their precursors. Its applicability in the opening of *Moses und Aron*, where the metaphoric meaning of revisionary ratios finds itself congruent with its positivistic meaning, is truly uncanny.

The row partition that dominates the opening seven bars is X+Y, but the emergence and subsequent disruption of X+Y foreshadows developments within the music that immediately follows in the confrontation of Moses with the Divine as well developments that will take place over the opera as a whole as Aron and the folk are added to the mix. The first sounds that we hear, the women's chords of m.1, are the X-chords from S_0, connected without their Y-component. The answering men's chords, the first disruption of the pulse stream, are X-chords from RI_0 and once again there is no Y-component. The combination of male and female voices is the source of the close and complementary relationship that we studied in Examples 6.3 and 6.4. The differentiation and combination is also suggestive of a basic principal of Being itself dividing into primal oppositions/complementarities. The X-progression from S_0 is reiterated in the woodwinds, and this time the piano responds, interposing the row's Y-component, albeit without the contour that will become normative only after Moses speaks. The radically differentiated pulse of Y, its dramatic registral ascent, and its linear rather than chordal texture, punctuate the emergence of the new component. The male X-chords, from RI_0, are reiterated, crashing into the ongoing texture more forcefully than before, now divided between the trombone combined with lower strings and the male voices (mm. 4–5). The *fpp* articulated by a tremolo in the strings and flutter-tonguing in the trombone extends the gamut downward and these elicit the piano and woodwind figure, the Y-component of I_0 (not RI_0), completing the aggregate but combining in ways that avoid the Y-comparisons still to come. The shattering effect of this second Y-component is intensified by its dramatic ascent, even higher than before, by the crescendo to *f*, and then by the trichords that emerge immediately out of it. These are the first three ordered trichords of S_0 (ordinals $\{1,2,3\},\{4,5,6\}$, and $\{7,8,9\}$). Although the trichordal subcomponents of X+Y are maintained, the ordering constitutes the first breakdown of X+Y and so the first manifest potential of X+Y to transmute into other partitionings. It is as though the genetic strands already show their capacity to recombine in ever more fanciful and unanticipated ways. The breakdown or transformation of X+Y continues as the trumpet plays the first linear hexachord of S_0. Linear S_0 is completed by the flute and then bassoon in the following measure: the trichordal components are articulated by changes of color and register, while the rhythmic articulation allows us to hear the linear hexachord as a whole. Moreover, even though there is a rhythmic shift between the hexachords as well as other sounds that are interposed, the soft staccato articulations help us to hear the linear row form that has emerged out of the X+Y texture. Interposed between the two hexachordal halves of S_0, the women's voices return to their original X-chord (the first X-chord in

Example 6.28b. Implicit voice leading in the combined female and male chords of the opening.

composite of opening
trichords P and RI

composite revoiced
showing voice leading

reduced and
respelled

Variant of the Grail
Motive from Parsifal

S_0, equivalent to the second X-chord in R_0) while the trombone and lower strings play the remaining ordered trichords of R_0.

Example 6.28b studies the voice leading that underlies the initial chord progressions in *Moses und Aron*. Either the female or male progression alone is missing voice-leading connections between the trichords. The composite of male and female chords, shown on the left side of the example, supplies the missing links. Needless to say, the idea of combining male and female elements as necessary complements in a creation act (here the creation of Moses' altered perception and all that it entails) has extraordinary dramatic resonance. In the middle of Example 6.28b, the composite chords are revoiced to make the parsimonious semitone voice leadings explicit – from the soprano down, B♭ to B, A to G♯, E to F, and D♭ to C. On the right side of the example, I strip away the B♭-B strand to reveal the underlying Grail motive from Wagner's *Parsifal*. Near the very end of *Parsifal* the final transformation of this motive signifies the lifting of Kundry's curse, her entry into Paradise (there the progression is D♭ major to A minor).[45] The opening trichords of *Moses und Aron*, signify an emanation from a Divine source: Moses, we are meant to believe, perceives not Paradise, but the source of being itself. To be sure, the ghostly presence of the Grail motive, the faint trace of Wagner deeply hidden within the workings of the *Moses und Aron* tone row, cannot have been conscious. We might even go a step further and ask ourselves if the presence of the motive is actual or imposed by analytic sleight of hand. Is it statistically convincing that six out of the opening eight tones can be rearranged to form a motive from Wagner? Well, not just any motive, this motive. Are the deeply hidden connections to *Parsifal* composed by the composer or imposed by the analyst? I suspect that neither option is correct and yet to say that they are composed by the musical language itself, with bows towards "the death of the author," where language composes its own manifestations, strikes me as wholly inadequate. And so, we will assert that the ghostly presence is one that defies a definitive "rational" explanation and so defies a clear attribution or understanding: in this it is just as Moses' vision itself.

As we have noted, the Voice sings the vowel "O," Moses responds using words (as in Example 6.19), and then the combined choirs continue with words as well. In thinking about Moses' words, I still find myself in agreement with an article that I wrote some twenty years ago, "Schoenberg's Representation of the Divine in *Moses und Aron*."[46]

> Moses' list of Divine attributes is interesting in a number of significant ways. For example, the first word "Einziger," would seem to preclude a series of Attributes. In the philosophical sense of the word, God is simple. The Divine nature defies being broken down into parts; as the Hebrew prayer of Moses would have it, "God is ONE." Thus, there is a paradox in the continuation. Nonetheless, God's simplicity cannot be encompassed by any single human concept, and the ideas contained within the outer terms attempt to come closer to articulating Moses' vision than "Einziger Gott" will allow.
>
> As it turns out the entire list of attributes is unified by a musical structure that refers back to the opening "O" and hints ahead to the problem of language that will plague Moses through the opera.
>
> The musical setting stresses the first vowel of each Attribute. The accented vowels form a progression that gradually moves from a relatively "high, front" vowel toward a "low, back" one, precisely toward the open vowel "O" that had been sung by the Divine Voice: *Einziger, ewiger, allgegenwärtige, unsichtbarer, und unvorstellbarer Gott!*
>
> The vowel progression moves chord by chord through the complete series, and falters, at thrice *un*, before reaching the last word, *Gott*. The Divine name, *Gott*, restates the "O" vowel, but with a crucial difference. Now "O" is conditioned and bounded by strong consonants. Thus the open unbounded "O" is not uttered by Moses. The Voice from the Bush and the 6 Solo Voices enter simultaneously with Moses' word *Gott*. They restate the original harmony, and now sing and speak with *words*.[47]

Whatever the open "O" signifies, it cannot be uttered, even by Moses.

How shall Moses speak these words? If performed according to Schoenberg's indications, Moses is the only one on stage. Schoenberg provides a note in the score indicating that Moses has a deep resounding voice (*tiefe, sehr grosse Stimme*). He is given freedom to be expansive in his declaration; indeed, the score indicates that he declaim as slowly as possible (*möglichst langsam*). And the dynamic, *mf*, indicates that Moses is to be clearly heard above the orchestral voices. The natural tendency for the singer will be to articulate with surety and strength: by this interpretation, *mf* made *f* might be even better! Moreover, a strong, confident Moses seems to be indicated in a letter that Schoenberg wrote in 1933: "My Moses more resembles – of course only in outward aspect – Michelangelo's. He is not human at all [*Er ist gar nicht menschlich*]."[48]

On the other hand, *gar nicht menschlich* might indicate that Moses' concerns are not normal human concerns, but not that Moses is fearless in the face of some overwhelming, indeed supreme force. We do see the wrathful, overpowering Moses later in the opera, at the moment when he first comes down from the mountain and commands *Vergeh du Abbild des Unvermögens* causing the golden calf to disappear. However, the Moses of the first scene is taken by surprise; the mystery of Divinity visits him unbidden. He must be shaken by this for the role to make dramatic sense. The attributes should convey mystery, awe, even bewilderment, but not swagger.

Example 6.29 shows the music the follows Moses' first words. This is the same passage that we had considered in Example 6.4, only now the example adds the Voice from the Thornbush, the speaking choir that complements the singing Voice for the remainder of the first scene.

Responding to Moses' words, the Divine Voice intensifies its contrapuntal prism. The winds and strings spin out an interweaving of Y-components that have taken on the contour somehow intuited by Moses. Their interrelations are those we studied in Example 6.4. The singing Voice recasts its polyphony of X-chords, now adding text (derived from Exodus, 3.5). And the Voice from the thornbush adds another layer of rhythm and timbre speaking the same text. Unlike the singing Voice, the spoken Voice is univocal: its timbre and inflection will change, but its constituent parts always participate in a monophonic rhythmic patterning. This will remain true for the entire scene, although the speaking Voice will develop more variety by dropping and adding parts to change its timbre and pitch envelope, as our study of subsequent passages will show.

The spoken lines integrate text from the female and male sung polyphony as they mimic tongues of flame flaring out from the bush, as though the Divine "light" emanating from the singing Voice is being brought down to a condensed focal point.[49] Thus, the spoken *Lege die Schuhe ab* is an approximate diminution of the same text sung by the female constituent of the singing Voice, its beginning and end approximately equidistant from the beginnings and ends of the sung thread. The spoken *bist weit genug gegangen* has the same relationship with the male strand. And then *du stehst auf heiligem Boden* continues the relationship with the female strand. The final sung text, *nun verkünde*, is not spoken.[50]

As the scene continues, the singing Voice will develop and intensify its tendency toward polyphony, while the speaking Voice will gain greater textual

Example 6.29. Act I, mm. 11–13.

Example 6.30. Act I, scene 1, mm. 16–22.

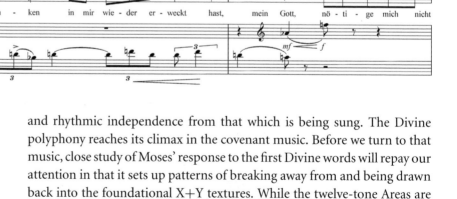

and rhythmic independence from that which is being sung. The Divine polyphony reaches its climax in the covenant music. Before we turn to that music, close study of Moses' response to the first Divine words will repay our attention in that it sets up patterns of breaking away from and being drawn back into the foundational X+Y textures. While the twelve-tone Areas are roughly analogous to the key areas of tonality, it is the play among relatively

Example 6.30. (*cont.*)

stable and unstable partitions that gives Schoenberg's twelve-tone music its sense of drama and momentum, a point about Schoenbergian twelve-tone syntax whose importance has been generally underestimated in the theoretical literature.

Gott meiner Väter,	God of my fathers,
Gott Abraham, Isaaks und Jakobs,	God of Abraham, Isaac, and Jacob
der du ihren Gedanken in mir wieder erweckt hast,	You who have again awoken their thoughts in me,
mein Gott, nötige mich nicht ihn zu verkünden.	My God, do not compel me to be your prophet.
Ich bin alt, lass mich in Ruhe meine Schafe weiden!	I am old, let me graze my sheep in peace.

In the biblical narrative God tells Moses that He is the God of Abraham, Isaac and Jacob (Exodus, 3.6). In Schoenberg's telling, Moses recognizes this without being told, at least not through words. The score indicates that Moses is fervent and imploring (*sehr innig, flehentlich*) as Schoenberg fancifully embroiders the biblical account of Moses' resistance and feelings of inadequacy. The music is unstable in terms of row areas, partitions, and the resulting textures. Rather than belaboring a note by note accounting of row derivations, let us concentrate on the most dramatic shifts of partitioning and how they express the musical drama.[51]

Example 6.31a. X+Y partition of S0 and RI11.

The first block of text, *Gott meiner Väter, Gott Abrahams, Isaaks und Jakobs,* is set to overlapping vertical trichords, beginning with an X-type and then overlapping chromatic trichords, at first derived from Y.[52] X is only momentarily projected and in the "wrong key"; Y is disoriented, its sinuous linearity changed into the dissonance of chromatic simultaneities. The overlapping chords seem to tug at one another and despite their *pp dolce* markings they convey inner conflict. X+Y come into better focus with the next block of text, *der du ihren Gedanken in mir wieder erweckt hast:* linear Y-components, broken into *staccato* punctuations, are heard in the trombone, and the remaining voices wobble back and forth between X-chords, the syncopated X-triplets creating a sense of unbalance. X+Y break down again into overlapping trichords with *mein Gott,* and then more fully dissolve in Moses' plea *nötige mich nicht, ihn zu verkünden,* eventually falling into Moses' ordered tetrachords. Moses' second sentence begins with X-chords in the woodwinds and a fractured Y divided between the horn and cello. This breaks down for the last part of the sentence, *Ruhe meine Schafe weiden!,* again reverting to ordered tetrachords. The effect of fracturing is intensified by the half-note quintuplets, further developing the rhythm first introduced with *nötige mich nicht.* When the Divine Voices respond in the following measure, A_0 partitioned into X+Y once again asserts control, although the tendency toward lyricism is increased.

The music that sets the singing/speaking of the covenant forms the sonic climax for the first scene. This music takes on much added significance in that it has a double reprise in the fourth scene of Act I, and a final statement in the last scene of Act II (with some significant changes that we will attend to in due course). The covenant music, whose *Hauptstimmen* and serial background we have studied in Examples 6.5 and 6.6, is preceded by a four-measure benediction comprising mm. 67–70 of the first scene. The underlying partition and row derivations for the benediction are shown in Example 6.31.

The inversion that moves S_0 onto I_{11} holds E-natural invariant, in other words S_0 inverted about E (I^E) yields I_{11}. E-natural is also the tacit pitch-class

Example 6.31b. Comparison of X-progressions.

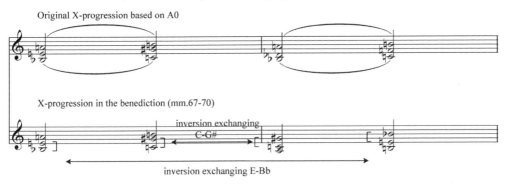

center of the Y_0 interval palindrome, $<D-E^\flat-C^\sharp-(E)-G-F-F^\sharp>$, so that Y_0 inverted about E yields its own retrograde. As a result, RI_{11} holds Y_0 invariant (or $Y_0=RI(Y)_{11}$). As we have seen, earlier passages in the scene develop the equivalence of $T_1(Y)$ to the retrograde of its combinatorial inversion (as discussed in relation to Examples 6.3,6.4, and 6.29). In those contexts, we have noted the perceptual difficulties surrounding the easily perceived transposition, versus the perceptually difficult (and hence concealed) retrograde inversion. The benediction incorporates a new Y-relation, invariance used as a pivot between two row forms (S_0 and RI_{11}).[53] The newly resulting X-progression is also interesting to compare with the combinatorial X-progression that has dominated earlier passages in the scene. We make that comparison in Example 6.31b. In the combinatorial X-progression, the repetition of the outer voices, $B^\flat$-A to C-B, helped to mask the underlying retrograde inversion. In contrast, the palindromic mirror in the benediction holds dyadic invariants between the mirrored chords. Thus, within the benediction, Schoenberg develops relations that emphasize its inversion about a center, a property that is more hidden in earlier manifestations.

Example 6.32 shows the actual passage, and Example 6.33 displays the same passage, baritones, basses and speaking voices omitted, with the voices arranged to show how the X+Y components combine to form an inversional balance about the central E, the pitch that begins and ends the symmetrically disposed augmented chord in the alto and tenor line (as always, sounding with their orchestral doubles).

The text for the central line is the single word *gesegnet* (blessed), iterated three times by the baritone and bass strands, while being expanded upon by the speaking Voice.

| Ihr werdet gesegnet sein. Denn das gelobe ich dir: | You will be blessed. For this I promise you: |

Example 6.32. Act I, scene 1, mm. 67–70.

Example 6.33. Inversional balance about E, mm. 67–70.

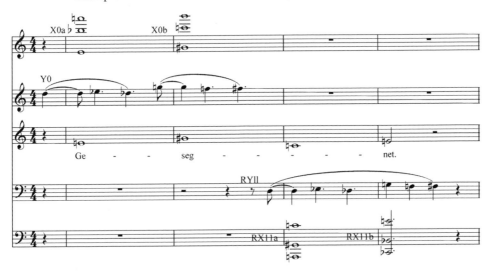

That an augmented triad should form the conceptual center for the benediction is striking, both in terms of its sounding characteristics, a remarkable departure from the intervallic structures that have dominated and will
subsequently dominate the musical textures, as well as in the ways that its
sonority reaches back to an earlier period in Schoenberg's creative life –
echoes of Wagner still emerge. The pitches of the central augmented triad
also participate in the structure of the X-chords, composing first the lowest
and then the highest voices in those chords. The labels in Example 6.33 make
this clear. The voicing of the X-chords forms a perfect mirror about the central E, the closing chords in the bassoon, tuba, and lower strings reflecting
those in high woodwinds, trombone, and violins. The linear Y-motives, first
in the trumpet and then in the horns, are also symmetrically disposed about
E; they are played for the most part without text, although the baritone and
bass voices join in for the final Y-trichord in m. 70, setting their third iteration of *gesegnet*. The Y-motives are syncopated with relation to the X-chords
and this helps to bring out the essential dissonance (*pace* Schoenberg's
"emancipation" of dissonance) between the X and Y components, properties
of rhythm and pitch that individuate the two strands, and refuse to let them
merge. Thus the central mirror about E is counterbalanced by elements of
individuation. The "perfection" of the pitch mirror is also challenged by
other means beyond the individuation and conflict among its constituents.
The first part of the baritone-bass lines, mm. 67–8, adds a contrapuntal
stratum to the texture that violates both the inversional balance and the X+Y

Example 6.34. Act I, scene 1, mm. 71–8.

Example 6.34. (*cont.*)

partition. Anticipating partitions that will be characteristic of subordinate voices within the covenant music proper, the initial iterations of *gesegnet* in the baritone and bass comprise contiguous hexachords, first S_0a and then R_0b, both sub-partitioned into harmonic dyads.[54] This same partitioning continues in the clarinet, oboe, and piano in m. 70, mirroring the baritone-bass lines of m. 68, while holding the initial dyad invariant ($D^\sharp$-$C^\sharp$ of m. 68 map onto $E^\flat$-$D^\flat$ of m. 70). The speaking Voice comprises yet another contrapuntal stratum that adds to the textual and rhythmic complexity of the benediction while providing its fullest textual message. Remarkably, the augmented triad at the center of the benediction becomes the sonic prototype and genetic source for the cascade of augmented chords that overcome Aron in Act II, the music we have already discussed in Examples 6.10 and 6.11.

The cognitive difficulties of the benediction become compounded as we move into the words and music of the covenant. Example 6.34 shows its initial seven measures.

The music of the covenant exemplifies the combined Voices at their most extravagant. The text is given below, that part in brackets goes beyond the confines of our musical example.

Dieses Volk ist auserwählt	This people is chosen
vor allen Völkern	before all peoples,
das Volk des einzigen Gottes zu sein,	to be the people of the One God,
dass es ihn erkenne,	that they will know Him,
sich ihm ganz widme;	and dedicate all to Him;
dass es alle Prüfungen bestehe	that they will endure all hardships
in Jahrtausenden	that thought has exposed
der Gedanke ausgesetzt ist.	over the millennia.
[Und das verheisse ich dir:	[And this I promise you:
Ich will euch dorthin führen,	I will lead you where you shall be
wo ihr mit dem Ewigen einig	one with the Eternal,
und allen Völkern ein Vorbild werdet.]	to become a model for all peoples.]

Schoenberg's own amalgam, the text is partly based on the Bible's scattered references to a "chosen people"; it makes a somewhat veiled reference to being led out of bondage, but is mostly of Schoenberg's own making. The speaking Voice (the Voice from the thornbush) presents the text in a straightforward manner. This in itself causes a cognitive difficulty in that it masks the elaborate polyphony in the remaining voices. The sound envelope changes by thickening and thinning the speaking choir, but the speaking Voice remains monophonic in delivering its text.

The principal line among the pitched voices comprises the *Haupstimmen* that we studied in Examples 6.5 and 6.6. It is a composite line with some overlapping threads, beginning in the alto voice (mm. 71–2), moving to the mezzo (72), alto (73–4), mezzo (74), and baritone and bass (75–8). The *Hauptstimmen* are doubled by the high strings for the first four measures and by the low strings woodwinds for the next three measures, diverging from and then returning to the vocal line in m. 78. Although it begins just before the speaking Voice, the main strand of sung text tends to lag behind the spoken words.

The remaining lines, in instruments and voices, repeat an isorhythmic pattern to form a contrapuntal *Gestalt* of interlocking voices: horns, tenor, baritone and bass (mm. 71–2); clarinets, soprano, baritone and bass (73–4); violins, alto, mezzo and soprano (75–6, adding the tenor in 76); and finally, tenor, alto, mezzo and soprano (77–8). The register of this contrapuntal *Gestalt* is essentially below the *Hauptstimmen* for the first four measures, and then moves above with striking effect as the *Hauptstimmen* become the bass line. The combined harmonies, widely spaced and rich in chromaticisms, have an opulent effect, but one that is greatly masked by the ongoing speaking Voice.

The arrangement of text in the subordinate *Gestalt* forms a kind of selective reading of the more comprehensive text in the *Hauptstimmen*. Transformations of the *auserwählt* figure, initiated by the tenor in m. 71, articulate the downbeats of each measure until the partial liquidation at m. 78, making "chosen" the central word of text for the entire first part of the covenant. During the first four measures, the bass voice echoes text from the *Hauptstimmen*, while the baritone alternates *Dieses Volk* and *auserwählt*. Then, once the *Gestalt* is transferred into the upper register, the text shifts to iterations of *auserwählt* in all the subordinate voices (until the alto and tenor sing *vor allen Völkern* in m. 78). Notably, the subordinate *Gestalt* omits the final part of the text: *dass es alle Prüfungen bestehe in Jahrtausenden der Gedanke ausgesetzt ist*, an omission that becomes all the more interesting in light of textual changes within the reprises of this music by Aron and the Israelites.

The trope of being "overwhelmed" is an essential element in Schoenberg's dramatic palette, one that he used in many works, spanning all of his creative periods. Schoenberg mimics being overwhelmed by creating passages of structural density, where the listener cannot take it all in. Such passages are used both to embody and to portray an overwhelming force. They embody such force by overwhelming our perceptual capacity, so that, as it were, cosmos verges on chaos. They portray such a force when such embodiments are taken as mimetic depiction. The force that overwhelms can be an influx or impact of things external to the self or portrayed self, or it can be the result of a welling-up of internal pressures, or it can be a combination of the two. The technique, already evident in Schoenberg's *Pelleas und Melisande*, and even earlier in the *Gurrelieder*, becomes especially important in the Five Pieces for Orchestra, op. 16, and in other works from the "atonal" period, including *Erwartung* and *Die glückliche Hand*. It remains part of Schoenberg's musical language and is particularly salient in the String Trio.

Being overwhelmed is absolutely central to Moses' experience in the first scene of *Moses und Aron*. As the opera unfolds, we come to recognize two overwhelming forces, God and the folk. Both have polyphonic sound mass at their disposal, something necessarily not granted to either brother. Moses will be overwhelmed by the Israelites in the fourth scene, as will Aron in Act II.ii, but the overwhelming of Moses in Act I.i is unique in that nowhere else is either brother reduced to utter silence.

Through the first half of the scene, Moses resists the Divine imperative with a series of objections each of which the Voices refute: *Ich bin alt* (I am old), *Wer bin ich mich der Macht der Blindheit entgegen zustellen?* (Who am I to oppose the might of blindness?), and so forth until Moses' final objection *Meine Zunge ist ungelenk: ich kann denken aber nicht reden* (My tongue is awkward: I can think but not speak). These will turn out to be Moses' final words within the first scene. Although he remains the sole presence on the stage, burning bush aside, he is silent for the rest of the scene, approximately its entire second half. The Divine Voices reply to Moses' final objection in two ways. The first response is concerned with the nature of thinking in the prophetic mode (the *denken* part of the *denken/reden* opposition): *Wie aus diesen Dornbusch . . . so vernimmst du meine Stimme aus jedem Ding* (As out of this thornbush . . . so you will perceive my voice in every thing). The second part of the response is a practical solution, *Aron soll dein Mund sein!* (Aron will be your mouth!). All of this leads up to the covenant itself.

As we have noted in our analyses of earlier passages within the first scene, it is by no means clear that Moses himself is able to perceive the paradoxes that underlie divinity. We understand the perceptual conundrums of the X+Y partition having had the leisure of analysis; Moses must catch the drift on the fly. The perceptual problems become intensified during the covenant music whose elaborate structure, rich polyphony, and juxtaposition of multiple strands of spoken words and sung words compound the difficulties.

The music of the covenant is simplified in all of its subsequent versions, in chief because the speaking choir, the Voice from the Thornbush, is absent. There are also significant changes in text. Aron is the first to reprise the covenant music, this toward the end of the long fourth scene of Act I (I.iv, beginning at m. 898). Aron's melody is what had comprised the earlier *Hauptstimmen*, beginning with the same text, but changing the words beginning in the fifth measure. The original words continue from that point: *dass es ihn erkenne, sich ihm ganz widme; dass es alle Prüfungen bestehe in*

Jahrtausenden der Gedanke ausgesetzt ist (that they will know Him, and dedicate all to Him; that they will endure all hardships that thought has exposed over the millennia). Aron's new words have a strikingly different content:

ihm allein zu dienen,	to serve Him alone,
keines andern Knecht!	bound to no other!
Ihr werdet frei sein von Fron and Plage!	You will be free of compulsion and plague!

The music that we have been calling "the subordinate *Gestalt*" is transferred to the orchestra and so Aron's textual message is particularly clear – greatly different in this respect from the original. The text of the second half of the covenant in Aron's version also departs from the original *Und das verheisse ich dir: Ich will euch dorthin führen, wo ihr mit dem Ewigen einig und allen Völkern ein Vorbild werdet* (And this I promise you: I will lead you where you shall be one with the Eternal, to become a model for all peoples). Aron's new version is:

Das gelobt ihr euch:	This He vows to you:
Er wird euch führen in das Land,	He will lead you into the land
wo Milch und Honig fliesst;	where milk and honey flow;
und ihr sollt geniessen	and you will enjoy
lieblich, was euern Vätern	in pleasure, in spirit,
verheissen geistig.	what was promised to your fathers.

Aron's words speak of pleasure and enjoyment, and, like the biblical account, of a land of milk and honey.

The version of the covenant sung by the Israelites follows (beginning at m. 919). Their music basically reiterates Aron's words (tellingly, the word *geistig* is omitted) while restoring the subordinate *Gestalt* to a sung version and still omitting the original speaking parts. In the Israelites' version of the covenant the rich harmonies and counterpoint that were originally masked by the speaking Voice and then understated in Aron's version are brought to the fore. As a result, the Israelites' version of the covenant is the most sensually beautiful of the three.

The folk sing one final version of the covenant, toward the end of Act II (beginning at m. 1084). This version, essentially reiterating their earlier text, is remarkably overlaid with music derived from the triumphant March, which then continues past the covenant music as the Israelites and Aron exit, leaving Moses once again, as at the beginning, alone on the stage. Many commentators have noted the poignancy of Moses' final utterance in Act II, a text we have already commented on twice. Moses is accompanied by the violins in unison as they play out the final seven notes of an unadorned tone row (RI_6). Ironically, A_6 was most fully developed in the music depicting the building of the golden calf.

Some closing thoughts

While almost all of Schoenberg's music pays close attention to detail, this quality seems to be particularly characteristic of *Moses und Aron*. The opera makes ways of knowing thematic and at the core of that remains its insoluble conflicts about the necessity of symbolic thought and representation. The things we know or recognize always distract us from knowing or recognizing other things. Schoenberg encoded this philosophy into his twelve-tone row, which always achieves part of its potential at the cost of another part.

Moses und Aron remains one of Schoenberg's most essential achievements. The internal conflicts that inhere within its germinal tone row are played out over the whole, generating the opera's personae, their driving forces, and their conflicting needs, abilities, desires, and destinies. Schoenberg's *Moses* is without final dramatic resolution, despite the composer's evident desire over many years to bring the conflict of the brothers to a close by Aron's death. As I have suggested earlier, I feel that Schoenberg had underestimated the importance of Aron. Perhaps he had underestimated or even repressed the importance of Aron-like tendencies within himself. More important, Schoenberg as critic and theorist had underestimated the power of his twelve-tone method to resist musical closure. The instincts of Schoenberg the composer, however, could find no solution of closure. There was none to be found.

7   The String Trio: metaleptic Schoenberg

Something *was* burning. And besides,
At the far end of the room a discredited waltz
Was alive and reciting tales of the conquerors
And their lilies – is all of life thus
A tepid housewarming? And where do the scraps
Of meaning come from? Obviously,
It was time to be off, in another
Direction . . .
John Ashbery: "April Galleons"

Introduction

Schoenberg composed his String Trio, op. 45, primarily during a period of convalescence following a nearly fatal heart attack that he suffered on August 2, 1946.[1] Schoenberg's own recollections of the events of his illness as well as a discussion of their relevance to programmatic elements in the String Trio have been studied by Walter B. Bailey. Bailey describes the original commission for the trio, Schoenberg's initial conception of its form, and the relation of that conception to the finished work.

> The dates on the manuscript of the Trio, 20 August – 23 September 1946, show that it was written largely during the period when Schoenberg was recovering from his heart attack. Leonard Stein, a frequent visitor in the Schoenberg home, recalls that Schoenberg worked on the score even before he was strong enough to leave his bed. The work, however, had been commissioned somewhat earlier by A. Tillman Merritt of Harvard University. In a letter of 28 May, 1946, Merritt asked Schoenberg to write a chamber composition of unspecified instrumentation for a concert that would accompany the "Symposium on Music Criticism" that Harvard would host the following May. . . . Schoenberg accepted the commission in a letter of 15 June 1946, where he noted that he had begun work on the score. An early sketch for the work, dated 7 June 1946, bears this out. Schoenberg explained further in the letter that he had decided on the ensemble of a string trio, that the work would be in one movement, perhaps shorter than the fifteen- to twenty-minute length suggested by Merritt, and that it would consist of three main sections interrupted by two "episodes," all to be played without pause. This description, which matches the external form of the finished Trio, shows

that Schoenberg remained true to his own dictum that a work must be conceived as a whole before any notes were written down. It also shows that the program dealing with his sickness, the advent of which was nearly two months in Schoenberg's future at the date of the commission, was not important for deciding the external form of the Trio. It was, however, as revealed by a closer examination of the work, very important for the general musical character of the Trio and for the relationship between the various sections of the composition.[2]

In the course of his study, Bailey cites numerous sources on the programmatic aspects of the Trio. Although those aspects of the work are personal and not part of the published score, Schoenberg had pointed out specific programmatic contents to his students and friends. Leonard Stein's recollections are particularly helpful in this regard.

> According to Stein, Schoenberg explained the many juxtapositions of unlike material within the Trio as reflections of the delirium which the composer suffered during parts of his illness. Thus, the seemingly fragmentary nature of the Trio's material represents the experience of time and events as perceived from a semiconscious or highly sedated state. These unusual juxtapositions also represent . . . the alternate phases of "pain and suffering" and "peace and repose" that Schoenberg experienced.[3]

Bailey also cites Schoenberg's unpublished essay "Mein Todesfall," his personal recollection of the heart attack and of the subsequent composition of the Trio. Schoenberg's description adds another, perhaps surprising perspective, that of humor.

> On August 2 of this year [1949] it will be three years since what I jokingly call "my fatality." . . . I began the Trio, of which I have told many people that it is a "humorous" representation of my sickness, soon after I was over the worst. But at that time I did not yet know the full reality of my sickness. It was kept a secret from me.[4]

In fact the Trio, as we shall see, does contain humorous passages, but humor is only one of a diversity of musical affects that are expressed through the course of the work. Biographical and autobiographical sources tell us that Schoenberg did not think of the String Trio as a piece of abstract design. And while there is no composer, including Beethoven, who traversed a greater imaginative space during the course of one lifetime, in this respect the composer of the String Trio is unchanged from the young man who composed *Verklärte Nacht* some forty-seven years earlier.

While Bailey argues that a depiction of the composer's illness functioned to inspire the surface character of the music for the Trio, he also recognizes that Schoenberg was wary of musical programs throughout most of his creative life. In short, Schoenberg felt that an accompanying program could in fact limit a listener's subjective response and, moreover, distract from the perception of the music itself.[5] The reader will recall the extended discussion of Schoenberg's deep ambivalence toward program music in the context of Chapter Three, our study of *Pelleas und Melisande.* Schoenberg's conflicted feelings about extra-musical programs continued to influence the reception of his music throughout his career – the Trio is certainly no exception.

The role of the program in the Trio is further complicated by the supposed "secret" nature of the program. In contrast to Bailey's position, Carl Dahlhaus argued that because the autobiographical elements in the String Trio are personal and private, "it would be inappropriate to describe it as programme music." He goes on to say that "the trio should be understood as autonomous music, as form and structure."[6] Our approach, while closer to Bailey's, will be less interested in the specific imagery associated with Schoenberg's illness – the kinds of representative detail that Schoenberg shared with students and friends – and more focused on the ways that the disruptions and diversity of the musical surface function in a wider context to evoke a host of associative memories in the context of a work stimulated by the composer's confrontation with death.

Surpassing *A Survivor from Warsaw* (1947) and the *Phantasy* for violin with piano accompaniment (1949) that followed, the Trio is the great masterpiece of Schoenberg's final period. And yet, some forty-nine years after its composition, the Trio remains a work that is profoundly difficult to interpret. This is largely due to the extreme contrasts and even apparent *non sequiturs* that fracture the work's surface. Schoenberg's depiction "of time and events as perceived from a semiconscious or highly sedated state" along with the "unusual juxtapositions" that represent "the alternate phases of 'pain and suffering' and 'peace and repose'" give rise to music that is full of abrupt and striking changes of texture and affect. Musical ideas are broken off before their completion, through abrupt shifts of texture and mood.[7] But the discontinuities of the work's surface go beyond the juxtaposition of conflicting affects, disruptions and apparent *non sequiturs.* In surprising ways the Trio seems to alternatively *remember* and then abandon the musical languages of its historical antecedents. Passages that employ harsh, strident dissonance give way to passages that evoke the sweetness of tonality only to reemerge and begin the process again. Passages where the shapes of musical phrase have only the most tenuous connection to Schoenberg's precursors give way to passages whose phrase shapes have clear connections to the past. Even the work's musical form presents a conflict between a striking departure from the past and evocations of tradition. We have seen that the musical encoding of remembering and forgetting had been central to Schoenberg's musical thought from early on. Our studies of *Gurrelieder*, *Pelleas und Melisande*, the First String Quartet, and *Moses und Aron* have all emphasized processes of musical recollection. Our theory of uncanny time, the principal topic of Chapter 5, derives its Freudian idea of the uncanny from the return of the repressed, itself a kind of forgetting and remembering. All of these tendencies take on special meaning within the Trio where a radically new musical discourse confronts a host of historical references.

The Trio's fragmented and even fractured surface, its stark contrasts of mood and texture, present enormous difficulties for the critic as well as for musicians who would perform the work. Indeed, much of Schoenberg's music is particularly performance dependent: a characteristic reflected perhaps in his almost excessive concern with rehearsals.[8] Yet an understanding required for a convincing critical interpretation or performance of the Trio will generally have little to do with the labeling of chords or row forms; it will have much to do with successful balances, inflections, and tempi, as well as with a convincing projection of musical drama and its structural correlate, musical form. Moreover, our understanding of these formal and expressive components is necessarily contingent upon the ways that we answer some version of the question that John Ashbery poses in the poem cited as our epigraph: "where do the scraps of meaning come from?" Our answer, in short, is that "the scraps of meaning" come from the ways that this work, or any work, engages, challenges and transforms a nexus of musical associations that ground the work in a larger affective, formal, and conceptual world. In turn, the ground of musical associations, within a work or among works in a larger tradition, is musical *memory*. From this point of view, the musical work is a repository of musical memories, memories that link ideas internal to the work with ideas that place the work into a larger historical context. The fact that *this* work expresses a near death experience brings the role of memory into a particular kind of focus, for the role of retrospection at the time of death is a powerful and virtually universal trope. Leonard Stein's account of the recapitulation of the Trio as "going back and 'reliving' that portion of his life found in the first section"[9] is but one instance of the diverse and pervasive evocations of memory that in many ways and on many levels are central to the Trio.

Because *remembering* is so basic to the work, it will be worthwhile to consider the ways that memory can be encoded within a musical composition. "Musical memory" operates in three conceptually distinct domains. First, memory allows us to perceive a network of time spans, musical events and their transformations to constitute a musical experience.[10] Our discussion of Bergson's two types of memory in Chapter Four, cumulative memory and memories of specific events stimulated by other specific events, are both part of this process. These are the kinds of memory typically invoked most explicitly in music analyses. A second kind of memory connects the first with a set of memories from other musical experiences. Both of Bergson's types are also operative here, only now they take us outside of the domain of the singular work. This is the type of memory involved in recognizing that a given work participates in a larger body of works by style, genre, orchestration, and so forth. It is through this second type of memory that traditions are constituted.

Music historians tend to make the second type of memory explicit. And though music theorists often leave it implicit, the two types of memory necessarily coexist. For example, even if we restrict our observations to purely formal matters, Schoenberg's use of hexachordally partitioned twelve-tone rows in the String Trio will interrelate (i.e. associate and contrast) this work with the larger body of his twelve-tone compositions. Together they form a canon of works that, among other things, explores aspects of hexachordal combinatoriality. Or if we view the work with more specificity, then the relative freedom with which Schoenberg uses his source hexachords, in the context of chamber music, will closely associate the Trio with the *Phantasy*. Indeed, this and other aspects of composition make the Trio and *Phantasy* very kindred works. Thus, memories of the first type evoke and merge with memories of the second type.

A third type of memory connects musical experiences with other kinds of experiences. As before, both of Bergson's categories might apply. Sometimes the third type of memory is merely the association of a musical composition with the time and place of another hearing of the same work. Such is suggested by the phrase "this is our song." And sometimes there are aspects of the musical events themselves that we perceive as analogous to non-musical events or emotions. In the misleading designation of common language, the third set of memories connects musical ideas to the so-called extra-musical.[11] Since any music can and most likely will evoke all three kinds of memory, there is nothing extraordinary in claiming that all three types are operative in Schoenberg's Trio. But the explicit autobiographical content makes the third category of memory particularly apposite to our understanding of the work.

As already noted, traditional analysis tends to focus, at least most explicitly, on the first type of memory: the recognition of themes and their transformations, the perception of musical form, the recognition of recurrent harmonic progressions, the deployment of partitioned row forms, and so forth. Our strategy here will be to use these types of observations not for their own sake, but in support of ideas that interrelate the first type of memory with the other two types. Schoenberg evokes our musical memories in (or *through*) the Trio in extremely varied ways. And because he draws upon so many different aspects of his own musical and extra-musical background in the context of this work's fractured surface, the means through which Schoenberg evokes memory are difficult to understand.

Our perception of the work's fractured surface is a function of what I will call its musical rhetoric. Apart from its place in the history of music theory, rhetoric is a word normally used to refer to the ways that we use language to persuade and influence others. The formal organization of prose as well as the formulation of figurative tropes are both traditionally parts of rhetoric. By musical rhetoric, we refer to the musical analogues to these language based ideas. These include aspects of musical narrative, but also analogues to rhetorical tropes such as metaphor, metonymy, synecdoche and irony. The reader will recall our discussion of these "master tropes" in the Introduction to this book.

Discussions of musical rhetoric necessarily take us into the realm of our third type of memory, the so-called extra-musical. Toward describing aspects of that rhetoric, we will define two key terms: *distraction* and *imperfection*. *Distraction* has a wide range of meanings, from benign to horrifying; here it describes the ways that an anticipated musical trajectory, such as phrase completion or thematic continuation, is disrupted. That disruption has formal as well as dramatic and emotional implications. *Imperfection* is a member of the tropical nexus developed in the Introduction to this book – also including conflict and flux – and developed intermittently throughout. As in its grammatical meaning, imperfection conveys a sense of incompletion. This sense of incompletion in our present context is the result of a *distraction*. Thus, the two tropes, distraction and imperfection, work as a pair, with the former leading to the latter. I will suggest that in the context of the Trio the closure that is avoided, the *perfection* that is never achieved, symbolizes death itself.

The impact of musical rhetoric is largely dependent upon the ways that formal constituents of the work intersect with a larger tradition. In studying the work's form, including its evocations of tonality and features of its phrase structures, we will argue that these design components within Schoenberg's Trio are specifically *memorial* in nature.[12] This is to say that aspects of form in the Trio are not simply means toward structural coherence, but in addition express specific kinds of recollection that are bound up with the work's narrative impulse. In addition to the memorial aspects of form, Schoenberg thematicizes memory by evoking a single most significant composer as precursor for the work's narrative. Musical memory within the work also focuses on a single privileged *genre*. The composer is Beethoven, and the work's many adaptations of a Beethovenian rhetoric are crucial to its design and content. Of course for Schoenberg, Beethoven, specifically late Beethoven, would have been nearly synonymous with the activity of deathbed composition. The privileged genre is that of the waltz, an emotionally loaded choice for a Viennese musician of Schoenberg's generation, especially for one whose life is coming to a close on soil far away from his native land and the culture of his youth. As we shall see, Schoenberg uses waltz fragments throughout the Trio to create a sense of repose and equilibrium that vividly contrasts with the more disruptive elements surrounding those fragments. That sense of repose and equilibrium in turn is remarkably congruent with Freud's concept of the death instinct, and so we shall see that Schoenberg's waltz fragments are specifically linked with the near death experience that the work portrays.

Given the centrality of memory in the Trio, it is only natural to ask if the status of Schoenberg as Jew is relevant in understanding that work. We need only recall the reasons behind Schoenberg's emigration to the United States to recognize the immense impact that Schoenberg's Jewish heritage had had upon his life. Of course, as discussed in Chapter Six, that heritage is engaged very explicitly in some of Schoenberg's works: *Moses und Aron, A Survivor from Warsaw, Kol Nidre*, Schoenberg's setting of *Psalm 130*, and his final work a *Modern Psalm*.[13] While it would be far-fetched to suggest that the String Trio is explicitly connected to Schoenberg's struggle with Judaism, a connection with specifically Jewish imagery can be made nonetheless. Alexander Ringer describes how Mahler in his Second Symphony "waived Christian notions of salvation in favour of Jacob's struggle with the angel."[14] Harold Bloom has suggested that the angel in Jacob's nightlong struggle is death itself.[15] I will suggest that similar imagery is not inappropriate in understanding the Trio.

The chapter closes with an analysis of one passage from the Trio, mm. 81–102. This passage contains the first presentation of what subsequently emerges as the "waltz strand," a discontinuous thread of waltz evocations that emerge and then disappear again and again until the work's final measures. The waltz itself is introduced by a passage marked *quasi recitativo* reminiscent of the similar passages in the late quartets of Beethoven. With the emergence of the waltz, the listener first apprehends the potential for repose and balance that the returning waltz fragments will cumulatively suggest as the work continues to unfold. The rhythmic constituents of the waltz, its regular meter (actually a slow 6/8 time) and its regular phrase rhythms are basic components of the perceived respite that the waltz fragments express. The phrase rhythm that brings the waltz into relief comprises the antecedent and consequent of a musical period, or rather what might have comprised a period were it not for the *distraction* that causes the music to spin off in another direction. In turn the resultant *imperfection*, the inability of the waltz to conclude, sets up the pattern of dissolution and reemergence – or to use Freudian tropes, *repression* and *return* – that I have already described. Toward similar ends, the passage incorporates evocations of tonal harmony.[16] Like the waltz itself, the implications of tonal function emerge and dissolve again and again. And all of this interacts with the underlying twelve-tone structure. Twelve-tone technique, the composer's ordering and reordering of the work's hexachordal components, along with the various ways that the resultant twelve-tone rows are used in combination with one another, provides Schoenberg with the technical means to generate the pitches at the work's fractured surface as well as the means to establish a more fundamental, if elusive, unity among the shards that comprise that surface.

Distraction and imperfection

The tropes of *imperfection* and *distraction* generalize well and can be used to inform interpretations of most of Schoenberg's music, as well as that of many other composers. Needless to say, the tropes take on specific dimensions within the Trio. As I have already indicated, the term *distraction* will be used to describe the ways that an anticipated musical trajectory, such as phrase completion or thematic continuation, is disrupted. Distraction also describes the dramatic or emotional affect of that disruption. Outside of musical contexts, in the mental and physical life of normal day to day existence, we can lose continuity of thought through a variety of means. To "drift off" would normally imply a benign diversion of consciousness; it is what happens, for example, when we are mentally fatigued or when something that has happened sets us off on a train of thought seemingly disconnected from whatever we had been paying attention to before. Much of our fantasy lives are distractions in just this sense. Yet being distracted can of course be more serious than a mere drifting off. Indeed, the original meaning of distraction denotes being torn asunder. Thus distraction at its extreme suggests *sparagmos* – the Dionysian rending and devouring of living flesh symbolic of rebirth through death, a topic Schoenberg had explored as early as the *Gurrelieder*.[17]

In contrast to distractions that yield imaginative play, or physical or emotional pain, there are distractions that yield darkness and silence. To "doze off" is like drifting off, except that it is followed by dream consciousness or unconsciousness; when consciousness is abruptly interrupted and followed by unconsciousness we call it "blacking out."

Example 7.1. Measures 41–51. Used by permission of Belmont Music Publishers, Pacific Palisades, CA 90272.

These various ways of breaking off continuity, expressed through Schoenberg's musical technique, are essential elements in the way that the story goes. For example, the fermata over the bar line between measures 44 and 45, near the end of Part 1, looks non-consequential enough on the page. In the *Sämtliche Werke* it is crowded into a space at the end of the printed line (see Ex. 7.1). In its graphic presentation, it appears almost as though it is an afterthought.

Yet the fermata arrives after an extended section of anguished passages all played *fortissimo*. And it is followed by a dramatic shift of texture, played *pianissimo*. There is a tendency in performance to give this fermata short shrift. But if we think of it as the moment where the preceding pain has become unbearable, as the moment where we "black out," then the events that follow measure 44, though only a measure later, are understood as dramatically and temporally removed from that which had come before. The fermata as "black-out" functions as an ellipsis, a break in consciousness separating the time and place of what came before from what comes after. We might not want to pin the image down, but nonetheless imagery of this sort will help a performance more than noticing, for example, that a new hexachord begins with the 2/2, *poco meno mosso*. However, the point is not that the articulation of the new hexachord is insignificant, but rather that its significance needs to be interpreted in terms of an unfolding drama.

The term *imperfection* has been a central trope throughout this study of Schoenberg. The term is taken from grammar, where an imperfect tense refers to action not yet completed. In medieval theology, God is conceptualized as "Perfect" in that God is not on the way toward becoming God, God simply *is*. Much closer to Schoenberg's generation, Nietzsche writes that *we* live our lives "in the imperfect tense."

> Existence fundamentally is – an imperfect tense that can never become a perfect one. If death at last brings the desired forgetting, by that act it at the same time extinguishes the present and all being, and therewith sets the seal on the knowledge that being is only an uninterrupted has-been, a thing that lives by negating, consuming and contradicting itself.[18]

Whereas the teachings of the Catholic Church had promised perfection in death through sharing in the glory of God, for Nietzsche, if we achieve "perfection," it is only through death which "extinguishes the present and all being." Whether or not Schoenberg shared in Nietzsche's metaphysics, the idea is remarkably congruent with Schoenbergian musical rhetoric, and uncanny in its relation to the life-and-death struggle depicted in the String Trio.

The term *perfection* has other points of contact with musical rhetoric as well. In music, we still use the term "perfect" to refer to intervals that earlier styles had thought suitable for closure. While Mozart or Haydn could use musical imperfection to express wit or to achieve lyric contemplation, closure, which is to say "perfection," no matter how much avoided, is always inevitable. In contrast, a profound shift occurs with the advent of the Romantic imagination. As closure becomes elusive it becomes that which needs to be achieved, and so it becomes something at risk. One already senses this to a degree in Beethoven. In Schubert, however, the impossibility of emotional closure becomes a recurrent trope, evidenced by many of his songs. Mahler's symphonies continue this development.

In the extreme, closure becomes that which *cannot* be achieved. To my mind, the works of the Second Viennese School are precisely works about "imperfection" in this sense. The vectors of musical imagination always seem to go beyond what is given, to disappear into silence. In this way, as well as so many others, Schoenberg receives and heightens the Romantic tradition. But none of this takes place in a vacuum. Freudian psychology, Einsteinian physics, and Schoenbergian musical ideas are all about the impossibility of closure. As explored in the Introduction to this book, closure is impossible in Freudian psychology in that the unconscious (or id), for Freud, remains inaccessible to direct knowledge. In this sense, we cannot get to the bottom of things. We have also seen how Kafka's stories obsess over variants of imperfection. In analogous ways, Einsteinian physics deprive us of a privileged vantage for reckoning time and space.[19] To use our trope, these four men provide a psychology, prose, physics, and music of imperfection.

The principal way that Schoenberg expresses this sense of imperfection is by composing musical ideas that suggest a continuation that is somehow diverted, disturbed or disrupted. Of course, this aspect of musical rhetoric is already well established by the "First Viennese School"; indeed, understanding Haydn, Mozart or Beethoven is quite impossible without having a sense of such diversions and disruptions. The impression of imperfection can also be achieved by juxtaposing musical ideas that are in irreconcilable conflict with on another. This is a technique developed extensively by Mahler, and remarkably foreshadowed in late Beethoven.[20]

Having developed an understanding of the roles played by distraction and imperfection in Schoenberg's musical rhetoric, we need to place these techniques in a more synoptic context which reflects the kind of coherence that grows out the very old-fashioned impulse of story-telling. The real work of interpretation lies in formulating a convincing sense of the flow of musical ideas, so that crowding-in, breaking-off and dozing-off become convincing variables in the overall flux of the work.

As the passage from Bailey cited earlier indicated, Schoenberg had settled on the main outlines of the Trio prior to his heart attack. The work is divided into five principal sections: Part 1 (mm. 1–51), First Episode (mm. 52–132), Part 2 (mm. 133–79), Second Episode (mm. 180–207) and Part 3 (mm. 208–93). These formal articulations are easily heard, and they are also clearly marked in the published score. The work's shattered surface is nowhere more evident than at its very beginning, where rapid and radical shifts of register, strident dissonance, and the juxtaposition of quickly changing musical fragments convey a sense of pain and disorientation (Ex. 7.2, see also Ex. 7.3).[21]

The Trio opens with a sudden calamity and world-changing event that separates us from all that had come before. In *Moses und Aron* it was the character of Moses whose world was transformed. Here the protagonist is

Example 7.2. The opening of the String Trio. Used by permission of Belmont Music Publishers, Pacific Palisades, CA 90272.

Example 7.2. (*cont.*)

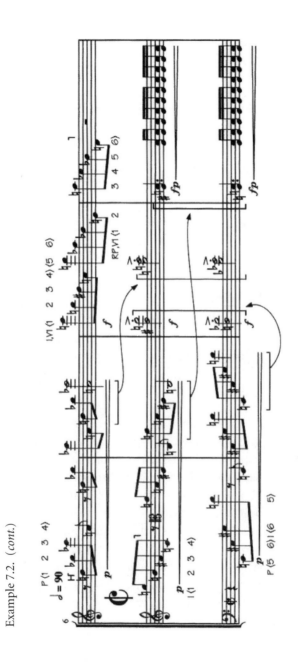

Example 7.3. Schoenberg's sketches. Used by permission of Belmont Music Publishers, Pacific Palisades, CA 90272.

(a) A1

(b) A49

(c) A13

Schoenberg himself, without the dramatic mask of another persona. Once again we recall Kafka's recurrent strategy of beginning the story just after or just as a world-changing event has taken place. The pain and confusion that is immediately available to our musical intuitions, is also reflected in Schoenberg's use of twelve-tone technique. The opening passage is generated from the row area A_D, as in Schoenberg's sketch "A1," shown in Example 7.3a, the source for the hexachords that compose its harmonic and melodic constituents.[22] At the outset, Schoenberg partitions his rows – one might say that he has "exploded" his rows – in such a manner that the linear order of A_D is impossible to perceive, at least in real time. For example, in the first measure the first hexachord of the prime form (labeled **P**) is fully intertwined with the first hexachord of the combinatorial inversion (labeled **I**). Thus the prime form alternates ordinals 1 and 3 in the viola (D-E♭), places ordinal 2 in the cello, and then moves on to ordinals 4 (violin A), 5 (cello E) and 6 (viola D♭). All of this is entangled with the inversion: ordinal 1 and 3 in the violin (G-F♯), ordinal 2 in the cello (B), and then ordinals 4 (viola C), 5 (cello F), and 6 (violin G♯). While the linear ordering of sketch A1 is effectively obliterated in its initial realization, what Schoenberg does project – and even this is tenuous – is the inversion that maps G onto D, A♯ onto B, F♯ onto E♭, and so forth (juxtaposing the first note of the violin trill and first note of the viola trill, second note of the violin trill and second note of the viola trill, first note of the cello and second note of the cello, etc.). Of course these pairs are the basis of the combinatorial inversion associated with A_D.[23]

As the passage continues, the linear order gradually clarifies. The deployment of the source materials, at first in disarray and then only gradually coming into focus, is undoubtedly programmatic, where disarray portrays mental confusion and anguish, and focus portrays something about at least recognizing the state of one's condition.[24]

In the greater scheme of the Trio's structural and expressive ideas, the dyadic couplings of the opening anticipate (and negate) an equilibrium that is suggested and evaded throughout the work. Indeed, the source idea and its complementary reflection might have been used to constitute a symbolic wholeness: a perfect equilibrium of forces to depict a physiological homeostasis.[25] Yet the opening expresses anything but an equilibrium of forces, anything but an inversional "balance."[26] While Schoenberg's concept of the *Grundgestalt* always includes a tension between centripetal and centrifugal forces respectively effecting coherence and dispersal, the centripetal forces are remarkably heightened here.[27] The potential for equilibrium is presented in the beginning as a shattering of equilibrium, or more precisely as the shattering of a relative equilibrium that must be imagined settled in silence just before we begin. Whatever that silence depicts, the opening is clearly a painful distraction that breaks into, and so emerges out of it.

As we progress through the first forty-four measures, the work's opening becomes a virtual study of disruption and distraction. In other places, for example, just before the beginning of Episode 2 (m. 179), the work seems to doze off, to drift into silence (Example 7.4).[28] This silence is followed by a quasi-comical *martellato*, which seems to function either as an "awakening," or an entering into dream consciousness (my choice) at the beginning of Episode 2. But, no matter how we interpret the *martellato*, its entrance is abrupt and disorienting.[29]

A similar effect of dozing off takes place, even more dramatically, at the very end of the Trio (Example 7.5b), this in conjunction with the unraveling of the consequent phrase in a musical period. At other places yet, the drift is into a *non sequitur* (see mm. 92–3, discussed in Example 7.9 below).

Form as memorial

A number of commentators have recognized that the Trio integrates or evokes formal procedures which predate Schoenberg's twelve-tone

Example 7.4. The conclusion of Part 2 and the beginning of Episode 2
(mm. 178–81). Used by permission of Belmont Music Publishers, Pacific Palisades,
CA 90272.

compositions, both within Schoenberg's own evolution, and beyond that
toward Schoenberg's precursors. For example, Dahlhaus recognized a return
to formal procedures that had concerned Schoenberg in his earliest works.

> The work realizes – albeit in a more complicated form in which the original
> scheme is hardly recognizable – a formal idea that had already been used
> by Schoenberg in *Pelleas und Melisande* and the First Chamber Symphony,
> Op.9: the idea of condensing the four movements of a sonata – Allegro, slow
> movement, scherzo and finale – into a single movement, in such a way as to
> identify the movements of the cycle with the sections of a sonata allegro
> (principal theme, subordinate theme, elaboration and recapitulation).[30]

Dahlhaus heard Part 1 as principal theme/first movement, the First
Episode as subordinate theme/slow movement, Part 2 as scherzo, the Second
Episode as "elaboration," presumably a development section, and Part 3

as finale/recapitulation. The Dahlhaus model is not altogether convincing. First, it ignores strong correlations that interrelate the two episodes and distinguish them from Part 1 and Part 2. In addition to the distinctive row ordering reserved for the episodes, both episodes move characteristically through row areas related by three semitones, a move not characteristic of the other sections of the work.[31] More important, however, the recapitulation of the cantabile theme from Part 2 (beginning originally in m. 159, recapitulated in m. 282), brings it into the row area of Part 1, while the recapitulation of the First Episode (beginning in m. 233) is without change of "key."

Example 7.2, together with Examples 7.5a and 7.5b are designed to show the apposite "key scheme." The examples label each row form, and also give the ordinal position of each pitch within that form. As we have already noted, the work opens in A_D. This row area comprises the entire Part 1 on into the opening five measures of the First Episode.

Example 7.5a shows the beginning of the cantabile theme from Part 2 and Example A_B; its recapitulation is in A_D. The reader will find that the row partitioning is much less complex than at the opening, and for our context requires no special explanation. More to the point, the recapitulation of the cantabile theme brings it into the row area of the work's beginning (which is identical to the beginning of the recapitulation).

If sonata principle is understood as bringing contrasting "keys" into reconciliation at the recapitulation, then Part 2, not Episode 1, would seem to constitute the subordinate group. On the other hand, this "reconciliation" comes far too late in the work to function as in the traditional sonata form. Moreover, if Episode 1 is not the "subordinate group," then what is its function in a larger sonata form? One alternative is to hear Part 1 as introductory, Episode 1 as principal group, and Part 2 as subordinate group. But skewed key relations still remain in that Part 1, not Episode 1, introduces the row area that returns to begin the recapitulation and also to bring the work to a close.

There are obviously many difficulties in trying to hear the Trio as sonata. Nonetheless, the recapitulatory function of Part 3 does bring the sonata principle to mind. More important still, the aspect of Dahlhaus' argument that centers on Schoenberg's return to a multi-movement/single movement conception of form remains compelling. Schoenberg combines the principal sections of the Trio, each of which can be heard as a movement in itself, into a unified single movement design in ways that harken back to procedures from the first period of his creative life. Dahlhaus, in cataloging earlier multi-movement/single movement forms, might have added to his list the First String Quartet, and more controversially, *Verklärte Nacht* as well.[32]

Example 7.5a. The cantabile theme of Part 2 (mm. 159–69). Used by permission of Belmont Music Publishers, Pacific Palisades, CA 90272.

Example 7.5a. (*cont.*)

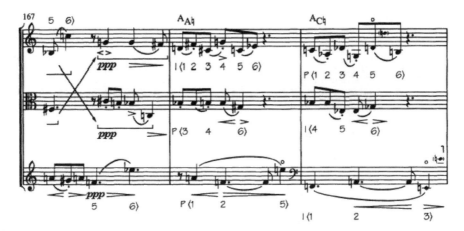

Had he done so, the final list would have comprised, with the exclusion of *Gurrelieder*, every major work of Schoenberg's first period. In composing such forms, early Schoenberg engages a tradition that goes back to the final movement of Beethoven's Ninth Symphony, and continues through the works of Liszt, Wagner and Strauss. Schoenberg had abandoned this type of formal design beginning with the Second String Quartet. That he should return to it late in life, after a close brush with death, is remarkable to say the least.[33] Form, in this context, is not merely "formal"; it is a specific locus of musical memory.

Another facet of memory has to do with the ways the work evokes memories of a specific musical lineage. As is well known, Schoenberg was particularly concerned with his relationships to specific composers in the Austrian and German tradition. In addition to his claims that his real teachers were Bach, Mozart, Beethoven, Brahms and Wagner, there was his lifelong engagement with Brahmsian "developing variations," and also the selfconscious synthesis of Brahms and Wagner so manifest in the early works.[34] The Trio evokes more than one voice, but the precursor most vividly present is Beethoven, specifically late Beethoven.[35] Dahlhaus understood and wrote about some aspects of this presence.

> Part III, the finale, is simply a recapitulation; indeed in stark contradiction to Schoenberg's principle of 'developing variation', a principle which aims at the constant transformation of themes and motifs, earlier groups of bars are recapitulated unchanged or with only slight variations. Even stranger than the literal nature of the reprise, however, is the procedure of patching together

Example 7.5b. The recapitulation of the cantabile theme (m. 282–end). Used by permission of Belmont Music Publishers, Pacific Palisades, CA 90272.

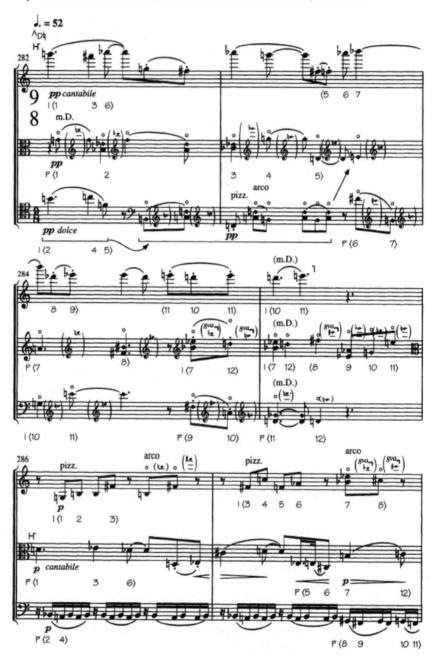

Example 7.5b. (*cont.*)

of what had initially been kept separate, or conversely, of cutting a few bars
out of an earlier phrase. This patchwork technique seems like a relapse into
formal simplicity or even primitivity. Yet it is just this paradoxical
interlocking of extreme complexity and a strange disregard for the postulates
of formal 'culture' that is one of the distinguishing feature of a late work, a
feature which Schoenberg's trio shares with the late Beethoven quartets.[36]

Dahlhaus need not have referred to the recapitulation in order to invoke Beethoven. His presence is vivid at many junctures throughout the Trio, including the work's remarkable opening.

The opening (see Example 7.2 above) can be understood as the shattering of an imaginary equilibrium that might exist only outside of the work's frame. Its musical ideas heap upon one another, disrupt continuity, displace or disallow musical consequence (that which *should* follow), break off stability of phrase, timbre, tessitura and meter.[37]

The anguish of the opening, so far as I know, is without precedent. However, its fractured rhetoric, its halting broken phrases, and its seeming inability to settle into an even relatively stable musical space do have a predecessor in Beethoven. Even in his early works, Beethoven occasionally breaks off a phrase midway, as though he has thrown his hands into the air rejecting that which has accumulated. It is in his late works, however, that this particular aspect of Beethovenian rhetoric becomes exaggerated. Examples we have noted in our discussion of the uncanny are apposite here as well: the opening of the last movement of the *Hammerklavier* Sonata, where it is as though Beethoven is groping for his fugue subject before our very ears, or the last movement of the Ninth Symphony, where he begins by recollecting and then rejecting the previous movements, "nicht diese Töne!" Perhaps most to the point there are the abrupt rhetorical shifts in the last quartets, especially in Op. 130, in the *Grosse Fuge*, and in Op. 131. And of course the association of these works with grave illness toward the end of life is well-known.

The role of dynamics is crucial in the portrayal of this emergence out of silence, even more crucial the second time around at the outset of the recapitulation. The opening of the recapitulation, which in a sense is very anti-Beethovenian, is particularly difficult to perform effectively. While Beethoven's sonata recapitulations tend to be moments of triumph, Schoenberg's recapitulation here is a moment of relapse, or even more convincingly a recollection of the pain depicted at the opening.[38]

There are other aspects of the opening that are Beethovenian as well. Its very first measures combine the effect of "slowly-coming-into-being" so often used by Beethoven to open works, with the effect of "entering in *medias res*," a rhetorical gesture also derivable from Beethoven.[39] Yet it is the shattered, disruptive qualities of the opening that are most salient. And these characteristics give rise to procedures of distraction and imperfection that ramify throughout the Trio.

Evocations of tonality

A Freudian reading of Schoenberg's "overcoming of tonality" might well insist that the tonal world that Schoenberg had overcome necessarily became the repressed world – a kind of musical id shadowing the surface – that is hidden by that which is explicitly manifest in his music.[40] In Freudian theory, repressed memories inevitably and inescapably take on subsequent manifestations, usually in transformed or hidden contexts of meaning. Freud's "return of the repressed" in some respects is similar to Proust's *mémoire involontaire*: the most powerful recollections are not under our rational control. Indeed, Walter Benjamin's reading of Proust emphasizes the complicity of remembering with forgetting in the sense that powerful memories are associated with things long forgotten.[41] In this light, the cogency of Schoenberg's earlier cited remark is underscored and given new meaning: "I was so weak that I don't know at all how I wrote it."

Charles Rosen, who also recognizes that Schoenberg reaches back into his own past within the Trio, emphasizes that the Trio "is a synthesis of much of Schoenberg's music, bringing together aspects that do not often coexist in the same work."[42] These aspects include evocations of tonal harmony.

> Like many of his later works, it is based on a series that permits the introduction of the perfect triads associated with tonality, although it avoids any implication of the harmonic function of tonality. Schoenberg uses these perfect triads for what might be called their latent sweetness and repose, but avoids using them for any sense of cadence; they initiate but do not close. To what extent these latent qualities are naturally inherent in the triads and to what extent culturally induced is not an answerable puzzle: the purity of the harmonic series in these chords plays an evident role, and so does their traditional association with the structural consonances of tonal music. Schoenberg uses the triads as background for his most expressive motifs, and he does not rely on the "innate" potency of the triads to make his point, which is always clarified essentially by texture.[43]

Rosen's claim that the Trio "avoids any implication of the harmonic function of tonality" does not seem to square with his observation that the triads at least in part evoke a "traditional association with the structural consonances of tonal music." The keen insight is in Rosen's phrase "they initiate but do not close." To initiate a tonal motion is to imply the conclusion of that motion. To be sure, the Trio never achieves a tonal cadence. Yet Rosen's idea of triads that "initiate but do not close" hits upon a fundamental aspect of the piece. That aspect is realized through versions of the rhetorical tropes of *distraction* and *imperfection*.

Voice-leading implications evocative of tonal functions are found within the sketches for the work's tone rows. In sketch A1 (Example 7.3a above), in addition to the beamed stems that divide each hexachord into disjunct trichords, the first and last notes of each hexachord are double stemmed.[44] The latter notation suggests a partitioning of each hexachord into "outer dyad"

Example 7.6. The triadic voice-leading implications of sketch "A1."

and "inner tetrachord," and moreover suggests a semitone voice leading connecting the first and last member of each hexachord. Both partitions of the respective hexachords (disjunct trichords and outer dyads plus inner tetrachords) are highly significant in the Trio, although numerous other partitions are used as well.[45]

Example 7.6, based on sketch A1, interprets Schoenberg's trichordal partitions as vertical chords and the double stemmed notes as voice-leading paradigms.

As can be readily heard, the progression of chords in P_D strongly suggests a tonal resolution to D (minor or major).[46] In earlier chapters we had seen that the key of D minor/major had special significance for Schoenberg. It is the repressed that returns at crucial junctures through the Trio as well.

The tonal implications for the inverted form are a bit more tenuous, but a resolution to G minor is suggested nonetheless. (I have added the resolutions to both progressions in parentheses.) In this context, the ordering of V2 takes on special significance in both $\mathbf{P_D}$ and $\mathbf{I_G}$. In $\mathbf{P_D}$, the exchange of D♯ and E – compare the first two chords to the last two – vitiates the "dominant" A major triad but allows the chromatic voice leading, E-D♯ [-D], to emerge. The alteration that opens $\mathbf{I_G}$,V2 introduces a "G dominant" chord, and then an "A♭ dominant," the latter suggestive of an augmented sixth chord. The augmented sixth is a function that Schoenberg had used as a dominant substitute in his early tonal works, and there is a return to that function here.[47] A recurrent realization of sketch A1 in the Trio progresses first through $\mathbf{P_D}$ and then through $\mathbf{RI_G}$. A trichordal progression based on this order is shown as Example 7.6c. The progression is remarkable in the way that the repeated descending bass line B♭-A-G♯-G binds the two row forms together, and also for the final bass descent, D-D♭-C-B, which can easily suggest a circular progression back to the first trichord of $\mathbf{P_D}$.

Schoenberg does not place the voice leadings extrapolated in Example 7.6 at the surface of the music, but they do emerge close to it. One remarkable passage in this regard is found at the beginning of Episode 1, shown in Example 7.7. Before changing to principal row area of the episode at m. 57, Schoenberg completes $\mathbf{P_D}$,V2, which begins with the trichord in measure 51, and completed by the trichord of mm. 52–6. The A-C♯ pedal, with arpeggiation of D♯-A-C♯-D♯ constitutes our "vitiated dominant." The poignancy of the D♯'s against the A-C♯ pedal is largely based on tonal memory.

A passage derived from the progression of our Example 7.6c occurs in mm. 267–75 (Example 7.8). This transitional section, which interconnects recapitulatory material in Part 3, modulates from $\mathbf{A_D}$ to $\mathbf{A_{A}}$♭, with a concomitant intensification of rhythmic displacement. The timbre and rhythms are distinctly Beethovenian, and the harmonies shown in Example 7.6c, along with their tonal evocations, are fairly clear, at least for the first six measures. Among the details of construction, we should note the reversal of several dyads. These affect the harmonies as well as the motivic interaction among the dyads as they are passed from voice to voice.[48] Placed in a slightly larger context, the "Beethoven passage" functions as a distraction from a waltz fragment that had emerged four measures previously (m. 263).[49]

Rosen's observation about triads that initiate but do not close also resonates with some points that Hans Keller made about Schoenberg's twelve-tone works in general and about the Trio specifically.[50] Keller cites Schoenberg's essay on twelve-tone composition: "Formerly the harmony had served not only as a source of beauty, but, more important, as a means

Example 7.7. The beginning of Episode 1 (mm. 45–58). Used by permission of Belmont Music Publishers, Pacific Palisades, CA 90272.

of distinguishing the features of form. For instance, only a consonance was considered suitable for an ending." And then continues as follows:

> Thus Schoenberg in "the" essay on twelve-tone composition. Thus and no further: the consonance did not identify the ending, since it appeared elsewhere, too; it was the total meeting of expectation, the perfect cadence, that did – and we have, in fact, lost the means of saying unambiguously, beyond musical doubt, that "this is the end." Through this loss, we have gained plenty of other things – the possibility of intensely meaningful open ends, and ends whose very ambiguity adds meaning – but the fact remains that while unification through tonality, stability through adherence to the

Example 7.8. Measures 267–75. Used by permission of Belmont Music Publishers, Pacific Palisades, CA 90272.

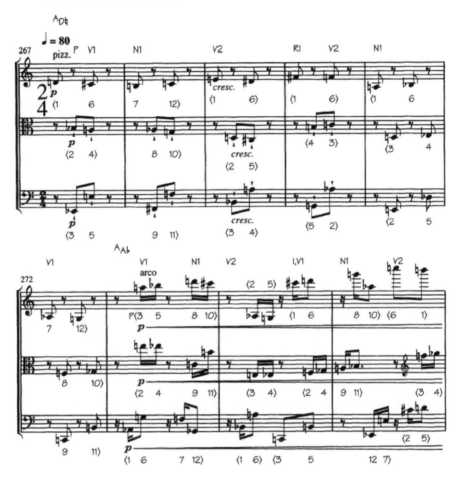

tonic and instability through modulation (development) have all found potent substitutes, or rather successors, at least in Schoenberg's dodecaphony, the unmistakable end, obvious to the naked ear of an infant, is a thing of the tonal past and the tonal present.

For Keller, *all* of Schoenberg's twelve-tone harmony represses a tonal basis, and so represses tonal closure. His view is stated succinctly a bit later in the same paper: "Harmonically, then, his dodecaphony is composed against the background – accent on the "against" – of well-defined, well-implied, but violently suppressed (and psychoanalytically speaking, repressed) tonal expectations . . ."[51].

One may doubt the universal validity of Keller's position, but it is convincing in many passages within the String Trio, and as we have seen in our analyses of the Third String Quartet and *Moses und Aron*, it is convincing in many passages of Schoenberg's other twelve-tone music as well. In fact, the only specific example in Keller's paper is taken from the opening of the First Episode in the Trio, the music we discussed in Example 7.7.[52] For Keller, this passage indicates a repressed tonal background that has suddenly emerged into the twelve-tone foreground. This is precisely congruent with the ideas from Freud and Proust that we have already developed. The emergence of tonality, powerful memories of "things long forgotten," exemplifies Freud's *unheimlich* and Proust's *mémoire involontaire* in that the force of the memory necessarily requires having first been forgotten.[53]

Memorial aspects of phrase structure

Within Schoenberg's theoretical and pedagogical works, his discussions of the musical phrase are primarily concerned with his historical antecedents. For this reason, and others such as Schoenberg's well known concern with his place in a larger tradition, I assume that phrase structure, in the context of Schoenberg's music, is often linked to memory. This is so not only in our first sense memory, as we group small events to form coherent larger events, but most crucially in our second sense as well, as we perceive a given musical work to participate in and thus transform a musical tradition.

Schoenberg's most developed discussion of musical phrase is in his book *Fundamentals of Musical Composition*.[54] It is here that he collects and discusses examples of his two basic models for phrase structure: the period and the sentence. Although the examples are numerous, the composer says nothing of his own practice. So, while we learn that he considers the two models to be basic to the music of the past and well as basic for one learning the craft in his own day, Schoenberg says nothing about their status within his own works. Webern, on the other hand, is explicit on this point. In the lectures posthumously published as *The Path to New Music*, Webern invokes the same models, sentence and period, and then goes on to say that both inform *all* music after Beethoven, including Schoenberg's.[55] While Webern's claim may be hyperbolic, the importance of the models for the Second Viennese is made clear nonetheless. And though Webern's lectures, from the early 1930s, predate Schoenberg's Trio by more than a decade, the relationships to the classical models are clearly still operative in the Trio.[56]

We have already noted how the evocations of tonality, built into the tone rows, imply and then deny closure. Schoenberg uses phrase structures toward similar rhetorical ends. One remarkable passage in this regard occurs at the very end of the Trio, the music shown in Example 7.5b. The music implies a vitiated period. The antecedent phrase comprises mm. 282–5. The consequent phrase begins in m. 286, but begins to unravel three measures later, and never achieves closure. The tropes of distraction and imperfection operate to disallow the conclusion of the period. The overall effect is stunning and the passage is worth studying in some detail.

The row components for the phrase – P_D and I_G – are, as already noted, derived from A_D. Significantly, $V2$ is omitted from the initial presentation. The partition of $I_G, V1$ into ordinals <1,3,6> and <2,4,5> allows the violin to project a double neighbor figure around G. The evocation of tonal harmonies is particularly lucid in m. 282, where there is an alternation between G major and D dominant seventh sonorities. To achieve this, Schoenberg manages a spectacular intertwining of the two row forms. The viola D and Bb, derived from P_D, unite with the outer voices to achieve Schoenberg's harmonic ends. The tonal function of D is clear. Bb substitutes for A, in the dominant chord, to create a whole tone structure of precisely the type and function that Schoenberg had discussed years earlier in the *Harmonielehre*.[57] After the initial measure, the harmonies become more difficult to understand, at least from a tonal perspective, and yet G continues to resonate in our ears. At the end of the phrase, m. 285, Schoenberg touches on D minor, and then in the high viola harmonics we hear the succession of ordinals <8,9,10,11> from I_G, C#-Eb-D-E. The first three pitches invert the contour of m. 282, now circling D, and this overlaps with the last three pitches, which replicate the G-F#-Ab contour, now beginning on Eb, Eb-D-E. The inversion of this contour beginning on D, D-Eb-Db, the retrograde of the previous viola C#-Eb-D, initiates the second phrase in m. 286.

This second phrase can be interpreted as the consequent of a musical period, or what might have been the consequent if not for its subsequent unraveling. A consequent with delayed closure is of course common in the classical style. But here closure is avoided altogether. Even beyond that, the passage is a bit more complicated than an evocation of the classical period. At m. 286, the change in timbre and register along with the crucial arrival of D, anticipated in m. 285, not only make m. 286 sound like the beginning of a phrase but more emphatically as a structural downbeat that usurps the function of the previous G downbeat (m. 282) and causes us to hear mm. 282–5, in retrospect, as an extended upbeat to m. 286. The model of a musical period is still operative, but not in the classical sense where the antecedent would typically initiate a tonic to dominant motion. Here D asserts itself as tonic.

The consequent begins to unravel halfway through m. 288; it is as though the viola loses its thread of thought. The distraction happens in several stages. The cello's accompaniment figure crowds in on itself, beginning in m. 287. At 288, the viola hesitates for an eighth rest and then plays its motive, B-C-E-D♯. The final pitch of this motive, D♯, is unsettling in part because D as tonic has just been so strongly projected. Heard in combination with the cello and the first two notes of the following violin figure, the harmony, although fleeting, hints at a dominant function. Schoenberg has used the hesitant B-C-E-D♯ motive to move us into **V2**, the part of the row avoided in the antecedent phrase. The rhythmic shape of this motive, along with that of the subsequent violin motive, gives rise to a series of echoes and mirror images as the musical idea drifts from voice to voice. The final iteration of this motive, anticipated in mm. 288–9, is derived from $P_D, V2$, a transformation of the idea we remember from the outset of Episode 1 and from its recapitulation in Part 3 (mm. 232–7). Just before this happens (in the violin figure beginning with the downbeat of m. 292) there is a final reminiscence of a rhythmic figure associated with earlier passages that form part of an intermittent thread of waltz evocations that have emerged and then disappeared again and again.[58] The two final pitch-classes in the violin are the lower and upper neighbors to D, so strongly associated with that note at the outset of the phrase. The final harmony throws even this dominant function into doubt by projecting another dominant, V of D♭. This is achieved by juxtaposing the final dyad of $I_G, V2$ against the close of **PD,V2**. The sense of incompletion, of imperfection, is vivid.

Schoenberg composes his "non-ending," to my ear one of the most beautiful in all music, by virtuosic manipulation of his tone rows. Yet one need not be aware of the twelve-tone logic to hear the musical idea drifting from voice to voice, unable or unwilling to find closure. The final suggestion and avoidance of closure through the completion of a musical period is one of numerous times that Schoenberg has used this strategy in the work, a strategy that is most vivid in the sections where the waltz emerges. The unraveling of the final waltz strand brings the central tropes of distraction and imperfection into poignant focus as the work drifts into silence.

The waltz as trope: repose, equilibrium and images of death

For a Viennese of Schoenberg's generation, evocations of waltz figuration are necessarily saturated with musical memory. The waltz along with its precursors and its close relations such as Ländler had been a pervasive fact of Viennese musical life, and so, a sense of nostalgia, bitter or otherwise, is inescapably linked to it.

Within the Trio, evocations of the waltz first emerge in Episode 1 (m. 86) and then form a conceptual thread that is repeatedly broken or submerged, only to reappear time and again throughout the remainder of the work.[59] Thus the waltz, in addition to its other functions, cuts across the boundaries of the work's principal sections to bind them together, despite the fractured musical rhetoric, and the impossibility of closure. Variously set in metric contexts of 6/8, 12/8 and ultimately in 9/8 (three threes), the waltz provides the work's most stabilizing passages.[60] When it is present, we are grounded through motivic and metric continuity, through a relative quietude of musical affect, and through the suggestion (significantly unfulfilled) of parallel phrases.

The passage containing the initial strand of the waltz enters the Trio relatively late in the work. As the work progresses the dance becomes more and more *cantabile*. Psychologically, it functions to bring us as close as we can get to the repose and stability we yearn for, the sense of closure that the work avoids. The tropes of distraction and imperfection allow the waltz strand to emerge, a *non sequitur* in its surroundings, and then to disappear as it in turn is subject to distraction and imperfection. I have suggested that the closure that is both yearned for and feared is death itself.

I have characterized the opening of the Trio as shattering an imagined equilibrium prior to, and thus outside of, the work's frame. Through their stabilizing effect, the waltz fragments bring a relative sense of equilibrium into the frame. Here I would suggest that the silence just before the sounds begin, immediately beyond the frame, can only be a *relative* equilibrium. And I furthermore suggest that in the context of *this* work, the greater equilibrium, the one desired and repressed, yearned for and fled from, represents the closure that Schoenberg denied to 1946 – the closure that we call *death*: death that we imagine, like Messianic ends of time, is always deferred.[61] If I come back to tell you about it, I've only flirted with the idea of its finality.

This striving for equilibrium, a matter of balance which affects phrase formation in conjunction with large and small scale compositional strategies for row deployment, becomes expressive of the life and death struggle that the music portrays. Freud's Death Drive, as discussed in the Introduction to this book, can be understood as yearning for a kind of equilibrium; for death, beyond the pleasure principle, is a yearning for the equilibrium of origins, the timeless preorganic state of repose antecedent to our finite organic lives. The potential toward death is a force in endless struggle with its counterpart, the one he names *Eros*, the one antithetical to repose. I would suggest that the equilibrium that is anticipated but avoided throughout Schoenberg's Trio is precisely analogous to Freud's Death Drive. If death too is a trope, a figurative place-marker for something not quite imaginable, non-existence, then the other tropes, our *loci* of memory throughout the Trio, are all in service of (and defense against) this most fundamental trope of all. The passage from Nietzsche cited earlier, now resonates all the more, "existence fundamentally is – an imperfect tense that can never become a perfect one. If death at last brings the desired forgetting, by that act it at the same time extinguishes the present and all being."

The image of death locked in embrace with life takes on various forms in various cultures. Chief among them is what we call "the dance of death." For the musical imagination coming of age in turn-of-the-century Vienna, the waltz is synecdoche for dance. The waltz had taken many turns by the time that Schoenberg's life, in incarnate bodily form, was soon to close. This is to say that the image had been troped, and so turned into another, several times over. In Schoenberg's Trio, that troping continues.[62] The troping of trope is metalepsis; it is the centrality of Schoenberg's re-imagining of the waltz that gives this chapter its title.

To make sense of all this, I fabricate a short story about the history of the dance from the First Viennese until the Trio. The story is simplistic history, but it is useful nonetheless. In the Classical style the dance movement had generally been a place devoid of the kinds of longing, struggle, and questioning that might be dramatically expressed in other movements. Even in Haydn's scherzi, there is no real *Angst*, no real yearning. The Classical dance is a most *heimlich* movement. Beethoven's scherzi up the ante. At times the metric and formal displacements suggest more than a playful joke. Later in the nineteenth century, anxiety within the dance intensifies, and in some works the dance becomes a macabre affair.[63] By the generation of Mahler, and most emphatically in Mahler's symphonies, the dance has become *unheimlich*, an ironic mockery of what it once was. The third movement of Mahler's Second Symphony or the third movement from his Seventh Symphony provide vivid examples. The dance as signifying *horror* takes its place within the semiotic code for the Second Viennese School, the waltz in Berg's *Wozzeck* being a prime example.

The role of the waltz in Schoenberg's music could easily be the topic of another chapter. Some remarkable examples include Tove's first song in *Gurrelieder* ("Sterne jubeln"), the grotesque Mahlerian parody of "Ach du lieber Augustin" in the Second String Quartet, the "Valse de Chopin" in *Pierrot lunaire*, the "Orgie der Trunkenheit" in the Golden Calf scene of *Moses und Aron* (Act II, beginning m. 605), and the waltz parody in the first movement of the Violin Concerto (beginning at m. 93). In all of these passages, with the exception of Tove's song (and even here there are foreshadowings of the tragedy to come) the waltz is used as an *unheimlich* parody of what it once was.

With Schoenberg's Trio, however, another turn of the spiral is complete, for the dance has once again become *heimlich*, even as it takes on its most *unheimlich* role of all. Death has been stripped of its macabre mask and has become peace. The waltz, or what it has now become, is a central image in the String Trio. Its play of threes suggests those various plays of three that comprise the basic musical substance of the work; a play of threes no doubt dear to the inveterate numerologist Schoenberg; metric closure always deferred, stopping but never concluding, always needing to go onward to a next downbeat, always deferring the final stroke of time.[64] And so, as we have noted, with the ending of the String Trio, we find not closure but a drowsy drifting off. This drifting off is most emphatically not death. We know this because Schoenberg came back to write his Trio down. Despite his claim "I have risen from real death," Schoenberg is not Orpheus returning from Hades to tell us of his triumph and loss. In any case that is a Greek story and Schoenberg is a Jew. Jacob wrestles with his Angel; he then lives on so that we remember his struggle.[65]

The image of Jacob wrestling has been used by Alexander Ringer to describe Mahler, who he characterizes as the "Jacob" to Schoenberg's "Moses." In doing so, Ringer develops George Steiner's concept of "meta-rabbi."

> George Steiner has coined the term 'meta-rabbi' in an effort to characterize in a culturally meaningful fashion an entire category of modern Jews who, in the very process of shaping the foundations of modern life and thought, practiced their 'Jewishness outside Judaism' and thus replaced the traditional 'expositors of the Law.' These 'high masters of modernity' include not only Marx, Einstein, and Freud, Bergson, Durkheim, and Lévi-Strauss, but also Kafka and Arnold Schoenberg, all of them 'exiles twice over: from their Jewish past and, therefore, from a fundamental strain in their own being.' . . . Gustav Mahler, the 'thrice alienated', virtually exemplified the concept [of 'meta-rabbi'] when, for his Second Symphony, he waived Christian notions of salvation in favour of Jacob's struggle with the angel. Considering that Mahler's identification with the patriarchal figure of Jacob directly preceded Schoenberg's with Moses, the prophet; considering too that their respective meta-rabbinical accomplishments account for so much in twentieth-century music as we know it, and that metaphorically Jacob and Moses represent two distinct historical stages of the Jewish people's continuous interaction with its non-Jewish environments, it appears, meta-rabbinically, that Mahler became the central figure in modern music's Genesis, whereas Schoenberg in turning his back on the fleshpots of Romantic harmony created its law.[66]

How well Ringer's assertations of Mahler as Jacob and Schoenberg as Moses hold up to scholarly scrutiny is certainly subject to debate, but the passage does hit on the idea of a Jewish struggle for life as opposed to a Christian faith in salvation. In my understanding of the String Trio, Schoenberg as law giver is not particularly relevant, whereas the image of Schoenberg struggling with his angel can be considered central to the work's ultimate *imperfection*. But, of course, the struggle against death is not restricted to Judaism. In truth, it is simply *human*. And while the story of Jacob wrestling with the angel is highly suggestive, it would be foolish to reduce the Trio to any single image or to any one spiritual or religious tradition.

The beginning of the waltz

By now it is clear that the emergent waltz fragments constitute a remarkable nexus for "memorial" aspects of phrase structure, tonality and the break-down of tonality, dance as *heimlich* and *unheimlich*, and for the central image of a struggle between life and death. Moreover, the contrast of those frag-ments with the other musical material in their environment brings the tropes of *distraction* and *imperfection* into particular relief. With the emergence of the waltz, the listener first apprehends the potential for repose and balance that the returning fragments will cumulatively suggest as the work continues to unfold. Our final musical example will place the first appearance of the waltz into a slightly larger context (Ex. 7.9).

The five bars of *quasi recitative* serve as an extended upbeat to m. 86. This function is not at all clear as we enter into m. 81, but becomes so in retrospect upon the arrival of m. 86. In using the instrumental recitative as extended upbeat, Schoenberg once again evokes late Beethoven. The principal line in the violin initiates a new row area, EA_G, composing a linear statement of EP_G. (Schoenberg modulates into the new area by opening the trichord $\{A\flat, G, E\flat\}$ held in common between EA_G and the previous area $EA_{B\flat}$.)[67] The rhythms and contours of this line, and the ways that it interacts with its accompanying voices, are unlike anything that we have heard before in the piece. Yet, because fragmentation and abrupt movement from idea to idea have been characteristic, the importance of this change can only be heard in retrospect. In mm. 81–2, the overall descent of the cello line, ending with a double neighbor figure around G, works in conjunction with the other lines to tenuously suggest G as tonic. Within this context, the "D dominant" arpeggio in the violin is salient. However, the final pitch in the violin (m. 82) transforms the sonority into a "G dominant" that functions as an augmented sixth leading into the next section of the recitative, which at first is suggestive of F♯ minor (m. 83). The tonal drift continues as the voice pile-up in the *saltando* passage effectively liquidates F♯ as local tonic, despite the persistence of that pitch throughout the passage. The recitative

Example 7.9. The first appearance of the waltz (mm. 81–102). Used by permission of Belmont Music Publishers, Pacific Palisades, CA 90272.

Example 7.9. (*cont.*)

Example 7.9. (*cont.*)

winds down in m. 85 terminating on F-natural, no clear dominant, to be sure, but enough for Schoenberg to use it as preparation for the B♭ downbeat at the *a tempo*.

As we enter into its space, the importance of m. 86 is not apparent. Yet the musical ideas that begin here will gain more and more emphasis as the work continues. In retrospect, or as we draw upon memories of earlier hearings of the work taking its later development into account, these evocations of the waltz become that toward which we were groping all along. Nonetheless, at its first appearance, there is nothing in the music to signal this importance. As m. 86 begins, it appears to be only another idea in the series of fragmented ideas that have comprised the work so far.

Example 7.9. (*cont.*)

The principal voice is heard for two measures in the violin and then two measures in the viola. Along with the accompanying figuration, these four measures comprise an antecedent phrase. The change of row area to EA_{Bb} constitutes a move back to the area that, after the completion of $P_D,V2$ (see Example 7.7), had initiated the episode at m. 57. The beginning of the episode had presented the listener with a striking change of affect, constituting the first glimmers of equanimity and repose after the fractured dissonance of the opening. Each two-bar subphrase completes a statement of EA_{Bb}, comprising EP_{Bb} and EI_{Eb}. The entire phrase constitutes an interval palindrome; thus, the second subphrase is a retrograde inversion of the first (with some octave displacements).[68] The interval palindrome, recognizable in the

Hauptstimme, is one facet of the relative equipoise suggested by the phrase. Tonal evocations are fairly clear at the outset of the phrase, yet even there the cello seems to gently mock what would otherwise be a lucid presentation of the dominant F. F reasserts itself at the downbeat of m. 88, but once again tonal reference becomes tenuous as the phrase continues. Both the phrase structure and the evocations of tonal function in the context of the emergent waltz have memorial implications of the kind that we have discussed.

The consequent phrase begins with the principal voice in the cello, m. 90, and continues for three measures as the cello waxes eloquent with its sixteenth-note figuration. Within m. 92, the cello and violin run through a complete row form, in a sense accelerating the harmonic rhythm. Their passage ends with a tentative suggestion of F, our dominant. Along with the harmony, the asymmetrical phrasing caused by the cello "done too soon" leads to a sense of incompletion. We are then diverted by the violin *scherzando* and the viola *spiccato*, which in lieu of concluding the cello melody, spin off on their own tangent. The twelve-tone structure contributes to this; we enter into a new area (A_B) that violates the normative diminished (or T_3) cycle relations among Episode row areas. As the *scherzando* marking would indicate, the diversion this time is apparently a pleasant one. In the following measure, the viola *spiccato* spins out of control. Beginning with the pickup to m. 96, it is as though the *cantabile* fragments try to regain the metric and phrase shape orientation of the dance, but to no avail. An *accelerando* follows, as once again the dance spins out of control. This in turn suddenly breaks off at the *meno mosso*, m. 101. What follows is an absurd, seemingly intoxicated pull-back. The comical *glissando* is reminiscent of the opening of the recitative, as though having lost our thread we try to start again. However, we are not quite able to pull that off either (*quasi recitative* does eventually return, at m. 105). The row structure is also part of the absurd situation. The cello and viola *glissando* composes the opening tetrachord of EP_F, and this associates with the opening tetrachord of EI_{Db}, which will be heard when the recitative successfully returns in m. 105. On the other hand, the violin *glissando*, the opening tetrachord of EI_{Bb}, associates with the opening tetrachord of P_D, a primary constituent of Part 1.

In a beer-hall setting, a tipsy dancer might be tottering back and forth dizzied by the dance and the drink, a parody perhaps of the famous waltz scene in Berg's *Wozzeck*. Only this is no beer-hall setting; the spinning out of control and the quasi-comical disorientations are placed in the larger context of a life-threatening illness. The effect is once again reminiscent of late Beethoven.[69]

The music that follows, after three more measures of disorientation, is once again the *quasi recitative*. Eventually the waltz idea returns, of course transformed, and eventually we are again distracted from its conclusion. The work insists on its own *imperfection*, and therein lies its greatest triumphs.

Again recalling John Ashbery's provocative question "where do the scraps of meaning come from?," our thoughts toward an answer in the context of the Trio have centered on the rich associations of our musical memories. The ways of remembering evoked by the Trio have included all three of the types suggested earlier on: the recollection and transformation of musical ideas within the work, the association of those musical ideas with a larger musical tradition, and the evocation of the "extra-musical" by the musical. Schoenberg, like all of our most original musical imaginations, engages our most significant musical memories – necessarily, of all three types – radically transforms them by filling them with new content, and brings the past into the present by way of the strangest of relations. In Schoenberg's case, "obviously, it was time to be off, in another direction." That *new direction* reached back to early musical memories and transformed them into the stylistic and expressive constituents of his final period.

Some final thoughts

We know ourselves through the stories that we tell about ourselves and about the universe that we inhabit. Story-telling, making "fiction," when degraded into a pastime, loses its sense as our most central and essential way of self-knowing. The great American poet Wallace Stevens wrote of "supreme fictions":

> What makes the poet the potent figure that he is, or was, or ought to be, is that he creates the world to which we turn incessantly and without knowing it and that he gives to life the supreme fictions without which we are unable to conceive of it.[70]

The word "fiction" is derived from an Indo-European root that denotes the kneading of dough or shaping of clay.[71] In this sense among others, clay-become-Adam is the fiction of the first man.[72] Behind the noun form "fiction" is a suppressed verb denoting an active shaping or kneading, working over the found materials – themselves fictions of a previous shaping – until they become what we need of them. The word "trope" is derived from the Greek word *tropos*, a turn, and it too has a verbal form, an active turning, as on a potter's wheel. Our fictions are a turning and returning.

We normally think of fiction as including only literature. But we do not only tell our stories through words, and we do not shape who we are only through books. Along with the other arts, music is a major force through which we humans self-create. In music we shape sound, her negative sister silence, and her necessary scenic context which is time. The composer, performer, critic, and audience member are all active participants in the making of musical fictions. Moreover, there is a mutual give and take among our ways of story-telling. Music is conditioned by other ways of knowing, and it in turn conditions other ways of knowing.

To write commentary is to base a new fiction on one's ongoing relationship with an earlier one, one to which we return again and again. My long meditation on Arnold Schoenberg is offered in that spirit. Writing at another time and place I might have chosen other of Schoenberg's works, ignored here not because I value them less, but because this book, like all books, must have its pages contained between its covers. Sooner or later, the author must stop writing. But in another sense, no book is contained between its covers, just as no piece of music is contained between its opening notes and final barline.

Falcon Heights, Minnesota
June 9, 2006

Notes

Introduction

1. Allan Janik and Stephen Toulman, *Wittgenstein's Vienna*, Simon and Schuster, 1973, 110.
2. The late David Lewin, my mentor and dissertation advisor, was an exception to this rule. He was one of very few music theorists whose Schoenberg scholarship ranged over all three periods. Unfortunately, Lewin never wrote an extended treatment of Schoenberg's music.
3. W. K. C. Guthrie, *A History of Greek Philosophy, Volume I, The earlier Presocratics and the Pythagoreans*, Cambridge University Press, 1962, 200–21 and 307–8.
4. *Ibid.*, 220–6, and 435–42.
5. The *perfect* intervals of medieval music theory were those that allowed conclusion. The idea was analogous to perfection in grammar (where an action is concluded), or, for that matter, to perfection in God (the Being who is not in a state of becoming). The categories of perfect intervals endure into the modern period. *Perfect cadences* are means by which musical phrases, and hence musical compositions are brought to completion in tonal works. The concept of *perfection* is studied further in Chapter Seven of this book.
6. Hannah Arendt, *Between Past and Future*, The Viking Press, 1961, 18.
7. The vast majority of technical descriptions concentrate on pitch relations. There are some exceptions: the permutational ordering and reordering of pitches in Schoenberg's twelve-tone music has been well addressed by Milton Babbitt and others; the quickness with which Schoenberg unfolds and transforms musical ideas, necessarily temporal in their nature, has also been noted by many scholars.
8. Carter develops the term "emancipated discourse" in his 1960 essay "The Recent Works of Goffredo Petrassi." See *Elliott Carter: Collected Essays and Lectures, 1937–1995*, edited by Jonathan Bernard, University of Rochester Press, 1997, 188. The parallels of an "emancipated discourse" in music with developments in the novel (e.g. Proust, Joyce, Kafka) and in poetry (e.g. Mallarmé, Rilke, John Ashbery) are as striking as they are pervasive.
9. Milton Babbitt's foundational work on twelve-tone theory emphasizes a break from the "combinational" systems of the past to the "permutational" nature of twelve-tone music. The pioneers of set theory, including George Perle and Allen Forte, developed ways of describing post-tonal harmony that were radically separate from the models of tonal practice. See Milton Babbitt, *The Collected Essays of Milton Babbitt*, edited by Stephen Peles et al., Princeton University Press, 2003; George Perle, *Serial Composition and Atonality*, Third Edition, 1972; Allen Forte, *The Structure of Atonal Music*, Yale University Press, 1973.

10. *The Formal and Dramatic Organization of Schoenberg's 'Moses und Aron'*. Ph. D. dissertation, Yale University, 1983.

11. "Schoenberg and *das Unheimliche*," *The Journal of Musicology*, vol. 11/3, Summer 1993, 357–73. Reinhold Brinkmann formulates related observations in "Schoenberg the Contemporary: A View from Behind," *Constructive Dissonance: Arnold Schoenberg and the transformations of twentieth-century culture*, University of California Press, 1997.

12. "Memory and Rhetorical Trope in Schoenberg's String Trio," *Journal of the American Musicological Society*, 51/3, Fall 1998, 559–602.

13. "Motive and Memory in Schoenberg's First String Quartet," in *The Music of My Future: The Schoenberg Quartets and Trio*, 61–80.

14. Gilles Deleuze, *Difference and Repetition*, translated by Paul Patton, New York: Columbia University Press, 1994, 36–7. Deleuze and Félix Guattari rename and further develop "nomadic" and "agrarian" space as "smooth" and "striated" space in their book *A Thousand Plateaus: Capitalism and Schizophrenia*, (Minneapolis: University of Minnesota Press, 1987, 474–550, and *passim*. In this context the authors specifically associate their discussion with music and with ideas derived from Pierre Boulez, *Boulez on Music Today*, translated by Susan Bradshaw and Richard Bennett (Harvard University Press, 1971). I find the earlier opposition of "nomadic/agrarian" more suggestive than the formal pair "smooth/striated" and use the earlier source for that reason.

    Agrarian space entails clear boundaries and hierarchical structures. In contrast, nomadic space entails vague boundaries, and movement through the whole of some space, rather than the division of that space into parcels. In the music of Schoenberg (and others) there is often a dialectic between the two kinds of musical space. For example, a theme that "belongs" to some well-defined area (e.g. the first theme group) will migrate into other areas, not properly its "home." I would argue that "overviews" of musical form, so typical in the theoretical literature, are absolutely agrarian in their conceptions (they divide the composition into discrete blocks), and are therefore inadequate representations of musical forms that are based on nomadic space or on a dialectic opposition of the two kinds of space.

15. "Dialectical Opposition in Schoenberg's Music and Thought," *Music Theory Spectrum*, 22/2, Fall 2000, 157–76.

16. Kenneth Burke, *A Grammar of Motives*, University of California Press, 1969, 503.

17. Bloom develops his extended theory of tropes in a number of works. Most pertinent is *A Map of Misreading*, Oxford University Press, 1975. Bloom's idiosyncratic understanding of hyperbole is clarified on pages 72–3:

    Influence conceived of as an hyperbole takes us into the realms of Sublime representation, restituting the emptyings-out of metonymy. The accent of excess here is allied to the defense of repression, for the high imageries of hyperbole conceal an unconsciously purposeful forgetting . . .

18. Hans-Georg Gadamer, *Truth and Method*, second revised edition, translation revised by Joel Weinsheimer and Donald G. Marshall, Continuum International Publishing Group, 2003, 9.

19. *Ibid.*, 11.

20. See Steven Cahn, "The Artist as Modern Prophet: A Study of Historical Consciousness and its Expression in Schoenberg's *Vorgefühle*, op. 22, no. 4," in *Schoenberg and Words: The Modernist Years*, Garland Publishing, Inc., 2000, 243–71. Cahn discusses Wilhelm von Humboldt's role on page 252.

21. An excellent discussion of *Bildung* in its German-Jewish contexts is found in the first chapter of Paul Mendes-Flohr, *German Jews: A Dual Identity*, Yale University Press, 1999.

22. *Ibid.*, 11–12.

23. Problematic aspects of a canon, and Schoenberg's uneasy place within it are discussed by Christopher Hailey in "Schoenberg and the Canon: An Evolving Heritage," in *Constructive Dissonance: Arnold Schoenberg and Transformations of Twentieth-Century Culture*, edited by Julie Brand and Christopher Hailey, University of California Press, 1997, 163–78.

24. Amos Elon, *The Pity of It All: A History of Jews in Germany, 1743–1933*, Henry Holt and Company, 2002, 9.

25. Paul Mendes-Flohr, *German Jews: A Dual Identity*, 27.

26. Leonard Stein notes the diagram and solicits responses as to its meaning in the first issue of the *Journal of the Arnold Schoenberg Institute*, vol. I, number 1 (1976), 5. The responses, found in vol. I, number 3 (1977), include a communication from Reinhold Brinkmann, 182–5, that suggests the row partition that Schoenberg had in mind and also connects the diagram to Goethe's concept of *Urpflanze*. The significance of the sketch in the evolution of Schoenberg's twelve-tone method is discussed in Ethan Haimo, *Schoenberg's Serial Odyssey*, 122–3.

27. Peter Gay writes of Freud that "He made a point of proclaiming his ignorance in musical matters and admitted that he could not carry a tune." *Freud: A Life for Our Time*, W. W. Norton & Co., 1988, 168. Schoenberg had no books by Freud in his library. See Clara Steuermann, "Schoenberg's Library Catalogue," *Journal of the Arnold Schoenberg Institute*, vol. III, no. 2 (1979), 203–18.

28. See Ritchie Robertson, *Kafka: Judaism, Politics, and Literature*, Oxford University Press, 1985. Kafka's readings in Freud are discussed on page 204.

29. Harold Bloom, "Freud and the Poetic Sublime," in *Poetics of Influence*, edited with an introduction by John Hollander, Henry R. Schwab, Inc., 1988, 195.

30. *Ibid.*, 196.

31. Philip Rieff, *Freud: The Mind of the Moralist*, University of Chicago Press, Third Edition, 1979, 28.

32. Sigmund Freud, "Beyond the Pleasure Principle," translated by James Strachey, included in *The Freud Reader*, edited by Peter Gay, W. W. Norton & Co., 1989. The passage cited is on page 613.

33. Rieff, *Freud: The Mind of the Moralist*, 13.

34. Bloom, "Freud and the Poetic Sublime," 199.

35. Bloom, *Ibid.*, 201.
36. Robertson, *Kafka: Judaism, Politics, and Literature*, 81.
37. *The Castle*, translated by Mark Harman, Schocken Books, 1988, 9.
38. *The Castle*, 24. The original reads as follows (*Das Schloss*, in der Fassung der Handschrift, Fischer Taschenbuch Verlag, 1981, 35):

   K. wußte, daß nicht mit wirklichem Zwang gedroht war, der fürchtete er nicht und hier am wenigsten, aber die Gewalt der entmutigenden Umgebung, der Gewöhnung an Enttäuschungen, die Gewalt der unmerklichen Enflüsse jedes Augenblicks, die fürchtete allerdings, aber mit diese Gefahr mußte er dem Kampf wagen.

39. Franz Kafka. *Diaries: 1910–1923*, edited by Max Brod, translated by Martin Greenberg with the cooperation of Hannah Arendt, Schocken Books, 1976, 398. I have altered the translation in a couple of places. The original reads as follows (Franz Kafka. *Tagebücher: 1914–1923*, Fischer Taschenbuch Verlag, 1990, 198):

   Es war in der letzten Woche ein Zusammenbruch, so vollständig wie nur etwa in der einen Nacht vor 2 Jahren, ein andres Beispiel habe ich nicht erlebt. Alles schein zuende und scheint auch heute durchaus nochnicht ganz anders zu sein. . . . Zusammenbruch, Unmöglichkeit zu schlafen, Unmöglichkeit zu wachen, genauer die Aufeinanderfolge des Lebens zu ertragen. Die Uhren stimmen nicht überein, die innere jagt in einer teuflischen oder dämonischen oder jedenfalls unmenschlichen Art, die äussere geht stokkend ihren gewöhnlichen Gang. Was kann anders geschehn, als dass sich die zwei verschiedenen Welten trennen und sie trennen sich oder reissen zumindest an einander in einer fürchtlichen Art.

40. Harold Bloom, editor. *Modern Critical Views: Franz Kafka*, Chelsea House Publishers, 1986, 2.
41. The essay "On Transience" is included in *Writings on Art and Literature*, Stanford University Press, 1997, 176–9. The quoted passage is on page 178.
42. *The Great Short Works of Franz Kafka.* Translated by Joachim Neugroschel, Simon & Schuster, 2000, 70.
43. *Ibid.*, 71.
44. *Ibid.*, 72. The original reads as follows (*Franz Kafka: Ein Lesebuch mit Bildern*, edited by Klaus Wagenbach, Rowohlt Taschenbuch Verlag, 2003, 36):

   Schon hielt er das Geländer fest, wie ein Hungriger die Nahrung. Er schwang sich über, als der ausgezeichnete Turner, der er in seinen Jungenjahren zum Stolz seiner Eltern gewesen war. Noch hielt er sich mit schwächer werdenden Händen fest, erspälte zwischen den Geländerstangen einen Auto-omnibus, der mit Leichtigkeit seinen Fall übertönen würde, rief leise: "Liebe Eltern, ich habe euch doch immer geliebt," und liess sich hinabfallen.
      In diesem Augenblick ging über die Brücke ein geradezu unendliche Verkehr.

45. Gilles Deleuze, *Proust and Signs*, translated by Richard Howard, University of Minnesota Press, 2000, 101.
46. Ken Frieden, *Freud's Dream of Interpretation*, State University of New York Press, 1990, 3.
47. Franz Kafka, *Parables and Paradoxes: Bilingual Edition*, Schocken Books, 1975, 12–15.

48. Scholem's idea is discussed by Robert Alter in *Canon and Creativity*, Yale University Press, 2000, 16 and 76–7.
49. Maurice Blanchot, *The Work of Fire*, translated by Charlotte Mandell, Stanford University Press, 1995, 1–2.

Chapter 1

1. Schoenberg makes the comment in a letter to Emil Hertzka dated 8 August 1912. See Brian G. Campbell, *Text and Phrase Rhythm in Gurrelieder: Schoenberg's Reception of Tradition*, University of Minnesota, Ph.D. dissertation, 1997, 8.
2. The Second Chamber Symphony, begun in 1906 and completed in 1939, is another exception, but one on a much more modest scale. See Jan Maegaard, "Schoenberg's Incomplete Works and Fragments," in *Constructive Dissonance: Arnold Schoenberg and Transformations of Twentieth-Century Culture*, edited by Julie Brand and Christopher Hailey, University of California Press, 1997, 131–45.
3. For background on the composition of *Gurrelieder* see Part I of Brian G. Campbell, *Text and Phrase Rhythm in Gurrelieder: Schoenberg's Reception of Tradition*.
4. Campbell, *ibid.*, 43.
5. This idea is thematic in Willi Reich's biography of Schoenberg: *Arnold Schönberg oder der Konservative Revolutionär*, Verlag Fritz Molden, 1968. Reich cites Schoenberg in the book's opening epigraph, "Ich bin en Konservativer, den man gezwungen hat, ein Radikaler zu werden" (I am a conservative who was compelled to become a radical), 8. The English translation of Reich's book alters the title and omits the epigraph. See Willi Reich, *Schoenberg: A Critical Biography*, translated by Leo Black, Praeger Publishers, 1971.
6. *Ibid.*, Chapter 3, 44–70.
7. Examples of works that incorporate significant musical depictions of light include the Five Orchestral Pieces, op. 16, *Erwartung*, *Die glückliche Hand*, and *Pierrot lunaire*.
8. Michael L. Klein insightfully discusses this aspect of the Wood Dove's song in his *Intertextuality in Western Music*, Indiana University Press, 2005, 85–7.
9. David Lewin, "Inversional Balance as an Organizing Force in Schoenberg's Music and Thought," *Perspectives of New Music*, vol. 6, no. 2 (1968), 1–21. In note 6 on page 6, Lewin divides the twenty-one songs of *Pierrot lunaire* into the three sections of Dionysian ritual: Sickness, Sparag..ios, and Satyr Play.
10. Campbell, *ibid.*, 11 and *passim*. Also see Campbell's "*Gurrelieder* and the Fall of the Gods: Schoenberg's Struggle with the legacy of Wagner," in *Schoenberg and Words: The Modernist Years*, edited by Charlotte M. Cross and Russell A. Berman, Garland Publishing, Inc. 2000, 31–63.
11. Geoffrey H. Hartman, *The Fateful Question of Culture*, Columbia University Press, 1997. See especially Chapter Three, "The Question of Our Speech," and Chapter Four, "Language and Culture after the Holocaust."
12. *Ibid.*, 73.

13. *Ibid.*, 76. Hartman parenthetically refers to Robert Musil's unfinished master-piece *Der Mann ohne Eigenschaften* (The Man Without Qualities).

14. Included in *Schoenberg and His World*, edited by Walter Frisch, Princeton University Press, 1999, 19–54.

15. *Ibid.*, 41.

16. *Ibid.*, 44.

17. Erich Auerbach, *Mimesis: The Representation of Reality in Western Literature*, translated by Willard R. Trask, Princeton University Press, 1953, 11–12.

18. Harold Bloom, *Ruin the Sacred Truths: Poetry and Belief from the Bible to the Present*, Harvard University Press, 1989, 150.

19. *Ibid.*, 149.

Chapter 2

1. An earlier version of this chapter appeared as "Dialectical Opposition in Schoen-berg's Music and Thought," *Music Theory Spectrum*, 22/2, Fall 2000.

2. Matters related to those that I explore in this chapter are central to Robert Fleisher, "Dualism in the Music of Arnold Schoenberg," *Journal of the Arnold Schoenberg Institute*, vol. XII, no. 1, June 1989, 22–42. Fleisher does not dis-cuss the philosophical roots of dialectical thought per se. His paper focuses on Schoenbergian "dualism" in a variety of contexts, including the opposition of the protagonists in *Moses und Aron*. For extended discussions of this conflict see Michael Cherlin, *The Formal and Dramatic Organization of Schoenberg's Moses und Aron* (Yale Ph.D. dissertation, 1983), *passim.*

3. Both topics, materialism vs. idealism and telos vs. a nonteleological view, are dealt with extensively in Stephen J. Cahn, *Variations in Manifold Time: Historical Consciousness in the Music and Writings of Arnold Schoenberg* (Ph.D. dissertation, State University of New York at Stony Brook, 1996), Chapter II, "On Historical Consciousness as an Ideological Source," 69–149.

4. W. K. C. Guthrie, *A History of Greek Philosophy, Volume I, The earlier Presocratics and the Pythagoreans*, Cambridge: Cambridge University Press, 1962, 220.

5. *Ibid.*, 435.

6. *Ibid.*, 437.

7. Andrew Barker, editor, *Greek Musical Writings: Vol. II, Harmonic and Acoustic Theory*. Cambridge: Cambridge University Press, 1989, 38. I owe the references to Philolaus to a conversation and subsequent correspondence with David E. Cohen.

8. *Ibid.*, 36.

9. David E. Cohen makes this point a central claim in *Boethius and the Enchiri-adis theory: The metaphysics of consonance and the concept of organum*, Ph.D. dissertation, Brandeis University, 1993.

   The concept of organum as symphonia can be explained in terms of a metaphysics of con-sonance taken from Boethius's highly influential *De institutione musica*. The metaphysics of consonance was a development of the Pythagorean-Platonic conception of music, in which the symphoniae represent the universal, divinely-ordained rational principles of cosmic order and harmony. The relationship between consonance and dissonance in Boethius's *Musica* is structured as an unequal, hierarchized opposition, in which consonance holds the dominant position because of its virtual identification with the metaphysical ideal of unity. Conversely, dissonance represents the negative values of duality and difference, and disorder. Consequently, through various textual strategies, consonance is identified with music itself, while dissonance is effectively excluded from that domain. The concept of organum in the Enchiriadis treatises is determined by this same metaphysics of consonance, with its consequent tendency to exclude or marginalize dissonance, a conceptual pattern that has resonated throughout the subsequent history of polyphonic theory and practice in the West.

Cohen continues to develop this line of thought in his paper "Metaphysics, Ideology, Discipline: Consonance, Dissonance, and the Foundations of Western Polyphony," *Theoria*, vol.7 (1993), 1–86. Cohen's opening epigram, taken from Schenker's *Kontrapunkt*, is in striking contrast to a Heraclitean view.

Consonance itself is sufficient evidence for itself; it rests in its euphony, signifying itself Beginning and End . . .
In this sense, consonance manifests an absolute character, dissonance, on the contrary, merely a relative and derivative [character]: In the Beginning is Consonance! – It is what is primary, dissonance is secondary!

10. Arthur O. Lovejoy, *Reflections on Human Nature*, (Johns Hopkins University Press, 1961), 38–40. Lovejoy subsequently demonstrates that principle of counterpoise later emerges, principally through the influence of James Madison, as the system of checks and balances embodied in the US Constitution (*ibid.*, 46–63).

11. *The Poetry and Prose of William Blake*, edited by David V. Erdman, commentary by Harold Bloom (New York: Doubleday and Company, 1965), 34. For a scholarly discussion of the role of the opposing contraries in Blake's thought see Harold Bloom, *The Visionary Company: A Reading of English Romantic Poetry* (Ithaca: Cornell University Press, 1971), pages 66 and 69. See also Northrop Frye, *Fearful Symmetry* (Princeton: Princeton University Press, 1969), especially pages 69 and 188–90.

12. Within Aristotle's discussion of friendship, in the *Nichomachean Ethics*, 1155^{b}5, he cites the Heraclitean principle "it is what opposes that helps." The correspondence of the Heraclitean principle with Blake's epigram in "The Marriage of Heaven and Hell" is too clear to be by chance. See *The Complete Works of Aristotle: the Revised Oxford Translation*, edited by Jonathan Barnes, (Princeton: Princeton University Press, 1984), Vol. 2, 1825–6.

13. The passage from *Athenäum Fragmente* (1797–8) is cited in John Daverio, *Nineteenth Century Music and the German Romantic Ideology* (New York: Schirmer Books, 1993), 13. Daverio's interpretation of the passage is at odds with my own. He asserts that "Schlegel embraces one of the Romantics' most cherished pipe dreams, the synthesis of opposites, only to explode it, by asserting a 'constantly self-engendering interchange.'" My own understanding is that

"self-engendering interchange" is the mechanism by which syntheses occur. Schlegel's concept of irony is discussed by Isaiah Berlin in *The Roots of Romanticism* (Princeton: Princeton University Press, 1999), 117.

> [Romantic] Irony was invented by Friedrich Schlegel: the idea is that whenever you see honest citizens setting about their business, whenever you see a well-composed poem – a poem composed according to the rules – whenever you see a peaceful institution which protects the lives and property of citizens, laugh at it, mock it, be ironical, blow it up, point out that the opposite is equally true. The only weapon against death, for him, against ossification and against any form of the stabilization and freezing of the life stream is what he calls *Ironie* . . . because that is the only way of escaping from the hideous logical strait-jacket which he is frightened of, whether in the form of physical causality, or of State-created laws, or of aesthetic rules . . .

14. Ian Bent, "Plato – Beethoven: A Hermeneutics for Nineteenth-Century Music?" *Indiana Theory Review*, vol.16 (1995), 1–33. Bent characterizes Schleiermacher's dialectical basis for hermeneutics on pages 14–18.

15. R. G. Collingwood, *The Idea of History* (Oxford University Press, 1956), 106.

16. From "Conflict and the Web of Group Affiliations," 1908 in *Georg Simmel: On Individuality and Social Forms*, 71–2.

17. See Thomas Christensen, "Fétis and emerging tonal consciousness," in *Music Theory in the Age of Romanticism*, edited by Ian Bent (Cambridge: Cambridge University Press, 1996), 49–56. Christensen also studies the dialectical model that Fétis develops for understanding the relation between sense perception and intellection that Fétis places at the core of understanding of *tonalité*. See p. 47.

18. Adolph Bernhard Marx, *Theory and Practice of Musical Composition*, translated by H. S. Saroni, P. J. Huntington and Mason & Law, 1852, 55.

19. Marx's dialectical description of a musical period is originally found in *Die Lehre von der musikalischen Komposition*, vol. 1, Breitkopf & Härtel, 1841. In English translation, the passage is found in *Theory and Practice of Musical Composition*, 88. Marx's description of sonata form is found in *Die Lehre von der musikalischen Komposition*, vol. 3, Breitkopf & Härtel, 1845, 217–18. For a more in-depth study of the role of opposition in A. B. Marx and stimulating discussion of gender in the context of Marx's dialectics, see Scott Burnham, "A. B. Marx and the gendering of sonata form," in *Music Theory in the Age of Romanticism*, 163–86.

20. I discuss this aspect of Hauptmann in "Hauptmann and Schenker: Two Adaptations of Hegelian Dialectics," *Theory and Practice*, vol. 13 (1988), 115–31.

21. *Neue Zeitschrift für Musik, Band* 68, *Januar bis December* 1872, pp. 279–82, 287–8, 353–5, 363–4, 373–4. Reprinted in Hugo Riemann, *Präludien und Studien*, vol 3, Leipzig 1901. Also see William C. Mickelson, *Hugo Riemann's Theory of Harmony and History of Music Theory, Book III*, University of Nebraska Press, 1977, 27–9.

22. See "Hauptmann and Schenker: Two Adaptations of Hegelian Dialectics," 115–31.

23. 'Der dialektische Komponist', Arnold Schönberg zum 60. Geburtstag (Vienna, 13 September, 1934), reprinted in Impromptus, Suhrkamp Verlag, 1968. For a complete bibliography and a well-rounded discussion of Adorno's writings on music, see Max Paddison, Adorno's Aesthetics of Music, Cambridge University Press, 1993. While it is not the goal of this chapter to present a critique of Adorno on Schoenberg (that would be an article or even a book in itself), it must be stated that for this reader Adorno's treatment of Schoenbergian dialectics is ultimately not satisfying. Despite his insistence that music forms an immanent critique of society, wherein the composer challenges the "givens" of musical composition within his works and so simultaneously challenges the assumptions of society, there is almost no close analysis of Schoenberg's musical compositions. Instead, Adorno tends to write in terms of "subjectivity/objectivity" or "authenticity/inauthenticity." Moreover, Adorno does not anywhere present close readings of Schoenberg's critical and pedagogical writings. These sources are invaluable in understanding Schoenberg's basic assumptions concerning the role of dialectical oppositions in his thought about music as well as in his musical thought per se. As a result, Adorno does not present any clear study of the technical means by which Schoenberg achieves his immanent critique.

    For further thought on a critique of Adorno's characterization of Schoenberg see Steven J. Cahn, Variations in Manifold Time, 109–12.

24. For example, the shift from a rhetorical to a dramatic basis for musical imagination is a key point in Charles Rosen, The Classical Style, W. W. Norton & Co., 1972, passim.

25. August Wilhelm von Schlegel, Friedrich von Schlegel's older brother, translated seventeen of Shakespeare's plays during the period 1797–1810.

26. A far-ranging discussion of Mehrdeutigkeit including its impact on Schoenberg is found in Janna K. Saslaw, Gottfried Weber and the Concept of 'Mehrdeutigkeit', Ph.D. dissertation, Columbia University, 1992. A brilliant, more recent adaptation of Mehrdeutigkeit is found in David Lewin, "Music Theory, Phenomenology, and Modes of Perception," Music Perception, 3/4 (1986), 327–92.

27. See Categories 11^{b}18–13^{b}36. Dialectics, in contrast, is a mode of argumentation involving contradictories. See Prior Analytics 24^{a}10–24^{b}15. It is not clear that the pre-Socratic would have made the Aristotelian distinction between dialectics and oppositions. It suffices to say that the term used in this chapter, dialectical opposition, combines the two meanings into a broader concept.

28. See Categories 11^{b}18–13^{b}36.

29. I would argue, contra Aristotle himself, that the Aristotelian categories of opposition do not divide the world into classes of opposed things, rather they provide different perspectives, different ways of understanding overlapping and even congruent things. From this it follows that the application of Aristotle's categories to musical oppositions will function in a similar way: the categories

as I apply them do not divide the world of musical objects into different *types* as much as they provide different perspectives through which we can understand even the same musical phenomena.

30. *Categories* 11^{b}24–6.
31. Edward Aldwell and Carl Schachter, *Harmony and Voice Leading*, second edition, Harcourt Brace Jovanovich, 1989, 60.
32. Arnold Schoenberg, *Theory of Harmony*, translated by Roy. E. Carter, University of California Press, 1978, 388.
33. The role of pattern completion in the compositions of Stravinsky is discussed by Joseph N. Straus, "A Principle of Voice Leading in the Music of Stravinsky," *Music Theory Spectrum* vol. 4 (1982), 106–24.
34. *Affirmation/negation* is at the heart of David Lewin's model for phenomenological hearings. See "Music Theory, Phenomenology, and Modes of Perception," 327–92.
35. Arnold Schoenberg, *Style and Idea*, edited by Leonard Stein, translated by Leo Black, University of California Press, 1975, 104. See the discussion of this passage in Steven J. Cahn, *Variations in Manifold Time: Historical Consciousness in the Music and Writings of Arnold Schoenberg*, 101–2.
36. *Ibid.* An excellent introduction to Hegel's thought is found in Charles Taylor, *Hegel*, Cambridge University Press, 1975. The force behind Schoenberg's anecdote is nicely paralleled by Taylor's description of "world-historical individuals."

> . . . the work of the *Weltgeist* is felt as an 'immanenter Trieb' [an immanent drive] among men, one that is merely 'instinctual', that is, not understood; and this is why the work of reason gets done among the clash of individual ambitions in history.
>
> Thus the greatness of world-historical individuals does not just lie in their being instruments of the Word-Spirit. They are also those who first sense and give articulation to what must be the next stage. Once they raise this banner men follow. In a time when one form is played out, when Spirit has deserted the reigning form, it is the world-historical individual who shows the way to what all men in their depths aspire to . . .
>
> Once they do articulate this new form, it has an irresistible force, even for those who are inclined by their own interest or judgment against it, because deep down they cannot help identifying with it. (393)

37. *Style and Idea*, 80–1.
38. *Adorno's Aesthetics of Music*, 72.
39. *Ibid.*, pages 22, 59, 72, 111.
40. *Style and Idea*, 76. A striking parallel to Schoenberg's comments is found in Adorno's paper "Arnold Schoenberg: 1874–1951."

> [Artistic extremism] receives its legitimacy from the tradition that it negates. Hegel taught that wherever something new becomes visible, immediate, striking, authentic, a long process of formation has preceded it and it has now merely thrown off its shell. Only that which has been nourished with the life-blood of the tradition can possibly have the power to confront it authentically; the rest becomes the helpless prey of forces which it has failed to overcome sufficiently within itself.

Theodor W. Adorno, *Prisms*, translated by Samuel and Shierry Weber, The MIT Press, 1981, 155.

41. *Style and Idea*, 76–7.

42. Charles Rosen, *Arnold Schoenberg*, The Viking Press, 1975, 2–3.

43. Arnold Schoenberg, *Fundamentals of Musical Composition*, St. Martin's Press, 1967, 94. This passage is cited in Robert Fleisher, "Dualism in the Music of Arnold Schoenberg."

44. This translation is taken from G. T. W. Patrick and I. Bywater, *Heraclitus of Ephesus*, Argonaut, Inc., 1969, 96. The original passage is in Aristotle, *Nicomachean Ethics*, 1155^{b}1.

45. See John Sallis and Kenneth Maly, *Heraclitean Fragments: A Companion Volume to the Heidegger/Fink Seminar on Heraclitus*, University of Alabama Press, 1980, 165–6 and *passim*.

46. On the other hand, the opening phrase of the Heraclitean fragment in Georg Burckhardt's German translation reads "Das in entgegengesezter Weise Gehobelte wird zusammengebracht." Georg Burckhardt, *Heraklit: Urworte der Philosophie* (Insel-Verlag, n.d.), 39. The word *entgegengesezter* can be translated as *contrasting* (or *contrary*), and this would correlate with Schoenberg's choice of terms. The choice of the word "Weise" in Burckhardt's translation is also interesting it that it can denote *manner* or *way*, but it also can be denote *melody*.

47. *Theory of Harmony*, 151.

48. David Lewin traces this way of thinking about the relationships among tonic, dominant and subdominant back to Rameau. See, "Inversional Balance as an Organizing Force in Schoenberg's Music and Thought," *Perspectives of New Music* 6/2, 2–3.

49. *Theory of Harmony*, 23–4.

50. "Inversional Balance as an Organizing Force in Schoenberg's Music and Thought," 1–21.

51. I explore contending the role of inversional balance in *Moses und Aron* in "Dramaturgy and Mirror Imagery in Schoenberg's *Moses und Aron*," *Perspectives of New Music*, vol.29/2 (Summer, 1991), 50–71.

52. Schoenberg's concept of *Grundgestalt* is discussed probingly in Severine Neff, "Schoenberg and Goethe: Organicism and Analysis," in *Music Theory and the Exploration of the Past*, edited by Christopher Hatch and David W. Bernstein, (Chicago: University of Chicago Press, 1993), 409–33. Also see Patricia Carpenter, "*Grundgestalt* as Tonal Function," *Music Theory Spectrum* 5 (1983), 15–38.

53. Similar observations are forcefully made by Patricia Carpenter and Severine Neff in their commentary to Schoenberg's *Der musikalische Gedanke und die Logik, Technik, und Kunst seiner Darstellung*.

> Such tonal functions present a set of balanced forces. Those close to or having the potential to move toward the tonic are termed *centripetal*, those far from or moving away from it *centrifugal*. Schoenberg viewed tonality as a necessary conflict, a battlefield upon which the struggle between centripetal and centrifugal forces is played out . . .

Arnold Schoenberg, *The Musical Idea and the Logic, Technique, and Art of Its Presentation*, edited by Patricia Carpenter and Severine Neff, Columbia University Press, 1995, 62.

54. The paper is ostensibly a critique of Ernst Kurth's concept of "linear counterpoint," however at one point Schoenberg assures the reader that "I have not read E. Kurth's book, *Der lineare Kontrapunkt*, and hardly know more than the title and the odd things I have heard or read. Even my pupils could not tell me anything about it." Given Schoenberg's disclaimer, it is difficult to read the paper as a serious critique of Kurth. Its value lies in the insights it gives us into Schoenberg's personal conception of counterpoint. Given that Schoenberg is surely among the most significant contrapuntalists of the twentieth century, the paper is of great interest indeed.

55. *Theory of Harmony*. The critique of "non-harmonic tones" is found on page 309; the critique of "atonal" is found on page 432.

56. Arnold Schoenberg, *Style and Idea: Selected Writings of Arnold Schoenberg*, edited by Leonard Stein, translated by Leo Black, University of California Press, 1984, 289.

57. Evidently, Schoenberg's students were acutely aware of these properties. Alban Berg's influential paper "Why is Schoenberg's music so hard to comprehend?" cites the earlier study of Schoenberg by Egon Wellesz to make the same point. (Berg's paper is included in Willi Reich, *Alban Berg*, translated by Cornelius Cardew, Vienna House, 1974, 189–204.)

As an aid to penetrating the psychology of his works, the sketchbooks he used during the period when this quartet [the First String Quartet, Op.7] was written are of the greatest importance. No one who has looked at them will be able to say that Schoenberg's music is constructed, intellectual, or whatever the rest of those clichés are which one uses as protection against the superiority of his teeming imagination. Because: '*Every thematic idea is invented complete with all of its counter-parts.*'

The thematic idea is invented "with all its counter-parts" because in a truer sense the idea requires those counter-parts for its realization.

58. *Style and Idea*, 289–90.
59. *Ibid.*, 290.
60. A discussion of polymorphous canons for English readers is found in Ebenezer Prout, *Double Counterpoint and Canon*, Augener Ltd., 1891, 249–53. Prout mentions Marpurg's discussion of a polymorphous canon by Valenti "which the composer worked in 2,000 different ways!" My thanks to Severine Neff for this reference.
61. *Style and Idea*, 290.
62. Compare A. B. Marx's conception of the musical period, endnote 19.
63. *Style and Idea*, 290.
64. The idea of imperfection, as explored in the Introduction to this book, can be thought of as a necessary aspect of all things from a Heraclitean perspective.
65. *Theory of Harmony*, 8.

66. *Theory of Harmony*, 47–8.
67. Schoenberg's recognition of musical practice as "second nature" anticipates Adorno's related discussions as discussed earlier.
68. *Theory of Harmony*, 48.
69. The translation is based on the 1922 edition of *Harmonielehre*. The passage reads differently in the 1911 edition. The German below intercalates both editions using curly brackets for text found only in the later edition and square brackets for text found only in the earlier edition.

> So kann man sich auch vorstellen, dass der Zufall einer dissonierenden Durchgangsnote, einmal schriftlich festgelegt, nachdem man erst ihren Reiz empfunden, des Bedürfnis nach einer weniger zufälligen, willkürlich hervorgebrachten Wiederholung provozierte; dass das Bedürfnis, diesen Reiz öfter zu empfinden, dazu geführt hat, von den Methoden, die ihn hervorrufen, Besitz zu ergreifen. {Doch: sollte der Reiz des Verbotenen zu unvermindertem Genuss führen, so musste jenes im Grund verächtliche Kompromiss zwischen Moral und Begierde geschlossen werden, welches hier in einer lässigeren Auffassung sowohl des Verbotes, als auch des Verbotenen besteht.} [Doch der Reiz der verbotenen Frucht sollte erhalten bleiben, deshalb durfte die Vorsicht wegen der Übertretung des Gebotes nicht so weit gehen, den Genuss zu verringern.] Die Dissonanz ward akzeptiert, aber an der Tür, durch die man sie entliess, ein Riegel vorgeschoben, {wenn} [der das] Übermass {drohte} [vermeiden sollte].

The suppression of the phrase "verbotenen Frucht" is a striking aspect of the reformulation.

Chapter 3

1. Schoenberg's remarks, originally in English, were made prior to a radio broadcast of *Pelleas und Melisande*, February 17, 1950. See *Arnold Schoenberg: A Self Portrait*, 116.
2. Schoenberg's move and the nature of his engagement at Überbrettl are discussed in H. H. Stuckenschmidt, *Arnold Schoenberg*, 47–60.
3. See Stuckenschmidt, 62–4. Stuckenschmidt reports that Schoenberg worked as a copyist for Strauss during this period. He suggests that Strauss's *Taillefer*, a work for chorus and orchestra that Schoenberg copied at the time, may have influenced the orchestration of Schoenberg's *Pelleas*.
4. Walter B. Bailey, *Programmatic Elements in the Works of Schoenberg*, UMI Research Press, 1984, 59.
5. Debussy's *Pelléas et Mélisande* was premiered in Paris on April 30, 1902 (Bailey, 59).
6. See Bailey, 52, and Walter Frisch, *The Early Works of Arnold Schoenberg, 1893–1908*, University of California Press, 1993, 158.
7. See Bailey, 52–73, for background on all of the primary sources for Schoenberg's *Pelleas*, including details on the early German editions and on the German edition in Schoenberg's library.
8. Mallarmé found the play so musical that he thought its intrinsic musicality denied the possibility of a musical setting. "*Pelléas and Mélisande*, on a stage,

exhales the delight of the page. [. . .] Almost silently and abstractly to the point that, in this art, where everything becomes music in the proper sense, the part of an instrument, even meditative, violin, would spoil things, by its uselessness." Cited in Patrick McGuinness. *Maurice Maeterlinck and the Making of Modern Theatre*, Oxford University Press, 2000, 125.

9. *Arnold Schoenberg: A Self Portrait*, 110.

10. Berg, *Pelleas and Melisande: Short Thematic Analysis*, translated by Derrick Puffett, in Derrick Puffett, "'Music that Echoes within one' for a Lifetime: Berg's Reception of Schoenberg's 'Pelleas und Melisande'," *Music and Letters*, 76/2 (1995), 250.

11. Aspects of Schoenberg's indebtedness to Wagner and Strauss in forming his characterizations are discussed by Puffett, *ibid.*, 226–9.

12. Rather than summarize the whole of Maeterlinck's play, much of which does not have analogues in Schoenberg's symphonic poem, my description here is generally restricted to the parts of the play that are either explicitly depicted by Schoenberg (according to Schoenberg and/or Berg) or that seem to influence the atmosphere and processes of dramatic and formal unfolding in Schoenberg's setting. For a succinct outline of Maeterlinck's play, see Bailey, *Programmatic Elements in the Works of Schoenberg*, 59–61.

13. We can be fairly certain that Schoenberg does not depict the supporting characters in his tone poem not only because Schoenberg (and Berg) do not identify supporting characters as being depicted among the work's motives and themes, but moreover because the motives and themes that are identified saturate virtually the entire musical texture, leaving no room for the representation of other characters.

14. In the play Melisande is delivered of a female child during the time she is comatose (the father is presumably Golaud, but this is not made explicit). This event does not seem to have any analogue in Schoenberg's setting.

15. The transcription of Schoenberg's letter in *Ausgewählte Briefe*, 52–4, and translated in *Schoenberg Letters*, 54–6, omits several crucial passages that are supplied in Walter B. Bailey, *Programmatic Elements in the Works of Schoenberg*, 66–9 (on the other hand, Bailey omits interesting passages found in the *Letters*). There is a discrepancy on the date of the letter. In the German edition it is dated 23 March, 1918; in the English edition the date is corrected to 20 March, 1918. Alban Berg's analysis, *Pelleas und Melisande (nach dem Drama von Maurice Maeterlinck): Symphonische Dichtung für Orchestra von Arnold Schönberg, Op.5 kurze thematische Analyse*, is available in two English editions, translated by Mark DeVoto in the *Journal of the Arnold Schoenberg Institute*, XVI numbers 1 and 2, 1993, and by Derrick Puffett, appended to his article " 'Music that Echoes within one' for a Lifetime: Berg's Reception of Schoenberg's 'Pelleas und Melisande', " *Music and Letters*, 76/2 (1995). Schoenberg's 1949 program notes are included in *Arnold Schoenberg: A Self Portrait*, 110–12.

16. Schoenberg may have had specific scenes in mind in composing the passages meant to capture Golaud's perspective, but the primary sources are not explicit on this. Possibilities include Act II, scene 2, where Golaud finds out that

Mélisande has lost their wedding-ring, Act III, scene 1, where Golaud comes upon Pelléas and Mélisande to find them weeping in the darkness of Mélisande's room, and the end of Act III, scene 2, where Golaud comes upon Pelléas and Mélisande as Pelléas plays entangled in Mélisande's long hair.

17. Act I, scene 1 connects chronologically to Act V, scene 1, and so, the remainder of Act I and all of Acts II, III, and IV are anticipated by the opening.

18. McGuinness, *Maurice Maeterlinck and the Making of Modern Theatre*, Oxford University Press, 2000, 133.

19. Most sources list the date as 26 January, 1905. According to Puffett, " 'Music that Echoes within one' for a Lifetime: Berg's Reception of Schoenberg's 'Pelleas und Melisande'," 211, n.16, the original concert poster lists 25 January as the date.

20. *Schoenberg Letters*, selected and edited by Erwin Stein, translated by Eithne Wilkins and Ernst Kaiser, St. Martin's Press, 1965, 52.

21. *Arnold Schoenberg Self Portrait*, edited by Nuria Schoenberg Nono, Belmont Music Publishers, 1988, 112.

22. Stuckenschmidt, *Arnold Schoenberg*, 134. In contrast, Willi Reich cites an incredibly hostile "open letter" from the critic Walter Dahms to Schoenberg. Among Dahms's bitter remarks are "The Berlin public's self-restraint was the only reason why the performance of your rubbish was allowed to continue . . ." Willi Reich, *Schoenberg: A Critical Biography*, translated from the German by Leo Black, Praeger Publishers, 1971, Reich, 62–3.

23. Stuckenschmidt, 163, 179–81, 259, 264–5.

24. Stuckenschmidt records that Schoenberg fell ill after the Boston premiere on 11 January, 1934, and then returned to conduct *Pelleas* on 16 March, 1934. Schoenberg had arrived in America on 31 October, 1933.

25. *Style and Idea*, 185–9.

26. As noted earlier, the transcription in *Schoenberg Letters*, 54–6, omits several crucial passages that are supplied in Bailey, *Programmatic Elements in the Works of Schoenberg*, 66–9. Frisch, *The Early Works of Arnold Schoenberg, 1893–1908*, 175–7, also discusses this correspondence, drawing some interesting parallels between Zemlinsky's request and Bruno Walter's request to cut passages from *Verklärte Nacht*.

27. Schoenberg's letter implies that while the passages in question employ irregular phrasing, the preceding parts of the work were too often four-square. Careful analysis does not particularly bear this out. While there are numerous two-bar ideas that are treated sequentially, the 2×2 bar pattern is generally disrupted by fragmentation and spinning out throughout the work.

28. The final paragraph describing the programmatic associations is omitted from the standard editions of the selected letters, both in German and English, but included in Walter Bailey's study, *Programmatic Elements in the Works of Schoenberg*. See Bailey, 66. I use Bailey's translation, correcting his inadvertent "E-flat trumpet."

29. The ambivalence in Schoenberg's letter to Zemlinsky finds a remarkable parallel in a letter that Schoenberg wrote to Alma Mahler on 7 October, 1910 concerning

Die glückliche Hand. Richard Kurth provides insightful commentary on that letter and its place within Schoenberg's evolving ideas concerning the *Bilderverbot* of the Second Commandment. See, "Schönberg and the *Bilderverbot,*" *Journal of the Arnold Schönberg Center,* vol. 5 (2003), 332–72. The discussion of the letter to Alma Mahler is found on pages 350–2.

30. From "On Revient Toujours" (1948), *Style and Idea,* 109.

31. Joseph Auner makes similar observations in his excellent article "The Second Viennese School as a Historical Concept," in Simms, *Schoenberg, Berg, and Webern,* 1–36. See especially 21–2.

32. The passages given in Schoenberg's musical examples (not identified in the original) are rehearsal 1.1–6, the principal Melisande leitmotiv; rehearsal 9.1–4, the initial presentation of the Pelléas motive; rehearsal 50.3–6, the motive associated with Mélisande's death; three presentations of the material depicting Golaud's jealousy (23, 27.7, and 29.5); and rehearsal 30.6, the opening of the vault scene.

33. *Arnold Schönberg,* Berg et al., R. Piper and Co., 1912, 27–30.

34. Berg, *Pelleas und Melisande (nach dem Drama von Maurice Maeterlinck): Symphonische Dichtung für Orchestra von Arnold Schönberg, Op.5 kurze thematische Analyse,* Universal Edition, 1920. Mark DeVoto, in addition to a full translation, provides historical background to this and Berg's other guides to Schoenberg's music. See *Journal of the Arnold Schoenberg Institute,* XVI (1993), 6–23, and 271–92. Derrick Puffett provides a critique of Berg's guide in his *Music and Letters* article (1995), 209–64.

35. Puffett, " 'Music that Echoes within one' for a Lifetime: Berg's Reception of Schoenberg's 'Pelleas und Melisande'," 209 and *passim.*

36. Egon Wellesz, *Arnold Schoenberg: The Formative Years,* translated from the German by W. H. Kerridge, J. M. Dent and Sons, 1925, 96.

37. Gould's remark is in his 1964 article "Schoenberg – A Perspective," Glenn Gould, "Schoenberg – A Perspective." In *The Glenn Gould Reader,* edited with an introduction by Tim Page, Alfred A. Knopf, 1984, 111.

38. See Frisch, *The Early Works of Arnold Schoenberg,* 158–77, and Puffett, " 'Music that Echoes within one' for a Lifetime: Berg's Reception of Schoenberg's 'Pelleas und Melisande'," 209–64.

39. Frisch, 177.

40. Puffett, 239. See also William Austin, *Music in the 20th Century,* W. W. Norton and Company, 1966, 214.

41. Puffett, 250.

42. It is possible to read Berg to mean that the scenes by the castle tower and the castle vaults complete a three-part Scherzo movement. That "explanation" of the formal function does not correlate with the normal ABA structure of a Scherzo, and Berg does not support this reading in his commentary.

43. In the musical substitution of Death Drive for Eros, Schoenberg's musical practice anticipates a development of late Freudian theory, remarkable to say the least. Freud posits the death drive (*Thanatos*) in his 1920 paper *Beyond the Pleasure*

Principle. Of course Freud's paper suggests a far more elemental and ramified opposition, Eros–Death Drive, than can be extrapolated from Schoenberg's representation.

44. Stanley Cavell suggests that "philosophy has to do with the perplexed capacity to mourn the passing of the world." (*This New Yet Unapproachable America: Lectures after Emerson after Wittgenstein,* Living Batch Press, 1989, 84). We work through the sorrow of mourning in order to learn how to let go of that which is past so that we may engage (embrace?) that which shall come. As Cavell strikingly puts it, "mourning" becomes "dawning."

45. Puffett, 219, hears this passage and the next (the beginning up through the end of Reh. 4) otherwise. He asserts that "much of it unequivocally expresses the tonic, D minor." In the entire span of 43 measures devoted to the exposition of MELISANDE LOST and MELISANDE there are no cadences on the tonic, and only two fleeting arrivals on the dominant (at Reh. 1, and at Reh. 4.3); neither of these is strongly cadential. Granted, the key signature would indicate D minor, but given the preponderance of chromatic harmonies, I doubt that we hear the key signature. Taking key and thematic content into account, Puffett criticizes Berg's characterization of this music as introduction. I believe that Berg may have decided to call the opening passages introductory because of two factors: the expression of tonality is tentative at best and, in contrast to the music associated with Golaud and Pelléas, the music associated with Mélisande does not cohere as a theme (at least not until the statement of MELISANDE embedded in the Love scene, at Reh. 43).

46. My imagery here is informed by Camille Paglia's discussion in the first chapter of *Sexual Personae*: "What is pretty in nature is confined to the thin skin of the globe upon which we huddle. Scratch that skin, and nature's daemonic ugliness will erupt." Camille Paglia, *Sexual Personae: Art and Decadence from Nefertiti to Emily Dickinson,* Yale University Press, 1990, 5.

47. See Puffett, 219, 253. After criticizing Berg on this account, Puffett suggests that we think of the manifestations of Fate as an adaptation of rondo technique. I find this solution no more appealing than Berg's. The cyclic returns of a rondo subject are vastly different in temperament and technique from the intrusions of Fate in Schoenberg's *Pelleas.*

48. Puffett notes that Schoenberg's "youthful and knightly" characterization of Pelléas has more in common with Wagnerian characters than with the "languid" Pelléas presented by Maeterlinck. See Puffett, 228.

49. The association of Fate with its new harmonies is noted by Berg (1920) and Schoenberg (1949).

50. Other subsequent presentations of Fate, "catastrophic" presentations aside, are sometimes supported by the characteristic harmonic progression (at 30.4–5, and 32.7–8), and sometimes not (as at 23.8–9, 49.7, 54.5, and 69.5–7).

51. The idea that Eros is bittersweet is an ancient one, developed by the poet Sappho. The idea is beautifully explored by Anne Carson in *Eros the Bittersweet,* Princeton University Press, 1986.

52. In most of the recordings that I have checked, the linear Fate motive is not even audible in the Pelléas theme. It is the chord progression and the motives in the upper woodwinds that are foregrounded.

53. Aspects of Schoenberg's portrayal of the enigmatic Mélisande anticipate his use of similar properties in his portrayal of the even more enigmatic qualities of divinity in *Moses und Aron*.

54. Readers familiar with David Lewin's "Music Theory, Phenomenology, and Modes of Perception" will recognize the C major chord as an example of an "external interrupt" as in "Sieglinde's suddenly noticing Hunding." *Music Perception*, vol.3, no.4, 327–92. The discussion of "external interrupt" is on 330–1.

55. Puffett calls the passage beginning at Reh. 43 "trio-like." See Puffett, 222.

56. Harold Bloom, *Ruin the Sacred Texts: Poetry and Belief from the Bible to the Present*, Harvard University Press, 1989, 4. Bloom's examples are from the Torah and Kafka.

57. Many differences aside, the parallels to the love-death idea in *Tristan* are obvious.

58. The situation once again resonates with Lewin's discussion in "Music Theory, Phenomenology, and Modes of Perception," 330–1.

59. The metaphor is borrowed from Edward T. Cone, "Schubert's Promissory Note: An Exercise in Musical Hermeneutics," in *Schubert: Critical and Analytical Studies*, edited by Walter Frisch, University of Nebraska Press, 1986, 13–30.

60. Anne Carson, *Eros the Bittersweet*, 3.

61. Puffett, 222, is highly critical of Berg's description of Reh. 33–35 ("An Introduction in the manner of an elaboration") saying "one has to deplore the poverty of the terminology". While Berg's terminology may not be particularly revealing, the passage clearly does set the stage for the larger Adagio that will follow. The role of EROS in this setting up of the Adagio LOVE theme is very much to the point.

62. *Eros the Bittersweet*, 26–7.

63. Puffett, 239, expresses extreme ambivalence about the end of this passage. "The chords that preface the Scene at the Castle Tower (from four bars before fig. 25) say it all: beautiful, highly expressive harmonies, as precisely calculated in the orchestration (first clarinet, then oboes, then flutes, finally strings) as they are in their voice-leading – but also in their plainness, verging on incoherence, as if, at the moment of ultimate expressivity, Schoenberg has decided to stop composing." It is hard to know how to respond. Suffice it to say that for me, the reduction of the texture from complex polyphony, to bare chords, and then on to the rich overlayered textures of Reh. 25 works beautifully. I find the chordal textures stunning, satisfying dramatically as well as formally.

64. In addition to noting correspondences between LOVE and PELLEAS, Berg asserts a connection between the contour of the opening of LOVE and MELISANDE LOST. The idea that LOVE is a synthesis of Mélisande- and Pelléas-derived materials is appealing, but as Frisch, 162 recognizes, the connection between the contour of LOVE and that of MELISANDE LOST seems

tenuous at best. On the other hand, analysis will show that the influence of MELISANDE (and FATE) is pervasive throughout the LOVE scene in controlling large scale harmonic motion and form.

65. The interaction of tonal space and symmetrical space was a stimulating topic of discussion in Richard Cohn's workshops on the application of Neo-Riemannian transformations to the study of *Parsifal* held in the Mannes Institute for Advanced Studies in Music Theory, summer 2003.

66. See Puffett, 221.

67. The conveyance of LOST INNOCENCE from Mélisande to Golaud poses a problem from a "realistic" point of view. That is, how can Mélisande's dreaming of lost innocence be conveyed to Golaud? Rather than a departure, however, this continues a practice found throughout *Pelleas und Melisande*. For example, Golaud somehow "knows" the EROS motive, and later the LOVE theme, without having participated in the events that gave rise to the motives. "Realism" is no more pertinent in Schoenberg's portrayal than it is in Maeterlinck's.

68. As has been noted by previous scholars, the $E^\flat$ pedal here complements the $C^\sharp$ pedal that is prolonged during what we have characterized as Mélisande's dream sequence. The two pedal tones are symmetrically disposed about the final tonic, D.

Chapter 4

1. An earlier version of this chapter appeared in *Music of My Future: The Schoenberg Quartets and Trio*, edited by Reinhold Brinkman and Christoph Wolff, Isham Library Papers 5/Harvard Publications in Music 20, 2000. The volume is dedicated to David Lewin and was generated out of a symposium held in his honor at Harvard University, February 26–27, 1999. My thanks to the Harvard University Department of Music for permission to publish this present version of the paper here.

2. Arnold Schoenberg, "Brahms the Progressive," in *Style and Idea*, edited by Leonard Stein, translated by Leo Black, University of California Press, 1984, 399.

3. Henri Bergson, *Matter and Memory*, translated by N. M. Paul and W. S. Palmer, Zone Books, 1991.

4. My thanks to Therese Muxeneder, archivist for the Arnold Schönberg Center in Vienna, for this information.

5. *Matter and Memory*, 79–83.

6. The *interval function* spans intervals (variously defined for temporal and/or pitch events) from one event (note, chord, motive, etc.) to another. These necessarily accumulate over time as a work (or passage) proceeds. See David Lewin, *Generalized Musical Intervals and Transformations*, (New Haven: Yale University Press, 1987), especially 88–104.

7. Lewin explores the implications of the second type of memory in his article "Music Theory, Phenomenology, and Modes of Perception," *Music Perception* 3/4 (1986), 327–92.

8. See Schoenberg's discussion of harmonic "regions" in *Structural Functions of Harmony*, edited by Leonard Stein, W.W. Norton & Co., 1969, 19–34. Also see his graphic representations of phrase shapes in *Fundamentals of Musical Composition*, edited by Gerald Strang and Leonard Stein, St. Martin's Press, 1967.

9. The program notes are included in Ursula Rauchhaupt, editor, *Schoenberg, Berg, Webern: The String Quartets, a documentary study*, (Hamburg: Deutsche Grammophon Gesellschaft Mbh., 1971) 11–13, 35–42.

10. *Ibid.*, 11.

11. *Ibid.*, 16.

12. Marx's dialectical description of a musical period is originally found in *Die Lehre von der musikalischen Komposition*, vol. 1, Breitkopf & Härtel, 1841. In English translation, the passage is found in *Theory and Practice of Musical Composition*, 88. Marx's description of sonata form is found in *Die Lehre von der musikalischen Komposition*, vol. 3, Breitkopf & Härtel, 1845, 217–18.

13. *Generalized Musical Intervals and Transformations*, 157–244.

14. See David Lewin, "Music Theory, Phenomenology, and Modes of Perception," 327–92.

15. See note 14 in the Introduction.

16. Gilles Deleuze, *Difference and Repetition*, 36–7.

Chapter 5

1. The term *time shard* is influenced by the literary theories of Harold Bloom, who is influenced in turn by Gershom Scholem's writings on Jewish mysticism. Scholem wrote numerous texts on the history of Kabbalah; *Major Trends in Jewish Mysticism* (Schocken Books, 1941) is a *locus classicus*. Chapter Seven of that text is devoted to the school of Isaac Luria, a Jewish Kabbalist writing after the catastrophic Spanish Inquisition and the Jewish exile from Spain.

The exiles from Spain must have held an intense belief in the fiendish realities of Exile . . . It expressed itself in a vigorous insistence upon the fragmentary character of Jewish existence, and in mystical views and dogmas to explain this fragmentariness with its paradoxes and tensions.   (249)

Lurianic doctrine posits a first creation in *Adam Kadmon*, "primordial man."

Adam Kadmon is nothing but a first configuration of the divine light which flows from the essence of *En-Sof* . . . From his eyes, mouth, ears, and nose, the light of the Sefiroth [the Divine Attributes] burst forth. At first these lights were coalesced in a totality . . . The lights coming from the eyes, however, emanated in an "atomized" form in which every Sefirah was an isolated point . . . it was necessary that these isolated lights should be caught and preserved in special "bowls" created – or rather emanated – for this particular purpose. The vessels which corresponded to the three highest Sefiroth accordingly gave shelter to their light, but when the turn of the lower six came, the light broke forth all at once and its impact proved too much for the vessels which were broken and shattered.

(265–6)

Harold Bloom adapts the phrase "breaking of the vessels" to express the means by which creative writers necessarily break the mold of their precursors, transforming tradition to keep tradition alive. Developments out of Bloom's confrontation with Lurianic Kabbalah are found in many of his books, including *Kabbalah and Criticism* (Seabury Press, 1975), *The Breaking of the Vessels* (University of Chicago Press, 1982), and *Genius* (Warner Books, 2002).

2. Martha M. Hyde discusses metric properties of twelve-tone music in "A Theory of Twelve-Tone Meter," *Music Theory Spectrum*, vol. 6, 14–51. Through numerous examples, Hyde shows how row segments, or "secondary dimension" constructs that are set-theoretic equivalents to row segments, are congruent with meter. Unfortunately, Hyde begs the question in asserting that "meter is not imposed upon Schoenberg's twelve-tone music, but rather evolves from its harmonic structure." (17) For Hyde, the row segments (or secondary dimension segments) articulate the meter. On the contrary, the harmonic structure might have been articulated in any number of ways, in any possible meter or outside of a metric structure altogether. A more realistic claim would be that the meter articulates the row structures (even this would be an exaggeration, but closer to the truth). Unfortunately, claiming that the row articulates the meter is a little like claiming that water shapes the bottle that contains it. On the other hand, it would be a mistake to simply assert that the meter is arbitrarily imposed upon the row. Something like this is the claim that Pierre Boulez makes in his famous article "Schoenberg is Dead." I would rather claim that there is an interactive relationship between the two forces, the imperatives of the *a priori* row structure and the imperatives of an *a priori* metric frame (a metric frame that recalls tonal idioms, but is not equivalent to them). This is like saying that the water can take the shape of its container because of properties that inhere within the water as well as in the container.

3. The Brahmsian influence comes first; Schoenberg's studies with Zemlinsky in the 1890s led to a period of intense involvement with Wagner's music. Of course, the rhythmic practices of Brahms and Wagner are themselves complex palimpsests.

4. For an extended discussion of Augustine's speculations on time see Paul Ricoeur, *Time and Narrative*, vol. 1, University of Chicago Press, 1984, 5–30.

5. Stephen Kern, *The Culture of Time and Space: 1880–1918*, Harvard University Press, 1983, provides a book-length study.

6. Writing about *Die glückliche Hand*, Schoenberg's student and biographer Egon Wellesz observes "One is likely to discover the lines on which this drama is written if one thinks of the chamber-plays of Strindberg, for whose works Schönberg had an extraordinary admiration." *Arnold Schönberg*, translated by W. H. Kerridge, J. M. Dent & Sons, n.d., 29.

7. The abstract nature of time had been a concern of philosophy as far back as the Pre-Socratics. During the Enlightenment Leibniz and Newton provided competing models; for the former, time was the "accident" of bodies in motion, while for Newton time was absolute, measured by a Divine clockwork. Time and space as *a priori* categories of perception are keystones in Kant's philosophy.

Yet no philosophers, to my knowledge, systematically considered the experience of passing time, what we might call psychological time, until the generation of William James, Henri Bergson, and Edmund Husserl.

The writings of Henri Bergson, and their application in studying Schoenberg, are discussed in Chapter Four of this book. Ideas adapted from Husserl's phenomenology are central to David Lewin's "Music Theory, Phenomenology, and Modes of Perception," *Music Perception*, 3:4, 327–92. I discuss the work of William James in musical contexts in my review of Elliott Carter's *Collected Essays and Lectures, Music Theory Spectrum*, 23:1, 2001. Also see Stephen Kern, *The Culture of Time and Space, passim.*

8. The role of advances in communication and transportation is nicely explored in Stephen Kern, *ibid.*

9. The scare quotes around "non-functional" indicate my own discomfort with the term. I would rather say that Debussy's harmonies function in new and different ways.

10. Freud, *Das Unheimliche, Imago*, Bd. V, 1919. The English translation is included in *Collected Papers* (New York: Basic Books, 1959), vol. 4, 368–407. I discuss Freud's paper and its usefulness in studying Schoenberg in "Schoenberg and *Das Unheimliche*: Spectres of Tonality," *The Journal of Musicology* 11:3, 1993. An excellent, more recent study of Freud's essay on the uncanny and issues surrounding relations among "hexatonic poles" (e.g. C minor and E major) in the music of Wagner and others is found in Richard Cohn, "Uncanny Resemblances: Tonal Signification in the Freudian Age," *Journal of the American Musicological Society*, 57/2, 285–323. Another insightful musical adaptation of Freud's essay is Nicholas Marston, "Schubert's Homecoming," *Journal of the Royal Musical Association*, 125 (2000), 248–70. Michael L. Klein makes an important contribution in his study of influence and intertextuality as signs of the uncanny, Chapter Four of *Intertextuality in Western Art Music*, Indiana University Press, 2005, 77–107.

11. My phrase "hierarchically disposed congruences," is a simplification of a more complex procedure. Tonal rhythms are hierarchically congruent when they entail strict multiplications/divisions of musical time-space; for example, musical measures embedded in four-measure groups, those embedded in eight-measure phrases, those in thematic units of sixteen measures, and so forth. In actual practice, the congruences are modified by expansion or contraction, for example when a four-measure antecedent is answered by a five- or six-measure consequent, the latter time-space being heard as a dilation of the former.

12. Of course, Mozart is able to pull this off only by composing the overture after the rest of the opera.

13. The web of leitmotivic recollections includes the passage later in the same scene, where the giant Fasolt, having obtained the ring, is killed by his brother Fafner; the end of II.1 in *Die Walküre*, when Wotan gives way to Fricka, promising that he will no longer allow Brünnhilde to serve as Siegmund's protector; II.2 of *Siegfried*, where Siegfried kills Fafner, himself obtaining the ring; and finally near

the end of *Götterdämmerung* when Brünnhilde takes the ring off of Siegfried's finger, before placing him on his funeral pyre, and returning the ring to the Rhinemaidens.

14. An excellent discussion of the George text is in Judith Ryan's "'Ich fühle luft von anderem planeten': Schoenberg Reads George," in *Music of My Future: The Schoenberg Quartets and Trio*, Harvard University Press, 2000, 81–93.

15. See Bryan R. Simms' discussion of this passage in *The Atonal Music of Arnold Schoenberg: 1908–1923*, Oxford University Press, 2000, 89–99.

16. Nicholas Marston develops very similar ideas in his "Schubert's Homecoming," cited above. See especially his comments on Schubert songs on page 269.

17. Richard Cohn's insightful discussion of voice leading between "hexatonic poles" applies as well to the *Tarnhelm* progression. The juxtaposition of E major and C minor creates one such hexatonic pole. From the perspective of E major, the third of C minor (E♭) is only apparent – it actually functions as a D♯ leading tone, while C functions as flat six leading to B. In contrast, from the perspective of C minor, the third of E major (G♯) is only apparent – it actually functions as an A♭ (flat six in C) leading to G, while B functions as a leading tone to C. Seen from either perspective, the "other" is dissonant, and not even a triad. Just so with the *Tarnhelm* progression. For example, in the passage from *Verklärte Nacht*, Schoenberg juxtaposes D♯ minor and B minor. From D♯ minor's perspective, the apparent D-natural in B minor actually functions as a C-double sharp leading tone, while from the perspective of B minor, the apparent D♯ functions as an E♭, voice leading downward to D, the third of B minor. As with the hexatonic opposition, from either perspective, the "other" appears as a non-triadic dissonance. The inherent instability of meaning (both chords are and are not triads depending upon one's fluctuating perspective) is primary toward achieving the uncanny effect. See Richard Cohn, "Uncanny Resemblances: Tonal Signification in the Freudian Age," *Journal of the American Musicological Society*, 57/2 (2004), 285–323.

18. The paradox of "up is down" and related metaphors is central to David Schur, *The Way of Oblivion: Heraclitus and Kafka*, Harvard University Press, 1998. Schur cites Heraclitus Fragment 59, "The way of writers, straight and crooked, is one and the same," (15) as well as Fragment 60, "The way up and down is one and the same," (20) contrasting the Heraclitean paradoxes with images of the "straight path upward" in Hesiod and others. Like Heraclitus, Kafka's prose is full of such paradoxical indirections. One striking parallel is in Kafka's "Reflection" on the downward path to eternity – "A man was amazed at how easily he went the way of eternity; that is, he raced down it." (*Einer staunte darüber, wie leicht er den Weg der Ewigkeit ging; er raste ihn nämlich abwärts*) (195).

19. This problem is already strongly manifest in many passages in Wagner.

20. Bryan R. Simms provides a useful overview of the George texts in *The Atonal Music of Arnold Schoenberg: 1908–1923*, 45–6.

21. The pitch configuration of the left hand chords, mm.17–18, is derived from the left hand motive of mm. 10–11. The earlier passage, along with the separate right hand motive in those measures, depicts a visual hallucination; starlight, as it flickers through the dense foliage is perceived as snowflakes.

22. As discussed in Chapter One, Schoenberg had used the tolling of time with great effect in the seventh song of *Gurrelieder*, *Es ist Mitternachtszeit*, to set the words *Unsre Zeit ist um* (our time is over) and then in the song of the Wood Dove. Schoenberg would use a similar musical image in the last of the Op. 19 piano pieces, to depict the tolling of bells associated with Mahler's funeral.

23. Bryan R. Simms discusses the complicated history of the names attached to the movements of Op. 16, as well as Schoenberg's misgivings about the names. See *The Atonal Music of Arnold Schoenberg*, 73–4.

24. In practice, the term *Klangfarbenmelodie* (tone color melody) has taken on two interrelated meanings. The more radical sense of the term is the topic of the justly famous final paragraph of Schoenberg's *Harmonielehre* (*Theory of Harmony*, translated by Roy E. Carter, 421).

> The distinction between tone color and pitch, as it is usually expressed, I cannot accept without reservations. I think the tone becomes perceptible by virtue of tone color, of which one dimension is pitch . . . Now if it is possible to create patterns out of tone colors that are differentiated by pitch . . . then it must also be possible to make such progressions out of tone colors of the other dimension, out of that which we will simply call 'tone color' progressions
>
> [*was wir schlechtweg Klangfarbe nennen*] . . .

Schoenberg's only realization of this ideal is the third movement of Op. 16, variously titled *Sommermorgen an einem See* and *Farben* ("Summer Morning by a Lake" and "Colors"). The secondary meaning of *Klangfarben* refers to passages where there is a melodic line that undergoes color transformations. This latter sense of *Klangfarben* has clear precedents in earlier music; for example, the first thirty-one bars of Brahms' Second Symphony passes the principal line from the basses, to the horns, then woodwinds, back to the horns, back to the woodwinds, and then to the strings. Anton Webern's arrangement of the ricercar from Bach's *Musical Offering* uses *Klangfarben* in the same sense. Examples of this kind of *Klangfarben* are extensive throughout Schoenberg's Op.16.

25. For a helpful discussion of the text's origin see Bryan R. Simms, "Whose Idea was *Erwartung*?," in *Constructive Dissonance: Arnold Schoenberg and the transformations of twentieth-century culture*, edited by Juliane Brand and Christopher Hailey, University of California Press, 1997, 100–11. See also Michael Cherlin, "Schoenberg's Music for the Theater," in *The Great Tradition and its Legacy*, edited by Michael Cherlin, Halina Filipowicz, and Richard L. Rudolph, Berghahn Books, 2003, 246–58.

26. Schoenberg's minimal emendations of Marie Pappenheim's text remove just those passages that would have made the murder explicit. To quote Bryan Simms,

"he did not wish the poem to be construed as a realistic or objective study but instead as hallucination." In Bryan R. Simms, "Whose Idea was *Erwartung?*," 104–5.

27. H. H. Stuckenschmidt calls this particular harmonic construct "the primal cell," locating examples of it throughout Schoenberg's life's works. See *Arnold Schoenberg*, 525–34. In the language of pc set theory, it is a [016] trichord.

28. Bryan R. Simms discusses the *Am Wegrand* quote and other passages influenced by it in *The Atonal Music of Arnold Schoenberg*, 97–9. See also Herbert Buchanan, "A Key to Schoenberg's *Erwartung*," *Journal of the American Musicological Society*, XX/3 (1967), 434–49, and Michael Cherlin, "Schoenberg and *Das Unheimliche*: Spectres of Tonality," *The Journal of Musicology*, XI/3, 357–73.

29. Time shards play an equally significant role in the sister work to *Erwartung*, Schoenberg's amazing dream sequence, *Die glückliche Hand*. If anything, the kinds of uncanny ostinati that we have identified in *Erwartung* are even more pervasive in *Die glückliche Hand*. One extraordinary example is the famous "color crescendo," mm. 125–53; this entire sequence is composed almost exclusively of shifting time shards, each of which is correlated to a color and intensity, as the overall process leads to an ever brightening and intensifying experience of color and light.

30. For an historic overview and commentary of all twenty-one songs see Jonathan Dunsby, *Schoenberg: Pierrot lunaire*, Cambridge University Press, 1992. Another very useful reference is the booklet *From Pierrot to Marteau* published by the Arnold Schoenberg Institute (then in Los Angeles) in 1987. The booklet contains essays by Pierre Boulez, Leonard Stein, Susan Youens, Reinhold Brinkmann, Christian Martin Schmidt, and others.

31. Although *Mondestrunken* does not share the sense of a lost past with *Vergangenes*, many of the songs in *Pierrot lunaire* do. In contrast to *Vergangenes* (or *The Book of the Hanging Gardens* for that matter), the nostalgia in *Pierrot* takes on an ironic, even sardonic edge. In this respect, and some others, *Pierrot* anticipates developments that will occur in Schoenberg's works from the 1920s.

32. Richard Kurth places the phantasmagoria of *Pierrot lunaire* into a larger context in Schoenberg's evolution in his paper "Schönberg and the *Bilderverbot*," *Journal of the Arnold Schönberg Center*, vol.5 (2003), 332–72. The discussion of "Gebet an Pierrot" is found on pages 353–61.

33. The trichordal pc sets expressed through simultaneities over mm. 23–4 run through the entire repertory of trichordal types that include a semitone: (012, 013, 014, 015, 016). No other trichordal types are included. It may not be trivial that all of these trichord types can be extracted from the original piano ostinato (none appear as contiguous members of that segment). Thus, it might not be too far-fetched to think of this shard as a shattering of the moonbeams in a rather technical sense. The voice crossings between the flute and the piano's upper line add to the effect.

34. The evolution of Schoenberg's twelve-tone method is carefully studied in Ethan Haimo, *Schoenberg's Serial Odyssey: The evolution of his Twelve-Tone Method,*

1914–1928, Oxford University Press, 1990. Because Haimo is concerned only with musical technique, and not with more general aspects of cultural history (or musical expressivity), the role of the World War and subsequent developments in Weimar Germany are not addressed in his study. The study that would place twelve-tone music into a larger historical frame is yet to be written, so far as I know.

35. Schoenberg states his position clearly in his article "Composition with Twelve Tones": "Composition with twelve tones has no other aim than comprehensibility." *Style and Idea*, edited by Leonard Stein, translation by Leo Black, University of California Press, 1975, 215.

36. On the Treaty of Versailles and its impact on post-war Germany see Peter Gay, *Weimar Culture: The Outsider as Insider*, W. W. Norton & Co., 1968, 13–16 and *passim*. The situation in post-war Austria is summarized by Howard M. Sacher:

> From a might conglomeration of 52 million inhabitants, Austria was now transformed into a hunchback republic of barely 7 million. The city of Vienna alone encompassed a third of the entire remaining population... Before the war, the empire had boasted highly of developed resources – Silesia's coal, Bohemia's steel, textiles, and quarries, Hungary's wheat, northeastern Italy's wharfage and maritime facilities – as well as a network of railroads and a huge administrative bureaucracy. Most of this vast reticulation was gone."
>
> *Dreamland: Europeans and Jews in the Aftermath of the Great War*,
> Alfred A. Knopf, 2002, 175.

Schoenberg lived in the midst of all of this. Before the war he had divided his career between Vienna and Berlin; after the war he lived in Mödling (near Vienna), until moving to Berlin in January of 1926. See H. H. Stuckenschmidt, *Arnold Schoenberg*, 309ff.

37. Schoenberg's 1912 essay "The Relationship to the Text" gives a fair indication of his position at that time. Schoenberg approvingly cites Schopenhauer: "The composer reveals the inmost essence of the world and utters the most profound wisdom in a language which his reason does not understand, just as a magnetic somnambulist give disclosures abut things which she has no idea of when awake..." *Style and Idea*, 142. The painter Wassily Kandinsky shared these views with Schoenberg. Schoenberg's January 24, 1911 letter to Kandinsky makes this clear: "what you call the 'unlogical'... I call the 'elimination of the conscious will in art.' ... art belongs to the *unconscious!*" *Arnold Schoenberg, Wassily Kandinsky: Letters, Pictures and Documents*, edited by Jelena Hahl-Koch, translated by John C. Crawford, Faber and Faber, 1984, 23.

38. Peter Gay writes about a backlash against "anti-intellectualism and vulgar mysticism" in *Weimar Culture*, 33ff.

39. See Peter Gay, *Weimar Culture*, 98.

40. See Hans Mommsen, *The Rise and Fall of Weimar Democracy*, translated by Elborg Forster and Eugene Jones, University of North Carolina Press, 1996, 19. Also, Peter Gay, *Weimar Culture*, 19.

41. Schoenberg and his family had decided to spend the summer" of 1921 at Mattsee, a resort near Salzburg. Their vacation was interrupted by anti-Semitic demonstrations, and by the request that all Jews leave the resort. See H. H. Stuckenschmidt, *Schoenberg*, 272–4.

42. Compare Schoenberg's 20 July 1922 letter to Kandinsky.

> I expect you know we've had our trials here too: famine! It really was pretty awful! But perhaps – we Viennese seem to be a patient lot – perhaps the worst was after all the overturning of everything one has believed in. That was probably the most grievous thing of all.
>
> When one's been used, where one's own work was concerned, to clearing away all obstacles often by means of one immense intellectual effort and in those 8 years found oneself constantly faced with new obstacles against which all thinking, all power of invention, all energy, all ideas, proved helpless, for a man for whom ideas have been everything it means nothing less than the total collapse of things, unless he has come to find support, in ever increasing measure, in belief in something higher, beyond.
>
> *Arnold Schoenberg Letters*, 70–1.

43. Gershom Scholem's description of the method for meditation developed by the thirteenth-century Spanish mystic Abraham Abulafia has an uncanny correspondence with the permutational aspects of twelve-tone music:

> Abulafia is . . . compelled to look for an, as it were, absolute object for meditating upon; that is to say one capable of stimulating the soul's deeper life and freeing it from ordinary perceptions . . . Basing himself upon the abstract and non-corporeal nature of script, he develops a theory of the mystical contemplation of the letters and their configurations, as the constituents of God's name. For this is the real and, if I may say so, the peculiarly Jewish object of mystical contemplation: the Name of God . . . Starting from this concept, Abulafia expounds a peculiar discipline which he calls *Hokhmath he-Tseruf*, i.e. the science of the combination of letters . . . Abulafia himself has already quite correctly compared it with music. Indeed, the systematic practice of meditation as taught by him, produces a sensation closely akin to that of listening to musical harmonies. The science of combination is a music of pure thought . . .
>
> *Major Trends in Jewish Mysticism*, 132–3.

The permutational basis of the twelve-tone system is first discussed by Milton Babbitt in "Twelve-tone Invariants as Compositional Determinants" (1960). See *The Collected Essays of Milton Babbitt*, edited by Stephen Peles et al., Princeton University Press, 2003, 55–69. In light of these parallels, Schoenberg's reputed remark to Josef Rufer, in 1921, takes on a special irony: "I have made a discovery that will ensure the supremacy of *German* music for the next hundred years" (my emphasis). Quoted in Stuckenschmidt, *Schoenberg*, 277.

44. Schoenberg wrote his program notes for the Quartet in 1936 to accompany the Kolisch Quartet recording. *Arnold Schoenberg: Self Portrait*, edited by Nuria Schoenberg Nono, Belmont Music Publishers, 1988, 82.

45. Jeff Nichols has written a very perceptive analysis of rhythmic conflict in the first movement of the Third Quartet: "Metric Conflict as an Agent of Formal Design in the First Movement of Schoenberg's Quartet Op. 30," in *Music of My Future: the Schoenberg Quartets and Trio*, Harvard University Press, 2000, 95–116.

46. Compare the opening sentence of Schoenberg's 1923 essay "Twelve-Tone Composition":

    In twelve tone composition consonances (major and minor triads) and also the simpler dissonances (diminished triads and seventh chords) – in fact almost everything that used to make up the ebb and flow of harmony – are, as far as possible, avoided.

    Style and Idea, 207.

47. In reflecting C major with C minor, Schoenberg incorporates a relationship that had been noticed in music theory since Zarlino. Less remote to Schoenberg's experience would have been the *Dual* worlds of Hugo Riemann, or their antecedents in the harmonic theory of Moritz Hauptmann. Both theorists, Hauptmann in the early nineteenth century, and Riemann closer to Schoenberg's own time, posited minor as a mirror image of major.

48. Schoenberg's pupil Erwin Stein provides a formal outline of the movement, and of the whole Quartet, printed as a preface to the score in the Universal Edition. The design of the movement is sonata form, with the order of the principal and subordinate themes reversed at the recapitulation. Stein identifies mm.278–341 as *codaartig*, "quasi Coda" in the English translation.

49. Schoenberg does cite a model for the First Quartet, Beethoven's *Eroica* Symphony. Oddly enough, there the connections are extremely tentative, whereas the connections between the Third Quartet and the Schubert A minor Quartet are considerable.

    So far as I have been able to trace it, Charles Rosen is the first in print to claim that Schoenberg's Third Quartet is modeled on Schubert's A minor Quartet. His brief discussion can be found in *Arnold Schoenberg*, The Viking Press, 1975, 88–90. Joseph N. Straus develops a much more detailed discussion of the relationships between the two works in his *Remaking the Past*, Harvard University Press, 1990, 161–8, and less directly 121–32. Martha Hyde builds upon Straus' analysis, adding her own perspective in "Neoclassic and Anachronistic Impulses in Twentieth-Century Music," *Music Theory Spectrum*, 18/2 (1996), 200–35 (223–35 are devoted specifically to the Schoenberg/Schubert modeling).

50. *Structural Functions of Harmony*, W. W. Norton & Co., 1954, 53–4, 138, 156–8. All three passages refer to the first movement. The first citation of the Schubert is concerned with the exchange of tonic minor and major, a quality that is quite salient in the A minor Quartet, as in many other works by Schubert; Schoenberg's musical example shows the recapitulation of the principal theme, and its moves between A minor and A major. The second mention of the A minor Quartet is without musical example, in the context of a discussion of pedal points. Schoenberg's comment ,"from the standpoint of structural functions there is not much interest in pedal points," is astounding given the central

role played by the ostinato (which embeds the pedal point) throughout the Schubert, and even more astounding once we recognize it as the source for the ostinato in Schoenberg's Quartet. The third citation of the A minor Quartet is a harmonic analysis of the entire development section. Schoenberg's opening comment is much to the point: "The richness of Schubert's harmony perhaps marks the actual transition to Wagnerian and post-Wagnerian composers' procedures."

51. "Metric Conflict as an Agent of Formal Design in the First Movement of Schoenberg's Quartet Op. 30," cited earlier.

52. See Nichols, Example 5.3, "Metric Conflict as an Agent of Formal Design," 104.

53. *Ibid.*, 101. Also much to the point is Nichols' reference to David Lewin's paper on "Vocal Meter in Schoenberg's Atonal Music." Writing about similar properties in Schoenberg's Fourth Quartet, "Lewin implies that this music transcends traditional metric structures – if not by denying them, then by placing them in new, relativistic contexts" (109). Lewin's article appears in *In Theory Only*, VI/4 (1982), 12–36. Lewin's ideas, as well as ideas developed out of the discussion of Schoenbergian dialectic that forms Chapter Two of the present work, are further developed in an insightful article by Richard Kurth, "The Art of Cadence in Schoenberg's Fourth String Quartet," in *Arnold Schoenberg in America*, Arnold Schoenberg Center, Vienna, 2002, 245–70.

54. Nichols argues that the movement has two culminating points of metric clarification. The first is the proliferation of triple versus duple groupings shown in his Example 1, the passage leading up to the climax at m. 277 that we have already considered. The second is the passage beginning at m. 311, with the emergence of 9/4. Nichols hears the later passage as a clarification of the two meters, first triple (at 311–20) and then duple (321–3). *Ibid.*, 113–14. While the clarification of the triples at 311 is particularly salient, I do not hear the duples that follow as a "clarification." The *alla breve* time signature is aurally salient for only three bars (321–3) before the cross currents of conflicted shards resumes.

55. See Martha M. Hyde, "Neoclassic and Anachronistic Impulses in Twentieth-Century Music," 232–5. Hyde's interpretation of Schoenberg's coda in its relationship to Schubert – claiming that Schoenberg used the coda to reaffirm the movement's axes of inversion, and in doing so leaves Schubert behind, as Dante did Virgil at the end of *Purgatorio* – is quite different from my own; however, I see no logical reason for our two interpretations to be mutually exclusive.

56. Of course, both the ostinato and the Adagio theme are based on the same twelve-tone row. Compositionally, the abstract row is the source, but experientially, it is the ostinato that has been burned into our consciousness, not some abstract source row. The confusion between analysis of row matrices and analysis of twelve-tone compositions has plagued the reception of twelve-tone composition, especially within the field of music theory.

Chapter 6

1. There is a formidable literature on Schoenberg's religious-philosophical thought. Pamela C. White, *Schoenberg and the God–Idea*, UMI Research Press, 1985, provides a useful overview of the genesis of *Moses und Aron* (Chapter 1) and of the development of Schoenberg's religious thought (Chapter 2). Bluma Goldstein, *Reinscribing Moses: Heine, Kafka, Freud, and Schoenberg in a European Wilderness*, Harvard University Press, 1992, is another excellent source; it places Schoenberg's thought into a larger context of Jewish thought in Europe. Alexander Ringer, *Arnold Schoenberg: The Composer as Jew*, Clarendon Press, 1990, discusses a wide range of issues specific to Schoenberg as Jew. *Political and Religious Ideas in the Works of Arnold Schoenberg*, edited by Charlotte M. Cross and Russell A. Berman, Garland Publishing, 2000, provides a variety of valuable perspectives on the topic. Stephen J. Cahn, *Variations in manifold time: Historical consciousness in the music and writings of Arnold Schoenberg*, Ph.D. dissertation, State University of New York at Stony Brook, 1996, is an important study of the historical and intellectual background for Schoenberg's musical and spiritual thought. Cahn's "*Kol nidre* in America," *Journal of the Arnold Schoenberg Center*, vol. 4 (2004), 203–18, addresses aspects of Schoenberg's return to Judaism during his years in America.
2. *Der biblische Weg* is discussed in White and Goldstein, cited above. A useful introduction to *Die Jakobsleiter* is found in Bryan Simms, *The Atonal Music of Arnold Schoenberg: 1908–1923*, Oxford University Press, 2000, 165–77.
3. The letter is cited and discussed in Pamela C. White, *Schoenberg and the God Idea*, 51.
4. See *Schoenberg and the God Idea*, 53, and Bluma Goldstein, *Reinscribing Moses*, 137–8.
5. *Schoenberg and the God Idea*, 55.
6. Schoenberg's changing attitudes toward performance of the text for Act III are nicely summarized in Bluma Goldstein, *Reinscribing Moses*, 149–50.
7. Among those who argue that the work should not or cannot continue after Act II are Theodor W. Adorno, George Steiner, and David Lewin. Adorno's views are developed in "Sacred Fragment: On Schoenberg's *Moses and Aaron*," included in *Quasi una Fantasia: Essays on Modern Music*, translated by Rodney Livingstone, Verso, 1992, 225–48. George Steiner's argument against Act III is in the closing remarks of his essay "Schoenberg's Moses and Aaron," included in *Language and Silence*, Atheneum, 1986, 127–39. David Lewin's position is found in his article "*Moses und Aron*: Some General Remarks, and Analytic Notes for Act I, scene 1," originally published in *Perspectives of New Music*, 6/1, 1–17, and also found in *Perspectives on Schoenberg and Stravinsky*, edited by Benjamin Boretz and Edward T. Cone, W. W. Norton & Co., 1972, 61–77. Among those who argue that Act III is necessary are Bluma Goldstein in *Reinscribing Moses*, cited above, and Philippe Lacoue-Labarthe, *Musica Ficta (Figures of Wagner)*, Stanford University Press, 1994.

8. George Steiner makes a similar argument: "As we have no music to accompany the words, it is difficult to judge their effect. But the third act is essentially static. There is no dramatic justification for Moses' triumph over a prostrate Aaron. Much is missing." "Schoenberg's Moses and Aaron," 139. David Lewin also argues forcefully along related lines:

> ... the libretto [for Act III] is unconvincing to me. The problem posed by the drama is not whether Moses or Aron is "right," but rather how God can be brought to the Volk. If the triple-play combination of God to Moses to Aron to Volk has broken down between Moses and Aron, and if the Moses-Aron link cannot be repaired, then the catastrophe of the philosophical tragedy has occurred in Act II and the drama is over. If there is a personal tragedy involved, it is surely that of Moses, and he, as well as or instead of Aron, should be the one to die (which in a sense he does at the end of Act II).

"*Moses und Aron*: Some General Remarks, and Analytic Notes for Act I, scene 1," 62.

9. The passage is cited and discussed in Lacoue-Labarthe, *Musica Ficta*, 139. It is also considered in Gary Tomlinson, *Metaphysical Song*, Princeton University Press, 1999, 151.

10. The passage is cited in *Musica Ficta*, 129.

11. *Metaphysical Song*, 150.

12. An excellent discussion of Schoenberg's evolving ideas concerning *Unvorstellbarkeit* with specific references to *Moses und Aron* is found in Richard Kurth, "Schönberg and the *Bilderverbot*," *Journal of the Arnold Schönberg Center*, vol. 5, 332–72.

13. The passage is cited in *Music Ficta*, 127.

14. The most extensive study of row properties in *Moses und Aron* is Christian Martin Schmidt, *Schönbergs Oper 'Moses und Aron'*, Schott, 1988. My doctoral dissertation, *The Formal and Dramatic Organization of Schoenberg's 'Moses und Aron'*, Yale University, 1983, devotes considerable attention to the tone row, its principal partitions, and their formal properties and dramatic associations. Many observations in the dissertation are integrated into this chapter. Needless to say, many of my views have been modified over the more than twenty years since the dissertation. An earlier study of row properties is Graham Hair, *Schoenberg's 'Moses und Aron'*, Ph.D. dissertation, University of Sheffield, 1973.

15. Babbitt discusses the various types of combinatoriality in "Set Structure as a Compositional Determinant" (1961). The essay is included in *The Collected Essays of Milton Babbitt*, Princeton University Press, 2003, 86–108.

16. See, David Lewin, "*Moses und Aron*: Some general remarks and analytic notes for Act I, scene 1," *Perspectives of New Music*, 6/1, 1–17 (1967). After almost forty years, Lewin's article remains the best short introduction to the work yet written. Christian Martin Schmidt's study of the opera uses the term *Region* to express the same set of relations as Lewin's 'Area'. See, *Schönbergs Oper 'Moses und Aron'*, 47.

17. This labeling system is a departure from the one most often used, where the number attached to a transposed or inverted row signifies the first pitch-class in that row, and where retrograde rows are given the same number as their non-retrograded forms. Using this system, and naming the source row for *Moses und Aron* S_0, the combinatorial inversion would be named I_3 (i.e. A=0, and the combinatorial inversion starts on C=3). The system adapted from Lewin, using the same number for each member of a combinatorial quartet, is less efficient for arithmetic calculations, but it is more efficient for indicating the most basic families among row forms.

18. Ordered pitch-class intervals are equivalent to the shortest distance from one note to the next in an ascending chromatic scale, measured in semitones. Pitch intervals are not an appropriate measure because the row is compositionally realized through variable pitch contours. A higher degree of abstraction can be studied through unordered pitch-class intervals, also known as interval classes. An interval class reduces pitch-class intervals to their shortest distances, ranging from 1 through 6. We will normally use ordered pitch-class intervals in studying row properties, although the higher level of abstraction will be useful at times.

19. Milton Babbitt uses the term in "Set Structure as a Compositional Determinant," page 93 and following, and it becomes normative in twelve-tone theory following Babbitt.

20. "*Moses und Aron*: Some general remarks and analytic notes for Act I, scene 1."

21. The inversional operation in this instance can be notated as I_3 (with A-natural as 0) or, following Lewin, as I^{A-C}.

22. David Lewin, with characteristic wit and insight, used a metaphor derived from baseball to describe the dramatic situation. The triple play combination of from God to Moses to Aron to the *Volk* breaks down when Moses cannot communicate his vision to Aron. The passage is cited in note 8 above.

23. The Divine "Voice" comprises two polyphonic ensembles. "Six solo voices" are instructed to sit in the orchestra; each is doubled at the unison by an instrument – soprano with second flute, mezzo-soprano with second clarinet, alto with English horn, tenor with 2nd bassoon, baritone with bass clarinet, and bass with second cello. In addition, there is a speaking choir identified as the "voice from the burning bush" (*Stimme aus dem Dornbusch*). This is composed of four to six voices on each part, soprano, boys, alto, tenor, baritone and bass. The stage instructions indicate that "One might consider having them speak over telephones from behind the scenes, separated aurally and only in visual contact with one another, each voice being carried to the front by its own line to different points and broadcast over a loudspeaker so that it is only in the concert hall that they become unified." (*Schoenberg: Moses und Aron*, Ernst Eulenburg Ltd., 1984, x–xi).

24. I so-characterized the relationship in my 1983 dissertation, *The Formal and Dramatic Organization of Schoenberg's Moses und Aron*, 60.

25. The music returns, with some minor changes in register, in I.iv, mm. 896–912 (with Aron singing the *Hauptstimme*), mm. 919–33 (with the folk singing the

Hauptstimme), and in II.5, mm. 1083–8 (with the folk singing the *Hauptstimme*). No other passage is repeated literally more than once.

26. The music for the Divine "*Aron!*" is derived from m. 59 of the first scene.

27. The pattern is the dyad reversing permutation OPTS-POST that relates permutes RS_2a onto I_6a, $RS_{10}b$ onto I_2b, and RS_6c onto $I_{10}c$. Schoenberg does not systematically explore this relation in the music.

28. The hexachord is also found, albeit less conspicuously, in one other place in *Moses und Aron*, I.4, m. 611. The earlier passage is the climax of the Israelites' song of ridicule, *Bleib uns fern!* The properties of the [014589] hexachord are systematically explored by Milton Babbitt in "Some Aspects of Twelve-tone Composition" (1955), where he characterizes the hexachord as a "third order all-combinatorial" source set. See *The Collected Essays of Milton Babbitt*, 38–47. Schoenberg was evidently not fully aware of this hexachord's special properties during the composition of *Moses und Aron*. He later uses the same hexachord type as the basic structure in his *Ode to Napoleon*, and then in his last unfinished work, *Der erste Psalm*, op.50c. For a discussion of the hexachordal properties in the *Ode to Napoleon* see Yuri Cholopov, "Ode to Napoleon Buonapart," *Journal of the Arnold Schönberg Center* 4/2002, 69–92. For Op.50c, see Alexander L. Ringer, "Faith and Symbol: On Arnold Schoenberg's last musical utterance," *Journal of the Arnold Schoenberg Institute*, VI/1, 80–95.

29. The names "odd" and "even" have no intended significance beyond pointing out their derivation for alternating ordinal members of the source row. If we were to use the ordinal numbers 0 through 11, as is normative in much twelve-tone theory, the "odd" and "even" elements would be reversed, the first note being even instead of odd.

30. The piccolo, flutes, and harp in mm. 125–6 are derived from the very opening of the scene, mm. 98–100.

31. One of the most interesting errors in the scholarly reception of *Moses und Aron* occurs in an early essay by Milton Babbitt, written before Schoenberg's sketches for the work became available for scholarly research. Babbitt ascribed the prime form of the row to Aron, because he, in the second scene, sings the first linear row form in the opera, and then continues to comprise the entire combinatorial quartet. This is indeed the most lucid presentation of tone rows in the entire opera. See "Moses and Aaron: An Introduction to the Music," *Perspectives on Schoenberg and Stravinsky*, edited by Benjamin Boretz and Edward T. Cone, W. W. Norton & Co., 1972, 53–60.

32. Xa for any row form in *Moses und Aron* can be understood as row-defining. That is, the opening trichord, comprising ordered elements 1 through 3, uniquely defines each row form (in contrast, the Y-component is not row-defining). Schoenberg uses a number of partitions that mimic X-chords through "partial ordering," the association of non-contiguous members of the row; odd/even is a case in point.

33. The first half of the I_8 Y-component is the basses and celli, m. 630, and the second half of the S_8 Y-component is in those same voices in the next measure.

The timpani plays the first two notes of the I_8 Y-component (twice), and the tuba plays the first two notes of S_8 Y-component and then the beginning of the second half of the I_8 Y-component.

34. The *Auserwähltes Volk* hexachord returns at m. 682 (slightly altered), 773, 778, and at 957 where it is developed until the end of Act I.

35. Moses, at Act II, scene 4, mm. 980–2, commands "*Vergeh, du Abbild des Unvermögens, das Grenzenlose in ein Bild zu fassen!*" (Be gone, you image of the unimaginable, that would grasp the boundless in an image), after which the golden calf vanishes. The contrast with Moses' inept handling of the signs in Act I could not be more vivid. Even more so than was the case in Act I, Schoenberg's representation is a broad departure from the biblical narrative. In the Bible, the golden calf is ground to powder, spread upon the water, and the Israelites are made to drink thereof (Exodus, 32.19–20). Later, according to the biblical account, the Levites, at Moses' bidding, execute some three thousand people. None of this is in Schoenberg's version.

36. Embedding Y_0 through the partial ordering (contiguous or non-contiguous ordered segments) of two row forms is not as rare as might be expected, although the property is used only once in the opera. Eight different row forms embed $<$D-$E^\flat$-$D^\flat>$ and eight embed $<$G-F-F$^\sharp>$. Thus Schoenberg might have embedded Y_0 through sixty-four different combinations.

37. This passage is discussed in the larger context of Schoenberg's representation of Divinity in my "Schoenberg's Representation of the Divine in *Moses und Aron*." *Journal of the Arnold Schoenberg Institute*, vol. IX/2 (November 1986), 210–16.

38. Interested readers may refer to Christian Martin Schmidt's study or to my own dissertation, both of which are cited in note 14 in this chapter.

39. David Lewin names this type of permutation FLIPSTART in *Generalized Musical Intervals and Transformations*, 189–90.

40. David Lewin defines and exemplifies *wedge* transformations in *Generalized Musical Intervals and Transformations*, 124–32.

41. The roles of speaking and singing are exchanged by the men and women in the first reprise of the march (m. 796). Men and women sing together in the third statement (m. 937) as well as in the final reprise (Act II, m. 1102).

42. I discuss this partition more fully in *The Formal and Dramatic Organization of Schoenberg's 'Moses und Aron'*, 88–92.

43. See note 23 for a fuller description of the speaking and singing choirs that represent the Divine.

44. See Chapter 5, note 1.

45. Richard Cohn discusses the uncanny aspects of Kundry's final transformation in "Uncanny Resemblances: Tonal Signification in the Freudian Age," 295–6.

46. *Journal of the Arnold Schoenberg Institute*, vol. X/2 (November 1986), 210–16.

47. "Schoenberg's Representation of the Divine in *Moses und Aron*," 214. The article goes on to compare Schoenberg's vowel progress to Wagner's fanciful theories of language, where the vowel is the fluid life-blood of language, capable of

expressing the unbounded "primal substance" of speech, whereas consonants function to bind the vowels so that they might refer to some concrete object, relationship, or action.

48. The letter dated 15 March 1933 is to Walter Eidlitz who had sent Schoenberg his book *Der Berg in der Wüste*. *Arnold Schoenberg Letters*, 172.

49. The correlation of flames and speaking choir is a visual aspect that seems to have eluded the productions that I have seen. In my dissertation, *The Formal and Dramatic Organization of Schoenberg's 'Moses und Aron'*, (178) I noted that the ancient Greeks used the name "burning mirror" to describe a concave lens used to concentrate light to a more intense focal point.

50. The omission of *nun verkünde* by the speaking Voice, here and elsewhere, led David Lewin to suggest that the speaking choir represents the *unvorstellbar* aspect of God, while the singing Voice represents the aspect that requires prophecy. While I agree with Lewin's assertion that these two aspects provide the central paradox of the opera, the core of Moses' dilemma, I am not comfortable with his characterization of the two choirs. I argue the pros and cons of Lewin's interpretation in "Schoenberg's Representation of the Divine in *Moses und Aron*," 212–13.

51. The row areas composing the passage are: I_9 (m. 16), R_8 (last beat of 16 through first half of 17), RI_5 (second half of 17 through first half of 18), S_5 (concluding 18), I_2 (first half 19), S_5 (second half 19 to downbeat 20), I_5 (remainder of 20), S_8 (21), I_9 (22). The progress through the areas comprises a rough-hewn palindrome $A_{9-8-5-2-5-8-9}$.

52. Had the final trichord of the initial I_9 (third beat of m. 16) followed the row structure, it would have contained a $B^\flat$ instead of F. As a result the aggregate is incomplete, and the final trichord a chromatic, Y-like chord instead of an X-type. R_8 that follows also violates serial structure; the flute C at the downbeat of m. 17 would have been an $E^\flat$ had the ordered trichords been derived from the row. In this case, the resulting trichord remains of the chromatic Y-type. Once again, the aggregate is incomplete as a result of the substitution. Because these two substitutions are not particularly emphasized, it is difficult to know what to make of them. Of course, they participate in Moses' overall disorientation.

53. This development of Y properties is anticipated in mm. 51–3 of the scene. I discuss this extraordinary passage in "Dramaturgy and Mirror Imagery in Schönberg's *Moses und Aron*," *Perspectives of New Music*, 29/2, 1991, 62–3. In that article I used the name MOSES to signify the row component the we are calling "Y." My rationale there was that Moses is the first to provide "Y" with its normative contour. In the context of that article, what we are calling the X-progression was named COVENANT. I am no longer happy with these designations. The name MOSES distracts us from the Divine source of Y, and COVENANT is too reductive. Nonetheless, the reader may still find the discussions of mirror imagery to be useful.

54. The published editions of *Moses und Aron*, based on Schoenberg's manuscript, place a B-natural as the terminal bass note of m.68. I have notated a $B^\flat$ instead.

The B-natural not only violates the serial order, but sounds like a weak doubling of the B in the violins. Moreover, the clarinet, oboe, and piano figure of m. 70 are the mirror image of the baritone and bass, m. 68. B-natural, in the printed score, disrupts that mirror as well. In addition B♭ and A in the baritone and bass voice lead smoothly by semitone descent into the following X-chord. Thus for contextual musical reasons as well as for reasons based on the serial logic of the passage, the printed B-natural appears to be incorrect.

Chapter 7

The research that led to the original version of this chapter was enabled through funding of a McKnight Summer Fellowship and a Summer Research Fellowship from the University of Minnesota. I wish to express my sincere gratitude for those sources of funding.

1. This chapter is a revision of my article "Memory and Rhetorical Trope in Schoenberg's String Trio," *Journal of the American Musicological Society*, 51/3, fall 1998, 559–602. My thanks to Joseph Auner for his careful reading and insightful criticism of earlier drafts.
2. Walter B. Bailey, *Programmatic Elements in the Works of Schoenberg*, UMI Research Press, 1984, 151–2.
3. Bailey, 156.
4. Bailey, 152. The translation is Bailey's.
5. Bailey, 160.
6. See "Schoenberg and programme music," in *Schoenberg and the New Music*, translated by Derrick Puffett and Alfred Clayton, Cambridge University Press, 1987, 103.
7. Arnold Whittall points out that "strong contrasts of mood, speed and texture play a peculiarly decisive part" in the Trio. He places these elements in opposition to the unifying aspects of its twelve-tone technique. See Arnold Whittall, "Schoenberg and the 'True Tradition': Theme and Form in the String Trio," *The Musical Times*, 115 (September 1974), 739–43.
8. Schoenberg's letter to Varèse, dated 23 October, 1922, gives a good indication of his attitude toward rehearsals.

What offends me equally, however, is that without asking me whether you *can and may* do so you simply set a definitive date for my 'Pierrot lunaire'. But do you even know whether you can manage it? Have you already got a suitable speaker [*Sprecherin*]; a violinist, a pianist, a conductor . . . etc.? How many rehearsals do you mean to hold, etc . . . etc.? In Vienna, with everyone starving and shivering, something like 100 rehearsals were held and an impeccable ensemble achieved with my collaboration. But you simply fix a date and think that's all there is to it!

Arnold Schoenberg Letters, selected and edited by Erwin Stein, translated by Eithne Wilkins and Ernst Kaiser, (New York: St. Martin's Press, 1965), 78–9.

9. See, Bailey, *Programmatic Elements in the Works of Schoenberg*, 156.

10. The formulation "network of time spans, musical events and their transformations," is indebted to the conceptual models developed in David Lewin's book *Generalized Musical Intervals and Transformations*, Yale University Press, 1987.

11. The extraordinary status of the designator "extra-musical" is made vivid by imagining a similar designator applied to spoken or written language when units of syntax and semantic seem to refer to things "in the world," as opposed to referring to other units of grammar in a self-enclosed, self-referential system. Or imagine using a similar designator when graphic design is perceived as pictorial representation.

12. My use of the word "memorial" is stimulated by Charles Rosen's comment that the Trio is "a memorial to [Schoenberg's] own momentary death." A memorial to someone's death is necessarily a remembering of their life. See, *Arnold Schoenberg*, The Viking Press, 1979, 94.

13. Numerous aspects of Schoenberg's relation to Judaism are discussed by Alexander Ringer, *Arnold Schoenberg: The Composer as Jew*, Oxford University Press, 1990. See also, Steven J. Cahn, *Variations in Manifold Time: Historical Consciousness in the Music and Writings of Arnold Schoenberg*, Ph.D. dissertation, State University of New York at Stony Brook, 1966.

14. *Arnold Schoenberg: The Composer as Jew*, 199.

15. Harold Bloom, *Ruin the Sacred Texts: Poetry and Belief from the Bible to the Present*, Harvard University Press, 1989, 6.

16. The role of tonal evocations in Schoenberg's twelve-tone music in general and in the Trio specifically are discussed by Silvina Milstein, *Arnold Schoenberg: notes, sets, forms*, Cambridge University Press, 1992, 162–72 and *passim*. More recently, Richard Kurth has written insightfully on the topic of tonal evocations: "Moments of Closure: Thoughts on the Suspension of Tonality in Schoenberg's Fourth Quartet and Trio," in *Music of My Future: The Schoenberg Quartets and Trio*, edited by Reinhold Brinkmann and Christoph Wolff, Harvard University Press, 2000, 139–60 and "Suspended Tonalities in Schönberg's Twelve-tone Compositions," *Journal of the Arnold Schönberg Center*, vol. 3, 2001, 239–65.

17. The mythical and ritualistic aspects of *sparagmos* are discussed in E. R. Dodds, *The Greeks and the Irrational*, University of California Press, 1951, 155. Also see note 9 to Chapter One of this book. Schoenberg composes a vivid and literal depiction of *sparagmos* during the Golden Calf scene of *Moses und Aron*. Of course, in that context, hopes of rebirth through death are delusional.

18. Friedrich Nietzsche, *Untimely Meditations*, "On the uses and disadvantages of history for life," translated by R. J. Holindale, Cambridge University Press, 1983, 61.

19. Arguments related to, but distinct from the one I develop here inform some aspects of deconstructive literary criticism in the sense that interpretive meaning is infinitely deferred and thus lacks the possibility of closure. An interesting discussion of these matters forms the first chapter of J. Hillis Miller, *The Linguistic Moment*, Princeton University Press, 1985.

20. Passages in Beethoven's *Grosse Fuge*, op. 133 are striking in this respect. Mahler often composes a conflict among voices, but the technique is used most extensively within his development sections.

21. Arnold Schoenberg, *Sämtliche Werke*, Abteilung VI: Kammermusik, Reihe A, Band 21, edited by Christian Martin Schmidt, B. Schott's Söhne, 1982, 127–51. The critical report for the edition, transcriptions of Schoenberg's sketches, and some commentary are in *Sämtliche Werke*, Abteilung VI: Kammermusik, Reihe B, Band 21, edited by Christian Martin Schmidt, B. Schott's Söhne, 1984, 93–131. Consistent with other volumes in the *Sämtliche Werke*, the edition of the String Trio is reluctant to change what well may be errors handed down from earlier editions. Performers of the work should especially consult the table of row deviations (Reihenabweichungen), beginning on page 129 of the critical report. Of the eleven passages listed, there are good musical reasons to make corrections in almost every case.

22. As is common in Schoenberg's twelve-tone practice, the source hexachord for the Trio is inversionally combinatorial. Schoenberg uses his hexachordal source to generate two distinct row forms. The first, as in sketch A1, comprises eighteen ordered pitch-classes, where the final six notes are a reordering of the first six. This form, transposed and inverted, generates Parts 1 and 2. A second tone row, this a more normative twelve-tone row derived from sketch A49, generates the Episodes. Part 3 is basically recapitulatory, recasting material from the previous Parts and Episodes.

The Critical Report labels the respective hexachords in row forms derived from sketch A1 *Vordersatz* 1 (antecedent 1), *Nachsatz* 1 (consequent 1), and *Vordersatz* 2, which are abbreviated V1, N1 and V2. For the sake of consistency, the present chapter adapts the same labels. I have modified the labeling system of the Critical Report only to avoid ambiguity. Readers used to the convention of P_0 to identify the prime form of the tone row may at first be confused by our adaptation of P_D. The reason for this is that the present chapter avoids integer notation for pitch-classes and instead adapts the traditional letter names for notes. In the context of this chapter, integers are reserved for ordinal purposes only. The combinatorial inversion of "B" (Basic) in sketch A1 is composed beneath "B" on the same grand staff. It follows the same disposition of V1, N1 and V2. The other sketches follow a similar procedure. In the context of the present chapter, I will name the row pair of sketch A1 "A_D" (area D, based on the first note of the prime row), comprising "P_D" (prime row, beginning on D), "I_G" (inversion, beginning on G), and their retrogrades. Transpositions of A_D are named accordingly after the first notes of their prime forms, and the same procedure will hold for the individual row components. To identify isolated hexachords, we use the row name followed by the hexachord name, e.g. $RP_D,V2$ names the retrograde of the final six notes of the (18-note) prime form P_D.

A final note on counting ordinal positions within row forms: I count beginning with 1 (not 0). Twelve note counts will be notated $<1,2,3,\ldots 9,10,11,12>$. Instead of counting from 1 through 18 for those rows comprising V1+N1+V2, we will number members of V2 as V2<1,2 . . . 6>. In counting ordinal members of retrograde rows we renumber the pitch-class members and maintain an ascending numerical sequence, e.g. RV2<1,2 . . . 6> is the retrograde of V2 <1,2 . . . 6>.

23. A penetrating analysis of pitch-class mappings in the opening bars of the Trio is found in David Lewin, "Generalized Interval Systems for Babbitt's Lists, and for Schoenberg's String Trio," *Music Theory Spectrum* 17 no. 1 (1995), 81–118. The competing perspectives explored in Lewin's Figures 16 through 21 resonate nicely with our own metaphorical reading of the passage. Lewin also explores ramifications of the opening transformational networks in the music of mm. 148–54 from Part 2 of the Trio. The latter comprises one of the most sublime passages in the work, and its deep formal correlations with what is perhaps the most anguished passage show an astounding underlying conceptual unity beneath the disruptions of the musical surface.

24. We explore similar strategies in *Moses und Aron* in Chapter 6.

25. Antonio Damasio explores and develops the meaning of homeostasis, physiological balance and well-being, in his *The Feeling of What Happens: Body and Emotion in the Making of Consciousness*, Harcourt Brace, 1999, and in his *Looking for Spinoza: Joy, Sorrow, and the Feeling Brain*, Harcourt Brace, 2003.

26. David Lewin briefly discusses this passage in his ground-breaking paper "Inversional Balance as an Organizing Force in Schoenberg's Music and Thought," *Perspectives of New Music* 6/2 (1968), 14. Within the paper, Lewin studies the establishment, disruption and reestablishment of inversional balances in Schoenberg's music. While Lewin shows the abstract inversional balance of pitch-classes in the the opening of the Trio, my own understanding of the passage emphasizes the overwhelming of that "balance" by other, disruptive aspects of musical rhetoric. My study of *Moses und Aron* (Yale University, Ph.D. Dissertation, 1983) discusses similar processes in the context of Schoenberg's largest twelve-tone work. See also, "Dramaturgy and Mirror Imagery in Schoenberg's *Moses und Aron*," *Perspectives of New Music* vol. 29/2 (1991), 50–71.

27. Schoenberg's concept of *Grundgestalt* is discussed probingly in Severine Neff, "Schoenberg and Goethe: Organicism and Analysis," in *Music Theory and the Exploration of the Past*, edited by Christopher Hatch and David W. Bernstein, University of Chicago Press, 1993, 409–33. Also see Patricia Carpenter, "*Grundgestalt* as Tonal Function," *Music Theory Spectrum* 5 (1983), 15–38. Because the opening of the Trio is so fragmentary and chaotic, it can be argued that it does not function as the work's *Grundgestalt*. Along these lines we might argue that the emergent waltz and the subsequent dialectic between the opening and the waltz comprise a richer conceptualizaton of the *Grundgestalt*. On the other hand, it can be argued that the fragmented sense of the opening itself necessitates the counterforce of the waltz.

28. The second principal row ordering, that which generates the Episodes, is shown in Example 7.3b and 7.3c. The example is a transcription of the sketches labeled A49 and A13 in the Critical Report. *Sämtliche Werke*, VI/B/21: 116 and 120. Sketch A49 is not significant in the piece (sketch A13 is highly significant) but

is included so that the reader may easily contrast its row ordering with that in sketch A1. V1 is left unchanged, the contents of N1 are reordered to comprise N2, and V2 is omitted. Sketch A13 is related to sketch A49 by transposition.

Following our earlier procedure for naming the rows, we will call the row pair of sketch A13 "$\mathbf{EA_{Bb}}$" (episode area Bb), comprising "$\mathbf{EP_{Bb}}$" (episode prime Bb), "$\mathbf{EI_{Eb}}$" (episode inversion Eb), and their retrogrades.

29. The mock heroics of the *martellato* are clearly a parody of heroic music normally associated with the nineteenth century. It is difficult to say whether or not a specific precursor is meant to be invoked.

30. Carl Dahlhaus, *Schoenberg and the New Music*, 103–4.

31. The structural basis of these three semitone moves in the episodes is a pivot trichord found in $\mathbf{T_3}$ related $\mathbf{EP_n}$ (and $\mathbf{T_3}$ related $\mathbf{EI_n}$) forms. For example, compare $\mathbf{EP_{Bb}}$ with $\mathbf{EP_G}$:

$$< Bb, \; Gb, \; B, \; F, \; C, \; A, \; D, \; Db, \; E, \; \underline{G, \; Eb, \; Ab} >$$
$$< \underline{G, \; Eb, \; Ab}, \; D, \; A, \; Gb, \; B, \; Bb, \; Db, \; E, \; C, \; F >$$

32. The incorporation of the four movements of sonata form into a large-scale single sonata movement in the First Quartet is well known. For a recent treatment of this and the other multi-movement/single movement works mentioned by Dahlhaus see Walter Frisch, *The Early Works of Arnold Schoenberg: 1893–1908*, University of California Press, 1993. Also see my review of Frisch in *19th Century Music*, XVIII, no. 2 (1994).

The inclusion of *Verklärte Nacht* is controversial because there is disagreement on its overall form. Richard Swift in his paper "Tonal Relations in Schoenberg's *Verklärte Nacht*," *19th Century Music*, vol. I (1977): 3–14, hears the work to embed two sonata forms. Frisch contests this hearing.

33. The Violin Phantasy, op. 47, the next major work after the Trio, can also be heard to incorporate multiple movements into a single movement design.

34. Schoenberg discusses these influences in his essay "My Evolution," *Style and Idea*, edited by Leonard Stein, translated by Leo Black, University of California Press, 1984, 80.

35. Rosen, *Arnold Schoenberg*, 104, makes a more sweeping case for the pervasive influence of late Beethoven in Schoenberg's twelve-tone works.

The periodic nature of serialism means, too, that the fundamental unit of music composed in this form is not the note but the series as a whole, a larger unit and harder to grasp – for the composer as well as listener ... This serial "rhythm" has classical roots, as it is obviously related to (and even derived from) the motivic structure of Beethoven, particularly late Beethoven, where the continuous recurrence of motifs throughout the texture does not always coincide either with the pulse or with the harmonic rhythm, although interlocking with both.

Rosen may well be correct; nonetheless, there are some works, or movements within works, that vividly evoke a Beethovenian rhetoric, while in others the specific connection is more tenuous. Schoenberg's Fourth String Quartet, op.

37, like the Trio, is a work with strong connections to Beethoven. Milstein finds specific correlations between the Schoenberg and the first *Razumovsky* Quartet, op. 59/1. See, *Arnold Schoenberg: notes, sets, forms*, 98–118.

36. Dahlhaus, *Schoenberg and the New Music*, 104.

37. H. H. Stuckenschmidt's commentary emphasizes the similar aspects, see *Schoenberg: His Life, World and Work*, translated by Humphrey Searle, Schirmer Books, 1978, 481.

38. Performers, recognizing the recapitulation, have a tendency to clearly define the beginning of m. 208. The effect of relapse, or of a painful memory slowly coming into consciousness, will work better if Schoenberg's marking of *pianissimo* is exaggerated.

39. Beethoven's opening strategies, in the context of his symphonies, are discussed by Leo Treitler in his essay "History, Criticism and Beethoven's Ninth Symphony." See Leo Treitler, *Music and the Historical Imagination*, Harvard University Press, 1989, 19–45.

40. Parallels between Freudian and Schoenbergian thought are explored in the Introduction.

41. Walter Benjamin's essay "The Image of Proust" contains a beautiful discussion of Proust's *mémoire involontaire*. The essay is included in *Illuminations*, translated by Harry Zohn, edited by Hannah Arendt, Schocken Books, 1969, 201–15.

42. Charles Rosen, *Arnold Schoenberg*, 94–5.

43. *Ibid.*, 95.

44. The double stemming within the sketch and its relationship to passages in the Trio are discussed by Silvina Milstein, *Arnold Schoenberg: notes, sets, forms*, 163–4. Milstein labels the double stemmed notes a "secondary set," and shows how they emerge to form the *Hauptstimme* at mm. 12–17 and 135–41. Milstein's book includes photo-copies of Schoenberg's sketches for the tone rows that generate the Trio. See Plates 19 and 20.

45. As in sketch A1, sketch A13 – the row form used in the Trio's Episodes – emphasizes a partition into disjunct trichords, this time using bar lines to separate the trichords. In contrast to sketch A1, there are no double stemmed notes. Unlike Parts 1, 2 and 3, the partition of outer dyad plus inner tetrachord plays only a minimal role in the Episodes.

46. Milstein's study of the Trio emphasises the tonal implications of a number of passages where G and D initiate or terminate tonal motions. See *Arnold Schoenberg: notes, sets, forms*, 164.

47. Schoenberg's substitution of an augmented sixth for a dominant is discussed by Walter Frisch, *The Early Works of Arnold Schoenberg: 1893–1908*, University of California Press, 1993, see especially page 135.

48. In terms of motive, the reversal of the cello dyad in m. 270 (G-A♭), makes it the retrograde of the violin A♭-G, m. 272. This is analogous to the relationship of the cello in m. 267 to the violin of m. 269 (E♭-E becomes E-E♭). In a similar way, the viola reversal in m. 270 (B-C), makes it the retrograde of the cello C-B in m. 272. The two dyadic reversals combined with the normative F♯-F in the

violin, produce a retrograde of the harmonies of m. 272. In the second part of the passage, the violin reversal C-B (m. 275) echoes the cello C-B of m. 274. Harmonically, the reversal allows m. 275 to end with a "B minor triad." The next downbeat brings the fifth related E.

49. The waltz fragment at mm. 263–6 is an inversion of the antecedent phrase of the original waltz fragment, mm. 86–9.

50. Hans Keller, "Schoenberg's Return to Tonality," *Journal of the Arnold Schoenberg Institute*, vol.V, no.1 (1981), 2–21, see page 3.

51. Keller, "Schoenberg's Return to Tonality," 7. I develop similar ideas in "Schoenberg and *das Unheimliche*," *The Journal for Musicology*, Fall 1993.

52. Keller discusses the passage at length, and his observations are well worth studying. See "Schoenberg's Return to Tonality," 16–18.

53. The *unheimlich* emergence of tonality in works like the String Trio intersects with another issue in Schoenberg studies, the status of late works such as the Variations on a Recitative for Organ, op. 40, and the Theme and Variations for Wind Band, op. 43a, in which Schoenberg explicitly returns to tonality. I am convinced that tonality in these works also functions as a locus of memory, as opposed to a simple and direct means of expression. It is ironic that the effects of tonal memory in these contexts are weakened by the absence of an active process of "forgetting."

54. Arnold Schoenberg, *Fundamentals of Musical Composition*, edited by Gerald Strang and Leonard Stein, St. Martin's Press, 1967.

55. Anton Webern, *The Path to New Music*, edited by Willi Reich, translated by Leo Black, Theodore Presser Company, 1963. Webern's discussion of musical phrase is found in the fifth, sixth and seventh lectures of the "Path to New Music" series.

56. Milstein, *Arnold Schoenberg: notes, sets, forms*, makes extensive use of Schoenberg's phrase models in her analyses of his music. Remarkably, her analysis of the Trio does not employ those models.

> The abandonment of classical phrase construction in the Trio and its replacement by a kind of 'musical prose', reminiscent of that of the Expressionist period, have been viewed as the counterpart of a more autonomous type of twelve-tone syntax (157).

Her discussion of the String Trio goes on to argue against the view of an "autonomous type of twelve-tone syntax" and in favor of understanding implicit or attenuated tonal functions. However, the assumption of "the abandonment of classical phrase construction" is not explicitly challenged. To be sure, there are passages in the Trio that cannot be explained in terms of periods and sentences. Yet the traditional period structure does play a central role, as our analysis shows.

57. Arnold Schoenberg, *Theory of Harmony*, translated by Roy E. Carter, University of California Press, 1978, 391–2.

58. The rhythm is derived specifically from m. 122, but related rhythms are pervasive in mm. 86–9, mm. 122–5, and mm. 263–6.

59. Stuckenschmidt, *Schoenberg: His Life, World and Work*, 479, notes the emergence of "a slow waltz" at the beginning of Part 2. Our placement is some fifty measures earlier.

60. The 12/8 setting, mm. 184–7, is remarkable in that the principal voice exclusively comprises groupings of three dotted quarter notes prefaced by a dotted quarter rest. In the context of the passage, it sounds as though 9/8 (three threes) has been expanded to fill out 12/8, with the subsidiary voices being responsible, in each case, for the metric expansion.

61. Deferrals of this sort are the central topic of Frank Kermode's important book *The Sense of an Ending: Studies in the Theory of Fiction*, Oxford University Press, 1967.

62. As noted in the Introduction, the idea of "troping tropes" is taken from the literary theories of Harold Bloom. John Hollander writes a succinct (and beautiful) explanation of the idea in his introduction to Harold Bloom, *Poetics of Influence*, Henry R. Schwab, 1988, xi–xlvi; see especially xxx–xxxix.

63. Carl Schorske discusses Ravel's *La Valse* as *danse macabre* in Chapter One of his book *Fin-de-Siècle Vienna*, Alfred A. Knopf, 1980. It is odd that Schorske turns to Ravel for an example of the crisis in *fin-de-siècle* Vienna. Dances from Mahler, Schoenberg or Berg would have made the point more vividly.

   The "intoxicating" quality of the waltz, and all that it repressed, is discussed by the art historian Allessandra Comini in her book *The Fantastic Art of Vienna*, Alfred A. Knopf, 1978, especially pages 6–7.

64. An interesting discussion of triple meter in this regard is found in Moritz Hauptmann, *Die Natur der Harmonik und der Metrik zur Theorie der Musik* (1853). For Hauptmann, who bases his theory on ideas derived from Hegel, duple divisions of time express identity through an expression of self and self-reflection. Triple divisions of time, according to Hauptmann, throw this rhythm of self-reflection into a state of imbalance. I discuss this and other matters in my paper "Hauptmann and Schenker: Two Adaptations of Hegelian Dialectics," *Theory and Practice*, vol. 13 (1988), 115–31.

65. The story of Jacob and the Angel is a recurrent image in the literary theories of Harold Bloom. In his essay "Wrestling Sigmund" Bloom asks and answers the following question:

   Who is that "man," later called one of the Elohim, who wrestles with Jacob until dawn? And why should they wrestle anyway? Nothing in any tradition supports my surmise that this daemonic being is the Angel of Death, yet such I take him to be.

   The essay is included in *Poetics of Influence*, edited by John Hollander. The passage quoted is found on pages 220–2.

66. *Arnold Schoenberg: The Composer as Jew*, 199–200.

67. This is the same property discussed in note 31 above.

68. The phrase (mm. 86–9) is recapitulated in an inversion beginning on E♭, mm. 263–6. The interval palindrome of the original presentation, which ends on E♭, allows the inverted form to be the retrograde of the original. For more on

Schoenbergian interval palindromes see my "Dramaturgy and Mirror Imagery in Schoenberg's *Moses und Aron*," *Perspectives of New Music*, vol. 29/2 (1991), 50–71.

69. I find the juxtapositions of the sublime and the absurd in Op. 131 particularly apposite in this regard. The Adagio section of the fourth movement, mm. 130–61, is stunning in this respect, as Beethoven interjects comic *pizzicati* into the context of his soaring melodic lines.

70. Wallace Stevens, *The Noble Rider and the Sound of Words*, cited in Harold Bloom, *Wallace Stevens: The Poems of our Climate*, Cornell University Press, 1977, 172.

71. See Joseph T. Shipley, *The Origins of English Words*, Johns Hopkins University Press, 1984, 68.

72. Harold Bloom makes this point on page 10 of *Ruin the Sacred Texts*:

To shape by molding, to make a fiction, is to fashion Adam out of the *adamah*, out of the red clay. Adam is not faked; he is fictitious and not factitious.

Bibliography

Writings of Arnold Schoenberg

Arnold Schoenberg, *Arnold Schoenberg: A Self Portrait*. Nuria Schoenberg Nono, ed. Belmont Music, 1988

Ausgewählte Briefe, Erwin Stein, ed. B. Schott's Söhne, 1958

The English translation of the letters is *Arnold Schoenberg Letters*, edited by Erwin Stein, translated by Eithne Wilkins and Ernst Kaiser, St. Martin's Press, 1965

Fundamentals of Musical Composition, St. Martin's Press, 1967

Stil und Gedanke: Aufsätze zur Musik, Ivan Vojtech, ed. S. Fisher Verlag, 1976

The English translation of most of Schoenberg's articles is *Style and Idea*, edited by Leonard Stein, translated by Leo Black, University of California Press, 1984

Structural Functions of Harmony, Leonard Stein, ed. W. W. Norton, 1969

Theory of Harmony, translated by Roy. E. Carter, University of California Press, 1978

Books and Articles about Schoenberg

Walter B. Bailey, *Programmatic Elements in the Works of Schoenberg*. UMI Research Press, 1984

Alban Berg, *Pelleas und Melisande (nach dem Drama von Maurice Maeterlinck), Symphonische Dichtung für Orchestra von Arnold Schönberg, Op. 5: kurze thematische Analyse*. Universal Edition, 1920

The Berg guide to *Pelleas* is available in two English translations, one in the *Journal of the Arnold Schoenberg Institute*, XVI numbers 1 and 2, 1993, translated by Mark DeVoto, and another appended to Derrick Puffett's article "'Music that Echoes within one' for a Lifetime: Berg's Reception of Schoenberg's 'Pelleas und Melisande.'" *q.v.*

Alban Berg *et al.*, *Arnold Schönberg*. R. Piper, 1912

Leon Botstein, "Schoenberg and the Audience: Modernism, Music, and Politics in the Twentieth Century," in *Schoenberg and His World*, Walter Frisch, ed. Princeton University Press, 1999

Juliane Brand and Christopher Hailey, editors, *Constructive Dissonance: Arnold Schoenberg and the transformations of twentieth-century culture*. University of California Press, 1997

Reinhold Brinkmann, Correspondence. *The Journal of the Arnold Schoenberg Institute* I/3, 182–5

"Schoenberg the Contemporary: A View from Behind," in *Constructive Dissonance: Arnold Schoenberg and the transformations of twentieth-century culture*. University of California Press, 1997

Reinhold Brinkmann and Christoph Wolff, editors, *Music of My Future: The Schoenberg Quartets and Trio*. Harvard University Press, 2000

Steven Cahn, "The Artist as Modern Prophet: A Study of Historical Consciousness and its Expression in Schoenberg's 'Vorgefühle, op. 22, no. 4'," in *Schoenberg and Words: The Modernist Years*. Garland Publishing (2000), 243–71

Brian G. Campbell, *Text and Phrase Rhythm in Gurrelieder: Schoenberg's Reception of Tradition*. Ph.D. dissertation: University of Minnesota, 1997

"*Gurrelieder* and the Fall of the Gods: Schoenberg's Struggle with the legacy of Wagner," in *Schoenberg and Words: The Modernist Years*, Charlotte M. Cross and Russell A. Berman, editors. Garland Publishing, Inc. (2000), 31–63

Michael Cherlin, "Dialectical Opposition in Schoenberg's Music and Thought." *Music Theory Spectrum* 22/2 (Fall 2000), 157–76

"Dramaturgy and Mirror Imagery in Schönberg's *Moses und Aron*: Two Paradigmatic Interval Palindromes." *Perspectives of New Music* 29/2 (Summer 1991), 50–71

The Formal and Dramatic Organization of Schoenberg's Moses und Aron. Ph.D. dissertation: Yale University, 1983

"Memory and Rhetorical Trope in Schoenberg's String Trio." *Journal of the American Musicological Society* 51/3 (Fall 1998), 559–602

"Motive and Memory in Schoenberg's First String Quartet," in *The Music of My Future: The Schoenberg Quartets and Trio*, Reinhold Brinkmann and Christoph Wolff, editors. Harvard University Press (2000), 61–80

"Schoenberg and *das Unheimliche*." *The Journal of Musicology* 11/3 (Summer 1993), 357–73

"Schoenberg's Representation of the Divine in Moses und Aron." *Journal of the Arnold Schoenberg Institute* IX/2, 210–16

Richard Cohn, "Uncanny Resemblances: Tonal Signification in the Freudian Age." *Journal of the American Musicological Society*, 57/2 (2004), 285–323

Carl Dahlhaus, *Schoenberg and the New Music*, translated by Derrick Puffett and Alfred Clayton. Cambridge University Press, 1987

Robert Fleisher, "Dualism in the Music of Arnold Schoenberg." *Journal of the Arnold Schoenberg Institute* XII/1 (June 1989), 22–42

Walter Frisch, *The Early Works of Arnold Schoenberg, 1893–1908*. University of California Press, 1993

Walter Frisch, editor, *Schoenberg and his World*. Princeton University Press, 1999

Bluma Goldstein, *Reinscribing Moses: Heine, Kafka, Freud, and Schoenberg in a European Wilderness*. Harvard University Press, 1992

Glenn Gould, "Schoenberg – A Perspective," in *The Glenn Gould Reader*, introduction by Tim Page, editor. Knopf, 1984, 107–22

Ethan Haimo, *Schoenberg's Serial Odyssey: The evolution of his Twelve-Tone Method, 1914–1928*. Oxford University Press, 1990

Martha Hyde, "Neoclassic and Anachronistic Impulses in Twentieth-Century Music." *Music Theory Spectrum* 18/2 (1996), 200–35

Hans Keller, "Schoenberg's Return to Tonality." *Journal of the Arnold Schoenberg Institute* V/1, 2–21

Richard Kurth, "Moments of Closure: Thoughts on the Suspension of Tonality in Schoenberg's *Fourth Quartet* and *Trio*," in *Music of My Future: The Schoenberg Quartets and Trio*, Reinhold Brinkmann and Christoph Wolff, editors. Harvard University Press (2000), 139–60

"Schönberg and the *Bilderverbot*: Reflections on *Unvorstellbarkeit* and *Verborgenheit*." *Journal of the Arnold Schönberg Center* 3 (2003), 332–72

"Suspended Tonalities in Schönberg's Twelve-tone Compositions." *Journal of the Arnold Schönberg Center* 3 (2001), 239–65

Phillip Lacoue-Labarthe, *Musica Ficta: Figures of Wagner*, translated by Felicia McCarren. Stanford University Press, 1994

David Lewin, "Generalized Interval Systems for Babbitt's Lists, and for Schoenberg's String Trio." *Music Theory Spectrum* 17/1, 81–118

"Inversional Balance as an Organizing Force in Schoenberg's Music and Thought." *Perspectives of New Music* 6/2 (1968), 1–21

"Moses und Aron: Some general remarks and analytic notes for Act I, scene 1." *Perspectives of New Music* 6/1, 1–17

Jan Maegaard, "Schoenberg's Incomplete Works and Fragments," in *Constructive Dissonance: Arnold Schoenberg and Transformations of Twentieth-Century Culture*. University of California Press, 1997, 131–45

Silvina Milstein, *Arnold Schoenberg: notes, sets, forms*. Cambridge University Press, 1992

Derrick Puffett, "'Music that Echoes within one' for a Lifetime: Berg's Reception of Schoenberg's 'Pelleas und Melisande.'" *Music and Letters* 76/2 (1995), 209–64

Ursula Rauchhaupt, editor. *Schoenberg, Berg, Webern: The String Quartets; a documentary study*. Deutsche Grammophon Gesellschaft, 1971

Willi Reich, *Schoenberg: A Critical Biography*. Leo Black, trans. Praeger Publishers, 1971

Alexander Ringer, *Arnold Schoenberg: The Composer as Jew*. Oxford University Press, 1990

Charles Rosen, *Arnold Schoenberg*. Viking, 1975

Bryan R. Simms, *The Atonal Music of Arnold Schoenberg: 1908–1923*. Oxford University Press, 2000

Bryan R. Simms (editor), *Schoenberg, Berg, and Webern: A Companion to the Second Viennese School*. Greenwood Press, 1999

Leonard Stein, "Noting the diagram and soliciting responses as to its meaning." *Journal of the Arnold Schoenberg Institute* I/1 (1976), 3–5

H. H. Stuckenschmidt, *Schoenberg: His Life, World and Work*. Humphrey Searle, trans. Schirmer, 1978

Gary Tomlinson, *Metaphysical Song: An Essay on Opera*. Princeton University Press, 1999

Egon Wellesz, *Arnold Schoenberg: The Formative Years*, translated by W. H. Kerridge. J. M. Dent and Sons, 1925

Pamela C. White, *Schoenberg and the God-Idea: The Opera Moses und Aron*. UMI Research Press, 1985

Arnold Whittall, "Schoenberg and the 'True Tradition': Theme and Form in the String Trio." *The Musical Times* 115, 739–43

Books and Articles by and about Schoenberg's Contemporaries

Robert Alter, *Canon and Creativity*. Yale University Press, 2000

Harold Bloom, "Freud and the Poetic Sublime," in *Poetics of Influence*, introduction by John Hollander, edited by Henry R. Schwab, 1988

Harold Bloom (editor), *Modern Critical Views: Franz Kafka*. Chelsea House Publishers, 1986

Gilles Deleuze, *Difference and Repetition*, translated by Paul Patton. Columbia University Press, 1994

   Proust and Signs, translated by Richard Howard. University of Minnesota Press, 2000

Gilles Deleuze and Félix Guattari, *A Thousand Plateaus: Capitalism and Schizophrenia*. University of Minnesota Press, 1987

Amos Elon, *The Pity of It All: A History of Jews in Germany, 1743–1933*. Metropolitan Books (Henry Holt), 2002

Sigmund Freud, "Beyond the Pleasure Principle," in *The Freud Reader*, translated by James Strachey, edited by Peter Gay. W. W. Norton, 1989

   "On Transience," in *Writings on Art and Literature*, edited by Werner Hamacher and David E. Wellbery. Stanford University Press, 1997

Ken Frieden, *Freud's Dream of Interpretation*. State University of New York Press, 1990

Peter Gay, *Freud: A Life for Our Time*. W. W. Norton, 1988

Susan A. Handelman, *Fragments of Redemption*. Indiana University Press, 1991

Allan Janik and Stephen Toulman, *Wittgenstein's Vienna*. Simon and Schuster, 1973

Franz Kafka, *The Castle*, translated by Mark Harman. Schocken, 1988

   Diaries: 1910–1923, edited by Max Brod, translated by Martin Greenberg, with the cooperation of Hannah Arendt. Schocken, 1976

   Franz Kafka: Ein Lesebuch mit Bildern, edited by Klaus Wagenbach. Rowohlt Taschenbuch Verlag, 2003

   The Great Short Works of Franz Kafka, translated by Joachim Neugroschel. Simon & Schuster, 2000

   Parables and Paradoxes: Bilingual Edition. Schocken, 1975

   Das Schloss. Fischer Taschenbuch Verlag, 1981

   Tagebücher: 1914–1923. Fischer Taschenbuch Verlag, 1990

Patrick McGuinness, *Maurice Maeterlinck and the Making of Modern Theatre*. Oxford University Press, 2000

Paul Mendes-Flohr, *German Jews: A Dual Identity.* Yale University Press, 1999

Max Paddison, *Adorno's Aesthetics of Music.* Cambridge University Press, 1993

Philip Rieff, *Freud: The Mind of the Moralist*, third edition. University of Chicago Press, 1979

Ritchie Robertson, *Kafka: Judaism, Politics, and Literature.* Oxford University Press, 1985

Ritchie Robertson and Edward Timms, editors, *Vienna 1900: from Altenberg to Wittgenstein.* Edinburgh University Press, 1990

Franz Rosenzweig, *The Star of Redemption*, translated by William W. Hallo, foreword by N. N. Galtzer. Holt, Rinehart, 1970

Howard M. Sachar, *Dreamland: Europeans and Jews in the Aftermath of the Great War.* Knopf, 2002

Christian Martin Schmidt, *Schönbergs Oper* Moses und Aron. Schott, 1988

Georg Simmel, *Georg Simmel: On Individuality and Social Forms.* Introduction by Donald N. Levine, editor. University of Chicago Press, 1971

Anton Webern, *The Path to New Music*, edited by Willi Reich, translated by Leo Black. Theodore Presser, 1963

General Background

Edward Aldwell and Carl Schachter, *Harmony and Voice Leading*, second edition. Harcourt Brace, 1989

Robert Alter, *Canon and Creativity.* Yale University Press, 2000

Hannah Arendt, *Between Past and Future.* The Viking Press, 1961

Erich Auerbach, *Mimesis: The Representation of Reality in Western Literature*, translated by Willard R. Trask. Princeton University Press, 1953

Milton Babbitt, *The Collected Essays of Milton Babbitt*, edited by Stephen Peles *et al.* Princeton University Press, 2003

Andrew Barker, editor, *Greek Musical Writings: Harmonic and Acoustic Theory* (vol. II). Cambridge University Press, 1989

Henri Bergson, *Matter and Memory*, translated by N. M. Paul and W. S. Palmer. Zone Books, 1991

William Blake, *The Poetry and Prose of William Blake*, edited by David V. Erdman, commentary by Harold Bloom. Doubleday, 1965

Maurice Blanchot, *The Infinite Conversation*, translated and with a foreword by Susan Hanson. University of Minnesota Press, 1993
The Work of Fire, translated by Charlotte Mandell. Stanford University Press, 1995

Harold Bloom, *A Map of Misreading.* Oxford University Press, 1975
The Ringers in the Tower: Studies in Romantic Tradition. University of Chicago Press, 1971
Ruin the Sacred Texts: Poetry and Belief from the Bible to the Present. Harvard University Press, 1989

Kenneth Burke, *A Grammar of Motives*. Prentice-Hall, 1945; repr. University of California Press, 1969

I. Bywater and G. T. W. Patrick, *Heraclitus of Ephesus*. Argonaut, 1969

Anne Carson, *Economy of the Unlost (Reading Simonides of Keos with Paul Celan)*. Princeton University Press, 1999

  Eros the Bittersweet. Princeton University Press, 1986

Stanley Cavell, *This New Yet Unapproachable America: Lectures after Emerson after Wittgenstein*. Living Batch Press, 1989

Michael Cherlin, "Hauptmann and Schenker: Two Adaptations of Hegelian Dialectics." *Theory and Practice* 13 (1988), 115–31

John Daverio, *Nineteenth Century Music and the German Romantic Ideology*. Schirmer, 1993

E. R. Dodds, *The Greeks and the Irrational*. University of California, 1951

Walter Frisch, editor, *Schubert: Critical and Analytical Studies*. University of Nebraska Press, 1986

Hans-Georg Gadamer, *Truth and Method*, second edition, translation revised by Joel Weinsheimer and Donald G. Marshall. Continuum, 2003

Peter Gay, *Weimar Culture: The Outsider as Insider*. W. W. Norton, 1968

W. K. C. Guthrie, *A History of Greek Philosophy: The earlier Presocratics and the Pythagoreans* (vol. I). Cambridge University Press, 1962

Geoffrey H. Hartman, *The Fateful Question of Culture*. Columbia University Press, 1997

Charles H. Kahn, *The Art and Thought of Heraclitus*. Cambridge University Press, 1979

David Lewin, *Generalized Musical Intervals and Transformations*. Yale University Press, 1987

  "Music Theory, Phenomenology, and Modes of Perception." *Music Perception* 3/4, 327–92

Arthur O. Lovejoy, *Reflections on Human Nature*. John Hopkins Press, 1961

Adolph Bernhard Marx, *Theory and Practice of Musical Composition*, translated by H. S. Saroni. Huntington, Mason & Law, 1852

Friedrich Nietzsche, *Untimely Meditations: On the uses and disadvantages of history for life*, translated by R. J. Holindale. Cambridge University Press, 1983

Camille Paglia, *Sexual Personae: Art and Decadence from Nefertiti to Emily Dickinson*. Yale University Press, 1990

Carl Schorske, *Fin-de-Siècle Vienna*. Knopf, 1980

David Schur, *The Way of Oblivion: Heraclitus and Kafka*. Harvard University Press, 1998

George Steiner, *Language and Silence: Essays on Language, Literature, and the Inhuman*. Atheneum, 1970

  Grammars of Creation. Yale University Press, 2001

General index
(Names and topics)

Index of Schoenberg's works and writings